MW00464911

"VanDoodewaard shows us real history is as good as epic—seemingly inexorable trends, alarming tolerance, and an ominous slide; compelling, illuminating, and more than a bit unnerving. Only with historical treatises such as VanDoodewaard's can we see clearly from where we came, how far we have slid, and yet how simple the answer is."

—Kurt P. Wise, professor of biology, Truett-McConnell College

"A very necessary book. In Brazil, where the influence of liberal theology and Darwinian evolution has eroded the confidence of many evangelicals in the historicity and reliability of the Genesis account of the creation and fall of Adam and Eve, such a work must be translated, published, and widely discussed, especially in theological schools of historical denominations. Dr. VanDoodewaard has given us a major contribution to the understanding and defense of the biblical narrative about the first Adam, and therefore has also strengthened our faith in the second Adam."

—Augustus Lopes Nicodemus, chancellor emeritus,
Mackenzie University, Sao Paulo, and professor of
New Testament, Andrew Jumper Post-Graduate
School of Theology

"The credibility of the Christian faith rests upon the historicity of two individuals: Adam and Jesus Christ. This claim is required not by a reactive and antiscientific reading of Genesis, but by reading Genesis in harmony with the theological arguments of St. Paul. This important new study illustrates some of the means by which Christians turned Adam into a character of myth—and how that move threatens our understanding of the work of Jesus Christ."

—Crawford Gribben, professor, School of History and
Anthropology, Queen's University, Belfast

"This book is an amazingly comprehensive and detailed documentation of views on the origins of Adam throughout church history, with particular attention to recent controversies. While he himself is convinced of the literal interpretation of the creation of humanity, the author allows alternate views to speak in their own words. That, in turn, enables insightful comparisons."

—Noel Weeks, honorary senior lecturer, ancient
Near Eastern studies, University of Sydney

"Theologians' attitudes toward the historical Adam and Eve and the uses to which they put the narrative of the fall in Genesis 3 reveal much about their hermeneutics and the entire structure of their thought. Building on a thorough and perceptive survey of the history of the use of the first parents in successive periods of the church's history and in modern secular philosophers, including Darwin, VanDoodewaard enters into the discussion of alternatives to acceptance of the historical veracity of Genesis 1–3 during the past sixty-five years. His sophisticated and sensitive analysis shows how vital affirmation of the historicity of Adam and Eve is for the entire corpus of biblical teaching."

—Robert Kolb, missions professor of systematic theology
emeritus, Concordia Seminary, St. Louis

"A comprehensive and well-documented historical analysis of theological responses to significant questions related to human origins. The author provides a much-needed perspective for those seeking to interpret the biblical text against the backdrop of scientific claims."

—Mohan Chacko, principal emeritus and professor of theology,
Presbyterian Theological Seminary, Dehra Dun, India

"A work of outstanding scholarship. *The Quest for the Historical Adam* by William VanDoodewaard provides an in-depth study of the varied Christian positions on human origins. This survey of past and present interpretations of Genesis 1–2 is foundational for future commentary."

—Emerson T. McMullen, associate professor, history of science,
department of history, Georgia Southern University

"It does not overstate to say that the gospel of Jesus Christ loses its biblical meaning and efficacy apart from Adam and Eve as the first human beings from whom all others descend. The author's thorough and instructive survey of the long history of interpretation down to the present, particularly of the opening chapters of Genesis, shows unmistakably how questionable hermeneutical commitments and unsound exegesis lead to denial or uncertainty regarding the Bible's clear teaching on common descent and, in conclusion, points out the disastrous consequences that follow for sound doctrine and the life of the church. One need not agree at every point with his own literal Genesis interpretation to appreciate the compelling value of his contribution. This is an important book and, given differences and confused thinking about the historicity of Adam increasingly among those claiming to be evangelical, particularly timely. It deserves careful reading and reflection by anyone interested in this crucial issue."

—Richard B. Gaffin Jr., professor of biblical and systematic
theology emeritus, Westminster Theological Seminary

"This is one of the best books, to my knowledge, on the controversy surrounding the interpretation of the first chapters of Genesis and its relation to modern science and the influx of Enlightenment thought, providing a historical survey on how Adam has been understood from the patristic era up to the past several decades. While holding to the literal interpretation of the Genesis account of creation of the first human being, Adam, VanDoodewaard presents alternate interpretations with a thorough and fair mind. This is a fine biblical-historical contribution to Adam scholarship."

—Daniel Hojoon Ryou, professor of Old Testament,
Baekseok University Divinity School, Seoul, Korea

"This is a bold and refreshing presentation of the literal hermeneutical approach to the creation and human origins story given in Genesis 1 and 2. Committed to the authority and priority of Scripture, focusing on the biblical theology of key Scripture passages, and with a balanced and comprehensive survey of the history of interpretation of early Genesis, VanDoodewaard gives us the fruit of a theologically sound quest for the historic Adam. I wholeheartedly recommend this fine scholarly work."

—Tewoldemedhin Habtu, associate professor of Old Testament,
Nairobi Evangelical Graduate School of Theology,
Africa International University, Nairobi, Kenya

"The biblical truth claims of the historicity of Adam and the reality of the fall are neither incidental nor insignificant to the Christian faith. They are matters of gospel importance. But in our time the validity of the church's doctrine of the special creation of Adam and Eve, body and soul, as our first parents, based on Genesis 1–2, and the corresponding affirmation of the historical reality of the fall, based on Genesis 3, have come under serious cross-examination. There are voices (some of whom self-identify as evangelical) calling on the church to abandon and to revise its historic teaching. Many reveal an unfamiliarity with the history of the church's exegesis on these issues and its assessment of their hermeneutical and theological significance. William VanDoodewaard's book, *The Quest for the Historical Adam*, then, arrives not a moment too soon. He provides us with a careful, clear, important, orthodox assessment of the question as well as a tremendously helpful survey of the history of interpretation (including current views). This will prove to be an enormously valuable resource to pastors and teachers wanting to get up to speed on the historical theology behind this discussion and to gain a quick grasp of the present theological lay of the land. Those arguing for a revisionist interpretation must now deal with the material VanDoodewaard has amassed and articulated."

—Ligon Duncan, chancellor and John E. Richards Professor of Systematic
and Historical Theology, Reformed Theological Seminary

"Dr. Bill VanDoodewaard has gifted the church with a work that began as a labor of love but has grown into a significant major study in which he marries the disciplines of a church historian and the concerns of a Christian theologian. The issues on which he touches reach down to the very foundations of the Christian worldview, to creation itself. Those who share the author's understanding of the early chapters of Genesis will deeply appreciate his detailed analysis and synthesis of how they have been interpreted throughout the Christian centuries. And those who differ, whether in fine details or in major ways, ought, in integrity, to familiarize themselves with the copious material that Dr. VanDoodewaard here presents. This is a valuable and significant contribution to a much-debated subject and from a perspective that has too often been overlooked."

—Sinclair B. Ferguson, professor of systematic theology,
Redeemer Theological Seminary, Dallas

"While scholarship may be turning away increasingly from the literal approach to the creation narrative of Genesis 1–3 and related texts, Dr. VanDoodewaard sets out in a fair and balanced manner the implications that such alternative hermeneutical approaches have not for just our understanding of creation and the origins of Adam, but even for basics such as our understanding of the inspiration and authority of Scripture and of Christ and His salvific work. This is a very informative and helpful overview of a fundamental aspect of the Christian faith."

—Brian Wintle, academic coordinator, Centre for Advanced Theological Studies,
SHIATS University, Allahabad, India; visiting professor of New Testament,
South Asia Institute for Advanced Christian Studies, Bangalore, India;
former regional secretary (India), Asia Theological Association

"I have found that often when I am wrestling with someone who holds on to a major doctrinal aberration, there is almost invariably a failure of sound hermeneutics in dealing with the first three chapters of Genesis. Equally true is the fact that a good understanding of these foundational chapters in Genesis is like the proverbial stitch in time that saves nine. Dr. VanDoodewaard's Herculean effort to get us back to a sure footing in this matter through this doctrinal and historical survey may prove to be that life-saving stitch. It is a scholarly work of the highest standard. Be assured you will be abundantly rewarded in reading it."

—Conrad Mbewe, pastor, Kabwata Baptist Church; chancellor,
African Christian University, Lusaka, Zambia

"An indispensable resource that puts the hotly debated hermeneutics of Genesis 1–2 in historical perspective. *The Quest for the Historical Adam* is staggering in its scope, rigorous in its documentation, and sobering in its conclusions. Whether subsequent writers are sympathetic to the author's anthropology and cosmology or not, their literature on this topic will either be in conversation with VanDoodewaard's work or be proportionately deficient. This church historian has made a lasting contribution to Old Testament studies."

—John Makujina, professor of biblical studies, Erskine College

"VanDoodewaard demonstrates that virtually the entirety of Christendom has held to the historicity of Adam and Eve as the first human pair, created in the manner described in Genesis 2:7 and 2:21–22. *The Quest for the Historical Adam* contains a wealth of information and research—it is clearly the most comprehensive treatment of the historicity and significance of the creation of Adam and Eve that exists. All future studies on Adam and Eve must now start with this tome."

—Mark F. Rooker, professor of Old Testament and Hebrew,
Southeastern Baptist Theological Seminary

"Dr. VanDoodewaard has served the church well in this labor. More than a history of interpretation, *The Quest for the Historical Adam* pulls a chair up for theologians of the past to join the church's present deliberation on a vital issue, and it clarifies the doctrinal stakes. A pathway of history stretches from the first Adam to the last—may this book foster the wisdom to not separate what God's Word has joined together."

—L. Michael Morales, professor of Old Testament,
Greenville Presbyterian Theological Seminary

"Modern scholarship on Genesis has confused the church with a tangle of speculations. Dr. VanDoodewaard skillfully exposes the problems of the new, 'scientific' Adam. He shows that recent debates on Adam do little justice to Scripture, ignore church history, and are scientifically ill defined."

—Neal A. Doran, professor of biology, Bryan College

"William VanDoodewaard's thoroughly documented survey of the history of interpretation of Adam and Eve is an essential entry point to understand the contemporary debate. Highly recommended."

—Iain Duguid, professor of Old Testament and religion, Grove City College;
professor of Old Testament, Westminster Theological Seminary, Philadelphia

The Quest for the Historical Adam

The Quest for the Historical Adam

Genesis, Hermeneutics, and Human Origins

William VanDoodewaard

Foreword by R. Albert Mohler Jr.

Reformation Heritage Books
Grand Rapids, Michigan

Reformation Heritage Books
2965 Leonard St. NE
Grand Rapids, MI 49525
616-977-0889 / Fax 616-285-3246
orders@heritagebooks.org
www.heritagebooks.org

Printed in the United States of America
16 17 18 19 20 21/10 9 8 7 6 5 4 3 2

Library of Congress Cataloging-in-Publication Data

VanDoodewaard, William.
  The quest for the historical Adam : genesis, hermeneutics, and human origins / William VanDoodewaard ; foreword by R. Albert Mohler Jr.
    pages cm
  Includes bibliographical references and index.
  ISBN 978-1-60178-377-6 (hardcover : alk. paper) 1. Adam (Biblical figure) 2. Theological anthropology—Biblical teaching. 3. Bible. Genesis—Criticism, interpretation, etc. 4. Bible and science. 5. Religion and science. I. Title.
  BS580.A4V36 2015
  233'.1—dc23
                          2014046792

For additional Reformed literature, request a free book list from Reformation Heritage Books at the above regular or e-mail address.

Contents

Foreword

Each generation of Christians faces its own set of theological challenges. For this generation of evangelicals, the question of beginnings is taking on a new urgency. In fact, this question is now a matter of gospel urgency. How are we to understand the Bible's story if we can have no confidence that we know how it even begins?

In terms of the gospel of Jesus Christ, the most urgent question related to beginnings has to do with the existence of Adam and Eve as the first parents to all humanity and to the reality of the fall as the explanation for human sinfulness and all that comes with sin.

This question has become especially urgent since the Bible's account of beginnings is being increasingly repudiated. We are not talking about arguments over the interpretation of a few verses or even chapters of the Bible. We are now dealing with the straightforward rejection not only of the existence of Adam and Eve but of both Eden and the fall. Though shocking, this line of argument is not really new. The new development is the fact that growing numbers of evangelicals are apparently buying the argument.

Especially since Darwin's challenge and the appearance of evolutionary theory, some Christians have tried to argue that the opening chapters of the Bible should not be taken literally. While no honest reader of the Bible would deny the literary character of Genesis 1–3, the fact remains that significant truth claims are being presented in these chapters. Furthermore, it is clear that the historical character of these chapters is crucial to understanding the Bible's central message—the gospel of Jesus Christ.

The apostle Paul in Romans 5, for example, clearly understood Adam to be a fully historical human who was also the genetic father of the entire human race. The fall of the human race in Adam sets the stage for the salvation of sinful humanity by Jesus Christ.

The implications for biblical authority are clear, as is the fact that if these arguments hold sway, we will have to come up with an entirely new understanding of the gospel metanarrative and the Bible's story line. The denial of a historical Adam and Eve as the first parents of all humanity and the solitary first human pair severs the link between Adam and Christ that is so crucial to the gospel. If we do not know how the story of the gospel begins, then we do not know what that story means. Make no mistake: a false start to the story produces a false grasp of the gospel.

This is one of the many reasons I am thankful for Dr. VanDoodewaard's new book, *The Quest for the Historical Adam: Genesis, Hermeneutics, and Human Origins.* VanDoodewaard's survey of the history of interpretation and subsequent application to modern theological controversy surrounding Genesis 1–3 is just the type of antidote needed to rectify careless theological reflection on this issue. This survey of the history of interpretation is a wonderful step forward in the conversation and a necessary project in the defense of biblical orthodoxy.

—R. Albert Mohler Jr.
President, The Southern Baptist
Theological Seminary

Acknowledgments

This book originated through an invitation to speak at the Origins Conference at Patrick Henry College, near Washington, D.C., in 2012. Little did I, or my wife, expect that nearly two years later what had been a short address on the theological importance of the historicity of Adam for visiting scientists, college faculty, and students would have grown into a project nearly as consuming as another doctoral dissertation. Initial reflections, reading, and conversations, particularly with Stephen Lloyd, led to the awareness that there was a paucity of scholarship on the history of the interpretation of Genesis in relation to human origins. And so the project began.

Many have helped along the way: Neal Doran, Kurt Wise, Todd Wood, and others, provided thoughtful engagement on both the history of science and interpretations of origins. Dariusz Brycko, Gregory Cumbee, Spencer Snow, and Pieter VanderHoek aided in research at points along the way, as did Gerald Bilkes, Gabriel Fluhrer, Laura Ladwig, Michael Lynch, Matthew Miller, Wayne Sparkman, Peter Williams, and Gregory Wills. Michael Barrett was an invaluable sounding board in his erudite knowledge of Hebrew and other ancient Near Eastern languages. Harold Schnyders provided thoughtful engagement on the wider issues of faith and science from the vantage of a Christian physicist. Fred Sweet gave numerous bibliographic recommendations. Others, including Adam Barr, Kevin DeYoung, John Fesko, Jason Helopoulos, Jeffrey Kingswood, Matthew Kingswood, Ryan McGraw, and Benjamin Short, gave encouragement and critical interaction with the manuscript along the way. Joel Beeke, Jay Collier, Annette Gysen, and the rest of the staff at Reformation Heritage Books were kindly helpful throughout.

The following libraries aided through staff and resources: Princeton Theological Seminary Library, Princeton, New Jersey; James P. Boyce Centennial Library, Southern Baptist Theological Seminary, Louisville, Kentucky; Theological University of Apeldoorn Library, Apeldoorn, the Netherlands;

Hekman Library and Archives, Calvin College, Grand Rapids, Michigan; Post-Reformation Digital Library, Calvin Theological Seminary, Grand Rapids; Puritan Reformed Theological Seminary Library, Grand Rapids; Miller Library, Cornerstone University, Grand Rapids; Concordia Theological Seminary Library, St. Louis, Missouri; PCA Historical Center, St. Louis. Without their assistance, this history and analysis of Christian interpretation of Genesis on origins would not be.

More than anyone, my wife, Rebecca, and children, Anna, Matthew, and Julia, deserve thanks for sacrifices made, loving encouragement in the work, and all the rest of life surrounding it. Thank you. Above all I thank our Triune God, the Creator of the heavens, the earth, and everything in them, and the provider of every good gift, for His incalculable goodness and grace. I pray He will prosper all that by His grace is good in this volume, and graciously override its weaknesses. To God alone be the glory.

Introduction

In the late eighteenth and early nineteenth centuries, a new movement developed among Protestant theologians engaging the claims of scientific naturalism and higher criticism: the search for the historical Jesus. Viewing the New Testament text as limited in its account and religiously or culturally conditioned to the point of fallibility, scholars devoted themselves to trying to discern who the historical Jesus "behind the text" actually was. What was He really like? What did He really do? Many were intrigued by the possibility that new textual approaches, in harmony with science, archaeology, and comparative studies, would bring forward a more accurate historical Jesus. This Jesus would be freed from the limitations of the inherently contextualized writings of the early Christian community (i.e., the New Testament), and also freed from millennia of "literalist," "unthinking" attachment of traditional Christianity to these texts. The result, as Albert Schweitzer noted in his *The Quest of the Historical Jesus,* was quite a variety of historical Jesuses, with some even arguing outright for the acceptance of a mythical Jesus.[1] None of these were the Jesus of Scripture. The undermining of Scripture's authority and scriptural doctrine among scholars and teachers in the academy led to an ensuing loss of scriptural doctrine in the life of many mainline Protestant denominations—not only due to the teaching of liberal theologians, but also because of broadly evangelical majorities which either refused or failed to act against them.[2] One result was

---

1. Albert Schweitzer, *The Quest of the Historical Jesus: A Critical Study of Its Progress from Reimarus to Wrede,* trans. W. Montgomery (London: Adam and Charles Black, 1910). Schweitzer presents his analysis and critique of the movement in this work but, in seeking to forge a better alternative, provides a devastating answer which is similarly far from historic Christianity: Jesus was a kingdom-of-God-seeking apocalyptic who challenged the powers of his day but was crushed by them, though his eschatology and "spirit" lived on.

2. Darryl Hart, commenting on the decline of Princeton Theological Seminary in the early twentieth century, states, "Conservatives were no longer in control…it was evangelicals who were not alarmed by liberals who took control of Princeton Theological Seminary [leading to

that as mainline churches moved into increasing theological declension, new conservative denominations and movements formed, whether under the lead of the "fundamentalists" or the confessionals of the early twentieth century.

Today, while most mainline Protestant churches continue along a now-advanced trajectory of decline into apostasy, a movement similar to, though not the same as, the old quest for the historical Jesus is gaining influence. This movement, while passé among mainline Protestants, is an innovative edge of theology among the evangelical and confessional heirs and supporters of the early twentieth-century "fundamentalists" and confessional Protestants.[3] Rather than Jesus Christ, whom Paul proclaims as the second Adam (cf. Romans 5; 1 Cor. 15:45), this quest centers on the first Adam. This "quest for the historical Adam" is not new—it has been pursued to some degree in evangelical academia for decades and has historical precedent going back to at least the nineteenth century. Its popularity is attested by the Biologos Forum, evangelical publishers, well-known preachers, and academics. Driven by arguments and conclusions from the scientific community, some, like Peter Enns, now argue that Adam is merely a mythical representative of early humanity.[4] Others, like John Collins, state that as long as there was "a" historical Adam, issues of who he was, when he lived, and what his origins are may be of little or no consequence to the Christian faith.[5]

Special and General Revelation

Like Schweitzer's *Quest*, this book narrates and assesses a vast topic while tackling "the quest for the historical Adam." It does so recognizing that engagement with evolutionary models of human origins from a scientific standpoint provides a needed and valuable contribution to Christian understanding,

---

its downfall]." Darryl Hart, *Machen and the End of Princeton* (lecture, Greenville Presbyterian Theological Seminary Spring Theology Conference, Greenville, S.C., March 13–15, 2012).

3. "Confessionals" or "confessional Protestants" refers to those Protestant denominations and individuals that continue to meaningfully maintain the commitment of their ministers, elders, congregations, and regional and denominational assemblies or synods to historic Protestant confessions of faith, including the Westminster Standards, the Three Forms of Unity (Belgic Confession, Heidelberg Catechism, Canons of Dordt), the Lutheran Confessions contained in the Book of Concord, and the various Baptist confessions, such as the London Baptist Confession of 1689. The evangelical heirs of the early fundamentalists tended to reflect a movement that subscribed to less comprehensive statements of belief.

4. Peter Enns, *The Evolution of Adam: What the Bible Does and Doesn't Say About Human Origins* (Grand Rapids: Baker, 2012), 122.

5. C. John Collins, *Did Adam and Eve Really Exist?: Who They Were and Why You Should Care* (Wheaton, Ill.: Crossway, 2011), 122, 130–31.

particularly when that engagement is undertaken with the conviction that Scripture has an authoritative and interpretive role where it speaks to comprehending human biological and geological history.[6] Special revelation (the Bible) and general revelation (the natural order) are in harmony with one another. Thus, an accurate understanding of Scripture will in most cases not contradict accurate scientific interpretations of present natural reality, nor vice versa.[7]

Most Christians, whether holding to literal six-day creation, or alternative hermeneutical approaches with a range of conclusions on origins and natural history (including theistic evolutionary models), agree at this point. There is also broad agreement that special revelation and the regenerating work of the Holy Spirit are necessary for salvation due to the fall into sin and the noetic effects of sin, in which men suppress the truth in unrighteousness. Yet, despite such common ground, divergence among evangelicals is widening—and individuals are diverging from historic Protestant evangelicalism—over the question of how to accurately interpret general revelation in coherence with special revelation in the area of creation history and human origins. There is also significant divergence in hermeneutical approaches to special revelation on creation history and human origins—and steady debate as to which are biblically warranted.[8]

Diverging Views of Hermeneutics and Human Origins

The crux of current division on creation and human origins is found where evolutionary theory stands in conflict with the traditional, literalistic reading of Genesis 1 through 5 common to the history of Christianity. Some attempt to harmonize Genesis with evolutionary theory by maintaining a literal reading of early Genesis but viewing it as a primitive conception. More often, evangelicals abandon the traditional literal reading to adopt an alternate hermeneutical approach to the text that allows for better coherence with an

---

6. Valuable areas for contribution in relation to human origins include engaging in the systematics and dating of early human and ape remains and in molecular, population genetics models for the understanding of origins and descent.

7. Exceptions to this include supernatural and miraculous events. It may also be stated that where science is defined, delimited, and epistemologically based in the overarching theology of reality rooted in divine self-revelation, these events should not be understood as contradictions, but rather as coherent in and congruent to a created order under the active sovereignty of God.

8. Andrew Kulikovsky provides a survey of this debate in his chapter, "Scripture, Science and Interpretation," in *Creation, Fall, Restoration: A Biblical Theology of Creation* (Fearn, U.K.: Christian Focus, 2009), 28–58.

evolutionary model of origins. Believing that contemporary scientific interpretation of natural evidence is usually accurate, proponents of these views
argue that the need for adjustment in Christian understanding falls in the area
of interpretation of Scripture and in Christian theology, resulting in a quest
for the historical Adam.[9]

In contrast, those who hold to a literal interpretation of early Genesis
argue that a literal reading, predicated by the textual form and content of early
Genesis, is the clear intent of divine revelation, which is further confirmed
in its harmony with the rest of Scripture. The origin, initial context and condition of man and the rest of creation, the fall into sin, the curse, and the
promise, indicate that early Genesis is innately part of what is necessary to be
known, believed, and observed for salvation.[10] Genesis 1 and 2 are seen as an
intentional and precise historical record of events—a narration of the divine
supernatural work of creation taking place within the space of six days of ordinary duration, with the diverse work of creation including the creation of time
and its measurement by days and weeks. Adam and Eve are understood to
be specially created by God in His image on the sixth day: Adam from the
dust of the earth, and becoming a living being after God breathed into him
the breath of life, and Eve from Adam's rib. As a result, proponents of the literal tradition's interpretation of the Genesis account either reject outright or
loosely hold aspects of mainstream scientific interpretations of human origins
and natural history. Some work toward alternative scientific models, pursuing alternate scientific hermeneutics for the interpretation of the evidence of
general revelation.

Aside from these two divergent groups, there is a third range of possibility which stands somewhat in the middle. It includes those who hold to
alternative hermeneutical approaches and at the same time posit a special,
"temporally immediate" creation of Adam and Eve, following a literal reading
of Genesis 2:7 and 2:21–22.[11] They tend to read at least Genesis 1:1–2:3 with an

---

9. Some of the proponents of alternate hermeneutical approaches reject arguments for a
literal reading of early Genesis, including reference to the doctrine of perspicuity of Scripture,
claiming the need for a more complex hermeneutic as much of this text is not necessarily
"plain in itself" and beyond that necessary for salvation. Westminster Confession of Faith, 1.7.

10 The first chapters of Genesis are seen as belonging to that which is "so clearly propounded, and opened in some place of Scripture or other, that not only the learned, but the
unlearned, in a due use of the ordinary means, may attain to a sufficient understanding of
them." Westminster Confession of Faith, 1.7.

11. The term "special" is used to describe the creation of Adam and Eve as distinct and
separate from the creation of other living things. The term "temporally immediate" refers to
the creation of Adam and Eve as occurring divinely and supernaturally over a relatively brief

overarching "nonliteral" hermeneutic, rejecting the text as a historical narration of God's work of creation, beginning with and spanning the first six ordinary days, while maintaining the text still does convey historical realities. Typically a transition to a more literal approach occurs in relation to some or all of the detail in Genesis 2:4 and following, usually due to the weight of theological and exegetical grounds from the rest of Scripture. This "middle way" receives critique from both literal creationists and full proponents of theistic evolutionary origins as lacking internal consistency.[12] Within the context of Genesis exegesis, such a transition in Genesis 2 arguably relies on what is at best a hermeneutically porous border and at worst a hermeneutical and exegetical inconsistency—despite the theological benefits to a historic confessional evangelical theology in retaining a literal view of the creation of Adam

---

duration of time (less than an ordinary day), a description in replacement of the sixth day "boundaries," which are removed in most of the hermeneutical approaches presented as alternatives to the literal tradition. The use of "temporally immediate" in relation to the creation of the first couple does not necessitate an ex nihilo act and reflects the fact that God used existing, nonliving matter, "the dust of the ground" (Gen. 2:7) in Adam's case and Adam's rib in Eve's case, in creating them. John Murray correctly notes that Reformation and post-Reformation theologians helpfully used the term "immediate" as a theological term in describing creation ex nihilo and "mediate" in describing "a creative action of God, using preexisting material"—speaking of the creation of the soul of man as "immediate" and the body of man as "mediate." While this was functional in the context of a popular conception of a young earth and a creation week of six generally ordinary days, the functionality of the term "mediate" diminished as its semantic range changed with the increasing acceptance of old earth and evolutionary hypotheses. Charles Hodge's adjusted use of the term "mediate" as including God's activity in the course of ordinary providence was commonplace in the nineteenth century and was often synthesized with evolutionary process to form a theistic evolution. B. B. Warfield notes the latter in his essay "Creation, Evolution, and Mediate Creation." While Warfield's argument for returning to the earlier definition of "mediate" creation is helpful in relation to the mode of creation, it nonetheless fails to eliminate the possibility of a theistic evolutionary model under supernatural influence when moved into an old earth context. The introduction of the common philosophical concept of temporal immediacy proves helpful here, just as Tertullian's introduction of a new use for the term "trinity" proved helpful to patristic theology. John Murray, "Immediate and Mediate Creation," *Westminster Theological Journal* 17, no. 1 (November 1954): 22–43; Charles Hodge, "Mediate and Immediate Creation," in *Systematic Theology* (Grand Rapids: Eerdmans, 1997), 1:556–74; B. B. Warfield, "Creation, Evolution, and Mediate Creation," in *B. B. Warfield: Evolution, Science and Scripture—Selected Writings* (Grand Rapids: Baker, 2000), 204–5.

12. See, for example, James B. Jordan's engagement with Waltke, Kline, Collins, Seely, and Futato in his *Creation in Six Days: A Defense of the Traditional Reading of Genesis One* (Moscow, Idaho: Canon, 1999); and Joseph Pipa's "From Chaos to Cosmos: A Critique of the Non-Literal Interpretations of Genesis 1:1–2:3," in *Did God Create in Six Days?*, ed. Joseph A. Pipa and David W. Hall (Greenville, S.C.: Southern Presbyterian Press, 1999), 153–98; as well as the critique by Daniel Harlow in his article, "After Adam: Reading Genesis in an Age of Evolutionary Science," *Perspectives on Science and Christian Faith* 62, no. 3 (September 2010): 179–95.

and Eve. Functionally, it appears to rely heavily on New Testament passages referring to Adam in building a "theology of retrieval"—lifting a specially created Adam and Eve, made as described in Genesis 2 and apart from any evolutionary origins, out of an otherwise substantially less literal Genesis 1 and 2. It shies from some mainstream scientific interpretations on origins for parts of the text (usually in relation to Adam and Eve and the ultimate origins of the universe) but accepts them and calls for adjustment in the interpretation of Scripture at others.

Defining the "Literal Interpretation" of Genesis 1 and 2

In the previous paragraphs, I referred to a "literal" six-day creation and interpretation of Genesis in contrast to alternative hermeneutical approaches. To avoid confusion, let me briefly explain how the term "literal" can be defined and how it is defined and used in this book.

In the field of hermeneutics, a reference to a literal reading of a text is commonly understood to refer to the reading of a text according to its literary genre. In this usage, the "literal" reading of a text could be primarily "figurative" in nature. It could be allegory, prophecy, parable, or poetry—or a mixture of these. This is not without historical precedent, even in application to the interpretation of Genesis 1 and 2. Augustine argued that the "literal sense" of much of the text of Genesis 1 was figurative. Some modern commentators on Genesis, such as Tremper Longman III and C. John Collins, follow a similar approach, stating that they hold to the "literal" reading of the text of Genesis 1 and 2, while maintaining that much of the text is figurative. The weakness of using "literal" in this manner in relation to the interpretation of Genesis 1 and 2 is that it conflicts with the more common use of "literal" in the context of Genesis interpretation—both in the present and through the history of the church.

While acknowledging the varied uses of the term "literal," this book follows the more popular usage in its focus on Genesis interpretation and commentary. It stands with Luther, Tyndale, and other Reformers in defining those who maintain the "literal sense" or "literal interpretation" of Genesis 1 and 2 as those who believe sound exegesis compels one to read this passage "literally"—as a nonfigurative, detailed, historical record of events and existence narrated as they actually were. For those who hold to the "literal interpretation of Genesis," the six days are ordinary days, the sun was created after the initial creation of light, the dust was real dust, the rib a real rib, and Adam and Eve the first people, specially created on the sixth day, without any evolutionary ancestry. Using "the literal interpretation of Genesis 1 and 2" to represent this major stream of Genesis interpretation helpfully delineates this interpretive tradition from alternatives, almost all of which adopt a more figurative reading of the text of Genesis 1 and 2.

Engaging the Quest

The quest for the historical Adam is intimately connected to the confession and life of the church in relation to the Word of God, as well as to an accurate reading of "the book of nature." The Holy Scriptures of the Old and New Testaments are the Word of God, divinely inspired, inerrant, and infallible—and as such authoritative and relevant; thus, the first chapter of this book gives a concise summary of Scripture passages relevant to Adam and Eve and human origins. Doing so provides the reader with God's revelation on human origins and the Hebrew to Christian understanding of the creation origins of humanity—from the first record in Genesis across the millennia of divine inscripturation to the completion of the New Testament canon.

Substantially removed from the apostolic era, we live in an era of extensive discussion and debate over hermeneutical issues and points of exegesis relevant to human origins. New books and articles appear almost monthly. However, the present quest for the historical Adam is often pursued with little attention to history—or at least little attention to historical theology. While it is in vogue to try to understand Genesis and human origins through the lenses of contemporary interpretation of pagan writings from the ancient Near East, scant attention is paid to the historical understanding of Genesis and human origins within Christianity. It is as if all that exists are discussions from the past twenty years or, at most, the last century or so. This historical amnesia obscures the fact that teaching on the early chapters of Genesis and human origins is hardly new. It has been engaged for millennia, from the Old Testament era onward. It would seem that this alone provides good reason to consider what has been said before us by those who sought to honor the true God and His Word.

Christian students of church history are (or should be) well aware that theology can (1) maintain faithful understanding of God's revealed truth, (2) develop a more full understanding of God's revealed truth, or (3) absorb error, leading to distortion and decline. The latter often occurs through the deconstruction and replacement of theology and exegesis. These realities press us to take serious stock of the history of biblical interpretation on human origins. There is a further, weighty reason to do so. Since the first century, Christ has given pastors and teachers of the Scriptures to equip and edify His church "till we all come to the unity of the faith and of the knowledge of the Son of God" (Eph. 4:11–13). Prior to His incarnation, Christ gave prophets and teachers to do the same through the millennia of Old Testament history (see Neh. 8:8). Christ promised that the Holy Spirit would guide the church into all truth, by the means of the Word (John 16:13). We are to search the Scriptures (Acts 17:11) to see whether any given teacher's teaching is true, yet this does not diminish the reality, nor the effectiveness, of Christ's promises. The implication is that apparently "novel" interpretations or expositions of Genesis on human origins require careful scrutiny—exegetically, theologically, and historically. Being aware of the Scripture exposition of those who have gone before us helps prevent us from being "tossed to and fro and carried about with every wind of doctrine" and better enables us to speak "the truth in love" (Eph. 4:14–15).

Chapters two through six of this book serve to recover and assess the teaching of those who have gone before us, providing a historical survey of Genesis commentary on human origins from the patristic era to the present. Reacquainting the reader with a long line of theologians, exegetes, and thinkers, these chapters trace the roots, development, and at times disappearance of streams of hermeneutical approach and exegetical insight relevant to human origins. The final chapter considers what difference it makes to hold to each of the presently offered alternatives on human origins. Welcome to the quest for the historical Adam.

1

Finding Adam and His Origin in Scripture

"Adam, where are you?" was God's call to Adam who was hiding in the garden shortly after he and Eve had fallen into sin. God called to Adam even though He knew exactly what had happened and exactly where Adam was hiding. In human terms, the situation was like a parent calling a child who is clearly visible under the dining room table to demand an account for some recent happening. In our age, interpretations of the realm of general revelation, including those on human origins, have made some Christians uncertain of who Adam was, how and when he came to be, or whether he even existed at all. The question "Adam, where are you?" echoes through the present quest for the historical Adam, though in a significantly different way than in the Genesis narrative.

So where do we begin in our quest? Undoubtedly a return to special revelation to examine what God has told us there is the best way to begin a historical and theological survey and evaluation. What does Scripture, the inerrant and infallible Word of God, say about human origins? What did the inspired authors, from Moses to the apostle John, understand regarding human origins? What did the ancient Hebrews and early Christians believe? This brief introductory overview will refresh your general awareness of key Scripture passages relevant to the origins of man, before turning to survey the postcanonical history of the interpretation of human origins, in the context of approaches to Genesis 1 and 2.

Key Passages in the Old Testament

Genesis 1–9

Genesis 1 opens with an account beginning "in the beginning": God creating the heavens and the earth ex nihilo. The revelation of God's work of creation is ordered by days, marked both by numerical sequence and by evening and morning, darkness and light, from the first day forward. The first "solar" day, day four, is marked by the same parameters. In a sequence of structured, creative activity, God brings the cosmos into being, forms the earth, and creates an abundant variety of life on earth.

The first mention of the origin, nature, and calling of man is found within the account of the sixth day, in Genesis 1:26 and following, "Then God said, 'Let Us make man in Our image, according to Our likeness'.... So God created man in His own image; in the image of God He created him; male and female He created them." Genesis 2:1–3 closes the creation days pericope, noting that the end of the sixth day marks the completion of the work of creation. The text then describes God resting on the seventh day, blessing the day and setting it apart as holy.

Genesis 2:4–7 reiterate with greater detail and context the creation of Adam.[1] God has created the surrounding creation, but neither man nor cultivated plants yet exist: "The LORD God had not caused it to rain on the earth, and there was no man to till the ground" (v. 5). In this setting, God creates Adam, an act of creation described with intimate detail: "The LORD God formed man of the dust of the ground, and breathed into his nostrils the breath of life, and man became a living being" (v. 7). God then plants an abundant garden, including "every tree...that is pleasant to the sight and good for food" (v. 9), and places Adam there to work it and keep it. This second account expands on the Genesis 1 account where God notes that He has given Adam plants and fruit for food. Following a geographical description of the garden's location, the text returns to the garden for a third time, noting God's generous command regarding which trees may be eaten from in the garden.

This is followed in Genesis 2:18–25 by the account of Adam's need for a helpmeet, God's design of the garden, a recapitulation of God's creation of birds and beasts of the field (v. 19), Adam's naming of them, and the lack of a

---

1. Verses 4–6 are a point of interpretive contention. This centers in part on use of the phrase "in the day that the LORD God made the earth and the heavens" which exegetes supportive of alternatives to the literal tradition use to argue that a "day" (Hebrew: *yom*) as used previously in Genesis 1 is not necessarily a twenty-four-hour day. However, literalist exegetes note three distinctions between the use of "day" in Genesis 2:4 and the use of "day" in Genesis 1: (1) the Hebrew word for "day" in Genesis 2:4 is prefixed with a Hebrew preposition which makes it semantically similar to the English "when"—the same form being used in Genesis 2:17. The use of the term "day" in Genesis 1 both lacks this prepositional prefix, and (2) is qualified with the terms "the evening and the morning were" as well as (3) a numerical prefix, as in "so the evening and the morning were the sixth day."

suitable helper among them.[2] In verses 21–25 the account focuses on the creation of the woman, Eve, from Adam's rib: "the LORD God caused a deep sleep
to fall on Adam, and he slept; and He took one of his ribs, and closed up the
flesh in its place. Then the rib which the LORD God had taken from man He
made into a woman, and He brought her to the man" (vv. 21–22). The passage
concludes with Adam's naming her, the paradigm of Adam and Eve for marriage, and their state of innocence.[3]

Genesis 3 and 4 chronicle the fall into sin, the curse and promise, and
the effects on Adam and Eve, Cain and Abel, along with further descendants
of Adam and Eve. Genesis 5, which turns to provide the genealogy of Noah,
begins in verses 1–4 with an account of the creation of Adam and Eve and a
brief synopsis of Adam's life and death. In narrating the reason for the Noahic
flood, Genesis 6:6–8 states, "The LORD was sorry that He had made man on the
earth…. So the LORD said, 'I will destroy man whom I have created…for I am
sorry that I have made them.' But Noah found grace in the eyes of the LORD."
In Genesis 9:6, after the flood, Noah is commanded: "Whoever sheds man's
blood, by man his blood shall be shed; for in the image of God He made man."

Exodus 20

In giving the fourth commandment to the Israelites, Moses declares that the
seventh-day Sabbath of the people of Israel is an ordinance patterned on the

---

2. There is some debate over the translation of the Hebrew term *yatsar* in Genesis 2:19:
some argue it is better translated in English as the perfect "formed," while others argue for the
pluperfect "had formed." Some proponents of figurative approaches to Genesis 1 and 2 argue
that the perfect is the best equivalent to the form of the Hebrew, going on to argue that this
stands as an indicator that there is a contradiction between the creation orders in Genesis 1
and 2, if they are taken literally. This becomes part of their case for a more substantially figurative approach to the text of Genesis 1. Counter to this, most current proponents of the literal
interpretation of Genesis, along with others, including C. J. Collins, Victor Hamilton, and
Kenneth Matthews, note that *yatsar* can be translated legitimately, and literally, as a pluperfect
following principles of Hebrew syntax and grammar, when understood in the wider context
of Genesis 1 and 2. There are also those, like Cassuto, who posit that the perfect is the better
option but argue it indicates that at this point God formed particular specimens for the purpose of presenting them to Adam. William Tyndale interpreted the Hebrew as pluperfect in
his translation, while the King James Version chose the perfect: both in the context of commitment to the literal tradition. Most modern English translations, such as the English Standard
Version and the New International Version, interpret *yatsar* in Genesis 2:19 as a pluperfect.

3. In Genesis 2:23, Adam names the woman, as recorded here in Hebrew, *Ishshah*, literally translated as "this one" or "woman" or "wife." The textual chronology of early Genesis
indicates that it is after the fall, the curse, and promise, when he renames her "Eve," in Hebrew
Chavvah, meaning "life" or "living" because "she was the mother of all living" (Gen. 3:20).
Many commentators see this as an act of faith in God's promise of redemption in Genesis 3:15.

seventh-day rest of God upon completion of the work of creation: "For in six days the LORD made the heavens and the earth, the sea, and all that is in them, and rested the seventh day" (Ex. 20:11). The creation origins of humanity are included in this passage by implication as part of the "all that is in them." Moses reaffirms that man, along with all the rest of creation, was created by God within the space of the first six days.

Deuteronomy 4

In this passage, Moses challenges the people of Israel to consider the immense wonder of God's awesome presence with them and audible speech to them at Sinai. Calling them to see its significance in human history since the creation of man, Moses declares, "Ask now concerning the days that are past, which were before you, since the day that God created man on the earth, and ask from one end of heaven to the other, whether any great thing like this has happened, or anything like it has been heard" (Deut. 4:32). The juxtaposition of Moses' use of "days" with "the day that God created man on the earth" points to the specific day, the sixth day on which man was created, and reaffirms that man was created by divine initiative and activity.

1 Chronicles 1

The historical narrative of the books of Chronicles begins with a genealogical list that spans from Adam through succeeding chapters to the returned exiles, with a particular focus on the genealogies and geographical locations of the twelve tribes and genealogies of the kings, Saul and David. The author views Adam as the beginning point of humanity, the genealogy itself as representative of God's covenant faithfulness. Consistent with the Mosaic account in Genesis, Adam is the first man.

Job 10

In this part of the book, Job laments his situation and pleads with God, echoing Genesis 2 as he recounts to God that he, as a man, is an intimate work of God: "Your hands have made me and fashioned me, an intricate unity; yet You would destroy me" (Job 10:8).

Job 38–40

These chapters comprise God's rebuke to Job, in which God reveals that He is the Creator and Sustainer of all, the One clothed in glory and splendor. In describing the most powerful and massive of created beasts, God notes, "Look now at the behemoth, which I made along with you" (Job 40:15). God declares that He is the Creator not only of these beasts, but also of man.

Psalm 8

Psalm 8 proclaims God's glory revealed in His creative works from the physical heavens to man. It then turns to trace God's creative works among living creatures, from the spiritual beings, such as the angels, to man and his place and role over the rest of God's creatures and creation. "For You have made him a little lower than the angels, and You have crowned him with glory and honor. You have made him to have dominion over the works of Your hands" (Ps. 8:5–6). David reflects the Mosaic understanding, first recorded in Genesis, that man was specially created, distinct from the rest of the "works of [God's] hands" in purpose and role.

Psalm 89

A psalm of praise and lament, Psalm 89 recounts God's covenant love toward his people and declares God's incomparable faithfulness and power as the sovereign Creator and Redeemer. Verses 38–48 lament God's wrath and judgment and the brevity and vanity of life in the face of death. In verse 47, the psalmist cries out to God as he reflects on Him as both the Creator and Judge of man: "Remember how short my time is; for what futility have You created all the children of men?"

Psalm 104

Psalm 104 praises God for His glory and grace, focusing on His providential sustenance of His gloriously complex and diverse creation, creation's continuing dependence on God, and His ongoing creative work flowing from the initial work of creation (cf. Pss. 102:18; 104:30). Verse 24 exalts God for His work of creation, including man (v. 23), declaring "O LORD, how manifold are Your works! In wisdom You have made them all; the earth is full of Your possessions."

Psalm 119

Here, the psalmist echoes the language of both Job and Genesis: "Your hands have made me and fashioned me; give me understanding" (Ps. 119:73).

Psalm 148

This psalm exalts the Lord for His glory and majesty, calling on all creation to praise Him. It calls angels, stars, sun, moon, and skies to "praise the name of the LORD, for He commanded and they were created" (v. 5). The psalmist calls the earth, its creatures, and mankind to praise God, again recounting His exalted majesty, as well as His salvation—the inference being that the earth and its inhabitants were created at God's command.

Ecclesiastes 3, 7, 12

In speaking of the apparent futility of life in the face of death, Ecclesiastes notes that the condition of men is like that of animals: "as one dies, so dies the other…all are from the dust, and all return to dust" (3:19–20). In noting these similarities, including their formation from the dust, the passage at the same time distinguishes man categorically from animals.

The book of Ecclesiastes refers two further times to the creation of man: the first time directly, with reference to man's original state of innocence, and the second by implication of man's relationship to God. Chapter 7 verse 29 states, "God made man upright, but they have sought out many schemes." The familiar call to "Remember now your Creator in the days of your youth" is in verse one of chapter 12.

Isaiah 40–45

Numerous passages in Isaiah reveal God's work as Creator, though the implications of this for human origins are most often by inference, rather than being explicit and direct. In Isaiah 40, the prophet contrasts God as the sovereign Creator with the idols created by men. God, speaking by His servant, declares, "'To whom then will you liken Me, or to whom shall I be equal?' says the Holy One. Lift up your eyes on high, and see who has created these things…. The everlasting God, the LORD, the Creator of the ends of the earth, neither faints nor is weary" (40:25, 28). This passage does not speak directly to the origins of man but to the created context of his existence, by inference including man who is encompassed by this creation.

Isaiah 42, a passage often referred to as one of the Servant Songs of the book, is a prophecy of coming redemption. It places the work of the redemption of God's people in the context of and being carried out by "the LORD, who created the heavens and stretched them out, who spread forth the earth and that which comes from it, who gives breath to the people on it, and spirit to those who walk on it" (42:5). In chapter 43, Isaiah prophesies of the work of the Redeemer who is also the Creator, gathering His people to Himself from across the earth: "Bring My sons from afar, and My daughters from the ends of the earth—everyone who is called by My name, whom I have created for My glory; I have formed him, yes, I have made him" (43:6–7).

Prophesying of Cyrus and the return of the exiles, Isaiah declares in chapter 45, "thus says the LORD…I have made the earth, and created man on it. I—My hands—stretched out the heavens, and all their host I have commanded" (45:11–12). Man is described here as a distinct creation of God, existing in the midst of the rest of God's creation.

Jeremiah 27

In this chapter of Jeremiah's prophecy, God calls the prophet to tell the kings of Edom, Moab, Ammon, Tyre, Sidon, and Zedekiah of Jerusalem, of His sovereignty in ordaining the reign of Nebuchadnezzar, the king of Babylon, and the futility of opposing him. Jeremiah proclaims, "Thus says the LORD of hosts, the God of Israel…'I have made the earth, the man and the beast that are on the ground, by My great power and by My outstretched arm, and have given it to whom it seemed proper to Me'" (27:4–5). The passage reflects God's work of special creation, distinguishing His creation of man from His creation of animals.

Ezekiel 28, 37

In Ezekiel 28 we find a prophecy of lament addressed to the king of Tyre. Verses 12–13 include a descriptive analogy between the king and Adam's creation and exalted position in Eden: "You were the seal of perfection, full of wisdom and perfect in beauty. You were in Eden, the garden of God…. The workmanship of your timbrels and pipes was prepared for you on the day you were created."

Ezekiel's vision of the valley of dry bones in Ezekiel 37 contains another apparent allusion to the account of Adam's creation in Genesis 2:7 when Ezekiel is called to prophesy: "O dry bones, hear the word of the LORD! Thus says the Lord GOD to these bones: 'Surely I will cause breath to enter into you, and you shall live. I will put sinews on you and bring flesh upon you, cover you with skin and put breath in you; and you shall live. Then you shall know that I am the LORD'" (Ezek. 37:4–6).

Malachi 2

Malachi 2:9–10 show the prophet addressing the sin of treachery in the covenant nation, calling them to reflect on both covenantal community and familial unity of race: "Have we not all one Father? Has not one God created us?" (Mal. 2:10). Malachi, a postexilic prophet, does so in clear continuity with the Genesis account of human origins.

Key Passages in the New Testament

Matthew 19; Mark 10

The gospels of Matthew and Mark both record Jesus' reference to the creation of Adam and Eve in relation to marriage and divorce. Mark notes Jesus saying, "From the beginning of the creation, God 'made them male and female.' 'For this reason a man shall leave his father and mother and be joined to his wife, and the two shall become one flesh'" (10:6–8).

Luke 3

As we turn to the New Testament Gospels, the first place we encounter reference to Adam is in Luke's genealogy. In contrast to the genealogy given by Matthew, which traces back to Abraham, Luke traces from Jesus back to "Adam, the son of God" (3:38). The significance of this genealogy is found in its connection to and indication of fulfillment of the promise of Genesis 3:15.

Acts 17

Acts 17 contains Paul's evangelistic address to the Athenians on Mars Hill. Using the altar to the unknown god as a point of contact, Paul declares, "Therefore the One whom you worship without knowing, Him I proclaim to you: 'God, who made the world and everything in it, since He is Lord of heaven and earth, does not dwell in temples made with hands. Nor is He worshiped with men's hands, as though He needed anything, since He gives to all life, breath, and all things. And He has made from one blood every nation of men to dwell on all the face of the earth" (17:23–26). Paul proclaims God as the Creator of both man and the rest of creation, and the unity of humanity in their common origin in Adam.

Romans 5

The apostle Paul here declares the reality of sin and death in Adam and life in Christ. Through Adam sin entered the world, and death through sin and so death spread to all men because all sinned (5:12). Paul describes Adam as the head of the human race, the one original man, "a type of Him who was to come" (5:14) and Jesus Christ as the fulfillment of God's promise of redemption, the one man in whom the gift of grace (5:15) is found. In doing so, the epistle rests on the Genesis revelation that Adam was the first man, the divinely created progenitor of the human race.

1 Corinthians 11, 15

In describing good order in the worship life of the church, including gender appropriate appearance, 1 Corinthians 11 makes several references to the original creation of man and woman, drawing on the pattern of Genesis 2: "Nor was man created for the woman, but woman for the man.... For as woman came from man, even so man also comes through woman; but all things are from God" (11:9, 12).

Paul's writings on the resurrection in chapter 15 make direct reference to Adam. The first reference closely parallels that of Romans 5, with Paul stating "since by man came death, by Man also came the resurrection of the dead. For as in Adam all die, even so in Christ all shall be made alive" (15:21–22). The second reference more directly refers to God's work of creation, beginning by distinguishing between different bodies and kinds of flesh as given by God to men, animals, and plants (15:37–39) and then drawing a parallel to the resurrection, differentiating between the present and resurrection states of the body.

Paul concludes this section of the first epistle to the Corinthians by drawing directly from Genesis 2: "And so it is written, 'The first man Adam became a living being.' The last Adam became a life-giving spirit.... The first man was of the earth, made of dust; the second Man is the Lord from heaven. As was the man of dust, so also are those who are made of dust; and as is the heavenly Man, so also are those who are heavenly. And as we have borne the image of the man of dust, we shall also bear the image of the heavenly Man" (15:45–49). The content and the way Paul uses the Genesis account of the creation of Adam in this epistle indicate that he views it as divinely authoritative historical narrative.

Colossians 3

Colossians 3 connects the unity of believers redeemed in Christ to the underlying reality of unity of race in the creation of man in the image of God: "You have put off the old man with his deeds, and have put on the new man who is renewed in knowledge according to the image of Him who created him, where there is neither Greek nor Jew, circumcised nor uncircumcised, barbarian, Scythian, slave nor free, but Christ is all and in all" (3:9–11).

1 Timothy 2

In this chapter of his first epistle to Timothy, Paul addresses gender roles and teaching in worship, drawing on the Genesis order of the creation of man and woman: "For Adam was formed first, then Eve" (2:13).

James 3

James, in the familiar chapter on the tongue, calls Christians to consistent holiness in speech in honor to God and out of respect to fellow men who are created in God's image: "With it we bless our God and Father, and with it we curse men, who have been made in the similitude of God" (3:9).

Jude

The short epistle of Jude makes the last direct reference to Adam in the New Testament, doing so in order to identify the historical person of Enoch: "Enoch, the seventh from Adam, prophesied about these men" (v. 14). In doing so, he infers the accuracy of Genesis as historical narrative, including the genealogical record.

Revelation 4, 10, 21–22

While the book of Revelation does not make specific reference to Adam or Eve, it does make general reference to God's work of creation and re-creation as encompassing man. The song of the redeemed in Revelation 4:11 proclaims, "For You created all things, and by Your will they exist and were created." The angel of Revelation 10 swears by "Him who lives forever and ever, who created heaven and the things that are in it, the earth and the things that are in it, and the sea and the things that are in it" (v. 6). Chapters 21 and 22 look forward to describe the new creation and the glorious condition of the redeemed in it, where "there shall be no more death…for the former things have passed away" (21:4), where the Tree of Life is, and where "they shall reign forever and ever" (22:5).

A Reflective Summary

From the positive teaching of Scripture, there is no inherent ground to posit anything aside from a special, temporally immediate creation of Adam and Eve as the first humans on the sixth day of creation. While God's mediate use of the "dust of the ground" in forming Adam is plain, as is His use of Adam's rib to form Eve, no indication is given of divine use of lengthy mediate processes in their creation, nor is there mention of a lineage of created ancestors of or predecessors to Adam and Eve. Scripture repeatedly distinguishes between man and animal as distinct and separate in created origins and continued existence.

The texts of Scripture positively declare the reality of God as the Creator of man and woman: Adam and Eve as the first human beings and the first parents of subsequent humanity by ordinary generation. References after early

Genesis, including those in the New Testament, view Adam and Eve as historical persons and their creation as a unique historical event, as recorded in Genesis. Scripture testifies to the uniqueness of humanity in relationship to God, as divine image-bearer and of humanity's role in and over the rest of creation. Turning to Scripture to answer the question, "Where are you, Adam?" unveils a wide and unified, divinely inspired testimony clearly locating both the man, Adam, and his creative origin and context. This divine testimony was revealed, proclaimed, and believed from the earliest beginnings to the days of the apostles. Now, however, a wide range of answers is given in the quest for the historical Adam.

Even a cursory comparison of the scriptural record and ancient belief with our contemporary diversity raises the questions: Why the apparent difference and discrepancy between then and now? What has changed; what has remained constant? The following chapters trace how Christians and the Christian church have understood Genesis and human origins across the nearly twenty centuries since the completion of the canon of Scripture.

2

The Patristic and Medieval
Quest for Adam

How has the "quest for the historical Adam" been pursued and resolved since the completion of the canon of Scripture? Where, and how, has Adam been found in patristic, medieval, Reformation, post-Reformation, and modern church history? In what context did his origin lie? What was his origin? For most of the history of the church, the quest for the historical Adam and his origin has been resolved primarily by turning to Scripture—especially to Genesis 1 and 2. This chapter narrates the history of patristic and medieval biblical interpretation and exposition of the origins of Adam and Eve as situated within the Genesis context of the origin of the rest of creation.

Patristic Theology on Origins
Near-eternal to eternal cosmologies were common to the religious and philosophical milieu of the Greco-Roman world. Some streams of Jewish tradition prior to and during the Roman era held to a literal understanding of creation, congruent with Second Temple writings including Tobit and Sirach, and more extensively displayed in the writings of Josephus.[1] In contrast, Philo of

---

1. Tobit (c. 250–175 BC) refers to the creation of Adam and Eve, as does Sirach (c. 196–175 BC), both in a manner congruent to the literal tradition. Sirach 17:1–5 states, "God created man of the earth, and made him after his own image...he created of him a helpmeet like to himself," with 33:10 stating, "And all men are from the ground, and out of the earth, from whence Adam was created." Tobit 8:6 (v. 8, Latin Vulgate, following Codex Amiantinus), states, "You made Adam out of the slime/mud of the earth, and gave him Eve for a helper." Robert Weber and Roger Gryson, eds., *Biblia Sacra Iuxta Vulgatam Versionem* (Stuttgart, Germany: Deutsche Bibelgesellschaft, 1994), 684. The Septuagint versions of Tobit do not include the clause "out of the slime/mud of the earth," raising the question as to whether this was an early Christian interpolation in the Vulgate—or whether the Aramaic version of the text used by Jerome, no longer extant, was the source of this statement, potentially allowing for it as original, with a subsequent removal in, or prior to, the creation of the Septuagint texts. Cf. Stuart Weeks, Simon Gathercole, and Loren Stuckenbruck, eds., *The Book of Tobit: Texts from*

Alexandria (20 BC–AD 50), a Hellenistic Jewish philosopher, exerted signifi-cant influence by using an allegorical hermeneutic while seeking to reconcile aspects of the Genesis creation account with Greek approaches to origins and existence. Appropriating significant aspects of allegory, "as it was practiced both in the Stoic interpretations of Homer and in the Middle Platonic inter-pretations of the *Odyssey*," Philo argued that the Mosaic account of creation was not to be taken literally.[2]

However, Philo was somewhat more guarded when the Greek philo-sophical approaches to their religious and mythical literature involved either a complete "rejection of the literal interpretation, or at least complete obliviousness."[3] Lest he be charged with nullifying the Mosaic law, part of the same corpus of writing, Philo stated that the literal sense of the early chap-ters of Genesis was adapted to human needs. The correct interpretation of this portion of the Mosaic record was allegorical: six days did not refer to time, but "to principles of order and productivity."[4] Philo would go on to accept a Hellenistic Jewish tradition of a double creation of man: a "heavenly man" in Genesis 1, and the "earthly man" in a material world in Genesis 2, further arguing that the Genesis 2 account was primarily intended as "an allegory of the soul"—"similar to Neoplatonic allegories which cluster around the figure of Odysseus."[5] Philo's somewhat gnostic approach to the Genesis text provoked debate in the Jewish community that continued well into the medieval period. Both Philo's allegorical method and the broader Greco-Roman philosophical context would prove influential, particularly in later Alexandrian Christian thought on early Genesis.[6]

---

the *Principal Ancient and Medieval Traditions: With Synopsis, Concordances, and Annotated Texts in Aramaic, Hebrew, Greek, Latin, and Syriac* (New York: de Gruyter, 2004), 2–3, 224–25. Titus Flavius Josephus, *Antiquities of the Jews*, 1.1.1.

2. Thomas H. Tobin, *The Creation of Man: Philo and the History of Interpretation* in *The Catholic Biblical Quarterly Monograph Series 14* (Washington, D.C.: Catholic Biblical Associa-tion of America, 1983), 154–55.

3. Tobin, *Creation of Man*, 155.

4. F. H. Colson and G. H. Whitaker, trans., *Philo* (Cambridge, Mass.: Harvard University Press, 2001), 1:2–5. Emil Hirsch notes that Philo is not always consistent in opposing a literal reading, as is evident in his "Questions and Answers on Genesis." "Philo," in *The Jewish Ency-clopedia* (New York: Funk and Wagnalls, 1925), 336–39.

5. Tobin, *Creation of Man*, 132–76. Tobin notes that "as in Philo's allegory of the soul, the Neoplatonic interpreters of the *Odyssey* no longer take the text to refer to events in the external world, but concentrate on the internal struggle of every human soul to transcend the material world and the vices connected with it." Tobin, *Creation of Man*, 150–51.

6. John Dillon, "Cosmic Gods and Primordial Chaos in Hellenistic and Roman Philoso-phy: The Context of Philo's Interpretation of Plato's *Timaeus* and the Book of Genesis"; Robert

Alexandrian Christianity and Allegory

The early Christian church was, of course, bequeathed with the Scriptures of the Old and New Testaments, but it also lived in a time when an increasing number of pagan intellectuals viewed works of popular Greco-Roman polytheism—represented by the *Iliad*, *Odyssey*, and *Aeneid*—as crude to embarrassingly barbaric. These intellectuals preferred Neoplatonic or gnostic readings that provided a more philosophical or spiritual alternative. They also posited an ancient earth.[7] While numerous patristic writers took up the pen against Greek philosophies that posited a progressively developing ancient earth, it was particularly in Alexandria that theologians like Clement of Alexandria (c. 150–211) and his successor Origen (c. 184–254) pursued a synthetic, allegorical approach to Genesis as they engaged with Greco-Roman philosophy and critics of Christianity.[8]

Origen, following Clement's lead, adopted a threefold hermeneutic, believing that every text of Scripture had "a deeper meaning requiring allegory."[9] Origen's hermeneutical method of allowing for multiple senses or layers of meaning (in his case *expecting* a deeper or hidden meaning), did not necessarily negate a remaining and literal sense. However, it certainly allowed interpretive fluidity and provided at least the potential of an alternative primary meaning. Using this hermeneutic, Origen, like Clement, criticized those who held to a "superficial interpretation" of the early chapters of Genesis and "say that the creation of the world happened during a period of time six days long."[10] Graeme Goldsworthy suggests that the motive of Christian

---

M. van den Berg, "God the Creator, God the Creation: Numenius' Interpretation of Genesis 1:2"; Teun Tieleman, "Galen and Genesis," in George H. van Kooten, ed., *The Creation of Heaven and Earth: Re-interpretations of Genesis 1 in the Context of Judaism, Ancient Philosophy, Christianity, and Modern Physics* (Leiden: Brill, 2005), 97–145.

7. Jan N. Bremmer, "Canonical and Alternative Creation Myths in Ancient Greece," in *Creation of Heaven and Earth*, 73–90.

8. James Mook cites Hippolytus's *Refutation of All Heresies*, 10.2; Basil of Caesarea's *Hexaemeron*, 1.2; and Lactantius's *Institutes*, 7.14 in "The Church Fathers: Young Earth Creationists" (lecture, Origins 2012 Conference, Patrick Henry College, Purcellville, Va., July 28, 2012). Herman Bavinck helpfully discusses the evolutionary concept of the Greek philosophers in his *In the Beginning: Foundations of Creation Theology* (Grand Rapids: Baker, 1999), 139.

9. Graeme Goldsworthy, *Gospel-Centered Hermeneutics* (Downers Grove, Ill.: IVP Academic, 2006), 95.

10. Origen, *Contra Celsum* (Cambridge: Cambridge University Press, 1980), 375. Robert Letham, "'In The Space of Six Days': The Days of Creation from Origen to the Westminster Assembly," *Westminster Theological Journal* 61 (1999): 147–74, gives an interpretive survey of a few key figures, including Origen, from each era of church history up to the Westminster Assembly.

interpreters of Scripture in Alexandria was to "avoid saying unworthy things about God" while also holding that "nothing should be affirmed against the rule of faith."[11] Origen's interaction with Celsus, a Greek philosopher, illustrates this approach, with Celsus exemplifying anti-Christian mockery of the Genesis text.

Origen believed that the Genesis description of six days of creation should be taken in a spiritual sense, a view at least partially due to the culturally pervasive influence of Neoplatonic thought. Believing that creation was a temporal expression of an eternal order necessarily implies that the act of creation essentially took place outside of time, in Origen's view. He combined this with a two-stage view of creation: God's original creation was spiritual, followed by subsequent creation of the material world. Origen held that the latter took place in one simultaneous act but is presented to us by God in sequential, "six-day" form to accommodate our capacity to understand. Despite the complexities, and at times arbitrariness, of his allegorical reading of early Genesis, Origen nonetheless held to a creation ex nihilo of the material world. He believed that Adam, though preexistent to the material creation in his spiritual being, was materially created by God from the dust of the earth, just as Eve was materially created from Adam's rib.[12] Aside from novel views of Genesis 1 and 2, Origen held to the literal sense of much of the Genesis text, believing "the Mosaic cosmogony…indicates that the world is not yet ten thousand years old, but is much less than that."[13]

Literal Interpretation and the Early Fathers

Despite the movement of the Alexandrian school of interpretation to both allegorize the six days and hold to a special, temporally immediate creation of Adam and Eve, many patristic writers continued to hold to the latter in the context of a literal interpretation of the early chapters of Genesis as historical narrative.[14] This interpretation is evident from the period of the formation of

---

11. Goldsworthy, *Hermeneutics*, 95.

12. Relating the creation of animals on the "sixth day," Origen states, "there is certainly no question about the literal meaning. For they are clearly said to have been created by God, whether animals or four footed creatures or beasts or serpents upon the earth." Origen, *Homilies on Genesis and Exodus* (Washington, D.C.: Catholic University of America Press, 1981), 60. See also Origen, *Contra Celsum*, 213.

13. Origen, *Contra Celsum*, 20. Michael Haykin provides a helpful assessment of Origen's exegesis in the chapter "Interpreting the Scriptures: The Exegesis of Origen" in his *Rediscovering the Church Fathers* (Wheaton, Ill.: Crossway, 2011), 69–90.

14. In doing so, they were not necessarily rejecting a further allegorical or typological

the New Testament canon onward. For example, *1 Clement* (c. 90–100) provides a short exposition of aspects of Genesis 1 and 2, giving no indication of treating as allegory its description of God's work of creation, including the creation of man: "Above all, as the most excellent and by far the greatest work of his intelligence, with his holy and faultless hands he formed mankind as a representation of his own image…and God created humankind; male and female he created them. So, having finished all these things, he praised them and blessed them and said, 'increase and multiply.'"[15] Justin Martyr (100– c. 165), in his "Dialogue with Trypho," is more extensive in his reflections on the creation of Adam and Eve, presenting a literal understanding of a special, temporally immediate creation of Adam and Eve.[16]

In Antioch, the theologian Theophilus (died, c. 183–185) wrote more extensively on creation in the second book of his *Apology*, which he addressed to "Autolycus, an idolater and scorner of Christians."[17] Theophilus challenged Greek philosophical conceptions of origins, maintaining that God created all things in six days, in the time and order stated in Genesis.[18] His literal approach was particularly evident as he argued that God created "plants and seeds…prior to the heavenly bodies."[19] God did so to display that His glory, power, and wisdom surpass that of man: "On the fourth day [God created] the luminaries…because God, who possesses foreknowledge knew the follies of the vain philosophers, that they were going to say, that the things which grow on the earth are produced from the heavenly bodies."[20] Theophilus referred to the Genesis 2 account of the creation of man "of the dust of the earth" as being a divinely given expansion of the Genesis 1 account of the sixth day, "since

---

sense at points in the text. A number of patristic theologians, while seeing the six days as real, ordinary days, at the same time held to the tradition of viewing them as typological, or eschatologically prophetic, of a six-thousand-year existence for the creation prior to the return of Christ.

15. "1 Clement," in *The Apostolic Fathers*, 3rd ed., trans. Michael Holmes (Grand Rapids: Baker, 2007), 88–89.

16. Justin Martyr, "Dialogue with Trypho," in *Ante-Nicene Fathers* (Peabody, Mass.: Hendrickson, 1989), 1:228, 241.

17. Theophilus of Antioch, "Theophilus to Autolycus: Book I," in *Ante-Nicene Fathers*, 2:89.

18. Andrew Louth argues that this is "the earliest Christian account of the six days of creation." "The Six Days of Creation According to the Greek Fathers," in *Reading Genesis After Darwin*, ed. Stephen C. Barton and David Wilkinson (Oxford: Oxford University Press, 2009), 40.

19. Theophilus of Antioch, "Theophilus to Autolycus: Book II," in *Ante-Nicene Fathers*, 2:101.

20. Theophilus of Antioch, "Theophilus to Autolycus: Book II," 2:101.

his [man's] creation was not yet plainly related."[21] Irenaeus (c. 115–202), in his "Against Heresies," describes the "only-begotten Son of the only God, who… became flesh for the sake of men…flesh is that which was of old formed for Adam by God out of the dust."[22] His acceptance of a literal reading of the Genesis text becomes more explicit later in the work when he states,

> Adam, had his substance from untilled and as yet virgin soil, and was formed by the hand of God, that is, by the Word of God, for "all things were made by him," and the Lord took dust from the earth and formed man…. If then, the first Adam had a man for his father, and was born of human seed, it were reasonable to say that the second Adam was begotten of Joseph. But if the former was taken from the dust, and God was his Maker, it was incumbent that the latter also, making a recapitulation in Himself, should be formed as man by God, to have an analogy with the former as respects His origin. Why, then, did not God again take dust, but wrought so that the formation should be made of Mary? It was that there might not be another formation called into being, nor any other which should [require to] be saved, but that the very same formation should be summed up [in Christ as had existed in Adam], the analogy having been preserved.[23]

Like his African contemporary Origen, Tertullian (c. 160 – c. 225) also engaged contemporary challenges to Christianity posed by Greek natural philosophers. Unlike Origen, Tertullian's debate with Hermogenes revealed a steady commitment to a literal hermeneutic. Drawing on Greek philosophy, Hermogenes rejected God's initial work of creation as ex nihilo, instead positing that God created all things out of eternally preexistent "matter." In his reply to Hermogenes's attempts to provide an alternate reading of the text in harmony with this belief, Tertullian states,

> The Holy Ghost made this the rule of His Scripture, that whenever anything is made out of anything, He mentions both the thing that is made and the thing of which it is made. "Let the earth," says He, "bring forth grass, the herb yielding seed, and the fruit-tree yielding fruit after its kind…and it was so. And the earth brought forth grass, and herb yielding seed after its kind, and the tree yielding fruit, whose seed was in itself, after its kind."… If therefore God, when producing things out of things which had been already made, indicates them by the prophet, and tells us what He has produced from such and such a source (although we might

---

21. Theophilus of Antioch, "Theophilus to Autolycus: Book II," 2:102.
22. Irenaeus, "Against Heresies," in *Ante-Nicene Fathers*, 1:329.
23. Irenaeus, "Against Heresies," 1:454.

ourselves suppose them to be derived from some source or other, short of nothing; since there already had been created certain things, from which they might easily seem to have been made); if the Holy Ghost took upon himself so great a concern for our instruction, that we might know from what everything was produced, would He not in like manner have kept us well informed about both the heaven and the earth, by indicating to us what he made them of…? Therefore just as He shows us the original out of which He drew such things as were derived from a given source, so also with regard to those things…which He confirms that they were produced out of nothing.[24]

Reflecting on the special creation of man, Tertullian further displayed the exegetical consistency of his hermeneutic:

The Scripture, which at its very outset proposes to run through the very order [of creation], tells us as its first information that it was created; it next proceeds to set forth what sort of earth it was…. Similarly (it afterwards) treats of man: "And God created man, in the image of God made He him." It next reveals how He made him, "And (the Lord) God formed man of the dust of the ground, and breathed into his nostrils the breath of life; and man became a living soul." Now this is undoubtedly the correct and fitting mode for the narrative. First comes a prefatory statement, then follow the details in full; first the subject is named, then it is described….

[Scripture] says that "God made the man of the dust of the ground and breathed into his nostrils the breath of life, and man became a living soul." Now, although it here mentions the nostrils, it does not say that they were made by God; so again it speaks of skin and bones, and flesh and eyes, and sweat and blood, in subsequent passages, and yet it never intimated that they had been created by God. What will Hermogenes have to answer? That the human limbs must belong to Matter, because they are not specially mentioned as objects of creation?… In the bodies the limbs are made, in the bodies the limbs too were mentioned.[25]

Patristic writers sympathetic to a literal reading of Genesis on origins reflected both thoughtful nuance and variety in their application of hermeneutical approaches to Scripture—in each case their view of the nature of the text at hand played a determinative role. Hippolytus of Rome (170–235), while adopting a strongly allegorical reading of the Song of Solomon, followed a literal reading of the text as a historical narrative in his exegetical comments on Genesis, arguing that not only does the text of Genesis 2:7 indicate the

24. Tertullian, "Against Hermogenes," in *Ante-Nicene Fathers*, 3:490.
25. Tertullian, "Against Hermogenes," 3:492, 495.

spiritual significance of man as created by God, but also that the "narrative tells 'how' He makes him."[26] In doing so, he demonstrates the reality that interpretive approaches—even among the patristic mainstream committed to a literal approach to Genesis and human origins—could and did vary depending on the text at hand. Within the wider patristic context, the Alexandrian school, as exemplified in Clement of Alexandria and Origen, stood distinct in its frequent, if not consistent, use of a strongly allegorical method. It appears to have been the primary source of a largely nonliteral, allegorical, or figurative approach to Genesis.

Antioch versus Alexandria

The most decided opposition to the Alexandrian hermeneutical tendencies to "over allegorize" was found in the hermeneutical tradition of Antioch, which appears to go back to Theophilus. One of the later Antiochian critics of the Alexandrian school, Diodore of Tarsus (died c. 390), stated, "The historical sense, in fact, is not in opposition to the more elevated sense; on the contrary, it proves to be the basis and foundation of the more elevated ideas."[27] Theodore of Mopsuestia (350–428), while accepting typological interpretations in Scripture where he believed textually warranted, similarly decried the Alexandrian approach. Theodore declares, "Whenever they speak of their allegorical interpretations, I say again and again that these are truly dependent on the pagans who have invented these [kinds of interpretation] in order to set aside their fables as they are [now] setting aside the true facts present in the divine Scriptures."[28] As one might expect, Theodore is decidedly literal in his interpretation of the Genesis 2 accounts of the creation of Adam and Eve.[29] Theodoret of Cyrus (c. 393–c. 457), another representative of the Antiochian stream, reflects the reality that the Antiochian approach, while strongly supportive of a literal hermeneutic, nonetheless saw a place for figurative interpretation where textually warranted and in harmony with the rule of faith. In commenting on Psalm 119:73, Theodoret notes, "'Your hands made me and shaped me,' [as penned by the Psalmist] reminds the Creator of his love for human nature:

---

26. Hippolytus of Rome, "Fragments from Commentaries," in *Ante-Nicene Fathers*, 5:163, 168.

27. Diodore of Tarsus, *Commentary on Psalms 1–51*, trans. Robert C. Hill (Atlanta: Society of Biblical Literature, 2005), xxv.

28. Theodore of Mopsuestia, "In Opposition to the Allegorists," in *Theodore of Mopsuestia*, trans. Frederick G. McLeod (London: Routledge, 2009), 76.

29. Theodore of Mopsuestia, "The Creation of Adam and Eve," in *Theodore of Mopsuestia*, 93–94.

having devised everything by a word, he is said to have formed humankind, not by use of hands, being incorporeal, but by giving evidence of greater affection towards this creature. So he begs the one who formed it to furnish the creature with understanding."[30] The Antiochian hermeneutical stream, along with the Alexandrian, exerted a significant and long-enduring influence in the history of Christianity.[31]

Basil of Caesarea

Numerous theologians in the East, including Basil of Caesarea (329–379), advocated a literal reading of early Genesis that was similar to the Antiochian approach.[32] In his work "The Hexaemeron," Basil states his familiarity with "the laws of allegory...from the works of others" and criticizes allegorists "who do not admit the common sense of the Scriptures, for whom water is not water...like the interpreters of dreams."[33] While "The Hexaemeron" ends prior to substantial engagement with the Genesis 1 and 2 accounts of the creation of man, Basil concludes his work by briefly noting the creation of man in the image of God on the sixth day.[34] In the context of his hermeneutical approach and his explicit reference to creation occurring over six twenty-four-hour days in his exposition of "evening and morning" as qualifiers for "day," there is every reason to expect Basil to hold to a special, temporally immediate creation of man.[35]

Robert Letham argues that viewing Basil's days as twenty-four-hour units may be somewhat complicated by Basil's earlier statement that "in the beginning God created...is to teach us that at the will of God the world arose in less than an instant"—inferring a potential similarity to Augustine's view of an instantaneous, rather than a six-day, creation. However, further clarity is

30. Theodoret of Cyrus, *Commentary on the Psalms, 73–150*, trans. Robert C. Hill (Washington, D.C.: Catholic University of America Press, 2001), 260.

31. The Antiochian school was not without its own weaknesses, including at times an extreme hesitation toward typology, as well as errors in Christology, which in time gave birth to Nestorianism.

32. Lactantius in his *Divine Institutes* affirms a six-ordinary-day creation, along with a special, temporally immediate creation of man. "The Divine Institutes," in *Ante-Nicene Fathers*, 5:58–63, 198–99; "On the Workmanship of God," in *Ante-Nicene Fathers*, 5:282–83. Methodius writes similarly in "The Banquet of the Ten Virgins," in *Ante-Nicene Fathers*, 6:316, 333, 339.

33. Basil of Caesarea, "The Hexaemeron," in *Nicene and Post-Nicene Fathers* (Peabody, Mass.: Hendrickson, 1989), 8:101.

34. Basil of Caesarea, "The Hexaemeron," 106–7.

35. Basil of Caesarea, "The Hexaemeron," 64–65.

gained when Basil's statement is read in the context of the prior statement: "You will thus find that this was the first movement of time; then that the creation of the heavens and the earth were like the foundation and the groundwork," as well as his subsequent exposition that the earth at this point was "unfinished and incomplete…the [heavenly] bodies were not yet created… man did not yet exist."[36] Basil's statement that "the world arose in less than an instant" appears to refer to the initial ex nihilo act of the creation of "the heavens and the earth" on the first day.[37]

With other patristic writers, Basil believed that the real six days of creation were also typological of God's plan for history, a view that may be traced back within the Christian community to the "Epistle of Barnabas" (c. 70–130). "Barnabas" draws a typological sense of eschatological significance from the Exodus reference to the completion of the six days of creation and the beginning of the Sabbath rest as meaning "that in six thousand years the Lord will bring everything to an end, for with him a day signifies a thousand years." The same typological view is related in the Jewish commenting traditions of the Talmud (c. 200–500) and would continue long into the medieval era, creating apocalyptic concern at various points, especially around the year 1000.[38] Interestingly, the unknown writer of "Barnabas" also makes an apparently literal reference to the creation of "Adam [who] was formed out of the face of the earth."[39]

Continuities of Literal Interpretation in East and West

The great preacher of Antioch and Constantinople, John Chrysostom (c. 347–407), although not detailing the length of the creation days by hours, appears to view them as ordinary, noting they were sequential and marked in transition by evening and morning. His Genesis commentary appears congruent with the Antiochian tradition of a literal interpretation of God's work of creation. At one point, Chrysostom states, "Consider…how everything came to being on the earth by the word of the Lord. I mean, it was no man who was the cause…[nor] effort towards it from any other source—simply that everything heard the command, and at once sprang from the earth into view." His

36. Letham, "In the Space of Six Days," 153; Basil of Caesarea, "The Hexaemeron," 55, 59.
37. Louth suggests the same in "Six Days of Creation," 44–55.
38. "Epistle of Barnabas," in *Apostolic Fathers*, 427; A. W. Streane, trans., *A Translation of the Treatise Chagigah from the Babylonian Talmud* (Cambridge: Cambridge University Press, 1891), 55–61. See also Richard Landes, "The Fear of an Apocalyptic Year 1000: Augustinian Historiography, Medieval, and Modern" in *Speculum* 75, no. 1 (January 2000): 97–145.
39. "Epistle of Barnabas," 397. A similar brief reference is found in the "Traditions of the Elders," in *Apostolic Fathers*, 769.

homilies on the creation of man maintain a special, temporally immediate creation of Adam, reading the Genesis 2 text literally while guarding against anthropomorphic error.[40]

The literal approach to early Genesis as historical narrative was not confined to the church in the East during the latter period of the patristic era. Ambrose of Milan (c. 330–397), who was influenced to some degree by Neoplatonism and adopted an allegorical approach to a variety of Old Testament texts, followed Basil's literal approach while expounding the creation days in his "Hexaemeron." He states, "Scripture established a law that twenty-four hours, including both day and night, should be given the name day only, as if one were to say the length of one day is twenty-four hours in extent.… The nights in this reckoning are considered to be component parts of the days that are counted. Therefore, just as there is a single revolution of time, so there is but one day."[41]

Ambrose's interpretation of the Genesis 1 text as a historical narrative continues into the Genesis 2 narrative of the creation of Adam and Eve. He states: "Let us consider the precise order of our creation: 'Let us make mankind,' He said, 'in our image and likeness.'"[42] While clearly retaining the literal sense in his exposition, like other later patristic writers, Ambrose freely moves far beyond the text in both broader reflection and application.

Augustine, Allegory, and Origins

In these latter centuries of the early church, even where there was divergence on the interpretation of the creation days, a significant clarity and unity existed on the creation of Adam and Eve. Augustine of Hippo (354–430), influenced by the Alexandrian or Origenist hermeneutic, posited that the entire work of creation might have in one aspect taken place instantaneously, followed by occurrences of spontaneous and natural generation over a series of "days," of

---

40. Anthropomorphism is an error which envisions God as having human form and attributes. John Chrysostom, "Homilies on Genesis," in *Fathers of the Church* (Washington, D.C.: Catholic University of America Press, 1986), 74:44, 72–73, 173.

41. Ambrose of Milan, "Hexaemeron, Paradise, Cain and Abel," in *Fathers of the Church*, 42:42–43. Letham suggests that Ambrose's statement "there is but one [recurring] day" is potentially inconsistent with a literal, six-day view of creation. Reading further in the "Hexaemeron," it appears that Ambrose applies this concept of a "recurring day" to every individual day in sequence, attempting to show the pattern and relationship of markers of time (days, weeks, etc.), with both sequential chronology in time, and beginnings and endings of ages. Letham, "In the Space of Six Days," 154.

42. Ambrose of Milan, "Hexaemeron, Paradise, Cain and Abel," 253.

which "we must be in no doubt that they are not at all like [our days], but very, very dissimilar."[43] Augustine held that this part of the text was figurative—a divine use of allegory to accommodate human weakness.

At points Augustine argued for a tentative approach allowing a latitude of conceptions but not the literal sense. At the same time, like Origen, he posited the real meaning of the text using a blend of Greek natural philosophy and creative philosophical theology, guided by the parameters of the "rule of faith." Even with this approach, Augustine continued to hold to a literal, supernatural, instantaneous creation of Adam from the dust and Eve from his rib.[44] In contrast to pagan cosmologies of an ancient earth, which posited "that out of its elements the human race was produced," Augustine placed the divine creation of man in a recent historical context, drawing on genealogies to posit that "according to Scripture, less than 6000 years have elapsed since he began to be."[45]

The Early Church and Finding Adam

During the patristic era, the mainstream of the church viewed the Genesis 1 and 2 accounts of the creation of Adam and Eve as a literal account of human origins.[46] According to patristic theology, the totality of God's work of creation took place in six ordinary days or in fewer than six ordinary days,

---

43. Augustine, "The Literal Meaning of Genesis," in *On Genesis* (Hyde Park, N.Y.: New City Press, 2006), 267.

44. Augustine, "The Literal Meaning of Genesis," 76–77, 131, 237. Louis Lavallee provides helpful insights in understanding Augustine's approach to Genesis and creation in "Augustine on the Creation Days," *Journal of the Evangelical Theological Society* 32, no. 4 (December 1989): 457–64. Augustine's own reflection on his work on Genesis is found in Augustine, *The Retractations*, trans. M. Inez Bogan (Washington, D.C.: Catholic University of America Press, 1999), 168–71. See also Thomas Aquinas's consideration of Augustine's thought in "The Production of the First Man's Body," in *Summa Theologica* (London: Burns, Oates & Washbourne, 1922), 4:266. On Augustine's commitment to a literal Adam, see also Peter Sanlon, "Augustine's Literal Adam," *The Gospel Coalition*, June 14, 2011, http://www.thegospelcoalition .org/article/augustines-literal-adam. By the time of publication this source had been removed from the Internet.

45. Augustine, *The City of God* (New York: Modern Library, 2000), 392.

46. Theophilus, "Theophilus to Autolycus: Book II," 2:98–105; Clement of Alexandria, "The Instructor" in *Ante-Nicene Fathers*, 2:210; Lactantius, "The Divine Institutes," *Ante-Nicene Fathers*, 7:58–63, 267–72; Basil of Caesarea, "The Hexaemeron," 8:64–65, 106–7. An intriguing area for further study on creation theology among the patristic fathers could be built around the question, "Why did writers holding to an allegorical understanding of the Genesis 1 and 2 text continue to hold to a literal understanding of human origins by a special, temporally immediate, divine supernatural act?" Was it because of a lack of alternatives? Was it because they viewed it as necessary in order to maintain the "rule of faith"?

according to the few proponents of an allegorical reading (Clement, Origen, and Augustine).[47] Scripture was understood by the patristic fathers to declare a temporally immediate creation of "the heavens and earth, and all that dwell therein" by God's supernatural acts. This included the special, temporally immediate creation of Adam—the first man, formed from the dust of the ground, with God breathing the breath of life into him so that he became a living soul. On the same day, Eve, the first woman, was created from Adam's rib. The creation of Adam and Eve was unique and separate from the creation of other creatures. As such, while Adam and Eve were God's creatures, they stood in a marvelous discontinuity from the rest of God's creation of living things. Whereas all other living things were created, "brought forth" by God's command "from the earth" each "according to their kind," God said, "Let Us make man in Our image, according to Our likeness."[48] The patristic writers understood that all of the supernatural, divine work of creation, including the creation of man, had occurred in a relatively recent past, with most holding it had occurred about five thousand years prior to their lifetimes. There is only one record of allowance for a somewhat greater span of no more than ten thousand years prior. The patristic interpretations of Genesis and genealogies provided this uniform result of a relatively recent creation.[49]

Medieval Theology on Origins

Medieval European theology mostly carried on with the patristic streams of thought regarding early Genesis. While the Genesis 1 and 2 accounts of the creation of Adam and Eve were commonly understood to be a literal account of human origins,[50] proponents of allegorical hermeneutics gained influence

---

47. Gregg Allison concurs that a literal, six-day, twenty-four-hour-day creation "became the standard view of the early church." *Historical Theology* (Grand Rapids: Zondervan, 2011), 260.

48. Genesis 1:24–26; 2:7, 21–23; Tertullian, "On the Resurrection of the Flesh," in *Ante-Nicene Fathers*, 3:548–52; Gregory of Nyssa, "On the Making of Man," in *Nicene and Post-Nicene Fathers Second Series*, 5:419–20; Leo the Great, "On the Feast of the Nativity," in *Nicene and Post-Nicene Fathers Second Series*, 12:134; Fulgentius of Ruspe, "To Peter on the Faith," in *Fulgentius: Selected Works*, trans. Robert Eno (Washington, D.C.: Catholic University of America Press, 1997), 99.

49. Origen stands as the only recorded exception to this, positing creation as taking place less than ten thousand years prior to his day; other patristic writers referring to the time of creation view it as taking place less than six thousand years prior to their day. This includes Clement of Alexandria, Julius Africanus, Hippolytus of Rome, Eusebius of Caesarea, and Augustine. Robert Bradshaw, "The Early Church and the Age of the Earth," in *Creationism and the Early Church*, http://www.robibradshaw.com/chapter3.htm.

50. Bede, *On Genesis*, trans. Calvin B. Kendall (Liverpool, U.K.: Liverpool University Press, 2008), 109–11; Anselm, *Cur Deus Homo*, in *St. Anselm: Basic Writings*, trans. S. N. Deane

in Europe, and gave fresh spin to patristic allegory. The medieval allegorist's hermeneutics were rooted in Origen's system and in part transmitted by Augustine, along with Augustine's view of the temporal realities of creation.[51] At the same time, among others, there remained a vibrant respect for the literal sense of the text of early Genesis, including the account of human origins.

Bede and a Literal Genesis

Bede (c. 673–735), one of the early medieval European theologians to write on Genesis and creation, had access in his English monastic setting to what was a significant library in his day—over 200 volumes, including the writings of Origen, Basil of Caesarea, Ambrose, and Augustine.[52] Bede notes his own consultation with Basil, Ambrose, and Augustine in penning his work *On Genesis*.[53] In *On Genesis, On the Nature of Things*, and *The Reckoning of Time*, Bede displays a steady dedication to the literal sense of the text of early Genesis, holding, like Basil, to six, twenty-four-hour creation days as typological of the six ages of world history.[54] For Bede, typology did not diminish the reality of the literal sense; he believed that the Scriptures were intended to have a historical accuracy in their numerical accounts, whether of days or genealogical records, and Bede even assigned a date to Adam's creation.[55] Bede

(La Salle, Ill.: Open Court, 1964), 184; Thomas Aquinas, "The Work of the Sixth Day," in *Summa Theologica*, 3:255.

51. The Eastern church would also see a continuing legacy of both Antiochian and Alexandrian influences. A representative example is John of Damascus (c. 676–749) who was influenced by Origen's hermeneutic but at the same time held to a literal description of the creation of man. He rejected the preexistence of souls, stating "body and soul were formed at one and the same time, not first the one and then the other, as Origen so senselessly supposes." "Exposition of the Orthodox Faith," in *Nicene and Post-Nicene Fathers Second Series*, 18, 29–31.

52. Benedicta Ward, "Bede the Theologian," in *The Medieval Theologians*, ed. G. R. Evans (Oxford, U.K.: Blackwell, 2001), 58. See also Roger Ray, "Bede," in *The Blackwell Encyclopedia of Anglo Saxon England* (Oxford, U.K.: Blackwell, 2001), 57–59.

53. See, for example, Bede's "Preface: Letter to Acca, Bishop of the See of Hexham," in *On Genesis*, 65–66.

54. Bede, "The Six Ages of the World" in *On Genesis*, 100–105. See also Verity Allan, "Bede's Commentary on the Six Days of Creation and the Six Ages of the World in *In Genesim* I. 1093–1224: Sources and Analogues" (bachelor's thesis, Cambridge University, 2000), 1–34; and "Theological Works of the Venerable Bede and their Literary and Manuscript Presentation, with Special Reference to the Gospel Homilies" (master's thesis, Oxford University, 2006), 24–37.

55. Bede, *On the Nature of Things*, in *Bede On the Nature of Things and On Times*, trans. Calvin Kendall and Faith Wallis (Liverpool, U.K.: Liverpool University Press, 2010), 74. Bede notes here that he speaks of the reality of the initial work of creation on the first day when "the

consistently views the first day of creation as "without a doubt a day of twenty-four hours."[56]

Robert Letham argues that Bede diverges from a strictly literal view in describing "an instantaneous act of creation, and a process of formation spread over six days," as such following Augustine's formulation of an instantaneously complete creation.[57] However, Bede not only explicitly rejects a primary allegorical reading of the days, but also rejects the instantaneously complete creation ideas of Origen and Augustine in his *The Reckoning of Time*. Here he criticizes them for "teach[ing] by a loftier scrutiny that everything which they read concerning the first seven days is of necessity otherwise than the custom of our age holds."[58] Bede goes on in his assessment to note that the approach of "equally catholic Fathers" such as Clement of Rome, Ambrose, Basil, and Jerome, is more exegetically compelling in maintaining a first "twenty-four hour" day of creation begun with God's instantaneous ex nihilo creation of a not yet "formed" heavens and earth.[59] Bede in *On Genesis* provides further context for his description in *On the Nature of Things* of a first instantaneous act of creation.[60] Here, Bede states that the use of "day" in Genesis 2:4 should be understood to mean

> that period of time of the first six days during which the whole creation of the world was fashioned. Therefore it is rightly stated that God did not rain upon the earth and that there was not a man to work the earth, in order that we might understand how much the first flourishing of the earth differed from the present one. For now not only does the earth blossom on its own accord by means of the watering of rains, but many things planted in gardens and groves are produced by the industry and cultivation of men. But the first creation of the green plants and trees was accomplished far otherwise. In it, under the new governance of the supreme Maker, the earth, which came into being dry, without rain and without human labor, was suddenly filled far and wide with diverse kinds of crops.[61]

---

elements of the world were made all at the same time in unformed matter," a description congruent to a literal reading of Genesis 1 and significantly different from the Augustinian view of an instantaneously complete creation.

56. Bede, *On Genesis*, 75.

57. Letham, "In the Space of Six Days," 157–59.

58. Bede, "The Day," in *The Reckoning of Time*, trans. Faith Wallis (Liverpool, U.K.: Liverpool University Press, 1999), 19–21.

59. Bede, *The Reckoning of Time*, 21.

60. Bede, *On Genesis*, 68–71.

61. Bede, *On Genesis*, 107–8.

Bede's commitment to a hermeneutic with a high regard for the literal sense of the text is further reflected in his exposition of Genesis passages on the creation of man. Commenting on the initial descriptive account of the sixth day in Genesis 1, Bede states,

> It is explained more fully in what follows whence and how God made the first man and woman.... For the sake of brevity they are only reported to have been created, so that the work of the sixth day and the consecration of the seventh along with other matters may be expounded.... Unlike the other animals which he created in their separate kinds not individually but many at a time, God created one male and one female, so that by this the bond of love might bind the human race more tightly to one another, because it remembered that it all arose from one parent.[62]

Turning to Genesis 2:7 Bede states,

> Here, then, is described at greater length the making of man, who was indeed made the sixth day; but there his creation was mentioned briefly, which here is expounded more fully, namely that he was fashioned into the substance of body and soul. Of these, the body was formed of the mud of the earth, but the soul was created out of nothing by the inspiration of God; but also the woman was fashioned from his side while he slept.... *He breathed into his face the breath of life, and man became a living soul,* when he created for him the substance of the soul and spirit by which he would live.[63]

Eriugena, Allegory, and an Androgynous Adam

Bede, as a proponent of the literal tradition, provided perhaps the most significant reflection on the creation of Adam and Eve among early medieval theologians. Others, following the interpretive stream of Philo, Origen, and Augustine, presented decidedly nonliteral approaches. The Irish monk Johannes Scotus Eriugena (c. 815–c. 877), an opponent of Gottschalk in the predestination

---

62. Bede, *On Genesis*, 92.
63. Bede, *On Genesis*, 109–10. Bede's reference to Adam's body being formed from the "mud of the earth" is reflective of the Genesis text of the Vulgate "formavit igitur Dominus Deus hominem de limo terrae," along with that of Tobit 8:6 (v. 8, Latin Vulgate). In the case of the Genesis text, it appears that the Hebrew term now commonly rendered "dust" was instead translated by Jerome as "slime/mud"—possibly in light of the context of the previous verse's reference to the "mist" that "watered the face of the whole ground." Another, though perhaps less likely, possibility is that Jerome allowed the now nonextant Aramaic text of Tobit 8:6, which he similarly translated, to influence his word choice in his Genesis translation.

controversy and translator of Pseudo-Dionysius, advocated an allegorical reading of Genesis 1 and 2 through the lens of Neoplatonic philosophy.[64]

Eriugena argued for a hierarchy of primordial causes, giving no indication of any chronological sequence following ordinary days. He bizarrely argued that Adam and Eve were created before all other things, and while being made of body and soul, prior to the fall had genderless bodies that were "incorporeal, spiritual" bodies, sharing in essence with the angels, having "no need of food, sleep, clothing, shelter."[65] According to Eriugena, the fall into sin resulted in corporeal or material bodies along with sexual differentiation and procreation "like that of the animals" rather than the spiritual multiplication of angels. He went so far as to argue that "if man had not sinned…he would not have suffered ignominious generation from the two sexes like irrational animals, as the wisest of the Greeks declare by the surest reasons."[66] At the resurrection, Eriugena claimed, man would return to his original incorporeal state and leave his corporeal body behind in the dust.[67] Eriugena viewed Genesis 1 and 2 as predominantly figurative or symbolic, including the descriptions of paradise, and he held that Adam and Eve spent no time at all in the garden, for any duration there would have enabled man "to acquire sufficient perfection to prevent sin from occurring."[68] Eriugena's teaching on human origins displayed the creative potential of the stream of allegorical interpretation—and carried Genesis commentary to new, unorthodox territory.

What about Anselm?

Compared with Eriugena, Anselm of Canterbury (c. 1033–1109), an Italian who ministered in France and became the archbishop of Canterbury after the Norman conquest of England, made less extensive but more conventional reference to the creation of Adam and Eve. Both Anselm's *Monologium* and *Cur Deus Homo* refer to God's work of creation in the context of theological dialogue.

---

64. Stanley Jaki, *Genesis 1 Through the Ages* (London: Thomas More Press, 1992), 112–13. Jaki's substantive work attempts to evaluate the influence of philosophy and science in textual interpretation. However, it fails to adequately distinguish between those who maintained the literal tradition, allowing for the use of philosophy and science as methods of explanation within the parameters of the literal interpretation of the text, and those who pursued figurative reinterpretations of the text in order to accommodate it to philosophy and science.

65. Johannes Scotus Eriugena, *Periphyseon: On the Division of Nature*, trans. Myra Uhlfelder (Indianapolis: Bobbs-Merrill, 1976), xxxii–xxxiii, 250–68.

66. Eriugena, *Periphyseon*, 251.

67. Eriugena, *Periphyseon*, 264.

68. Eriugena, *Periphyseon*, 265.

Anselm's rationale for understanding the length of days seems to rest partly in a literal reading of "Moses' account" but more particularly in what he views as a corollary to answering questions regarding the relationship of the number of angels, the fall of some angels, and the elect among mankind.[69] Anselm posits that the angels' creation prior to man's proves less problematic than the Augustinian tradition of an instantaneous creation, which raises greater difficulties by forcing limitations in relation to medieval theological understandings of the temporal origin and number of angels and men. In this context, Anselm indicates both a hermeneutical and theological rationale supporting why "those days in which Moses appears to describe a successive creation are...to be understood like such days as ours."[70] Anselm later notes in his discussion of the number of angels and the elect from among men that "the opinion of the majority" in his day is that men and angels "were created at the same time...because we read 'He who lives forever, created all things at once.'"[71] In *Cur Deus Homo* Anselm appears to hold to a sequential creation, but he also seems to imply that an Augustinian understanding of creation was the predominant view in his day.

In *Monologium* Anselm argues that an orthodox doctrine of God which maintains the Creator-creature distinction necessitates an ex nihilo creation. In this work, Anselm appears to posit both the sequential six-day view and an instantaneous view as options, stating that God created through "intimate expression, whether separately, by the utterance of separate words, or all at once, by the utterance of one word."[72] While Anselm's hermeneutic in relation to Genesis 1 and 2 remains unclear, by either description, he held to a special, temporally immediate creation of Adam and Eve, apart from any previous ancestry.

Did Augustine's Allegory Dominate Medieval Europe?

Anselm's suggestion of the pervasiveness of an Augustinian view is difficult to corroborate. It may have been the case at least in a limited geographical region surrounding Le Bec, but its reach beyond this area is uncertain at best. Other medieval writers indicate a significant continuity of a more fully literal hermeneutic among Christian theologians of the high medieval period. Jewish philosophers and rabbis during this era in Europe seem to

---

69. Anselm, *Cur Deus Homo*, 213.
70. Anselm, *Cur Deus Homo*, 213.
71. Anselm, *Cur Deus Homo*, 214.
72. Anselm, *Monologium*, 51–52.

perceive their scholastic Christian counterparts as commonly holding to an ordinary six-day creation. In Spain the Jewish poet and philosopher Yehudah ha-Levi (1075–1141), like his French contemporary Shlomo Yitzhaki, "Rashi" (c. 1040–1105) and successors, argued for a largely traditionalist literal reading of the Mosaic text, defending it against Neoplatonic interpretations as "an authentic chronology of the world" from the beginning of the Pentateuch through the prophets.[73]

Intriguingly, ha-Levi, in his *Kitab al Kuzari*, depicts a representative Christian scholastic—in contrast to a Muslim philosopher—as stating, "I believe that all things are created, whilst their Creator is eternal; that He created the whole world in six days; [and] that all mankind sprang from Adam."[74] The grandson of Rashi, Samuel ben Meir, "Rashbam" (c. 1085 – c. 1174) wrote commentary on Genesis from the commitment "that a verse never departs from its plain meaning."[75] In it he argued that the "light" and "darkness" of day one each consisted of twelve hours, and explained that the sixth-day creation of man in Genesis 1 was revealed in detail in Genesis 2.[76] It appears that among the Jewish community, a substantial number continued to hold to a literal reading of Genesis on origins and believed that most Christians held to the same.

Lombard, Literalism, and the Creation of Man

The fact that allegorism did not dominate Genesis interpretation among high medieval Christians is immediately evident in the writings of Peter Lombard (c. 1100–1161), a theologian who was bishop of Paris. Lombard's *The Four Books*

---

73. See Deborah Abecassis, "Reconstructing Rashi's Commentary on Genesis from Citations in the Torah Commentaries of the Tosafot" (PhD diss., McGill University, 1999), 1–14; A. K. Offenberg, "The Earliest Printed Editions of Rashi's Commentary on the Pentateuch," in *Rashi 1040–1105, Hommage à Ephraim E. Urbach*, ed. Gabrielle Sed-Rajna (Paris: Éditions du Cerfs, 1993), 493; A. J. Rosenberg, ed., *The Complete Tanach with Rashi's Commentary* (Brooklyn: Judaica Press, 2012), http://www.chabad.org/library/bible_cdo/aid/ 63255/jewish /The-Bible-with-Rashi.htm. John Sailhamer argues that Rashi was opposed to the traditional view; however, in Rashi this appears limited to his engagement with verse 1 on the basis of his understanding of the basic elements of the universe in line with Greek thought and his query as to why "water" is not mentioned—leading to his reinterpretation of the phrase "in the beginning." "Genesis," in *The Expositor's Bible Commentary* (Grand Rapids: Zondervan, 1990), 2:21–23.

74. Yehudah ha-Levi, *The Kuzari: In Defense of the Despised Faith*, ed. David Kahn (Nanuet, N.Y.: Feldheim, 2009), 59–60.

75. Samuel Ben Meir, *Rabbi Samuel Ben Meir's Commentary on Genesis*, trans. Martin I. Lockshin (Lewiston, N.Y.: Edwin Mellen, 1989), 28–29.

76. Meir, *Commentary on Genesis*, 54–55.

of Sentences gained the stature of the preeminent medieval systematic theology, eclipsed only by Thomas Aquinas's *Summae Theologiae* (written 1259–1273) among Roman Catholics in Europe in the sixteenth century. Lombard opens his discussion of the Genesis account of the days of creation by noting,

> Some have handed down that all things had been created together in their matter and form; which Augustine seems to have thought. On the other hand some have proved and asserted this more, that first there was created the rude and formless matter…but afterwards through the intervals of the Six Days there was formed out of that matter the genera of corporal things according to their own species. Which sentence Gregory the Great, Jerome, Bede and several others commend and prefer, which even seems to be more congruent with the Scripture from Genesis…. And so according to this tradition, let us inspect the order and manner of the creation and formation of all things.[77]

Lombard explicitly follows Bede in defining the days, arguing that they should be accepted as comprising "the space of twenty four hours" in light of the textual addendum of "there was made evening and morning, one day."[78] Lombard states,

> There was made first the evening, and afterwards the morning, and thus there was one day comprising twenty four hours, namely a natural day which had an evening, but not a morning. For the end of the preceding and the start of the following day is called the 'morning,' which is the dawn, which has entirely neither the full light nor the darkness. Therefore the First Day did not have a morning, because neither had a day preceded it, which would be terminated at the start of the following day, and for this reason chiefly, because with the light appearing, there soon stood forth upon the Earth the full and very clear day, which did not start from the dawn, but from the full light and which was consummated on the morning of the following day.[79]

Not surprisingly, Lombard's commentary on the creation of man in Genesis 2 also follows the tradition of a literal hermeneutic guarded by the rule of faith against anthropomorphic error in relation to the Creator. Lombard affirms:

> God formed man's body from the slime of the earth, "into" which "He

---

77. Peter Lombard, "On the Creation and Formation of Things Corporal and Spiritual and Many Others Pertaining to This," in *The Four Books of Sentences*, trans. Alexis Bugnolo, Distinction 12, http://www.franciscan-archive.org/lombardus/opera/ls2–17.html. By the time of publication this source had been removed from the Internet.

78. Lombard, *Sentences*, Distinction 13.

79. Lombard, *Sentences*, Distinction 13.

breathed" a soul...not that he blew upon him with his throat, and/or formed his body with corporeal hands, for God is a spirit and He is not composed with the features of members. Therefore let us not think carnally.... He rather formed man from the slime of the earth according to the body by commanding, by willing, that is He willed and He commanded by His Word, so that he would thus be made; and He breathed into his face the breath of life, that is He created the substance of his soul, in which he would live, not from some corporal and/or spiritual matter, but from nothing.[80]

Lombard's use of a literal approach is further substantiated in his commentary on the creation of Eve from Adam. In part drawing on Augustine via Hugo of St. Victor, he notes,

In the same paradise...God formed a woman from the substance of the man.... Scripture says: God sent a deep sleep upon Adam. And when he had fallen asleep, He took one of his ribs and formed it into the woman.

Here one must attend why He did not create man and woman together, just as He did the angels, but first the man, then the woman from the man. For this reason, that is, that the one would be the beginning of the human race....

Woman was made from man, not from any part of the man's body, but she was formed from his side, so that there might be shown, that she was created in a partnership of love, lest perchance, if she had been made from his head, she might seem to be preferred to man for his domination, or if from his feet, to be subjected to him for his service. Therefore because for man there was prepared neither a lady nor a handmaid, but a companion, she was to be produced...from his side...that she might recognize that she was to be placed alongside him....

The body of the woman is said to have been made from the very substance of the rib alone, without any extrinsic addition, multiplied in its very self through the Divine Power, indeed by that same miracle, by which there were afterwards satiated from five loaves, multiplied by the heavenly blessing of Jesus, five thousand men.[81]

The writings and influence of Peter Lombard's *Sentences* attest to the pervasiveness of a medieval acceptance of the literal sense of Genesis 1 and 2, including a special, temporally immediate creation of Adam and Eve. However, there were also further proponents of the allegorical tradition exemplified in Origen and Augustine.

---

80. Lombard, *Sentences*, Distinction 17.
81. Lombard, *Sentences*, Distinction 18.

Maimonides: An Allegorical and Literal Blend

Intriguingly, it was not a Christian, but the Jewish philosopher Mosheh ben Maimon, also called Maimonides (1135–1204), who was one of the first medieval writers to propose a more limited allegorical or figurative approach to Genesis 1 and 2. His approach, which was less figurative than the approaches of Philo, Origen, or Augustine, and certainly less than that of Eriugena, would be particularly influential on the thought of Thomas Aquinas, who referred to him as "Rabbi Moses."[82] In his *Guide for the Perplexed*, as well as his commentaries on rabbinic tradition, Maimonides sought to both evaluate and harmonize aspects of Neoplatonic and Aristotelian philosophy with Jewish tradition. Philosophically, Maimonides did not reject a sequential creation over a period of six days as impossible.[83] However, his hermeneutic was directed by what he viewed as philosophical necessity and possibility, rather than a historical-grammatical approach guided by literary genre and the rule of faith.[84]

Maimonides critiqued the concept of the eternity of the universe as unproved, noting that it did not give "sufficient reason for rejecting the literal meaning of a Biblical text and explaining it figuratively, when the opposite theory can be supported by an equally good argument."[85] At the same time, in reference to Genesis 1 and 2, Maimonides stated, "the account given in Scripture of the Creation is not, as is generally believed, intended to be in all its parts literal...[as] the literal meaning of the words might lead us to conceive corrupt ideas and to form false opinions about God...superficially and unscientifically."[86] Maimonides affirmed a rabbinical tradition of a creation ex

---

82. David Novak, "Maimonides and Aquinas on Natural Law," in *St. Thomas Aquinas and the Natural Law Tradition*, ed. John Goyette, Mark Larkovic, and Richard Myers (Washington, D.C.: Catholic University of America Press, 2004), 43–65.

83. Moses Maimonides, *The Guide for the Perplexed*, trans. M. Friedlander, 2nd ed. (London: George Routledge & Sons, 1919), 294.

84. Maimonides argued that the incorporeality of God was demonstrated by philosophical proof, and, as such, "those passages in the Bible, which in their literal sense contain statements that can be refuted by proof, must and can be interpreted otherwise"—the necessary implication being that anthropomorphisms in the Bible were to be understood figuratively. Maimonides, *Guide for the Perplexed*, 317.

85. Maimonides, *Guide for the Perplexed*, 317.

86. Maimonides, *Guide for the Perplexed*, 331–32. It is interesting to note that Maimonides, like Yehuda ha-Levi and in contrast to Anselm, posits that a literal reading of Genesis 1 and 2 is "generally believed." As a contemporary to Maimonides, Lombard exemplifies the more fully literal approach, leaving the question open as to whether a comprehensively instantaneous view of creation really was predominant as Letham claims. Letham, "In the Space of Six Days," 160.

nihilo in which "all things were created together, but were separated from each other successively…[as] undoubtedly correct."[87]

Despite Maimonides's philosophical preference for an instantaneous, complete creation, his description of what he viewed as the remaining work of separation appears to take a largely literal reading of the Genesis text of the six days of creation as the completion of God's work. In relation to the creation of Adam and Eve he states,

> The account of the six days of creation contains, in reference to the creation of man, the statement: "Male and female created he them" (i.27), and concludes with the words: "Thus the heavens and the earth were finished, and all the host of them" (ii.1), and yet the portion which follows describes the creation of Eve from Adam, the tree of life…the history of the serpent and the events connected therewith, and all this as having taken place after Adam had been placed in the Garden of Eden. All our Sages agree that this took place on the sixth day, and that nothing new was created after the close of the six days. None of the things mentioned above is therefore impossible, because the laws of nature were then not yet permanently fixed.[88]

Elsewhere, Maimonides makes it clear that he assumes there was "a first man, who had no parent, viz. Adam…made out of earth"—a description which, when placed in the context of his wider discussions, indicates support for a special, temporally immediate creation of Adam and Eve, in the context of a supernatural work of creation, initial and separated, taking place within a span of six days.[89]

Maimonides's milder allegorism on Genesis was not uncontested among medieval Jewish scholars. Another influential Spanish Jew, Moshe Ben Nachman, also known as Ramban or Nachmanides (1195–1270), interacted critically with Maimonides, taking a more strongly literal approach to the

---

87. Maimonides, *Guide for the Perplexed*, 334.

88. Maimonides, *Guide for the Perplexed*, 338. Maimonides here displays his overriding concern not to violate what he views as philosophical necessities, seeking to explain the work of creation in a manner that does not violate "the laws of nature." He rejects Aristotle's belief in the eternity of the universe and his corresponding concept "that everything in the Universe is the result of fixed laws…that there is nothing supernatural" as the Aristotelian cosmology would place him "necessarily…in opposition to the foundation of our religion, [and then] we should disbelieve all miracles and signs, and certainly reject all hopes and fears derived from Scripture, unless the miracles are also explained figuratively. The Allegorists among the Mohammedans have done this, and have thereby arrived at absurd conclusions." Maimonides, *Guide for the Perplexed*, 318.

89. Maimonides, *Guide for the Perplexed*, 235.

interpretation of the Genesis creation account, despite Kabbalistic influences in his thought.[90] His aim in expositing Genesis was to provide "the correct and clear explanation…in its simplicity."[91] Nachmanides elucidated six days of creation of ordinary duration, while allowing they typologically pointed "to all the days of the world…that its existence will be six thousand years."[92] Not surprisingly, Nachmanides also followed a literal interpretation of the creation of Adam and Eve, from the dust of the ground and the rib, respectively.[93]

Grossteste: Expanding Allegorical Possibilities

Going beyond Maimonides was Robert Grossteste (c. 1168–1253), an English theologian and bishop, who wrote *The Hexaemeron*. Letham notes that Grossteste "builds on Origen's fourfold method of interpretation" combined with Augustine, consistently positing that the fuller—if not the correct—meaning of the text lies beyond the literal sense.[94] Grossteste's comments on the planting of the garden of Eden in Genesis 2 and other passages clearly indicate that he favored Augustine's figurative or allegorical interpretation to the literal interpretation:

> But according to the view of those who say that the first seven days ran in time through the period of twenty-four hours, we should understand that this planning was the perfect drawing out of the trees of paradise from the earth…. The "beginning" referred to here means that first revolution of seven days, by the repetition of which all the time that follows is measured. But according to the view of Augustine we should understand the word "beginning" here to mean the first instant and the indivisible beginning of time, in which the first seven days were made perfect in a non-temporal way in the minds of the angels. That is when God planted the paradise in a causal and potential way. This planting, according to Augustine, brought forth in time the complete formation according to the visible species.[95]

Liberated by allegory from a close adherence to the text, Grossteste, like Eriugena, proffered a variety of alternative readings, including one where each

---

90. Moshe ben Nachman, *Ramban (Nachmanides) Commentary on the Torah*, trans. Charles B. Chavel (New York: Shiloh, 1971), v-vi.

91. Nachman, *Commentary on the Torah*, 3.

92. Nachman, *Commentary on the Torah*, 31, 60–64.

93. Nachman, *Commentary on the Torah*, 77–79.

94. Letham, "In the Space of Six Days," 160.

95. Robert Grossteste, *On the Six Days of Creation: A Translation of the Hexaemeron by C. F. J. Martin* (Oxford: Oxford University Press for the British Academy, 1996), 314.

day is figurative for something other: "the second day the created intelligence of the angels," the "third day the bringing of matter and form into existence out of nothing," the fourth day the "formation and ordering of the church," the fifth day "the formation of the wavering soul," and "the sixth day is the making of the visible world over six days."[96] Commenting in greater detail on the third day, Grosseteste states,

> "Earth" can also mean the literal sense of Scripture, which feeds the simple with the humble simplicity of a moral interpretation, just as animals are fed by some herbs. The lofty heights of the allegorical and anagogical interpretation give fruit to the wise, and are like great trees that give food to rational human beings. This spiritual sprouting from the spiritual earth is seen by God with a gaze of good pleasure: he sees that it is good. He also sees the natural sprouting from the natural earth and sees that this is good, as signifying the spiritual sprouting in all its natural properties and benefits.[97]

As with Maimonides and other allegorists, Grosseteste's adoption of an allegorical hermeneutic appears to occur in a context of wanting to synthesize Scripture with aspects of prevailing natural philosophy. Developing his own model of creation with this potentially widely variable approach enabled Grosseteste, like Eriugena, to adopt a somewhat unique understanding of the creation of Adam and Eve. Positing that the six days are figurative and outside of time, but noting the difficulty that the chronology of Adam sleeping after being awake and engaging in conversation requires time, Grosseteste argues that "the man and the woman were created on the sixth day...both of them in their causes and potentialities only."[98] They were "not made perfect on the sixth day according to the visible form of the body" for the text notes that "she was made from the side of the man who was asleep."[99] It was "when time was flowing, they were made

---

96. Robert Letham sees in Grosseteste "the roots of what eventually became known as the framework hypothesis." Letham, "In the Space of Six Days," 160–61. I concur, noting, however, that these same roots run far further—through Eriugena, Augustine, Origen, and Philo. The history of this stream strongly suggests that adopting a figurative or allegorical approach to the text of Genesis 1 and 2 allows for a significant interpretive liberty with a nearly endless possibility of meanings and a loss of the literal meaning in the process. In each case, the adoption of an allegorical hermeneutic appears to occur in the context of seeking to harmonize Scripture with Greek natural philosophy. James McEvoy provides a helpful analysis of these trajectories in "The Place of Man in the Cosmos," in his *The Philosophy of Robert Grosseteste* (Oxford: Clarendon, 1986), 369–78.

97. Grosseteste, *Six Days of Creation*, 154.

98. Grosseteste, *Six Days of Creation*, 305.

99. Grosseteste, *Six Days of Creation*, 305–6.

formally and perfectly according to the visible form of their bodies" and could sleep and engage in conversation.[100] However, Grossteste takes a decided turn to a literal interpretation in stating:

> It is clear enough what was the manner of the establishment of the human being in so far as the body is concerned: that God, by his word, formed the body of the first human being from red dust, that is to say, from natural earth not infected or corrupted by any extraneous accident. The dust was dampened to cling together as slime. This moisture seems probably to have come from the spring [mist] which welled up and watered all the surface of the earth....
>
> He created the rational soul, and infused it into the body he had formed in order to make one person.... Scripture says that God blew the breath of life into the human being by breathing in his face, when he became a living soul.[101]

Grossteste's rejection of a chronology of six ordinary days in creation enabled him to posit a two-stage special creation of man: an initial creation occurring outside of time followed by a formal and visible perfecting of the work of creation in an indeterminate, albeit apparently short, period of time. By now well-established in Europe, allegorical Genesis interpretation continued to enable alternative views of human origins.

Aquinas's Angelic Knowledge

Thomas Aquinas (1225–1274) exerted some influence among medieval theologians in Europe, though his most substantial impact came long after his death with his writings gaining significant regard among Roman Catholics in the Reformation and post-Reformation eras. A teacher of theology in Paris, Cologne, and Italy, Aquinas had great regard for Aristotle, engaging with both the methods and content of Greek philosophy in his theological endeavor.[102] Aquinas stands as the last significant proponent of medieval allegorism in Genesis interpretation. In his vast *Summa Theologiae*, he reflects a continuity

---

100. Grossteste, *Six Days of Creation*, 306.

101. Grossteste, *Six Days of Creation*, 296–97.

102. Horst Seidl, "Is Aristotle's Cosmology and Metaphysics Compatible with the Christian Concept of Creation?," in *Divine Creation in Ancient, Medieval, and Early Modern Thought*, ed. Willemien Otten, Walter Hannam, and Michael Treschow (Leiden: Brill, 2007), 85–94. Seidl argues that Aquinas grants allowance for Aristotle's view of the eternal preexistence of matter due to his statement that "nothing in real things" existed prior to time.

of the Philo-Origen-Augustine stream of a figurative interpretation of Genesis 1 and 2, similar to his predecessors Grossteste and Eriugena.[103]

While aware that others view the six days of creation as literal days, Aquinas sees them as figurative, with the entire work of creation potentially occurring simultaneously, or possibly following an ordered sequence within one day. He appears to disagree with Augustine that part of the work of creation, that of angelic nature and formless matter, preceded time.[104] Aquinas believes it is "more probable...that the angels were created at the same time as corporeal creatures."[105] Following Augustine, Aquinas states that "by the expression 'day' the knowledge of the angels is to be understood." That gave Aquinas the challenge of seeking to discern the figurative meaning of what "morning and evening knowledge" was for the angels.[106] His explanation provides a clear medieval example of the consequences of speculative philosophical theology wedded to an allegorical hermeneutic.

Aquinas's work on the six days unfolds what he views as "the knowledge of angels" regarding the creation: the first three "days" are works of distinction, where the second three "days" are works of adornment.[107] Aquinas follows the sequential structure of the text in describing the work of creation. He finds a challenge to his division into works of "distinction" and "adornment" in the production of plants on the third day, noting,

> It would seem that it was not fitting that the production of plants should take place on the third day. For plants have life, as animals have. But the production of animals belongs to the work, not of distinction, but of adornment.[108]

Aquinas responds to this difficulty by arguing that the plants aided in the distinction of the surface of the earth from its former formlessness and further argues that these plants were created only in their causes, akin to seeds buried in the soil, but actual production of plants did not occur until later.[109]

---

103. Leo Elders, "Les citations de saint Augustin dans la Somme," *Doctor Communis* 40 (1987): 115–67.

104. Thomas Aquinas, *Summa Theologica*, Q. 66, 204. Aquinas devotes significantly more space to an allegorical-philosophical examination of the creation and nature of angels than he does to the work of the six days of creation. See Aquinas's "Treatise on Angels" in *Summa Theologica*, Q. 50–64, 1–175.

105. Aquinas, *Summa Theologica*, Q. 61, Art. 3, 121.

106. Aquinas, *Summa Theologica*, Q. 58, Art. 7, 92.

107. Aquinas, *Summa Theologica*, Q. 67–Q. 72, 206–56.

108. Aquinas, *Summa Theologica*, Q. 69, Art. 3, 235.

109. Aquinas, *Summa Theologica*, Q. 69, Art. 3, 235–37.

Continuing through the work of the six days, he makes no mention of the creation of man, turning to this following his summary of the seven days and an extensive excursus on the nature of the soul and its relationship to the body. Aquinas defends the immediate creation of the soul by God as occurring either at the same time as, or right after, the creation of the body. He viewed man's body as being specially and immediately created by God "from the slime of the earth; because earth and water mingled are called slime," and as a microcosm of the rest of creation.[110] According to Aquinas, a potential implication of Augustine's thought on "causal virtues" was that "the human body was produced by some created power."[111] Arguing against this, he stated, "The first formation of the human body could not be by the instrumentality of any created power, but was immediately from God.... [He] alone by his own power [can] produce matter by creation: wherefore he alone can produce form in a matter, without the aid of any preceding material form.... The first human body was of necessity made immediately by God."[112]

Lyra and the Literal Sense

Where Grosseteste and Aquinas indicate a significant and perhaps growing stream of allegorical interpretation of Genesis 1 and 2 through the late high medieval era, this was within the context of the at-least equally significant, continuing influence of Peter Lombard's *The Four Books of Sentences*, with its literal hermeneutic toward Genesis 1 and 2. Lombard's writings on Genesis form a historical backdrop to those of Nicholas of Lyra (c. 1270–1349), a minister provincial in the Franciscan order, teacher, and theologian. Lyra established a Burgundian Franciscan college at Paris in 1330, fulfilling the will of the late queen of Burgundy.[113] Unlike Eriugena, Grosseteste, and Aquinas, Lyra was an avid promoter of the literal sense of Scripture as primary, and he wrote extensively as a Bible commentator.[114] His *Literal Postill on the Whole Bible* (1331), which was widely read, helped maintain the continuity of the literal approach to Genesis 1 and 2.

Lyra was clearly acquainted with Aquinas's work on creation. Partly drawing from Aquinas, he divided the seven days of creation into an initial act and

110. Aquinas, *Summa Theologica*, Q. 91, Art. 1, 263.
111. Aquinas, *Summa Theologica*, Q. 91, Art. 2, 266.
112. Aquinas, *Summa Theologica*, Q. 91, Art. 2, 266–67.
113. Philip D. W. Krey and Lesley Smith, eds., *Nicholas of Lyra: The Senses of Scripture* (Leiden: Brill, 2000), 3–6.
114. A. Skevington Wood, "Nicholas of Lyra," in *Evangelical Quarterly* 4 (1961): 196–206.

works of distinction in the first three days, followed by three days of adornment.[115] However, Lyra goes on "to reject the Thomist interpretation of God's creative activity," generally preferring that of Bede.[116] He sees the text of Genesis 1 and 2 as a chronology of literal historical reality. As Patton notes, Lyra rejects the view of Augustine and Aquinas that the days refer to "angelic knowledge as far from the literal sense."[117] Instead, he argues that the modifiers of evening and morning indicate twenty-four-hour days, though marked by a light and darkness in a different way than it was after the creation of sun, moon, and stars.[118] Lyra also follows the literal sense of the text in describing the special, temporally immediate creation of Adam and Eve "in a perfect state" of maturity on the sixth day.[119] Even with Lyra's advocacy of a literal interpretation of Genesis on origins, by the late fourteenth century it seemed uncertain at best whether the literal tradition or its allegorical alternative would prevail, had the trajectories of medieval theology continued unchanged.

Medieval Shifts and Continuity in Finding Adam

Similar to the patristic era, a mainstream of the European church in the medieval era viewed human origins in harmony with a literal understanding of the Genesis 1 and 2 accounts of the creation of Adam and Eve.[120] However, a growing stream of the church, exemplified in Eriugena, Grosseteste, and Aquinas, did so in the context of an allegorical hermeneutic that viewed much of the text of Genesis 1 and 2 as figurative—in continuity with earlier efforts to accommodate the text to Greek natural philosophy. Nonetheless, there remained a fair degree of theological commonality across the medieval church. Most theologians believed the totality of God's work of creation took place in six ordinary days (as exemplified in Bede, Lombard, and Lyra), or in the case of the allegorists, in less than six ordinary days. The vast majority understood Scripture to declare a temporally immediate, ex nihilo creation of "the heavens

---

115. Corrine Patton, "Lyra's Commentary on Genesis 1–3," in *Nicholas of Lyra: The Senses of Scripture* (Leiden: Brill, 2000), 25. See also Nicholas of Lyra, *Postilla super totam Bibliam* (Rome: Conradus Suueynheym Arnoldus Pannartzque magistri…impresserunt, 1471–1472), 1:1–449.

116. Patton, "Lyra's Commentary," 25.

117. Patton, "Lyra's Commentary," 27.

118. Patton, "Lyra's Commentary," 27. Patton notes that Lyra avoids making excursus on "issues not raised by the text at hand, such as the creation and fall of the angels."

119. Patton, "Lyra's Commentary," 28–29.

120. Brian Murdoch, *The Medieval Popular Bible: Expansions of Genesis in the Middle Ages* (Suffolk, U.K.: Boydell & Brewer, 2003), 4–5.

and earth, and all that dwell therein" by God's supernatural acts within a relatively recent time frame.[121] With the exception of the allegorists Eriugena and Grosseteste, all appear to have held to a special, temporally immediate creation of humanity. Adam was the first man, formed from the dust of the ground, with God breathing life into him, so that he became a living soul.[122] On the same day, Eve was created from Adam's rib. The creation of Adam and Eve was viewed as unique and separate from the creation of other creatures. Thus, while Adam and Eve were God's creatures, the medieval and patristic theologians viewed their origin as gloriously distinct from the rest of God's creation of living things.

---

121. Like the patristic fathers, medieval commentators indicate a belief that a six-day or instantaneous work of creation took place within the past six thousand to ten thousand years.

122. In contrast to the medieval literalists, the allegorists, due to their hermeneutical approach, had surrendered compelling exegetical warrant within the Genesis text to counter Eriugena's interpretation.

3

Adam in the Reformation and Post-Reformation Eras

A significant movement away from an allegorical approach to the Scriptures occurred with the rise of northern Renaissance humanism and the dawn of the Reformation, when the allegorical approach came to be seen as either obscuring or denying outright the literal or historical sense in scriptural texts.

The Reformation Recovery of the Literal Sense

Early Reformers like William Tyndale (c. 1492–1536) recognized and promoted the value of this recovery of the literal sense of Scripture. Reflecting on late medieval hermeneutics, Tyndale notes,

> They divide the scripture into four senses, the literal, tropological, allegorical, and anagogical. The literal sense is become nothing at all: for the pope hath taken it clean away, and hath made it his possession. He hath partly locked it up with the false and counterfeited keys of his traditions, ceremonies, and feigned lies; and partly driveth men from it with violence of sword: for no man dare abide by the literal sense of the text, but under a protestation, 'If it shall please the pope.'…
>
> For Origen and the doctors of his time drew all the Scripture into allegories: whose ensample they that came afterward followed so long, till they at last forgot the order and process of the text, supposing that the scripture served but to feign allegories upon; insomuch that twenty doctors expound one text twenty ways, as children make descant upon plainsong.[1]

In rejecting the late medieval allegorical tendency that made the "literal sense nothing at all" and advocating one literal sense for every text, Tyndale was not promoting a simplistic biblicism. He noted that parts of Scripture by their literary form "make proverbs and similitudes, or allegories, in fact the

---

1. William Tyndale, "Four Senses of the Scripture," in *Works of William Tyndale* (Edinburgh: Banner of Truth, 2010), 1:303–5.

similitudes of the gospels are allegories…to express spiritual things."[2] Neither was Tyndale denying typological patterns or prophecy. Rather, he argued that the exegete must "find out the literal sense of the scripture by the process of the text, or by a like text of another place," discerning the intended meaning through a historical-grammatical and text contextual interpretation.[3]

Martin Luther, Genesis, and Greek Natural Philosophy
While Tyndale only made brief reference to the work of creation in his prologue to the book of Genesis, calling the reader to "note with strong faith the power of God, in creating all of nought," Martin Luther's (1483–1546) commentary on Genesis provides an extensive example of this hermeneutical shift among Reformation Protestants. Despite Tyndale's more bleak assessment of late medieval exegesis, this shift among Protestants was not completely disconnected from medieval approaches. Rather, it was a significant realignment to and further development of the stream of thought that held the literal sense of the text as the primary intended meaning; this stream had flowed from the patristic to the medieval eras. Luther himself reflected this continuity in his interactions on Genesis with Augustine and Aquinas and his preference for the exegetical approach of Nicholas of Lyra. Regarding the description of God's works of creation in Genesis 1 and 2, Luther states,

> These, then, are all historical facts. This is something to which I carefully call attention, lest the unwary reader be led astray by the authority of the fathers, who give up the idea that this is history and look for allegories. For this reason I like Lyra and rank him among the best, because throughout he carefully adheres to, and concerns himself with, the historical account. Nevertheless, he allows himself to be swayed by the authority of the fathers and occasionally, because of their example, turns away from the real meaning to silly allegories.[4]

Luther criticizes Lyra because "he enumerates [the opinions of philosophers] without comment" and was favorable to categorizing the days into works of creation, distinction, and adornment, even while maintaining the primary literal sense of the text. To this Luther responded, "I am disregarding [this] division…. I do not know whether this tallies well with the facts in every case…if anyone finds pleasure in that sort of thing, let him consult Lyra."[5]

2. Tyndale, *Works*, 304–5.
3. Tyndale, *Works*, 305.
4. Martin Luther, *Lectures on Genesis*, in *Luther's Works*, trans. Jaroslav Pelikan (St. Louis: Concordia, 1958), 1:93.
5. Luther, *Works*, 1:5.

Not surprisingly, Luther held "that Moses spoke in the literal sense, not allegorically or figuratively, i.e., that the world, with all its creatures, was created within six days, as the words read."[6] Turning to the Genesis 1 account of the creation of Adam and Eve on the sixth day, Luther states,

> Here our opinion is supported: that the six days were truly six natural days, because here Moses says that Adam and Eve were created on the sixth day. One may not use sophistries with reference to this text. But concerning the order of creation he will state in the following chapter that Eve was created sometime after Adam, not like Adam, from a clod of earth, but from his rib, which God took out of the side of Adam while he slept. These are all works of time, that is works that require time. They were not performed in one moment; neither were these acts: that God brings to Adam every animal and there was none found like him, etc. These are acts requiring time, and they were performed on the sixth day. Here Moses touches on them briefly by anticipation. Later on he will explain them at greater length.[7]

Commenting on the Genesis 2 account of the creation of Adam and Eve, Luther states that "if Aristotle heard this, he would burst into laughter and conclude that although this is not an unlovely yarn, it is nevertheless a most absurd one."[8] Challenging the long influential stream of Greek natural philosophy on origins, and its impact on Genesis interpretation, Luther goes on to argue that it is "folly for human reason to be so offended...reason shows in this way that it knows practically nothing about God, who, merely by a thought, makes out of a clod, not the semen of a human being but the human being itself, and, as Moses states later, makes the woman out of the rib of the man."[9]

Luther goes on to note that the language of Genesis 1 and 2 regarding the creation of man is marked as unique and distinct from the creation of the animals: "'God formed man from the clay of the earth' but...did not speak in these terms about the other living beings." He also notes "that God breathed a breath into his face.... It [is] stated in this passage concerning man alone that he was made a living soul...he was created after the image of God."[10] Luther

---

6. Luther, *Works*, 1:5. Following the pattern of previous literal interpreters of early Genesis, Luther later distinguishes that the unqualified use (by number, or "evening and morning") of the word "day" in Genesis 2:4 differs from the use in Genesis 1, and as such "is to be understood in the sense of indefinite time." Luther, *Works*, 1:83.

7. Luther, *Works*, 1:69.

8. Luther, *Works*, 1:84.

9. Luther, *Works*, 1:84.

10. Luther, *Works*, 1:85–86.

placed this special, temporally immediate creation of man on the sixth day in the context of a relatively recent (six thousand years before present) ex nihilo creation of the world.[11]

Melanchthon and Brenz

Luther's approach was a harbinger of what became the predominant, if not exclusive, hermeneutical approach to Genesis 1 and 2 among Reformation and post-Reformation Lutherans. Philip Melanchthon (1497–1560) was likely directly engaged in the formation of Luther's lectures on Genesis, and his article "Of Creation" in his *Loci Communes* appears to reflect this shared endeavor.[12] Like Luther, Melanchthon was committed to the recovery of the literal interpretation of Genesis and viewed Origen and Aquinas as corrupting influences on biblical interpretation and theology.[13] Another German Lutheran theologian, Johannes Brenz (1499–1570), in his 1553 commentary on Genesis, stated,

> When the world was created by God, not everything in this world was created at once, but each thing in its place and over the course of six days. Indeed, there are some who have said that God did not create on distinct days but rather everything in a single moment and that Scripture speaks of the six days allegorically.… Certainly, God could have created all things in a single moment, but what is to be sought here is what God did, not what he could do. Thus, he completed the work of creation not in one instant but in six continuous days.
>
> First of all, Scripture itself clearly testifies that the days during which creation was completed are natural days, not mystical or allegorical.

---

11. Gregg R. Allison, *Historical Theology: An Introduction to Christian Doctrine* (Grand Rapids: Zondervan, 2011), 263.

12. Jaroslav Pelikan, "Introduction," in *Luther's Works*, 1:66.

13. E. P. Meijering argues that Melanchthon's view of the authority of Scripture and his hermeneutic significantly impacted his theology as a Reformer: "Melanchthon's attitude towards Thomas can be compared with his view on Origen.… Origen was his most important target in his criticism of the corruption of truth which began in the early church, Thomas Aquinas is his most important target when he attacks the almost total corruption of the truth in Scholastic theology.… According to Melanchthon the original truth revealed in the Bible was gradually more and more corrupted in the course of time…until it was restored again in the Reformation." He further notes that Melanchthon nonetheless did at points draw on Origen and Aquinas, but only where he saw them in harmony with Scripture. E. P. Meijering, *Melanchthon and Patristic Thought: The Doctrines of Christ and Grace, the Trinity and the Creation* (Leiden: Brill, 1983), 180. Melanchthon's brief explanation of Genesis 1 and 2 in his *Commentary on Genesis* (1523) observes the literal sense of the text, and at points draws secondary figurative and typological conclusions from the text. Philip Melanchthon, *Commentarius in Genesin*, in *Corpus Reformatorum*, ed. Carolus Gottlieb Bretschneider (Halis Saxonum, Germany, 1846), 13:760–76.

Indeed if they weren't natural days, then the creatures made on those days wouldn't be natural creatures but only allegorical ones. But it is clear that they are truly external, real or natural creatures. So the days that are numbered in this chapter were also truly real or natural days.

In the second place, God preferred to create the world and its parts in orderly succession rather than all at once to show that he is a God not of confusion but of order.[14]

Brenz went on in his comments on the sixth day in Genesis 1 and Genesis 2 to describe the creation of man, noting that God "does not create human beings from nothing in the way that he previously created the mass of heaven and earth, but used the clay that he had created earlier."[15] Brenz's clear commitment to the literal tradition and open rejection of figurative approaches exemplified the significant hermeneutical recalibration taking place through the Protestant Reformation.

The Swiss Reformed

Numerous further Protestant Reformers exemplify the Reformation realignment to reading the early chapters of Genesis including the creation origins of Adam and Eve in a literal, historical sense. In Zurich, Huldrych Zwingli (1484–1531) posited six days of creation with the special creation of Adam from the clay on the sixth day.[16] Reflecting on the state of his generation and belief in Genesis in his *Commentary on True and False Religion*, Zwingli elucidated the difference between mere hearing of the Word and true faith in the Word, stating, "It is not the fact, as most men have thought, that the faithful become faithful because they hear Moses say (Gen. 1:1), 'In the beginning God created the heaven and the earth'; for those are numberless who hear this but do not believe the world was made according to the Mosaic tradition."[17]

Heinrich Bullinger (1504–1575), who took up Zwingli's position in Zurich, did address the days of creation although not speaking explicitly in the *Decades* to the creation of Adam and Eve. This work, as Letham notes, "became staple reading for English clergy and many who were later members

---

14. Johannes Brenz, *Commentary on Genesis*, in *Reformation Commentary on Scripture*, ed. John L. Thompson (Downers Grove, Ill.: InterVarsity, 2012), 1:23–24.

15. Brenz, *Commentary on Genesis*, 72.

16. Huldrych Zwingli, *Farrago Annotationum in Genesim* (Zurich, 1527), 16–17, 19–21.

17. Huldrych Zwingli, *Commentary on True and False Religion*, ed. Samuel Jackson and Clarence Heller (Durham, N.C.: Labyrinth, 1981), 60–61.

of the Westminster Assembly [were] likely to have read them."[18] In his exposition of the fourth commandment, Bullinger stated,

> Last of all, the Lord adds his own example, by which he teaches us to keep holy the sabbath-day. "Because," he says, "in six days the Lord made the heaven and earth, the sea, and all that in them is, and rested the seventh day…." The Lord our God wrought [or made; formed] six days in creating heaven and earth, the sea, and all that in them is; and the seventh day he rested, and ordained that to be an appointed time for us to rest in. On the seventh day we must think of the works that God did in the six days.[19]

In his *A Hundred Sermons on the Apocalypse of Jesus Christ*, Bullinger appears to further reflect a literal view of the creation of man in reference to the Triune involvement in his creation: "God looked upon the countenance of his Christ, when he first made man, for Christ is the beginning…[and] the preserver of human nature."[20] Bullinger went on to state that for God "it was enough to have said, it was enough to have willed…and they [created things] were created."[21]

Wolfgang Musculus (1497–1563), a teacher of theology in Bern, wrote more extensively on creation and human origins in his commentary *On Genesis*. Like other Protestant Reformation theologians, Musculus pursued a literal explication, engaging the Hebrew text as he interacted with Greek and Latin works, including those by medieval church fathers. He notes that the first day is to be understood as a natural day, the evening and morning together constituting "twenty four hours"; this day in turn forms the basis for weeks of seven days and in turn months and years.[22] His exposition of the Genesis 1 and 2 passages on Adam's and Eve's creation notes the distinct and separate creation by God of Adam from the dust, differentiating Adam's origin as separate from that of the animals, as well as the subsequent creation of Eve from Adam's rib. Both

---

18. Robert Letham, "'In the Space of Six Days': The Days of Creation from Origen to the Westminster Assembly," *Westminster Theological Journal* 61, no. 2 (1999): 164.

19. Heinrich Bullinger, *The Decades of Heinrich Bullinger* (Grand Rapids: Reformation Heritage Books, 2004), 258.

20. Heinrich Bullinger, *A Hundred Sermons on the Apocalypse of Jesus Christ* (London, 1561), 125.

21. Bullinger, *Sermons on the Apocalypse*, 155.

22. Later in his Genesis commentary, when expositing the phrase "the sun had risen on the earth when Lot entered Zoar," Musculus comments that "from the beginning of creation" God has used the sun to mark "the natural day" made up of "the period of twenty four hours." Wolfgang Musculus, *In Genesim Mosis Commentarij plenissimi: In quibus veterum et recentiorum sententiae diligenter expenduntur…* (Basel, 1554), 9, 14–15, 477.

are directly created by God in His image.[23] In his exposition, Musculus guards against the errors of both the "Anthropomorphites…and the Manichees."[24]

John Calvin

During his extensive ministry in Geneva, John Calvin (1509–1564) also gave significant attention to both the exposition of Genesis and the creation origins of Adam and Eve.[25] Calvin was firmly committed to a literal hermeneutic which held God's work of creation occurred over the span of six ordinary days.[26] Commenting on the text's description of the first day, Calvin notes,

> The error of those [which] is [here] manifestly refuted, who maintain that the world was made in a moment. For it is too violent a cavil to contend that Moses distributes the work which God perfected at once into six days, for the mere purpose of conveying instruction. Let us rather conclude that God himself took the space of six days, for the purpose of accommodating his works to the capacity of men.[27]

Like Bullinger's, Calvin's commentary on the fourth commandment stands in harmony with his ideas about creation: "I do not, however, doubt but that God created the world in six days and rested on the seventh…proposing Himself as the model for our imitation."[28] Calvin commended the works on Genesis by the patristic theologians Basil and Ambrose—both of whom articulated a creation period of six twenty-four-hour days. In his *Institutes*,

---

23. Musculus, *In Genesim*, 53–57, 68–80.

24. Musculus, *In Genesim*, 44.

25. John Calvin, *Commentaries on the Book of Genesis* (Grand Rapids: Baker, 2003), 111–12; John Calvin, *Institutes of the Christian Religion* (Philadelphia: Westminster Press, 1960), 1:161, 183–84.

26. Letham seeks to argue to the contrary that Calvin "does not deal directly with the details of the discussion on the days of creation." Letham, "In the Space of Six Days," 164. Alister McGrath makes a similar case in his *Foundations of Dialogue in Science and Religion* (Malden, Mass.: Blackwell, 1998), 125. The Biologos website goes further, positing that "Calvin supported the idea of accommodation…in the accommodation view, Genesis 1–2 was written in a simple allegorical fashion to make it easy for people of that time to understand." "Common Questions: How Was the Genesis Account of Creation Interpreted before Darwin?," *Biologos*, 2013, http://biologos.org /questions/early-interpretations-of-genesis. While a case may be made that Calvin believed the text was written in a manner to accommodate the reader, this idea did not lead him to depart from any aspect of the literal tradition: God had both acted and spoken in a way accommodated to man. Hoon J. Lee, "Accommodation—Orthodox, Socinian, and Contemporary," *Westminster Theological Journal* 75 (Fall 2013): 335–48. See also Stanley Jaki, *Genesis 1 Through the Ages* (London: Thomas Moore Press, 1992), 164–65.

27. Calvin, *Commentaries on the Book of Genesis*, 78.

28. John Calvin, *Commentaries on the Last Four Books of Moses* (Grand Rapids: Baker, 1983), 1:43.

Calvin further addresses a literal reading of the days, stating, "Moses relates that God's work was completed not in a moment, but in six days.... By this circumstance we are drawn away from all fictions to the one God who distributed his work into six days.... Until human reason is subjected to the obedience of faith...it grumbles, as if such proceedings were foreign to God's power."[29]

Turning to the creation of Adam and Eve on the sixth day, Calvin notes that a right understanding of the origins of man is essential: "We cannot have a clear and complete knowledge of God unless it is accompanied by a corresponding knowledge of ourselves.... [We must] know what we were like when we were first created and what our condition became after the fall of Adam."[30] Calvin criticizes Jewish rabbinical traditions which held that the statement "Let Us make man in Our image" (Gen. 1:26), refers to God holding "communication with earth or with angels." He writes, "Where, indeed, will they find that we were created after the image of the earth, or of angels? Does not Moses directly exclude all creatures in express terms, when he declares that Adam was created after the image of God?"[31] Calvin's hermeneutic brings him to see the Genesis 2 narrative of the creation of Adam and Eve as an expansion of Genesis 1:26–31. On Genesis 2:7 he comments, "[Moses] now explains what he had before omitted in the creation of man, that his body was taken out of the earth.... The body of Adam is formed of clay, and destitute of sense."[32] He adds, "Moses first speaks of the breath; he then adds, that a soul was given to man by which he might live, and be endued with sense and motion.... Three gradations, indeed, are to be noted in the creation of man; that his dead body was formed out of the dust of the earth; that it was endued with a soul, whence it should receive vital motion; and that on this soul God engraved his own

---

29. Calvin, *Institutes*, 1:161. Calvin here draws on his statement in his commentary on Genesis 1:26: "We have before observed, that the creation of the world was distributed over six days" the only difference being "over" versus "into" six days. Calvin, *Commentaries on the Book of Genesis*, 92.

30. Calvin, *Institutes*, 1:183.

31. Calvin, *Commentaries on the Book of Genesis*, 92. Some historians, like Letham, have sought to argue that because Calvin does not describe these as twenty-four hour days means their length was inconsequential, or potentially greater or less than twenty-four hours. This seems an anachronistic, twentieth-century argument, as no theologians known to Calvin appear to posit any possibility beyond an instantaneous creation, an *extratemporal* creation (in which the days were figurative), or a six-ordinary-day creation in time. There is no record of anyone positing that any creation days were longer than twenty-four hours—a position that would have once again made the days figurative.

32. Calvin, *Commentaries on the Book of Genesis*, 111.

image, to which immortality is annexed."[33] The latter part of Genesis 2:7, "man became a living being," Calvin states, "refers to nothing more than to explain the animating of the clayey figure, whereby it came to pass that man began to live."[34] Turning to the creation of Eve in Genesis 2:21, Calvin comments,

> Although to profane persons this method of forming woman may seem ridiculous, and some of these may say that Moses is dealing in fables, yet to us the wonderful providence of God here shines forth; for, to the end that the conjunction of the human race might be more sacred, he purposed that both males and females should spring from one and the same origin. Therefore he created human nature in the person of Adam, and thence formed Eve, that the woman should be only a portion of the whole human race.... Something was taken from Adam, in order that he might embrace, with greater benevolence, a part of himself. He lost, therefore one of his ribs; but instead of it, a far richer reward was granted on him, since he had obtained a faithful associate of life; for he now saw himself, who had before been imperfect, rendered complete in his wife.[35]

Capito, Vermigli, and Zanchi

While Calvin was in Strasbourg in 1539, Wolfgang Capito (1478–1541), one of his fellow Reformers in the city, published a substantial work on the six days of creation. Capito's *Hexemeron Dei opus explicatum* was unique in its extensive interaction with Jewish commentaries; like Calvin he advocated a literal interpretation of both the days and God's creation of Adam and Eve. Capito argued that textual cues specify the days as "natural"—"twenty four hours in length."[36] He also viewed God's work of the special creation of Adam and Eve as taking place on the sixth day, after the creation of all other living creatures.[37]

The keen interest in and concern of the Reformers for both the book of Genesis and the doctrine of creation origins are reflected in yet another Reformer, Pietro Martire Vermigli (1499–1562). Vermigli, who served as a theologian in Strasbourg, Oxford, and Zurich, also appears to view the literal sense of the text of early Genesis as primary. In his *Loci Communes* Vermigli

---

33. Calvin, *Commentaries on the Book of Genesis*, 112. In his *Institutes*, Calvin states, "When [Adam] was taken from earth and clay, his pride was bridled," 1.15:184. Calvin also addresses the creation of Adam and Eve in his sermons on Genesis. John Calvin, *Sermons on Genesis, Chapters 1–11*, trans. Rob Roy McGregor (Edinburgh: Banner of Truth, 2009), 1–124.

34. Calvin, *Commentaries on the Book of Genesis*, 112.

35. Calvin, *Commentaries on the Book of Genesis*, 132–33.

36. Wolfgang Capito, *Hexemeron Dei opus explicatum* (Argentorati per Vuendelinum, 1539), 144, 248–49.

37. Capito, *Hexemeron Dei*, 270–99.

states, "Let us beware of the error of them in old time, which thought there was an eternal and uncreated chaos, or unformed mass, existing before: and that God only drew out those things which were there mingled together. But we say that the same unformed mass was made the first day. Some in response demand, that seeing God could have brought forth the world long before, why did he do it so recently? This is an arrogant and impertinent question, wherein man's curiosity cannot be satisfied, but by beating down the folly thereof."[38]

In his commentary on Genesis, Vermigli further expounds his understanding of the first and subsequent days of creation. Interacting with the Jewish commentator Abenezra, Vermigli notes that the light and darkness marking the first day functioned differently than it would after the creation of the sun and other luminaries, with God sending the light for the "period of time set by God" as needed to constitute the day. As to why the use of the Hebrew term "day one" rather than the "first day," was significant, Vermigli argued that this was to indicate the fact that the period of light and the period of darkness together form one day.[39] Vermigli's description of the creation of Adam and Eve on the sixth day closely adheres to the literal tradition: Adam's body was created by God from the dust of the earth and made alive as the "breath of God" animated him to become a living soul. Eve was subsequently created from Adam's rib. Both were created in the image of God; Vermigli notes that their created nature marked them as distinct from created animals.[40]

Girolamo Zanchi (1516–1590), who served as an Old Testament scholar at Oxford, Strasbourg, and Heidelberg, was perhaps the most prolific Reformer on the exegesis of Genesis and the doctrine of creation. In *Confession of Christian Religion*, Zanchi states, "We believe that after all other things were created, man also at the last was created to the image and likeness of God, his body being fashioned out of earth, and his soul, being a spiritual and immortal substance, made of nothing, and inspired into that body; and that shortly after the woman was given him, made (concerning the bodily parts) of his bones, and formed to the same image of God."[41] Zanchi comments much more extensively on the doctrine of creation, including the creation origins of Adam and Eve, in his

---

38. Pietro Martire Vermigli, *Loci Communes* (Londini, 1576), 88–89.

39. Pietro Martire Vermigli, *In primum librum Mosis qui vulgo Genesis* (Zurich: Christophorus Foschouerus, 1579), 3–4. Letham argues somewhat anachronistically that "there is no evidence that Vermigli understands the days of Genesis 1 as twenty-four hours." Letham, "In the Space of Six Days," 169.

40. Vermigli, *Loci Communes*, 98–102.

41. Girolamo Zanchi, *H. Zanchius: His Confession of Christian Religion* (Cambridge, 1599), 4.

massive work, *Concerning the Works of God in Creation during the Space of Six Days* (1591). In his introduction, Zanchi argues for the perspicuity of the text of Genesis in its literal description of the creation of the visible world as given by the Holy Spirit through Moses.[42] Throughout the work he repeatedly refers to God's work of creation taking place within the span of six ordinary days.

One example is found in his discussion of the dispute concerning the creation of the angels, where he states that while this is not described by Moses in his description of the "visible creation," it is referred to in Colossians 1:16.[43] Zanchi then posits hypothetical possibilities as to the time of the creation of the angels, arguing that there are three: either the angels were created before the six days, during the six days, or after the six days. He argues, like Calvin, that when Colossians 1 is read in harmony with Genesis 2:1–3 that it is "beyond dispute" and "manifestly clear from Genesis 2 and Exodus 20" that all of God's work of creation, including the creation of angels, was perfected and completed within the six days.[44]

In commenting on the phrase "the evening and the morning were the first day," Zanchi provides an extensive excursus concluding that this is an explicit statement of "nothing shorter or longer than a natural day of twenty four hours."[45] Consistent with his literal hermeneutic, Zanchi describes Adam and Eve as specially created by God on the sixth day, in the manner described in Genesis 2.[46]

Lambert Daneau and a Christian Natural Philosophy

Lambert Daneau (c. 1530–1595), a student of John Calvin who later served as professor of theology at the Academy of Geneva and then at Leiden, was intrigued by the relationship between Scripture and science, which he explored in his writings on Genesis and human origins. According to David Sytsma, Daneau was a proponent of what would be termed "Mosaic physics," a "tradition which sought to meld theological views of creation drawn especially from Genesis chapter one with existing physics to create a pious or Christian natural philosophy purged of erroneous philosophical foundations."[47] Its

---

42. Girolamo Zanchi, *De operibus Dei intra spatium sex dierum* (Neostadii in Palatinorum, Germany, 1601), 1.1.4:4.

43. Zanchi, *De operibus Dei*, 1.1.2:6, 15.

44. Zanchi, *De operibus Dei*, 1.1.2:6, 15. See also Calvin, *Institutes*, 1.14:163–64.

45. Zanchi, *De operibus Dei*, 2.1.2:220–21.

46. See "De Hominis Creatione," in Zanchi, *De operibus Dei*, 3:1.1:416ff.

47. David Sytsma, "Calvin, Daneau, and *Physica Mosaica*" (paper presented at Calvin Theological Seminary Colloquium, November 12, 2013), 1.

theological tenets included what Sytsma describes as "an opposition to double truth (i.e., an affirmation of the unity of rational and revealed truths), the use of the Bible for deriving truths about nature where sense or reason were most inclined to ignorance or error (e.g., things far removed in place or time), and a desire to reform Aristotelian philosophy according to the standards of sense, reason, and Scripture."[48]

Daneau's thought drew on that of his mentor, Calvin. As Sytsma notes, Calvin held that where philosophers at best arrived at a "corrupt knowledge of God" as "the mind of the universe…God provided the Mosaic Genesis account in order to remove ambiguity or doubt and provide a clearer and more familiar knowledge of himself. The Genesis account thus acts as spectacles by which we are restrained from speculation regarding infinity of time and space and given an alternative finite account of these aspects of reality…. Calvin stated that while the heavens, apart from Scripture declare that God made them, 'the time and manner of the creation' is to be found in Scripture."[49]

Some modern scholars have sought to argue that Daneau's pursuit of a "Christian natural philosophy" was a misguided endeavor having little or nothing in common with Calvin. However, David Sytsma, following Richard Muller, has shown substantial continuities between Calvin and Daneau.[50] Sytsma states:

> Many of the questions handled by Daneau reflect the same traditional concerns of Calvin. Among these are not only the refutation of notions of the infinity or eternality of the world, but also the affirmation of creation ex nihilo, the chief end of creation as the glory and knowledge of God as creator, and other questions arising from the Genesis narrative…. A line of continuity between Calvin and Daneau [is evident in] their shared respect for early church hexaemeral tradition…. Daneau's method of

---

48. Sytsma, "Calvin, Daneau, and *Physica Mosaica*," 1.

49. Sytsma, "Calvin, Daneau, and *Physica Mosaica*," 8. Calvin, *Institutes*, 1:159–62, 179–80; Calvin, *Sermons on Genesis, Chapters 1–11*, 4, 8.

50. Lambert Daneau, *The Wonderfull Woorkmanship of the World Wherin Is Conteined an Excellent Discourse of Christian Naturall Philosophie*, trans. Thomas Twyne (London, 1578), 1–4. Sytsma, "Calvin, Daneau, and *Physica Mosaica*," 1–21; Richard A. Muller, *Post-Reformation Reformed Dogmatics* (Grand Rapids: Baker, 2003), 370; John Dillenberger, *Protestant Thought and Natural Science* (New York: Doubleday, 1960), 31–32, 36–37, 59–60; Ernst Bizer, *Frühorthodoxie und Rationalismus* (Zurich: EVZ Verlag, 1963), 35, 42; Donald Sinnema, "Aristotle and Early Reformed Orthodoxy: Moments of Accommodation and Antithesis," in *Christianity and the Classics: The Acceptance of a Heritage*, ed. Wendy Helleman (New York: University Press of America, 1990), 119–48.

eschewing allegory in favoring of the literal sense did follow in the steps of Calvin.[51]

Underlying Daneau's pursuit of a scriptural understanding of the natural order was his doctrine of faith and of Scripture. Responding to a question regarding the relevance of Scripture for natural philosophy he stated,

> The first testimony is that which is written…in the epistle to the Hebrews in these words: Through faith we understand that the world was made by the word of God. Wherefore we understand these things by faith. If by faith, then by the Holy Scripture, for there can be no faith without the Scripture. And therefore we must certainly conclude that the true and certain knowledge concerning these matters is declared unto us by Holy Scripture. The second authority is the first chapter of Genesis. For Moses, who at the appointment and command of God wrote that history of all others most excellent and wonderful, of the beginning of the world, and creation of all things, is either a vain fellow, or a liar, if the knowledge of natural philosophy be not contained in the Holy Scripture. For what other thing does he in that book, than briefly, howbeit truly and orderly, set down the origin of all things…. The selfsame thing S. Basil and S. Ambrose, and S. Chrysostom in the prefaces of their hexameron, or six days work, do with one consent, and plainly confirm, that whoso shall deny that the knowledge of natural philosophy may not truly and commodiously be learned out of holy Scripture gainsay the sacred Word of God.[52]

Daneau's further comments on the Genesis account of creation were significant in their implications for hermeneutics and creation origins:

> As it is to be granted that [Moses] spoke simply, so it cannot be proved that he spoke or wrote lyingly, falsely and ignorantly of those things…. [He spoke] simply but truly, barely but rightly, commonly but purely…. Some are of the opinion that all those things which he wrote in the first chapter of Genesis are to be interpreted allegorically. So neither do they think those six days are the space of time, neither indeed that the woman was made from Adam's rib…. Which opinion if it be true, what shall be sure or certain in all that whole chapter, and such like writings of other prophets, as appertaining to the knowledge of natural philosophy…? Shall we say, against the assured faith of Scripture that any one of the chiefest philosophers, to wit, Plato or Aristotle, which were heathen men, were called by God to counsel when he went about framing and creating the world, that they should know more than Moses the servant of

---

51. Sytsma, "Calvin, Daneau, and *Physica Mosaica*," 11–16.
52. Daneau, *Christian Naturall Philosophie*, 7–8.

God, whom God himself taught, and showed unto him such things as he should commit to writing…and especially for the instruction of his most dearly beloved church? Surely this cannot be taught, much less spoken, without notorious blasphemy against God himself.[53]

As Sytsma notes, Daneau's "Christian natural philosophy" did not preclude or reject the use of philosophy, nor did he deny the realm of general revelation.[54] Daneau did not claim that the Scriptures provided an exhaustive account of natural philosophy; rather, he held that Scripture provides the essential contours, with clarity. The Genesis text, written in accommodation to our senses, was literal, not allegorical. Genesis communicated the events of the first six days, including the creation of man, as would have been seen, heard, and felt through ordinary human experience as these things happened.[55]

The Reformation and the Literal Tradition

To be sure, there were those among the early Reformers, including Philip Melanchthon, Wolfgang Capito, and Pietro Martire Vermigli, who did not reject aspects or levels of meaning beyond the literal sense even while they held to a creation ex nihilo and viewed the days of creation as ordinary due to the markers of evening and morning. Thus, there were varying degrees of hermeneutical and expository continuity between the Reformers and their allegorist medieval forbears.[56] However, what does appear distinct among the first generation of the magisterial Reformers is that all promote a primary literal sense rather than a figurative sense in Genesis 1.

This approach was exemplified in an overwhelming defense of creation "in the space of six days"—a phrase to this point seen as affirming six twenty-four-hour days or ordinary, natural days, against an instantaneously complete or an extratemporal creation. Why the recurring emphasis on six ordinary days of creation? Undoubtedly it was not merely interaction with patristic and medieval sources but also the reality that figurative interpretations holding to an instantaneous or extratemporal work of creation remained influential in Roman Catholicism. The Reformers seem to have been as concerned with hermeneutical approaches and their broader implications as they were with the temporal realities of creation. The Reformation recovery of a literal hermeneutic brought

---

53. Daneau, *Christian Naturall Philosophie*, 9–10.

54. Sytsma, "Calvin, Daneau, and *Physica Mosaica*," 19.

55. Sytsma, "Calvin, Daneau, and *Physica Mosaica*," 17–19.

56. See for example, Iohannes Oecolampadius, *An Exposition of Genesis*, trans. Mickey L. Mattox (Milwaukee, Wisc.: Marquette University Press, 2013), 47–155.

with it a literal exegesis of the Genesis 1 and 2 texts describing the special creation of Adam from the dust and Eve from Adam's rib. It was also key to the
broader Reformation recovery of and growth in scriptural doctrine.

The first generation of Reformers and their followers viewed the text
of Scripture on creation, including the creation origins of man, as divinely
authoritative. For them, giving significant attention to the exposition of early
Genesis and creation doctrine was part of the exercise of their divine calling to
scriptural teaching and proclamation—an act of worship and wonder. Unlike
some patristic and medieval theologians, the Reformers were significantly
more at ease maintaining a literal reading even where this brought conflict
with Greek natural philosophies, including the science of their own day.[57]
Undoubtedly this was in part because they believed, as Richard Muller notes,
that "there is a regenerate view of the created order, which by the grace of God
and with the aid of Scripture, recognizes the revelation of God in the created
order for what it is—a manifestation of the greatness and goodness of God
to his eternal glory.... Only the regenerate who have learned from Scripture,
can return to creation and find there the truth of God."[58] For the Reformers, committing themselves to a literal Genesis that was occasionally at odds
with Greek natural philosophy did not negate the legitimacy of using human
reason to gain understanding of God's creation. Rather, it indicated that they
believed Scripture, as God's special revelation, took priority of authority in its
descriptions of the origins and history of the realm of God's creation.

Genesis and Origins in Post-Reformation Theology

Through the post-Reformation era, Lutheran orthodoxy appears exclusively
committed to a literal interpretation of Genesis, including the sixth-day creation
of Adam from the dust of the ground and Eve from his rib. Johann Gerhard
(1582–1637), perhaps the most influential and prolific of the post-Reformation
Lutheran orthodox theologians, set the stage for an era of thorough Lutheran
attention to theology. Among Gerhard's writings, the massive *Loci Theologici*
gives the most substantial attention to the doctrine of creation.[59] Engaging with
a host of patristic, medieval, and contemporary theologians, Gerhard continued
his Lutheran predecessors' commitment to the literal interpretation of Genesis.
At the same time, like Aquinas and some of the early Reformers, Gerhard paid

---

57. Jaki, *Genesis 1 Through the Ages*, 170.

58. Richard Muller, "Scripture as Word of God and *Principium Cognoscendi Theologiae*"
in *Post-Reformation Reformed Dogmatics*, 154.

59. Johann Gerhard, *Loci Theologici Cum Pro Adstruenda Veritate...* (Jena, 1611), 1–1093.

less attention to the Genesis account of the creation of man than he did considering questions related to the creation and fall of the angels.[60]

Across the Channel, in post-Reformation England, with all its shifts and changes, the Church of England, while Protestant, aimed to create an approximate middle way between Roman Catholicism and the magisterial Reformation. Individuals and congregations within it reflected a significant theological spectrum—a latitude enabled in part by the brevity of the Church of England's confession (the Thirty-Nine Articles). During the seventeenth and eighteenth centuries, the Church of England included some significant warmth toward aspects of medieval and contemporary Roman Catholic theology.[61] As one might expect, English post-Reformation theology on the historical context and origins of Adam and Eve varied more than did other streams of Protestantism. However, even within the greater breadth of theological opinions in the Church of England, only a small minority, best characterized as early Enlightenment thinkers, would challenge the dominant literal interpretation of the Genesis account of the creation of Adam and Eve.

The English Puritans, Genesis, and Adam

The English Puritans were representative of the vast majority of the Church of England in their commitments on the interpretation of Genesis and creation of humanity. Living within the wider latitude of the Church of England, they were committed to the pursuit of recovering godly piety, worship, and doctrine that was in close accord with the theology of the magisterial Reformation. At the same time, they lacked unity in their doctrine of the church, which precluded the more thorough ecclesial transformations seen in many of the Protestant city-states and state churches of the European continent, as well as the Church of Scotland to the north. The later ejections of Puritan ministers from the Church of England swelled the ranks of diverse ecclesial bodies (Congregationalist, Presbyterian, Baptist, and others) outside of the Church of England but significantly diminished Puritan influence within the Church of England.

---

60. Gerhard, *Loci Theologici*, 1–54.

61. It should be noted that while the writings of both Augustine and Thomas Aquinas on creation continued to exert significant influence among Roman Catholic theologians, some like Marin Mersenne (1588–1648) continued to see the literal sense as primary. Mersenne was a French theologian and mathematician who strongly supported the work of Galileo—assisting him in the translation of his works. While engaging extensively with figurative approaches to the days, Mersenne nonetheless argued that the work of creation was completed in a sequence of "six twenty four hour days"; though toward the end of his life he appeared to be intrigued by the early pre-Adamite thought of Isaac La Peyrère. Marin Mersenne, *Quaestiones Celeberrimae In Genesim…* (Lutetiae Parisiorum, 1623), 788–94.

Nicholas Gibbons: "A Sound Exposition of Genesis"

Though some recent scholarship has argued that the English Puritans had "a virtually complete absence of interest in creation," the writings of English Puritans reveal significant interest both in the doctrine of creation and in the Reformation hermeneutic of a literal interpretation of the early chapters of Genesis.[62] Nicholas Gibbons (c. 1585–c. 1602), an English Puritan minister and a skilled Cambridge Hebraist and exegete, provides one early example.

The title page of Gibbons's *Questions and Disputations Concerning the Holy Scripture* (1601) declared his intent to deliver "the everlasting truth of the Word of God…from the errors and slanders of atheists, Papists, philosophers and all heretics." Gibbons proposed to do this by providing "brief, faithful and sound expositions" of passages from the book of Genesis.[63] He did so displaying both a high level of interaction with patristic, medieval, and Reformation scholarship, and also a typical Puritan relish for application. Describing the creation of light and the days prior to the creation of the sun, Gibbons states,

> Half the earth (being as yet unformed) was in the light, the other half in darkness and without light. And withal he made it to run, as it were a race with time, by which means after the space of twelve hours, in which the light had shined, darkness came in place of the light, and night succeeded the first day. Now after three days were finished, he gathered the same light that was dispersed in the firmament into certain bodies, the Sun, the Moon, and the Stars, which should in more royal order govern the day and the night. Hereby the Lord would show, that although he commonly uses the means, which he himself has set, for the preservation of his creatures, yet he is not bound or tied unto the means, but of his good pleasure uses them. He hath made the Sun to give us light, yet he is able to give light without the Sun, and so he did, before he made the Sun…. Wherefore we ought to learn hereby, that when we see no means whereby we may enjoy the promises of God, we distrust not his power, who is able without means and against means to work our preservation; and when we have means, we should not trust in the means, but in the Lord.[64]

---

62. Letham, "In the Space of Six Days," 173. Recent publications in the field of English Puritan theology offer little on the Puritan doctrine of creation. Volumes such as Philip C. Almond's *Adam and Eve in Seventeenth Century Thought* (Cambridge: Cambridge University Press, 1999), 1–240, indicate significant ground for further research.

63. Nicholas Gibbons, *Questions and Disputations Concerning the Holy Scripture Wherein Are Contained, Briefe, Faithfull, and Sound Expositions of the Most Difficult and Hardest Places…* (London, 1601), title, epistle dedicatory.

64. Gibbons, *Questions and Disputations*, 13–14.

Gibbons followed his description of the work of the six days by discussing why "God chose six days space to make the world in."[65] He argues,

> He performed not the work of creation all at once as some suppose; the Scripture does expressly reprove that error. Neither yet is the Creator constrained unto time, unto whom one day is as a thousand years; neither was it for want of ability, in him that is omnipotent; or for weariness, that formed them all with the breath of his mouth. But for our sakes, for our instruction he divided the creation of the world into six day works, that he might temper his workmanship with our understanding. Things that are heaped or knit together, cannot be so well examined, as when everything is sorted by itself; wherefore God does also divide his works, that we might with due consideration, as it were, go in between them, view them, and discuss them, and by diligently examining his power, his wisdom, his greatness in them, we should return the glory unto him.[66]

Gibbons's literal approach to the days of Genesis 1 was maintained in his expositions of the creation of man from Genesis 1 and 2. Gibbons stated that man was made last on the sixth day "as it were the end and perfection of his work."[67] God did not say "let man be made" but "let Us make man." This was not because of the difficulty of the work but "in respect of the greatness of the work: the Scriptures speaking after our capacity, for as much as men of wisdom when they are to handle matters of importance do use the deeper consultation and greater care in the performance of them."[68] Gibbons went on to say, "the Spirit of God commends the excellent workmanship of God, performed in the creation of man…[and] also the dignity of man [and] the exceeding care and love the Lord does bear toward man even from the creation."[69]

Later, in commenting on Genesis 2:7, Gibbons affirmed the creation of man from the "dust of the ground, that is to say, consisting chiefly and wholly of earth as the same is mixed with other elements…the more base the matter is, the more excellent is the power and wisdom of the workmaster; the more man ought to be humble in himself and to glory in the Lord."[70] Gibbons connected the first creation from the earth to the resurrection of the body: "seeing the Lord has the power to make the earth out of nothing, and the body of the earth, how easily can he restore the same body being returned to the dust, and

65. Gibbons, *Questions and Disputations*, 45.
66. Gibbons, *Questions and Disputations*, 45.
67. Gibbons, *Questions and Disputations*, 29.
68. Gibbons, *Questions and Disputations*, 29.
69. Gibbons, *Questions and Disputations*, 29.
70. Gibbons, *Questions and Disputations*, 57.

make of an earthly body a spiritual body!"[71] Turning to the completion of the creation of man, Gibbons stated, "the body thus being created, he added thereunto a soul.... He breathed into his face: the substance or form thereof is called the breath of life...not that God hath mouth or organs of breathing, but that we might discern that he received life immediately from God."[72]

William Perkins: Six Days and Adam

Another Cambridge Puritan and fellow theologian to Gibbons was William Perkins (1558–1602). Perkins most extensively addressed the doctrine of creation in his section on the Creator of heaven and earth in *An Exposition of the Symbole or Creed of the Apostles*.[73] Perkins's literal hermeneutic becomes evident as he states,

> Some may ask in what space of time did God make the world? *I answer,* God could have made the world, and all things in it in one moment: but he began and finished the whole work in six distinct days.... The first day he made the matter of all things and the light; in the second the heavens.... In the sixth day he made the beasts of the field, and all cattle, and in the end of the sixth day he made man. Thus in six distinct spaces of time, the Lord did make all things.... If God had made the world in a moment, some might have said, this work is so mystical, that no man can speak of it. But for the preventing of this cavil, it was his pleasure to make the world and all things therein in six days....
>
> God made the world, and everything therein in six distinct days, to teach us, what wonderful power and liberty he had over all his creatures: for he made the light when there was neither Sun nor Moon, nor stars... in giving light.... He is not bound to the Sun, to any creature, or to any means.... God can make trees, plants, and herbs to grow without the means of rain, and without the virtue and operation of the Sun.[74]

---

71. Gibbons, *Questions and Disputations*, 57.

72. Gibbons, *Questions and Disputations*, 57.

73. William Perkins, *An Exposition of the Symbole or Creed of the Apostles* (Cambridge, 1608), 142–56. Perkins first discusses the doctrine of creation in his *A Golden Chain or the Description of Theology...* (Cambridge, 1597), 14–19.

74. Perkins, *Exposition of the Symbole*, 146. In the same work, speaking of the creation of the angels, Perkins notes, "The time and day of their creation cannot be set down further than this, that they were created in the compass of the first six days" (150). Perkins later refers to the days of creation in the context of Sabbath worship: "Touching the time of God's worship, it was the seventh day from the beginning of creation, the Sabbath day.... Adam had a set Sabbath to worship God his creator: and therefore much more need hath everyone of us of a Sabbath day" (155).

Going on to describe the creation of man, Perkins stated, "The body of man at the first was formed by God of clay, or of the dust of the earth, not to be the grave of the soul, as Plato said, but to be an excellent and most fit instrument to put in execution the powers and faculty of the soul.... As for the soul, it is no accidental quality, but a spiritual and invisible essence or nature."[75]

Henry Ainsworth: "The Literal Sense...the Ground of all Interpretation"

Less than a decade after Perkins's publication, Henry Ainsworth (1571–c. 1622), while noting the legitimacy of "allegories, types and shadows" in his detailed explanation of hermeneutics in the preface to *Annotations Upon the First Book of Moses, Called Genesis* (1616), argued that "the literal sense of Moses' Hebrew, is the ground of all interpretation."[76] Ainsworth's exposition of Genesis 1 and 2 reflected his adherence to the literal sense of the text.

Commenting on Genesis 1:5, he stated, "The evening which was the beginning of the night, and the morning, which is the beginning of the day, are here used for the whole time of the light and darkness in one succeeding course, which is with us, the space of 24 hours, which also in a more large sense is here called a day...because darkness was in time before the light, therefore is the evening set before the morning, and so among the Jews, they began their large day at evening."[77] Ainsworth noted that the statement about Adam's creation "*of* the dust" stands in unity with the rest of Scripture, including the New Testament, where the apostle Paul declares "the first man was of the earth, dusty."[78]

John Donne: God Did Not Need the Help of Nature

During this earlier part of the English Puritan era, the topic of creation was considered in the highest levels of English society. Toward the end of his life, the Anglican-poet-turned-preacher John Donne (1572–1631) preached to King Charles I on the creation of Adam. Donne marveled at the majesty of God displayed in the vastness of creation.[79]

---

75. Perkins, *Exposition of the Symbole*, 155.

76. Henry Ainsworth, *Annotations Upon the First Book of Moses, Called Genesis* (Amsterdam, 1616), preface.

77. Ainsworth, *Annotations*, Genesis 1:5. In relation to the use of "the day" in Genesis 2:4, Ainsworth follows in the literal hermeneutical tradition of noting that "day is used [here] for the time wherein anything is done; as in the day of salvation." Ainsworth, *Annotations*, Genesis 2:4.

78. Ainsworth, *Annotations*, Genesis 2:7.

79. For a helpful assessment of John Donne's place in the early Stuart church, see Daniel W. Doerksen, "Polemist or Pastor: Donne and Moderate Calvinist Conformity," in *John Donne*

Filled with wonder at creation and God's declaration of it in His Word, Donne states, "that earth, and that heaven, which spent God himself, Almighty God, six days in finishing, Moses sets up in a few syllables, in one line…. God required not nature to help him do it; Moses required not reason to help him believe…. Now, if all this earth were made in that minute, may not all come to the general dissolution in this minute?"[80] While moving quickly beyond the literal sense of the text to draw colorful allegorical connections and pithy applications, the foundation of Donne's exposition was nonetheless rooted in a literal approach to the text, evidenced both in his certainty that "God made man of earth" and the plentiful and wide-ranging applications he chose to draw from this reality.[81]

William Ames: Scripture's Answer to Our Queries

Among the English Puritans of this era was William Ames (1576–1633). Ames had studied under William Perkins at Cambridge, and he ministered and taught for the remainder of his life in the United Provinces (Dutch Republic). In *The Substance of Christian Religion*, Ames devoted one Lord's day of teaching to God's work of creation.

In his lecture, Ames argued that the authority of Scripture, as the Word of God, necessitates a creation occurring according to the description of Scripture, "for by this foundation we may forearm our faith against the curious queries of some men, who are used to ask, or wonder why the world was not created before that time, in which it was indeed created; or why such a part of it was not in such and such a manner. The Scripture answers, that God created all things by his own free choice, wisdom, and will; so that in this work, he was neither subject to any necessity, neither should any other reason be enquired for."[82] Following the text of Genesis 1, Ames held to the initial act of the creation of the heavens and the earth ex nihilo "in that [God] by his word, and his command he made the whole world suddenly, and of nothing."[83] In his *Marrow of Theology*, Ames notes that this world created by God "has parts distinguishable" and "the creation of these parts of the world did not occur at one and the

and the Protestant Reformation: New Perspectives, ed. Mary Arshagouni Papazian (Detroit: Wayne State University Press, 2003), 12–34.

80. John Donne, *Two Sermons Preached Before King Charles, Upon the xxvi verse of the first Chapter of Genesis* (Cambridge, 1734), 2–3.

81. Donne, *Two Sermons*, 28–31.

82. William Ames, *The Substance of Christian Religion* (London, 1659), 67–68.

83. Ames, *Substance of Christian Religion*, 71.

same moment, but was accomplished part by part in the space of six days."[84] Correlating his commentary on Psalm 104 with the work of the six days, Ames argued that the creation of light on the first day was in part for the purpose of "setting the order of time" prior to the third-day creation of the luminaries.[85]

His literal hermeneutic was further illustrated in his statement that "the power of God shone forth in that he first created the plants, the herbs and the trees before the sun and stars which customarily are causes in their production."[86] Completing his description of the sequence of God's work of creation across the six days, Ames described Adam's creation:

> Man as the last of the creatures is also the summary of all.... Therefore man is said to be created in a different manner from the other creatures; they were brought forth by a word only...but man was brought forth, as it were, with greater counsel and deliberation, Let us make man, Gen. 1:26. The body was first prepared and afterwards the soul breathed in, Gen. 2:7. The body was made of elementary matter, but the soul was produced not out of matter existing before, but rather by the immediate power of God. The excellency of man was chiefly fixed in this: he bore the image of God.[87]

Like his English Puritan contemporaries, Ames believed that God created man on the sixth day.[88]

The Dutch Reformed: Adam's Origin on the Sixth Day

Post-Reformation promotion of a literal interpretation of early Genesis was found beyond the English Puritans and can be seen in *Annotations on the Whole Bible ordered by the Synod of Dordt* (1637), commissioned by the Synod of Dordt (1618–1619) and financed by the Estates-General of the United Provinces. The Old Testament translation and annotations were the work of three Dutch Reformed theologians: Wilhelmus Baudartius (1565–1640), Johannes Bogerman (1576–1635), and Gerson Bucerus (c. 1565–1631). They commented on Genesis 1:5

---

84. William Ames, *The Marrow of Theology* (Grand Rapids: Baker, 1997), 102. Ames's work on the Sabbath, *Sententia de Origine Sabbati & Die Dominico...* (Franeker, 1653) views Genesis 2 as the historical origin of the Sabbath day as a day of rest, and he goes on to argue that issue should not be made of whether it begins in the evening, or the morning, nor should it be debated whether it should be kept for twenty-four hours or for twelve; rather the day should be a day of rest. Ames, *Sententia de Origine Sabbati*, 19–29.

85. Ames, *Lectiones in CL Psalmos Davidis* (Amstelodami, 1635), 357.

86. Ames, *Marrow of Theology*, 105.

87. Ames, *Marrow of Theology*, 105.

88. Ames, *Lectiones in CL Psalmos Davidis*, 357.

that "the meaning of these words is that night and day had made up one natural day together, which with the Hebrews began with the evening and ended with the approach of the next evening, comprehending twenty-four hours."[89] Regarding the creation of Adam and Eve on the sixth day, they noted, "The Lord God had formed man out of the dust of the earth…or shaped, fashioned, viz. as a potter forms some vessel out of clay…. The soul of man is not created out of any precedent matter, like the souls of beasts, but put into him without, out of nothing, from the Spirit of God. Thus man became a living soul…a creature endued with life, consisting of a body and a rational immortal soul, making up man together."[90] The *Annotations* were later translated into English by Theodore Haak, with the prefatory commendation of thirty-five English Puritans and Scottish Presbyterians, including William Twisse, Francis Roberts, William Greenhill, Thomas Goodwin, Alexander Henderson, Samuel Rutherford, and George Gillespie.[91] Like previous Reformation and post-Reformation works on early Genesis, Protestant orthodoxy raised no controversy, criticism, or discussion over the widespread use of a literal hermeneutical approach which read the six days as being ordinary days. Nor was there any critique of the literal reading of a special, temporally immediate creation of Adam and Eve.

During the *Annotations* production period, the influential *Leiden Synopsis* (1625), authored by the Dutch Reformed theologians Antonius Walaeus (1573–1639), Antonius Thysius (1565–1640), Johannes Polyander (1568–1646), and the French Huguenot André Rivet (1572–1651), similarly defined "the creation of the world as the external action of God omnipotent, incommunicable to his creatures, by which of himself and his most free will, moved by no other, he created heaven and earth out of nothing at the beginning of time, and fashioned certain things which he willed to form out of that primary material, by his arrangement within the space of six days, in order that he might make known to his creatures, especially to rational beings, the glory of his great wisdom, power, and goodness, and invite them to the celebration of his name."[92] The *Leiden Synopsis* went on to affirm that God created man after His image, fashioning him from the moist

---

89. Theodore Haak, trans., *The Dutch Annotations Upon the Whole Bible* (London, 1657), Genesis 1:5. See also C. C. de Bruin, "De Bijbelvertaling," in *De Synode van Dordrecht in 1618 en 1619* (Houten: Den Hartog, 1994), 121–56.

90. Haak, *Dutch Annotations*, Genesis 2:7.

91. Haak's 1657 translation of *The Dutch Annotations* noted the prefatory commendation as a "copy of the certificate or attestation about the general desire in both kingdoms (England and Scotland) to have the Belgick or Dutch annotations upon the Bible."

92. Antonius Walaeus, Antonius Thysius, Johannes Polyander, and André Rivet, *Synopsis purioris theologiae*, 3rd ed. (Leiden, 1642), 101–2.

soil of the earth and animating him with life in a moment, thereby completing His work of creating man.[93] Guarding against an errant anthropomorphic view of God in reading Genesis 2:7, the authors further argued that the point of the text in referencing man's formation from the earth was to emphasize both the unique divine care in this work as well as the supernatural reality of man's creation from matter unsuited by nature to this purpose.[94]

Puritans and the Westminster Assembly

Back across the Channel, English Puritans were coming into their ascendancy in the 1640s, and they continued creating substantial publications on Genesis and creation origins.

Arthur Jackson: Six Days of God's Power

Arthur Jackson (c. 1593–1666), a Presbyterian-minded Puritan clergyman, published his *Exposition Upon the Five Books of Moses* in 1643, providing a careful commentary in direct continuity with the Reformation tradition of a literal hermeneutic toward early Genesis. Jackson viewed the days of creation as ordinary in length, the "evening and the morning…comprehending both night and day…the space of twenty four hours."[95]

Commenting on the latter part of Genesis 2:7, Jackson stated, "By his almighty power the Lord did create and infuse into the yet lifeless body of Adam a living reasonable soul, which being instantly united to the body in an incomprehensible manner, his body was quickened and enlivened…. Thus the soul was not, as the body, made of the earth, but created of nothing, and so joined to the body."[96] For Jackson, the Genesis text, literally understood, was a display of the power of God—whether in the creation of all things within the space of six ordinary days, or in the particular creative acts of God within any of those days. His passion in explaining the text was that "the glory might resound" to God.[97]

The Westminster Assembly: It Pleased God to Create All Things

With the English Parliament at odds with Charles I, and the outbreak of the Civil War, reform-minded Puritans and Parliamentarians had soon called the Westminster Assembly (1643–1653) to provide a stronger doctrinal and

---

93. Walaeus et al., *Synopsis*, 133–42.
94. Walaeus et al., *Synopsis*, 133–42.
95. Arthur Jackson, *A Help for the Understanding of Scripture…* (Cambridge, 1643), 3.
96. Jackson, *The Understanding of Scripture*, 9.
97. Jackson, *The Understanding of Scripture*, preface.

ecclesial system for the Church of England. The fruit of the Assembly, though never enacted in the Church of England, included the Westminster Confession of Faith and Shorter and Larger Catechisms. Whereas the Thirty-Nine Articles of the Church of England (1563, 1571) gave no attention at all to creation, the English Puritan and Scottish Presbyterian delegates to the Assembly did, which is perhaps not surprising. They viewed themselves as the heirs and continuity of the Reformation and its literal hermeneutic toward the creation account, even as some in the broader Church of England advocated for a figurative interpretation of early Genesis—an approach more commonly found in the Roman Catholic Church on the European continent.

William Barker notes one example, citing that "Sir Thomas Browne, an Anglican physician, in his *Religio Medici*, published in 1643, the year of the Westminster Assembly's beginning," promoted an instantaneous creation.[98] By contrast, while the minutes of the Westminster Assembly reveal little of participants' discussions surrounding the doctrine of creation, the content of the Confession of Faith and Catechisms strongly indicates the approach of the Assembly to early Genesis and the creation origins of Adam and Eve.[99]

Continuing the Reformation recovery of a hermeneutic that primarily viewed Genesis in a literal sense, the Confession of Faith stated, "It pleased God the Father, Son, and Holy Ghost, for the manifestation of the glory of His eternal power, wisdom, and goodness, in the beginning, to create, or make of nothing, the world, and all things therein whether visible or invisible in the space of six days; and all very good."[100] The statement of God's work of creation occurring "in" or "within the space of six days" was reiterated in the Assembly's production of the Shorter and Larger Catechisms.[101]

The Assembly's statement "in the space of six days" has prompted vexed debate regarding its meaning among American Presbyterians adhering to the Westminster Standards in the late twentieth and early twenty-first centuries. Studies tallying how many of the Westminster divines explicitly held to a six, twenty-four hour, day creation have been meticulously reported and debated. The

---

98. William S. Barker, "The Westminster Assembly on the Days of Creation: A Reply to David W. Hall," *Westminster Theological Journal*, 62, no. 1 (Spring 2000): 115.

99. Chad VanDixhoorn, ed., *Minutes and Papers of the Westminster Assembly: Volume IV Minutes, Sessions 604–1163 (1646–1652)* (Oxford: Oxford University Press, 2012), 404–5, 408–9, 518.

100. Westminster Confession of Faith, 4.1, in Morton Smith, *Harmony of the Westminster Confession and Catechisms* (Taylors, S.C.: Presbyterian Press, 1990), 22. All subsequent citations of the Westminster Standards are from this source unless noted otherwise.

101. Westminster Shorter Catechism, Q&A 9; Westminster Larger Catechism, Q&A 15.

Westminster divines who explicitly stated the days of Genesis were twenty-four hours in length include John Lightfoot, John White, John Ley, George Walker, and William Twisse; debates exist over whether others should be included.[102] Supporters of modern figurative readings of the days of Genesis 1 argue that because there is no explicit statement by the Westminster Assembly that these days were "twenty-four hours," there is no definitive evidence that the Confession (to which they subscribe) originally intended six ordinary, or natural days.[103]

However, this contemporary debate fails to reckon with the broader Reformation and post-Reformation context and the precedent for the English Puritans who engaged in or supported the work of the Westminster Assembly. Rather than requiring the mention of "twenty-four hours" as the sole legitimate evidence for commitment to a six-ordinary-day span of God's work of creation, it would be better to see references to "twenty-four hours" as one good indicator among a variety of others that shows the Assembly's continuity of a literal hermeneutical approach in its interpretation of the early chapters of Genesis.[104] Correctly interpreting the English Puritan view of creation also requires an awareness of the limited alternatives to a literal, six-ordinary-day

---

102. Barker, "The Westminster Assembly on the Days of Creation," 117. Barker includes Lightfoot in this list, later noting Lightfoot's calculation that the first day must have been thirty-six hours in length. Lightfoot drew this conclusion from the light being created after the darkness of Genesis 1:2 as being parallel to "the evening and morning." Positing twelve hours of darkness, followed by twelve hours of light, Lightfoot inferred (assuming rotation of, and light on only one side of, the globe) that for the opposite hemisphere from that being described in the text this must assume an initial twenty-four hours of darkness, followed by twelve hours of light: "so the first natural day to that part of the world was thirty-six hours long." John Lightfoot, *A Few and New Observations on the Book of Genesis* in *The Whole Works of the Rev. John Lightfoot, D. D.*, ed. John Rogers Pitman (London, 1822), 2:333–34.

103. See for example, David Hall's "What Was the View of the Westminster Assembly Divines on Creation Days?" in *Did God Create in Six Days?*; and Barker's "The Westminster Assembly on the Days of Creation," 115. David Hall, at times using more circumstantial evidence, argued that as many as twenty-one Westminster divines give indication of literal days—an extensive list including men such as Joseph Caryl, Edmund Calamy, William Gouge, Jeremiah Burroughs, and others. Hall, "What Was the View," 52.

104. Other helpful indicators include qualifiers such as "natural," "ordinary," "in the space of," "in the time of," "across," "over," as well as the juxtaposed contrast of "instantaneous" or "extratemporal" creation with "six day" creation. References to "figurative" or "allegorical" versus "literal" or "plain" interpretation are also contextually helpful. Aside from Lightfoot's positing the first day to be thirty-six hours in length for the opposite hemisphere (which nonetheless retains a literal twenty-four-hour first day for the hemisphere of the writer) and the standard guarding against anthropomorphism in Genesis 2:7, no historical evidence indicates any figurative, primary sense interpretation of the days or any other part of Genesis 1 and 2 within the stream of Reformation to post-Reformation Reformed and Lutheran orthodoxy up to and including the time period of the Westminster Assembly.

interpretation that existed in the early to mid-seventeenth century, when a figurative reading of Genesis included either an instantaneous or *extratemporal* creation. In this context, arguments that the Westminster Assembly's statements of creation taking place "in" or "within the space of six days" potentially communicate something other than a space of six ordinary days appear anachronistic, if not simply revisionist.

The underlying literal hermeneutical approach to early Genesis by the delegates to the Westminster Assembly was further exemplified in their statement on the creation of man: "After God had made all the other creatures, he created man male and female; formed the body of man out of the dust of the ground, and the woman of the rib of the man, endued them with living, reasonable, and immortal souls; made them after his own image, in knowledge, righteousness, and holiness; having the law of God written on their hearts, and power to fulfil it, and dominion over the creatures, yet subject to fall."[105] The doctrinal statements of the Westminster Assembly, including these statements on the doctrine of creation, were adopted outside of England by the Church of Scotland at her General Assembly of 1647. Despite the failure to gain a full implementation of the Westminster Confession and Catechisms within the Church of England, many English Puritans continued to promote the same doctrine, including devoting energy to writing and preaching on Genesis.[106]

Ley, White, and Lightfoot on Origins
Among the participants in the Westminster Assembly, John Ley (1583–1662) and John White (1575–1648) wrote commentaries on Genesis. Both Ley in *Annotations on the First Book of Moses Called Genesis* and White in *A Commentary upon the Three First Chapters of the First Book of Moses Called Genesis* took a literal approach to the text of Genesis 1 and 2.[107] Together with specifying six days of ordinary length, Ley and White expounded a special, temporally immediate creation of Adam and Eve, Adam from the dust of the ground and Eve from his rib.[108]

---

105. Westminster Larger Catechism, Q&A 17. See also Westminster Confession of Faith, 4.2, and Westminster Shorter Catechism, Q&A 10.

106. See for example, Edward Leigh's chapters on creation in *A System or Body of Divinity Wherein the Fundamentals and Main Grounds of Religion Are Opened* (London, 1654), 225–95.

107. *Annotations on the First Book of Moses Called Genesis* was the first part of the *Annotations upon All the Books of the Old and New Testament*, a project led by John Downame that involved a number of other Puritan exegetes, including William Gouge.

108. John Ley, *Annotations on the First Book of Moses Called Genesis*, in *Annotations upon All the Books of the Old and New Testament*, ed. John Downame (London, 1645), Genesis 1–2;

John Lightfoot (1602–1675) was another of the more prolific writers on creation among the Westminster divines. In *Rules for a Student of the Holy Scriptures*, he provided an exposition of the days of creation following a literal hermeneutic. Lightfoot saw God's creation of Adam from the dust as a reason for the hope of the resurrection: "If God made man of dust, he can raise him."[109] While committed to the literal interpretation, Lightfoot at the same time was intrigued by potential inferences from the text, harmonization with natural philosophy, and the possibility of a chronological narration of history from the beginning of creation. Lightfoot began his chronology and dating of the history of the Old Testament in *A Chronicle of the Times* (1647) with the six days of creation. At times Lightfoot's deductions arguably went beyond the "good and necessary consequence" of the text.[110] He argued on the basis of Genesis 5:2 that the fall of Adam must have taken place on the sixth day, prior to the seventh day of rest: "God having thus created all things in six days, and man having thus fallen, and heard of Christ, and of death, and eternal life, and other like things on the sixth day,—the Lord ordained the seventh day for a Sabbath, or holy rest."[111] Working through Old Testament genealogical and other chronologies, Lightfoot further calculated that creation must have taken place some 3,519 years prior to Nehemiah's return to Persia.[112] Lightfoot's writings, despite occasionally speculative inferences, testified to the continued post-Reformation commitment to a literal Genesis understanding of human origins.

James Ussher: "Adam the Man, Eve the Woman"
James Ussher (1581–1656), a Puritan Episcopalian who served as archbishop in the Church of Ireland, did not take part in the Westminster Assembly although he was invited. Like his Puritan contemporaries, Ussher was committed to a literal hermeneutic of early Genesis. Significantly before the Westminster Assembly, he was the leading influence in the formation of the Irish Articles of Religion (1615), which stated that "God by his word alone, in the space of six days, created all things"—language similar to that later

John White, *A Commentary upon the Three First Chapters of the First Book of Moses Called Genesis* (London, 1656), 1:32, 2:27–32.

109. John Lightfoot, *Rules for a Student of the Holy Scriptures*, in *Whole Works of the Rev. John Lightfoot*, 2:10–11.

110. *Westminster Confession of Faith*, 1.6.

111. Lightfoot, *A Chronicle of the Times*, in *Whole Works of the Rev. John Lightfoot*, 2:72–74.

112. Lightfoot, *A Chronicle of the Times*, 2:326.

adopted in the Westminster Confession of Faith and Catechisms.[113] In the 1630s, Ussher wrote of the days of creation as "the beginning of the works of God (those six working days putting as it were an end to that long Sabbath that never had a beginning)."[114]

During the Westminster Assembly, Ussher published a catechism, *The Principles of Christian Religion* (1644), stating, as in the earlier Irish Articles, that "in the beginning of time…God by His Word alone, in the space of six days, created all things."[115] After noting the formation of Adam from the dust of the earth and Eve from Adam, Ussher states, "At the beginning of time two [were created]. Adam the man, and Eve the woman, from both whom, afterwards all mankind did proceed."[116] The origin of man was further expounded in his later work, *A Body of Divinity*, where Ussher stated that the totality of the creation period covered "six days and six nights."[117] In his comments on the creation of man he noted,

> [The body of Adam was made] of the very dust of the earth, Gen. 2.7. in which respect the work of God in making him is set forth by a similitude of the potter which of his clay makes his pots; Rom. 9.21…. His soul was made a spiritual substance, which God breathed into that frame of earth to give it life, whereby man became a living soul…. God made it immediately not of any earthly matter (as he did the body) nor of any of the elements, (as he did the other creatures) but of a spiritual matter, whereby is signified the difference of the soul of man…from the soul or life of beasts…which dies with them, whereas the soul of man comes by God's creation…that it might be immortal.[118]

Like Lightfoot, and numerous other contemporaries, Ussher's interest in biblical history extended beyond the immediate text. In his chronology of world history, he exemplified the contemporary fascination with attempting to precisely date the events of history back to the first moment of creation. Whereas in *Body of Divinity*, he stated that the creation of the world took place

---

113. "The Irish Articles of Religion," in Philip Schaff, *The Creeds of Christendom* (Grand Rapids: Baker, 1996), 3:529–30.

114. James Ussher, *Immanuel, or Mystery of the Incarnation of the Son of God* (London, 1638), 3.

115. James Ussher, *The Principles of Christian Religion…* (London, 1644), 5–6.

116. Ussher, *Principles of Christian Religion*, 7–8.

117. James Ussher, *A Body of Divinity or the Summe and Substance of Christian Religion* (London, 1653), 96–97. In his *Annals*, Ussher describes this period as "the first week of the world." James Ussher, *The Annals of the World Deduced from the Origin of Time…* (London, 1658), 2. Ussher's *Annals of the World* was highly regarded by many of his contemporaries.

118. Ussher, *A Body of Divinity*, 102–3.

"four thousand years before the birth of our Saviour Christ, and so about 5614 years before this time," in *Annals of the World* he refined the date of creation to the year 4004 BC. More precisely, he stated, "I incline to this opinion, that from the evening ushering in the first day of the world, to that midnight which began the first day of the Christian era, there was 4003 years, seventy days, and six temporary hours."[119]

Thomas Goodwin: "Nothing Was Your Great Grandmother"
In contrast to the expository works on Genesis and creation and the chronologies of world history by English Puritans, Thomas Goodwin's (1600–1680) *Of the Creatures, and the Condition of their State by Creation* was a more general, systematic treatise on creation.[120] Though he did not provide a sequential commentary on the works of the days in his treatise, Goodwin's work clearly evidenced a literal interpretation of man's creation origin, describing it as a cause for humility: "Your pedigree is from nothing; your ancestry, and that not far removed, is nothing…. Your body was immediately made from dust, that was your next mother by that line; but that dust was made of the first rude earth, without form, and that was your grandmother; but that earth was made purely of nothing; so then nothing was your great grandmother. Thus of your body. Then for your soul, that was immediately created by God out of nothing, and so by that line your next mother was nothing."[121]

At the same time, Goodwin noted the blessedness of Adam immediately following his creation:

> Man came forth of God's hands by immediate creation…. No sooner did he open his eyes, but he saw himself most happy. He had a world about him new made, and in its freshness and best hue, and furnished with all sorts of creatures, all of them well suited to his body (the epitome of them all), and to his senses…. And he was made the centre of all the goodness that was in those creatures…. God seated him in a garden planted by himself, in the richest and most pleasant soil in the world, Eden… planted by God himself, the best gardener for skill that ever was.[122]

Like many English Puritans writing on Adam and Eve in their original creation context, Goodwin marveled at the beauty and happiness of man in his

---

119. Ussher, *A Body of* Divinity, 98; Ussher, *Annals*, preface.
120. Thomas Goodwin, *Of the Creatures, and the Condition of their State by Creation*, in *The Works of Thomas Goodwin, D. D.* (Edinburgh, 1863), 1–128.
121. Goodwin, *Of the Creatures*, 17.
122. Goodwin, *Of the Creatures*, 34, 41–42.

first estate. The perfect goodness of Adam and Eve and their creation context illuminated the hard reality of their fall into sin, with its stark consequences for man and creation. As a result, the ensuing grace of God in the unfolding history of redemption in Christ stood sublime and utterly glorious.

Richard Baxter: "His Will Must Satisfy Us"

Where Thomas Goodwin's work on creation appeared to be directed toward ministers and an educated laity, Richard Baxter's (1615–1691) aimed to teach children the truths of Scripture, including the doctrine of creation and human origins, in *The Mother's Catechism*. This did not reflect any lack of intellectual acumen on Baxter's part—he engaged with and challenged the thought of contemporaries including René Descartes, Thomas Hobbes, and Baruch Spinoza—but rather reflected his awareness of the significance of the doctrine of creation.[123] Devoting his "fourth lesson" to the creation, Baxter drew up the following questions and answers:

C. [Child] What is it that the Bible tells us?

M. [Mother] The first thing is, how God made the world.

C. I would fain know that. How was it?

M. In the beginning, God made the heaven and the earth. And the earth was first like a great puddle of dirty water, without light or shape; and God did take six days' time to shape it out of this confused heap, and to adorn it with all the creatures which it possesses.

C. Why did God take just six days to do it?

M. We must not ask why God did it [in just six days]: his will must satisfy us: but this helps us the more distinctly to take notice of God's work....

C. What did [God] make the sixth day?

M. All sorts of beasts on the earth; and, lastly, man.

C. How did God make man?

M. He made his body of the earth, and then breathed his soul into it.

C. Did not God make woman?

M. When he made the man, he took a rib out of his side, and made it a woman, to be his wife, to show that a man and his wife should be, as it were, one.

---

123. David Sytsma, "Richard Baxter's Philosophical Polemics: A Puritan's Response to Mechanical Philosophy" (PhD diss., Princeton Theological Seminary, 2013), 270–74.

C. Who were the first man and woman?

M. Adam and Eve.[124]

Baxter's catechism for children reflected his concern, like that of the Westminster Assembly, that the English Church as a whole would grasp God's revelation of His work of creation, including human origins—in a manner consistent with a literal sense interpretation of Genesis 1 and 2. His commitment to educate the young in this way may well have been heightened by his awareness of rising challenges to the literal understanding of Genesis on creation and human origins.

John Owen: From "Contemptible Matter" to "Excellent, Curious, and Glorious Fabric"

John Owen (1616–1683), though primarily focused on other areas of theology and practice, also reflected the steady interest of Puritan theologians in God's work of creation. Like that of many of his contemporaries, Owen's work demonstrated his adherence to a literal hermeneutic characteristic of the Reformation and Reformed orthodoxy, including referring to God's work of creation occurring in a "duration of time [of] six days."[125] In his work *The Holy Spirit*, Owen substantively addressed the role of the Holy Spirit in the work of creation, particularly focusing on the creation of Adam. Expounding Genesis 2:7 Owen stated,

> 1. There is the matter whereof he was formed; 2. The quickening principle added thereunto; and, 3. The effect of their conjunction and union. For the matter he was made of, it is said he was formed [of] "dust of the ground" or dust gathered together on a heap from and upon the ground.... God... first prepares his matter, and then forms it as seems good to him.... This is mentioned for two ends:—First, to set forth the excellency, power, and wisdom of God, who out of such vile, contemptible matter as a heap of dust, swept it as it were together on the ground, could and did make so excellent, curious, and glorious fabric as the body of man, or as was the body of man before the fall....
>
> Into this formed dust, secondly, God breathed the "breath of life...a vital immortal spirit." This God breathed into him, as giving him something of himself, somewhat immediately of his own, not made out of any procreated matter.... His body was formed, as the beasts, from the

---

124. Richard Baxter, *The Mother's Catechism, or, A Familiar Way of Catechising Children, in the Knowledge of God, Themselves, and the Holy Scriptures* in *The Practical Works of The Rev. Richard Baxter* (London, 1830), 18:528–29.

125. John Owen, *The Works of John Owen* (Edinburgh: Banner of Truth, 2000), 3:165.

matter made the first day.... His soul was an immediate production... from the divine power.... This heavenly breath, was unto man a quickening principle...the effect [was that] man became a living soul...capable of all vital acts.... He could move, eat, see, hear, etc.... This was the creation of man.[126]

Owen went on to relate the creation of man from the dust to the consequences of the fall into sin: the curse of God in Genesis 3, "for dust you are and to dust you shall return."[127] His literalist view of human origins was plainly evident, consistent with his Puritan contemporaries.

Thomas Manton: The Manner of Creation Hidden from Reason, Supplied by Revelation

Sermons on the topic of creation were not uncommon for the English Puritans of the mid to late seventeenth century. Thomas Manton (1620–1677), preaching on Hebrews 11:3 stated, "In these words the apostle begins the history of faith, and therefore goes so high as God's ancient work of creation. His drift is to prove that faith satisfies itself in the word of God, though nothing be seen; and he proves it in the first instance and exercise of faith that ever was in the world— the creation."[128] Manton went on to argue "that it is of great profit and comfort to believers to consider the creation [and] that we can only understand the truth and wonders of the creation by faith...the whole creation is a standing monument of God's power."[129] Manton also followed in the Reformation and English Puritan tradition of holding to a literal interpretation of early Genesis. Describing the sequential work of creation as intended, he declared, "God provided for the necessities of beast, ere he would bring them into the world. God made first plants, that have but a growing life; then beasts, fishes, fowls, that have a feeling life; then man that hath a rational life.... Man was made last, as most excellent; his palace furnished with all things necessary, and then like a prince he is sent into the world to rule and to reign...all things are wonderfully made."[130]

---

126. Owen, *Works*, 3:100–101.

127. Owen, *Works*, 3:101.

128. Thomas Manton, "Sermons Upon Hebrews XI," in *The Complete Works of Thomas Manton, D. D.* (London, 1873), 13:388.

129. Manton, "Sermons Upon Hebrews XI," 389–91.

130. Manton, "Sermons Upon Hebrews XI," 391. For more from Thomas Manton on the creation of man, see his sermon on Psalm 119:73 in *The Complete Works*, 7:270–79. In this sermon, Manton comments on Genesis 2:7: "Before we read that man was created, here we see in what sort: his body was framed with great art, though of base materials; a handful of dust did God enliven and form into a beautiful frame. But for the frame within, he had a more excellent

Manton proclaimed,

> This was God's great aim and end in making man, that he might have a witness and publisher of his own glory. That this was the aim of God, to have his works viewed distinctly, may be discovered by many things; that he did prolong his work for six days, when he might have made all things in one day. And this was the reason he made man last, that when he was made he might contemplate all the rest of the creatures...to admire the greatness and goodness of it.... The first Sabbath was appointed for contemplation; it is the sweetest rest we can enjoy, to view the works of God.... Now what prospect is more various and beautiful than the works of God? Unclasp the book of nature, turn over a few leaves of that large volume, see what delight and contentment reason will find.[131]

Manton preached several further sermons on the value of meditation on God's works of creation, noting that "if you have rightly meditated upon the works of creation, there will be more fear and dread of God, that will arise from the consideration of his majesty and power impressed upon the creature... there will be more love to God for all his kindness, and for all...his goodness to the creature.... Meditation on the creature will beget trust and dependence on God."[132]

Turning from the value of meditation to the necessary means for a right understanding of creation, Manton argued, "The doctrine of the creation is a mixed principle; much of it is liable to reason, but most of it can only be discovered by faith. We must consider the creation in two ways, either *ex parte rei* or *ex parte modi*; either the thing itself, or the necessary circumstances. For the thing itself, that was known to the heathens, that there was a creation; but the manner how was wholly hidden from reason, and can only be supplied by revelation of the word. Nature doth confess a creation, but faith must teach us what it is."[133]

English Puritans like Manton held to the necessity of special revelation for the correct understanding of the manner of creation. His view resided squarely within the English Puritan commitment to a literal hermeneutic toward early Genesis—including the understanding of a special, temporally immediate creation of Adam and Eve on the sixth day.[134]

---

and perfect soul than God gave to any other creature; by union of both of these, man became a living soul. Heaven and earth were married in his person" (272).

131. Manton, "Sermons Upon Hebrews XI," 13:394.

132. Manton, "Sermons Upon Hebrews XI," 13:408–9.

133. Manton, "Sermons Upon Hebrews XI," 13:410.

134. David Hall comes to similar conclusions in "A Brief Overview of the Exegesis of Genesis 1–11: Luther to Lyell," in *Coming to Grips with Genesis: Biblical Authority and the*

Post-Reformation Orthodoxy: Adam and Eve, Created on the Sixth Day

During the post-Reformation era, both English Puritans and Dutch Reformed theologians continued to display a strong commitment to the Reformation hermeneutical recalibration back to the literal tradition. To a man it appears they held to a creation ex nihilo and viewed the days of creation as ordinary due to the markers of evening and morning. This did not mean they rejected aspects or levels of meaning beyond the literal sense—many, like Gibbons and Manton, saw rich theological significance and beautiful typology in the creation account. Some, like Lightfoot and Ussher, pursued detailed inferences of timing and chronology and considered possibilities that went beyond the literal interpretation of the text, though their ideas usually were not in any necessary conflict with the literal view. Post-Reformation Reformed theologians clearly viewed the Genesis creation account as perspicuous, literal, and cause for wonder- and awe-filled worship of God. Included within this commitment to the literal tradition was a literal exegesis of the Genesis 1 and 2 texts describing the creation of Adam from the dust and Eve from Adam's rib. The first man and woman were created specially, separate from the animals, and unique as God's image-bearers. They were the glorious, sixth-day crown of God's creation, made sinless and very good.

Like the first generation of the magisterial Reformers, the post-Reformation Reformed orthodox promoted a literal rather than a figurative sense in Genesis 1. Before, during, and after the Westminster Assembly, their desire to maintain the literal tradition was exemplified in their defense of creation "in the space of six days"—affirming six twenty-four-hour days or ordinary, natural days, against an instantaneously complete or an extratemporal creation. Why the recurring emphasis on six ordinary days of creation? Undoubtedly it was not merely in response to patristic and medieval sources. Figurative interpretations that posited an instantaneous or extratemporal work of creation continued among post-Reformation Roman Catholics, Socinians, and Anabaptists. Like the early Reformers, the post-Reformation Reformed theologians were concerned with hermeneutical principles and patterns as much as they were with the temporal realities of creation and were well aware of the devastating theological implications of wrongly adopting a figurative hermeneutic.

Like the Reformers, the post-Reformation Reformed orthodox in England and the Netherlands also displayed significant commitment to maintaining a

Age of the Earth, ed. Terry Mortenson and Thane H. Ury (Green Forest, Ark.: Master Books, 2008), 53–78.

literal reading of Genesis, even where this brought conflict with still-popular Greek natural philosophies in the science of their own day. Committing to the literal interpretation of Genesis did not negate their dedication to the legitimacy of using human reason in understanding God's creation. Rather, it indicated that they believed Scripture, as God's special revelation, should take priority in addressing the origins and history of the realm of God's creation.[135]

As Jae-Eun Park states, "subordinating philosophy to theology…[was] the shared thought and blueprint [of] the Puritan tradition of that time."[136] Those committed to this approach, like the English Puritan theologian and philosopher Theophilus Gale (1628–1678), believed ideas of natural philosophers or pagan traditions about human origins that cohered with the literal interpretation of Genesis reflected truth; ideas that stood in contradiction had suppressed the truth in unrighteousness.[137]

The prevailing paradigm among the Reformed orthodox was that the pursuit of natural philosophy in relation to creation and human origins was a legitimate and potentially helpful endeavor—when pursued within the parameters set by the literal interpretation of the Genesis text. Anything that contradicted or failed to cohere with the literal reading of the Genesis text was rejected as subversive to God's revelation. However, post-Reformation Protestants committed to the literal tradition, like their patristic, medieval, and early Reformation predecessors, also faced substantial challenges from those who accommodated the authority, sufficiency, and perspicuity of the Genesis account of creation and human origins to Greek natural philosophy.

New "enlightened" forms of thought that threatened to erode the literal interpretation of the Genesis account were evolving—entering the realm of Protestantism from its fringes. A crucial theological struggle was about to ensue, with Genesis, hermeneutics, and human origins a key battleground.

135. The widely popular commentaries of the Presbyterian-minded English Puritan, Matthew Poole (1624–1679), further attest to the breadth of the English Puritan commitment to a literal hermeneutic toward the early chapters of Genesis during the seventeenth century. Matthew Poole, *Annotations upon the Holy Bible* (London, 1683), Gen. 1–2.

136. Jae-Eun Park, "Theophilus Gale's Reformed Platonism: Focusing on His Discourse of 'Creation' and 'Providence' in the Court of the Gentiles," *Mid-America Journal of Theology* 24 (2013): 121–42.

137. Theophilus Gale, *The Court of the Gentiles: Or a Discourse Touching the Original of Human Literature, Both Philologie and Philosophie, from the Scriptures…* (Oxon, 1660), 315–40.

4

Adam in the Enlightenment Era

One novel challenge to the literal hermeneutic that grew during the latter part of the seventeenth century can be traced to Europe from at least the early sixteenth century, apparently originating in the early period of European seafaring exploration and discovery of "new" continents. In the 1530s Philip von Hohenheim (1493–1541), a Swiss physician, astrologer, and occultist, suggested the possibility that the "hidden islands" were populated "by people [which] are from a different Adam" and that African pygmies were not of Adamic descent.[1] He also postulated that they might lack language and souls and thus not be human.

Occultists, Socinians, and Atheists: The New Opposition to the Literal Tradition

Where von Hohenheim had suggested pre-Adamitism as a possibility, Jacob Palaeologus (c. 1520–1585), a Socinian with Roman Catholic roots, actively promoted the idea "that Adam and Eve were not the ancestors of all people" in his tract *Ad omnes ab uno Adamo descenderit* (1570), written fifteen years prior to his execution in Rome for heresy.[2] Giordano Bruno, a Dominican friar turned Renaissance freethinker, drew on medieval Jewish Kabbalist and Chinese sources when he also hypothesized on separate origins for Indians and Africans, suggesting in *The Expulsion of the Triumphant Beast* (1584) that "those of the new land are not of the human generation" despite their resemblance to humans.[3]

---

1. Von Hohenheim is also known as "Paracelsus." Philip C. Almond, *Adam and Eve in Seventeenth Century Thought* (Cambridge: Cambridge University Press, 1999), 49–50.

2. Almond, *Adam and Eve in Seventeenth Century Thought*, 49.

3. Giordano Bruni, *The Expulsion of the Triumphant Beast*, trans. and ed. Arthur D. Imerti (New Brunswick, N.J.: Rutgers University Press, 1964), 249–50; Almond, *Adam and Eve in Seventeenth Century Thought*, 50. Richard Popkin argues that the sources used by Bruno,

Thomas Nashe (1567–c. 1601) recounted claims of atheism in Sir Walter Raleigh's circles in 1585: the Anglican astronomer and mathematician Thomas Harriot (1560–1621), back from a voyage to Virginia with Raleigh, had apparently stated in a lecture that the natives of the new world had origins predating Adam by as much as ten thousand years.[4] The pre-Adamite theories had no precedent within the history of Christian thought on early Genesis and human origins. Their origins lay in non-Christian religious and philosophical influences.[5] These novel challenges influenced Genesis hermeneutics in the seventeenth century much as Greek natural philosophy had influenced ideas about Genesis in the patristic and medieval periods.

The historian Richard Popkin notes that for a significant period of the seventeenth century, no further publications proposed pre-Adamite theories. This lack of published theories did not mean the idea did not exist in some fashion—a number of writers in the English Civil War era mentioned individuals from sectarian groups like the Ranters and Diggers, "who said the world was created long before the time Scripture speaks of."[6] However, it appears that these ideas were held by only a fringe minority in society. The concept of

---

and later La Peyrère, included Yehudah ha-Levi and Maimonides, both of whom criticized pre-Adamite theories in the medieval traditions of the occultic and mystical Jewish Kabbalah and its precursors. Richard H. Popkin, "The Pre-Adamite Theory in the Renaissance," in *Philosophy and Humanism: Renaissance Essays in Honor of Paul Oskar Kristeller*, ed. Edward P. Mahoney (Leiden: Brill, 1976), 52–54.

4. Popkin, "Pre-Adamite Theory," 50–64. Nashe would also claim that Christopher Marlowe had taught similarly "that the Indians…have assuredly written of above 16 thousand years ago, whereas Adam is proved to have lived within 6 thousand years." Almond, *Adam and Eve in Seventeenth Century Thought*, 51.

5. David Livingstone argues that Joseph Justus Scaliger (1540–1609), a French Protestant classicist and historian (and a feared historical critic of Roman Catholic tradition) who taught at Leiden, challenged accepted chronologies of world history in a "troublesome" manner. This appears to be a dubious contention, however. Although Scaliger did engage in comparative study of Old Testament and Egyptian, Persian, and Babylonian chronologies, where these accounts conflicted with accepted Old Testament chronologies, he maintained a world chronology within the range accepted by adherents of the literal interpretive stream on Genesis. At most it may be argued that Scaliger's comparisons would later be revisited by individuals who were willing to reject both traditional chronologies and the literal approach to Genesis—which Scaliger did not do. Livingstone later notes that the standard approach during the post-Reformation era was "either to reduce all human histories to sacred history by a range of calculation translations…or deny the validity of nonsacred sources." David Livingstone, *Adam's Ancestors: Race, Religion & The Politics of Human Origins* (Baltimore: Johns Hopkins University Press, 2008), 9–10; Joseph Justus Scaliger, *Opus de Emendatione Temporum* (Geneva, 1629), 667–68.

6. John Holland, *The Smoke of the Bottomless Pit. Or a More True and Fuller Discovery of the Doctrine of Those Men which Call Themselves Ranters: or, the Mad Crew* (London, 1651) as cited by Almond, *Adam and Eve in Seventeenth Century Thought*, 51.

pre-Adamite human existence appears to have become significantly influential both in Europe and England only through the writing of the "Enlightenment" thinker Isaac La Peyrère (1596–1676).[7]

Isaac La Peyrère's Men before Adam

La Peyrère, who was born into a French Huguenot family of Portuguese Jewish origins, was fascinated by Judaism and in time ostensibly converted to Roman Catholicism, albeit under pressure due to heresy charges. La Peyrère shocked Europe by arguing for both an eternally preexisting world and pre-Adamic humanity in *Men before Adam*, first published in Latin in Amsterdam in 1655. Following a line of occult Judaism criticized by Jewish commentators like Maimonides, La Peyrère argued that only the Jews were the descendants of Adam. He claimed that Scripture was only intended to tell their history—Gentiles had an alternate history and line of descent. Placing a greater credence in indigenous pagan histories than in genealogical chronologies derived from Scripture, he posited that mankind must have existed at least as far back as fifty thousand years before Christ.[8]

Central to La Peyrère's exegetical argument on human origins was his separation of the creation accounts of Genesis 1 and 2; he proposed that Genesis 1 revealed the creation of the Gentiles and Genesis 2 was an account of the origin of the Jews.[9] He further argued that Adam and his posterity were also distinct from other men by virtue of the way Adam was created, saying Adam's "creation [was] from God himself."[10] Thus, he implied that other streams of humanity did not share in the mode of creation of Adam described in Genesis 2. Believing that the Genesis 1 account was both primitive and vague, La Peyrère argued that the best answers on origins could be found in the various histories and accounts of other people:

> It is a natural supposition that the beginning of the world is not to be received according to that common beginning which is pitched in Adam…for that beginning seems enquirable, at a far greater distance, and from ages past very long before, both by the most ancient accounts of the Chaldeans, as also by the most ancient records of the Egyptians,

---

7. Popkin argues that "in the period from Bruno and the Raleigh group to La Peyrère, practically nothing seems to have contributed to the theory." Popkin, "Pre-Adamite Theory," 64.

8. Popkin cites that this included accounts from Mexico, Greenland, and China. Richard H. Popkin, *Isaac La Peyrère (1596–1676): His Life, Work, and Influence* (Leiden: Brill, 1987), 47.

9. Isaac La Peyrère, *A Theological Systeme upon the Presupposition, that Men Were before Adam* (London, 1655), 88–118.

10. La Peyrère, *A Theological Systeme*, 330.

Ethiopians, and Scythians, and by parts…of the world newly discovered, as also from those unknown countries, to which the [Dutch] have sailed of late, the men of which, as is probable did not descend from Adam.[11]

La Peyrère's alternative view of origins required rejecting the idea that the complete divine work of creation literally took place in the space of six days, and his pursuit of philosophical and theological consistency necessitated further revisions. Realizing that his new scheme begged engagement with both the New Testament and covenant theology, La Peyrère proposed an elaborate reinterpretation of Romans 5, arguing that "there must have been a lawless world before Adam, containing people" and stating that "men that were born before Adam did sin."[12] However, he argued their actions were not really counted as sin until Adam was given and subsequently broke God's law in the garden, after which sin was imputed backward to previous humans "by a mystery for their salvation."[13] La Peyrère also posited that the Noahic flood must have been a local event, due to the continuity of pre-Adamic streams of humanity to the present, while Noah's family belonged to the Adamic stream.[14]

La Peyrère's critical spirit led him to reject Mosaic authorship of the Pentateuch, as had Thomas Hobbes in *Leviathan* (1651), which had been published just a few years earlier. La Peyrère's statements on the nature of Scripture, however, went significantly beyond those of Hobbes, with La Peyrère explicitly describing Scripture as a humanly formed tradition containing numerous inconsistencies and discrepancies.[15] Only through biblical criticism, he argued, could an accurate Bible be reconstructed. La Peyrère's thought would significantly influence others, including Baruch Spinoza (1633–1677) who was similarly critical of both traditional Judaism and Christianity.[16]

---

11. La Peyrère, *A Theological Systeme*, preface.

12. La Peyrère, *A Theological Systeme*, 336; Almond, *Adam and Eve in Seventeenth Century Thought*, 52–53.

13. La Peyrère, *A Theological Systeme*, 337–42.

14. Several other works in the late seventeenth century also posited a less than universal flood, though these works, in contrast to La Peyrère's, maintained that it nonetheless destroyed all existing humanity, apart from Noah and his family. These included Isaac Vossius, *Dissertatio de Vera Aetate Mundi* (Hague, 1659); Abraham van der Mijle, *De Origine Animalium et Migratione Populorum* (Geneva, 1667); Edward Stillingfleet, *Origines sacrae, or, A Rational Account of the Grounds of Christian Faith…* (London, 1675); and Matthew Poole, *Synopsis Criticorum…Sacrae Scripturae* (Francofurti ad Moenum, 1678). All held to Adamic origins for humanity in contrast to La Peyrère's pre-Adamite theory.

15. Richard H. Popkin, "Spinoza and Bible Scholarship" in *The Cambridge Companion to Spinoza*, ed. Don Garrett (Cambridge: Cambridge University Press, 1996), 387–91.

16. Popkin, *Isaac La Peyrère*, 84. Popkin notes that La Peyrère and Spinoza were both in Amsterdam over a six-month period in 1655, though there is no evidence the two met.

De Foigny: Australian Hermaphrodites and Serpentine Europeans
The Frenchman Gabriel de Foigny popularized La Peyrère's pre-Adamite concept in his fictitious travel account, *A New Discovery of Terra Incognita Australis* (1676). De Foigny stated that the Australians were hermaphrodites who argued that their origins lay in three men created three thousand years prior to Europeans. Europeans, it was posited, were descended from the union of a serpent and a woman—a significant alteration of the Genesis 1 and 2 account of the creation of Adam and Eve and the Genesis 3 revelation of the seed of the woman and the seed of the serpent.[17]

De Foigny's main character's beliefs were profoundly challenged through his travels. Engaging in debate with one of the "Australians," he came to believe that the traditional European view of husband-wife roles and relation was "rather the effect of an odious tyranny, than a legitimate authority."[18] The character was further challenged to view the concept of clothing for modesty as a European custom rather than a universally applicable normative principle, eventually concluding that the Australians "confound the vanity which we draw from our pretended knowledge, and by the assistance of which we only live like beasts."[19]

Protestant Orthodoxy's Response

There was a significant response to the unorthodox views of La Peyrère, de Foigny, and others who advocated erosive models for a "wonderful reconciliation" of Genesis with "all profane records whether ancient or new...those of the Chaldeans, Egyptians, Scythians, and the [Chinese]."[20] One influential response came from the Reformed theologian Francis Turretin (1623–1687), who in *Institutes of Elenctic Theology* (1679–1685), posed the question, "Was Adam the first of mortals, or did men exist before him? And is the epoch of the created world and of men's deeds to be referred much farther back than

---

However, Spinoza owned a copy of La Peyrère's *Men before Adam* and used arguments from the book in his own writing.

17. Gabriel de Foigny, *A New Discovery of Terra Incognita Australis, or, The Southern World* (London, 1693), 63, 118–19.

18. De Foigny, *New Discovery*, 72, 75–77.

19. De Foigny, *New Discovery*, 78.

20. La Peyrère, *Men before Adam*, 29–30. Richard Popkin lists some forty works published in following decades that either in part or whole were aimed at refuting his arguments. Popkin, *Isaac La Peyrère*, 80–81.

Adam?"[21] As an answer, he stated, "The former we affirm, the latter we deny, against the Preadamites."[22] Turretin continued:

> Although the Preadamic fiction is so absurd in itself and foreign to all reason (no less than to the Scriptural revelation itself) as to deserve rather the contempt and indignation of believers than a laborious refutation, yet in this very latest age (so productive of most dangerous heresies) there was found not so long ago one who did not blush to obtrude this fiction or fable upon the world. He endeavored to confirm it by various arguments...(cf. Isaac de la Peyrère, *Preadamitae sive exercitation*...[1655]) and systematic theology (*A Theological System upon that Presupposition that Men were before Adam* [1655]) prepared for this purpose. Thus the question must be touched upon briefly that not only its folly and falsity, but also its impiety may be the more clearly seen....
>
> He with whom we here treat, pretends that Adam, whose creation is recorded in Gen. 2, was the father only of the Jew and not of all men, and that his formation was different from the creation of the man referred to in Gen. 1.... Thus even before Adam, many myriads of men inhabited the earth, and many ages intervened between Adam and these other men. But the constant opinion thus far not only among Christians, but also among the Jews (yea even among the Mohammedans themselves) has been that Adam was created in the beginning of the world and was the first man, the father not only of the Jews, but also of all men universally. Of this assertion there are many invincible proofs.[23]

Turretin's invincible proofs began with "first...the voice of Scripture itself, which often sets Adam before us as the first of mortals, before whom no man existed and from whom all have sprung."[24] He cited and exposited passages including 1 Corinthians 15:45–47; Genesis 3:20; the genealogies of Genesis 5 and Luke 3; and Paul's assertion of unity of race in a mutual origin in Acts 17:26.[25] He also examined Paul's declaration of Christ as the second Adam in conjunction with 1 Corinthians 15:22, maintaining that the "words of the apostle imply that [Adam] is called not only first in the order of sinning (although this is also true), but also in the order of being."[26]

---

21. Francis Turretin, *Institutes of Elenctic Theology*, ed. James T. Dennison (Phillipsburg, N.J.: P&R, 1992), 1:431–88.
22. Turretin, *Institutes*, 1:457.
23. Turretin, *Institutes*, 1:457.
24. Turretin, *Institutes*, 1:457.
25. Turretin, *Institutes*, 1:457–58.
26. Turretin, *Institutes*, 1:458.

Using exegetical and philosophical theology, Turretin argued that the accounts of human origins in Genesis 2 are an expansion of the same in Genesis 1. In his final argument, he states, "If innumerable men had existed before Adam, a new world, a new church, and a new method of salvation would have to be devised for these new men. For the whole economy of salvation pertains to the posterity of Adam, not to the race of Preadamites."[27]

In his work, Turretin displays substantial commitment to a literal hermeneutic of the early chapters of Genesis. He viewed the creation of Adam and Eve as taking place on the sixth day of creation, when God "molded Adam from the dust of the earth…[and having] sent sleep upon him [taking] a rib out of his side…of it formed Eve."[28] Addressing the question "Was the world from eternity, or at least could it have been?," Turretin notes that "the pseudo-Christians and atheists of our day (who advocate the eternity of the world or at least of matter)" were aligned with the Greek natural philosophies of Plato and Aristotle.[29] He states that the first argument in the twenty he provided against "the actual eternity of the world" is "the voice of the Scriptures…what is said to have been made in the beginning cannot be said to have existed in eternity."[30] Turning to refute those who argued that "the six days must be understood allegorically of angelic cognitions," his first response was again drawn from Scripture:

> There are the following objections to this opinion: (1) the simple and historical Mosaic narration, which mentions six days and ascribes a particular work to each day; (2) the earth is said to have been without form and void and darkness rested upon the face of the deep (which could not have been said if all things had been created in one moment); (3) in the fourth commandment (recommending the sanctification of the seventh day), God is said to have been engaged in creation six days and to have rested on the seventh…. This reason would have had no weight, if God had created all things in a single moment. (4) No reason can be given for the order of Moses in his narration, if all things were not made successively.[31]

---

27. Turretin, *Institutes*, 1:460.

28. Turretin, *Institutes*, 1:458–59.

29. Turretin, *Institutes*, 1:436.

30. Turretin, *Institutes*, 1:437.

31. Turretin, *Institutes*, 1:444–45. Turretin indicates the days as ordinary in length: "God, on each of those distinct days, produced nothing besides [the distinct work assigned to each day]. Otherwise, if he had occupied the whole of the first day in the creation of light, he would have finished it only at the beginning of the following night (which is absurd)."

Hottinger, Heidegger, and the Continuity of the Literal Tradition
In marked contrast to La Peyrère's explanations, European theologians contemporary to Turretin continued to promote the literal interpretation of
Genesis common to Protestant orthodoxy. Theologian and linguist Johann
Heinrich Hottinger (1620–1687), in *De Ktisis Historiae Creationis* (1659),
examined Genesis 1:5 in the broader context of Genesis 1 and 2, writing "the
first day was the natural, made up of 24 hours, or an entire day and night."[32]
Hottinger, who taught in Zurich and Heidelberg, wrote extensively on the creation of Adam and Eve, following the tradition of a literal hermeneutic.[33]

Johann Heidegger (1633–1698) was Hottinger's successor at Zurich; like
Hottinger, he had also taught at Heidelberg. Heidegger briefly addressed creation in *Medulla Medullae Theologiae Christianae*, rejecting an instantaneous
or figurative view of the Genesis account, arguing that the six days were "distinct days" occurring in immediate succession, and providing a brief exposition
of the work of each day.[34] His account of the sixth-day creation of Adam and
Eve was somewhat more extensive and distinctly literal in its approach.[35]

And Many Will Follow: Jean Le Clerc and the Erosion
of Hermeneutical Orthodoxy
Despite the continuity of Protestant orthodoxy's literal tradition on Genesis
on the European Continent, further inroads of alternative, nonliteral, critical
thought were being made. One of Francis Turretin's former students, Jean Le
Clerc (1657–1736), the son of a Genevan professor of Greek, left Geneva and
Calvinism for Amsterdam and the Remonstrant cause. There Le Clerc also
adopted aspects of Socinian thought and became a critic of Scripture.

He grew increasingly sympathetic to the argument that the initial period
of darkness in creation was immense, allowing for a first day significantly longer than twenty-four hours. However, Le Clerc did argue that the days after
the creation of light and the ordering of the cycle of night and day (begun on
the first day) were distinctly twenty-four hours long.[36] Unlike La Peyrère, Le

---

32. Johann Heinrich Hottinger, *De Ktisis Hexaemeros. Id est, Historiae Creationis Examen Theologico-Philologicum* (Heidelbergae, 1659), 68.

33. Hottinger, *De Ktisis Hexaemeros*, 246–83.

34. Johann Heinrich Heidegger, *Medulla Medullae Theologiae Christianae* (Tiguri, 1697),
46–47.

35. Heidegger, *Medulla Medullae*, 50–53. Like previous Reformed orthodox theologians
Heidegger viewed God's breathing the breath of life into Adam as giving life to his body and
animating him so that the work was completed and "man was created body and soul."

36. Jean Le Clerc, *Genesis Sive Mosis Prophetae Liber Primus* (Amstelodami, 1710), 7.

Clerc held Adam as the first parent of the "whole of the species" of the human race, but like La Peyrère and others, Le Clerc was deeply skeptical of a global flood and denied the miracles found in Scripture.[37] With La Peyrère, Le Clerc represented a small but increasing number who were departing Reformed orthodoxy and taking steps away from the literal approach toward the early chapters of Genesis.

Bernard Pictet: Ready to Give an Answer

Turretin's defense of a literal reading of Genesis 1 and 2 was carried forward in the succeeding generation by Bernard Pictet (1655–1724), Turretin's son-in-law and successor at the Genevan Academy. In 1696 Pictet published a systematic theology: *Theologia Christiana*. Aware of both figurative and novel approaches to the Genesis account of creation origins, Pictet stated, "The narrative of Moses does not permit us to believe that the world was created in a single moment; for he expressly mentions six days, and ascribes to each day its particular work; and it is a proof of absurd infatuation to turn this narrative into a mere allegory."[38] He went on to state,

> God forbid that we should be of their opinion, who maintain that the story of the creation is a mere parable, only related by Moses because, they say, he was not at liberty entirely to leave out the subject of the world's origin, and the creation of things, since the surrounding nations had their cosmogonies (or stories of the world's creation) which were, for the most part, false and inimical to the true religion, which traditions the Israelites would have embraced, had they not been taught differently. Who can endure that the earliest narrative of an inspired writer should be reckoned among the mythologies of heathens; or is it likely that Moses would deliver fables to the people, in order to divert their attention from other fables![39]

Like many of his contemporaries, Pictet was critical of both the increasing departures from the literal hermeneutical approach to Genesis 1 and 2 and the further implications of those departures. Turning to the creation of Adam and Eve, Pictet noted that the creation of man "was the last of God's works"

---

37. Le Clerc, *Genesis*, 12; Jean Le Clerc, *Twelve Dissertations out of Monsieur Le Clerk's Genesis*, trans. Thomas Brown (London, 1696), 152–69.

38. Bernard Pictet, *Christian Theology*, trans. Frederick Reyroux (Philadelphia, 1890), 121. Pictet further notes the significance of the first and succeeding days of creation as indicative of the reality that "together with the world, time was created, which is nothing else than the duration of a created thing, or that mode of thinking, by which we measure the duration of a created thing" (136).

39. Pictet, *Christian Theology*, 122.

of creation.[40] Like many theologians before him, Pictet saw this as God's gracious and wise plan: "God was pleased to build the house, and furnish it with everything, before the inhabitant of it was introduced."[41] He went on:

> In the creation of man, we must consider the distinct formation of his body and soul—for of these he consists. His body, Moses teaches us, was formed of the dust of the ground (Gen. ii.7); not of rich materials or precious metal, but of the earth which we tread under our feet.... God was pleased to create man in this way, that he might remember his origin, and thus constantly carry with him grounds for humility, nor ever set himself up against his Creator. On this body the Lord bestowed an erect form, that man might be admonished to look down upon this earth and all earthly things, as placed beneath him, and look up to heaven, and God his Creator.... Into the body thus formed, God is said to have "breathed the breath of life" (Gen. ii.7. 1 Cor. xv.45), that is, "a living soul," which inspiration or breathing is not to be taken literally, as if God had a mouth to breathe with, like man; but...to signify...the human soul...is of heavenly origin.[42]

Pictet argued that when Adam's body received the "breath of life," "by the omnipotent will of God the nostrils of Adam began immediately to send forth breath."[43] Where there was no life in the body, God imparted the soul and made man "a living soul."[44] Pictet further defended the literal historicity of Genesis in his systematic theology. On one hand, he avoided "vain speculations," such as when Adam fell into sin, while on the other he defended the idea that the devil assumed the form "of a real serpent...and that the devil spoke by this serpent."[45] His comments on the fall reflected further consistency with the literal view of Adam and Eve as the original humans: "the effects of the first sin...[were] very great...it drew with it the most evil consequences, both to our first parents, and to all their posterity."[46]

The Dutch Reformed: Literal Orthodoxy versus Socinian Sophistry

Contemporaneous with though some twenty years senior to Pictet, Dutch Reformed theologian Wilhelmus à Brakel (1635–1711), continued the

---

40. Pictet, *Christian Theology*, 141.
41. Pictet, *Christian Theology*, 141.
42. Pictet, *Christian Theology*, 142–43.
43. Pictet, *Christian Theology*, 144.
44. Pictet, *Christian Theology*, 143.
45. Pictet, *Christian Theology*, 189–90.
46. Pictet, *Christian Theology*, 199.

mainstream Protestant literal approach to early Genesis in *The Christian's Reasonable Service*. According to à Brakel, the light God created on the first day—prior to the creation of the sun on the fourth day—revolved around the "mass of matter" of the unformed earth "during a twenty four hour period, thus creating day and night."[47] Regarding human origins he states, "Upon the sixth day God created the final creature, man.... God formed the body out of the earth...wondrously and in an artful manner.... The fact that God brought forth the soul of man out of nothing rather than from some dust is confirmed in Genesis 2:7. When God formed the body of man from the dust of the earth it was lifeless. God, however, 'breathed into his nostrils the breath of life; and man became a living soul.'"[48]

Another Dutch Reformed theologian, Herman Witsius (1636–1708), reflected a similar literal approach in *Sacred Dissertations on the Apostles' Creed*.[49] Witsius firmly defended—against the "sophistry...employed by those followers of Socinus"—that the world was finite in "extent" and "duration." He observed that "Scripture everywhere teaches, that its existence had a beginning...'in the beginning God created the heaven and the earth'...intimates the beginning of time, by which the duration of all created things is circumscribed."[50] Avoiding the detailed disputes over "how many years has elapsed since the creation of the world," which Witsius viewed as "hopeless," he stated, "Let it suffice to know in general, that the world has not yet reached six thousand years."[51]

On the days of creation, Witsius argues, "Though it would have been easy for God to create all things in full perfection, 'in a single moment, and by a single act and movement,' he was pleased to employ six days in this work; as the Mosaic history, which ought by no means to be debased by rash and unnecessary allegories, expressly states."[52] As to whether "each of the works of a day was perfected in a single moment, or in some period of time," he states:

> I rank it among those doubtful points, which may be disputed among
> the reformed, without any prejudice to faith and charity; provided it be
> firmly and conscientiously held, that there is a vast difference between

47. Wilhelmus à Brakel, *The Christian's Reasonable Service*, trans. Bartel Elshout, ed. Joel R. Beeke (Grand Rapids: Reformation Heritage Books, 1999), 273–74.

48. Brakel, *Reasonable Service*, 307–10.

49. Herman Witsius, *Sacred Dissertations on the Apostles' Creed* (Grand Rapids: Reformation Heritage Books, 2010), 1:178–230.

50. Witsius, *Sacred Dissertations*, 1:205.

51. Witsius, *Sacred Dissertations*, 1:207.

52. Witsius, *Sacred Dissertations*, 1:208.

the first *creation* of things, which was accomplished by the command of God, (in a manner quite different from that order which was subsequently to be observed,) and *natural generation*, which proceeds gradually from suitable matter, according to the rules of motion.... The denial of instantaneous creation is a step by which some proceed to maintain the most absurd hypothesis respecting all things spontaneously rising into existence by mere motion, the ordinary concurrence of God being supposed,—I utterly detest the denial of such creation.... It is impossible for us to assign the moments of the commencement and termination of the works of each day to their own hours respectively,— Divines justly say, according to Scripture, that six days, not six moments, were employed in the creation of the world.[53]

Apparently Witsius was aware of not only pre-Adamite theory, but also of the postulation of potential inhabitants of the sun, moon, and stars—narrated earlier, ostensibly by Johannes Kepler (1571–1630), "who relates that he saw through an optical tube…that the moon is inhabited, and that its inhabitants are short-lived, but of a stupendous size, fifteen times larger than the men of the earth."[54] Responding to both ideas in light of Genesis and the person and work of Jesus Christ, Witsius writes,

Moses, by the distinct account which he gives of the counsel of God respecting the creation of man, sufficiently shows, that at that time no living creature similar to him existed in the universe. Why should God be introduced, saying, "Let us make man in our image," etc., as if he were preparing for the chief of his works, if, perhaps only two days before, he had peopled the Moon, or the Sun, or even the other stars with men? For what purpose is it related, that, having discovered, so to speak, that it would not be good for man to remain alone, he thought at last of forming a companion for him…. The expressions would be utterly void of propriety, and could afford no meaning worthy of God, if several pairs of the human kind had already existed elsewhere….

Christ…assumed a human nature of the same blood [as Adam]. Neither is there salvation in any other; nor would it become a Most Holy God to admit sinful men to communion with himself, without a satisfaction to his justice. Such a satisfaction, besides, can be made by none but a person who is a God-Man…as we have elsewhere proved at large. Indeed new schemes of Divinity widely different from that which our churches maintain, must be framed for the benefit of the men inhabiting the Moon, as

---

53. Witsius, *Sacred Dissertations*, 1:208–9, 213.
54. Witsius, *Sacred Dissertations*, 1:216.

has been avowedly done of late, for the sake of his pre-Adamites, by him who has been the first to discover their existence.[55]

While not mentioning La Peyrère by name, it seems likely Witsius was thinking of him, as La Peyrère's writings proposed the most extensive "new schemes of Divinity" in relation to the origin of man to this point.

Van den Honert, Venema, and Dutch Resilience on Origins

A generation after Witsius, theologian Taco Hajo van den Honert (1666–1740) came to be viewed by contemporary Dutch theologians, including Antonius Driessen and Bernardus de Moor, as too sympathetic to Enlightenment thought. Nonetheless, he also exemplified the Dutch Reformed continued adherence of a literal hermeneutic toward the early chapters of Genesis. In *Dissertation on the Creation of the World*, van den Honert, like Witsius, à Brakel, and others, viewed the "mornings and evenings" and days as ordinary twenty-four-hour days, standing in continuity with the scriptural annotations commissioned by the Synod of Dordt.[56]

His commentary on the Genesis passages dealing with man's creation continued in the same approach, interpreting the text as indicating that God's special creation of Adam from the dust of the earth and Eve from Adam's rib took place on the sixth day. Man was specially created in the image of God and distinct in origin from other creatures.[57]

Another Dutch Reformed theologian viewed as a more liberal thinker, Herman Venema (1697–1787), also maintained a literal approach to the early chapters of Genesis. Venema, well aware of both natural philosophy and scientific endeavor in his day, stated that in regard to the manner of God's work of creation,

> [Scriptural] revelation is the only source of our information on this point.... God, by Moses, provided that this information should be communicated to us, that we might know his goodness, that we might distinguish the God of Israel as creator from false gods and that we might have disclosed to us the origin of the human race, Gen. i. Moses has left us this remarkable account, from which it is evident that the universe was produced by the command of God in the space of six successive days.... He gives an account of the formation not only of our earth as designed

---

55. Witsius, *Sacred Dissertations*, 1:216–20.

56. Taco Hajo van den Honert, *Dissertationes Historicae…* (Lugduni Batavorum, 1739), 27–28.

57. Van den Honert, *Dissertationes Historicae*, 78–97.

for the use of man and of the inferior animals, but of the universe itself and of all its parts, especially however in reference to us, and not, as some suppose, that he recorded not the production of the material universe but only the appointment of it to our use and as it first presented itself to our senses. This latter opinion is directly opposed to the simplicity of the text…[and] is opposed also to the order of the Mosaic narrative.[58]

His adherence to the literal hermeneutical tradition was further evidenced in his argument that

Moses simply mentions six days as the space of time occupied in the work of creating. Nor are there any reasons for departing from the ordinary acceptation of the word day. The affirmation of some that Moses speaks not of ordinary days but of years and of centuries is made carelessly and springs from the preposterous idea that creation proceeded according to mechanical laws. It is besides contrary to the meaning and scope of the narrative. That Moses understood the word [day] in its usual acceptation is plain from these two things, first that the day is distinguished in the ordinary way into evening and morning, and secondly, that the Sabbath is mentioned as recurring each seventh day as a memorial of creation, and therefore only six days properly so called must have been employed in the work.

In regard to the manner in which objects were created on each of the days Moses simply states they sprang into being at God's command and thus instantaneously,—not therefore, according to mechanical laws, as has been held by some.[59]

Consistent with this, Venema viewed human origins as beginning in the special, temporally immediate creation of Adam on the sixth day.[60] Both Venema and van den Honert stand as examples of eighteenth-century Dutch Reformed theologians most sympathetic to aspects of Enlightenment thought, and yet both held to a literal approach to early Genesis. Thus, it is perhaps not surprising that the Dutch Reformed tradition would continue to maintain its significant commitment to the literal approach—even in the midst of rising criticisms of the literal tradition. While no less aware of contemporary currents, the Dutch Reformed, like the mainstream of English Puritans to this point, were markedly less influenced by the philosophical and comparative

---

58. Herman Venema, *Institutes of Theology*, trans. Alex W. Brown (Edinburgh, 1850), 340–41.

59. Venema, *Institutes*, 342.

60. Venema, *Institutes*, 345–47.

religious critiques of Genesis than were their English Anglican and French Roman Catholic neighbors.

The Lutherans: Adam, the First of All Men

In nearby Germany, patterns of hermeneutic and theology on origins were similar. Among Lutheran theologians of the late seventeenth and early eighteenth centuries, Johann Wilhelm Baier (1647–1695) continued in the Reformation and post-Reformation literal hermeneutical tradition common to Lutheranism, positing that "according to the history of creation God completed the production of this universe within a space of six days."[61] He went on to state that on the sixth day God created man, "making his body from the ground, and a true spirit produced from nothing and joined to the body."[62]

Baier's contemporary and strong defender of Lutheran orthodoxy, Abraham Calov (1612–1686), also maintained the literal approach to both the days and the creation of Adam and Eve. Like his Dutch Reformed contemporaries, he explicitly rejected the teaching of Isaac La Peyrère, among others.[63] Johannes Andreas Quenstedt (1617–1688), also responding to pre-Adamite theory, "asked the question whether Adam was indeed the first of all men and whether there were men before Adam. His answer was that Adam was created by God on the sixth day of the hexameron and was the first man in point of time, the parent of the whole human race throughout the entire world."[64]

The later Lutheran orthodox theologian, David Hollaz (1648–1713) also explicitly rebutted pre-Adamite theory in his dogmatic text *Examen Theologicum Acroamaticum* (1707).[65] William Hausmann states, "The [Lutheran] dogmaticians were uniformly agreed that there was no race of men before Adam, no group or class of humans known as pre-Adamites. They regarded the concept of pre-Adamites as a fiction which would only corrupt the whole of theology."[66] Like many of their Reformed contemporaries, the Lutherans understood Adam and his origins according to the literal reading of Genesis and also realized the devastating potential of the new thought on origins.

61. Johann Wilhelm Baier, *Compendium Theologiae Positivae* (Lipsiae, 1750), 196.

62. Baier, *Compendium*, 202–8; 248–63.

63. Abraham Calov, *Commentarius in Genesin* (Wittebergae, 1671), 153–55, 208–13, 253–57.

64. William Hausmann, *Science and the Bible in Lutheran Theology: From Luther to the Missouri Synod* (Washington, D.C.: University Press of America, 1978), 66.

65. David Hollaz, *Examen Theologicum Acroamaticum Universam Theologam Thetico-polemicam Complectens* (Lipsiae, 1763), 357–58, 361–64, 406–7.

66. Hausmann, *Science and the Bible in Lutheran Theology*, 66.

Challenging the Literal Tradition in England

While Lutheran orthodoxy maintained a literal hermeneutic to the Genesis account of creation and human origins, further challenges to and abandonments of a literal interpretation were stirring back in England.

Thomas Burnet: Philosophy as the Interpreter of Scripture

The Anglican Thomas Burnet (1635–1715) studied at Cambridge where he was influenced by the "Cambridge Platonists" Ralph Cudworth (1617–1688) and Henry More (1614–1687). Intrigued by Greek natural philosophy, More taught an essentially eternal universe while holding to a young earth, and he also believed in other populated worlds.[67] After his studies, Burnet served some twenty years as a tutor and school master, eventually becoming a chaplain to William III—a position he lost because of his views of Genesis.

Burnet's perspectives on Genesis were first publicized in *The Sacred Theory of the Earth* (1681, 1689). In the preface, he stated, "'tis a dangerous thing to engage the authority of Scripture in disputes about the natural world, in opposition to reason."[68] Where La Peyrère had once felt concern about moving into heresy, Burnet appeared blithely unaware of the danger of undermining the authority of Scripture in disputes about the natural world.[69] In this early work, he sought to develop an explanatory hypothesis for the sources of water for the Noahic flood, which he held to be universal—in knowing contrast to La Peyrère.

However, Burnet's later writing departed significantly from a literal approach to Genesis. In *Archaelogia Philosophica* (1692), Burnet postulated that the "Mosaical epoch of about six thousand years, does not comprehend the origins of the universe, but the age of our earth" and further argued that those who held this did "violence to the laws of nature."[70] Presenting his reasons for the unlikelihood of each day's works being accomplished in twenty-four-hour periods, Burnet claimed "the vulgar never regard these niceties."[71] He went on to state,

> But because [Moses] had resolved (or at least as I suppose) to hold and consecrate the seventh day for a Sabbath, it was necessary for him to spin

---

67. Phil Jones, "Thomas Burnet's Sacred Theory of the Earth, Part I," *Genesis and Geology*, http://genesisandgeology.wordpress.com/2012/08/03/thomas-burnets-sacred-theory-of-the-earth-part-1/. By the time of publication this source had been removed from the Internet.

68. Thomas Burnet, *The Sacred Theory of the Earth...* (London, 1726), xix.

69. Le Peyrère, *Men before Adam*, preface.

70. Thomas Burnet, *Archaelogia Philosophica, or the Ancient Doctrine Concerning the Originals of Things...* (London, 1729), 35–37.

71. Burnet, *Archaelogia Philosophica*, 42.

out his creation to six days…that the seventh day might be forever solemnly observed.… Even in the making each of the Planets there ought to be six days employed…but Moses follows the philosophy of the vulgar.… It was not this favored author's design to represent the beginning of the world, exactly according to the physical truth.[72]

Burnet realized that he faced significant opposition among "those who adhere to the literal sense of the account of the creation in six days."[73] And he understood how others would object "that if we may depart from the letter of the Mosaical history, in the first chapters of Genesis, why not in others also? And where must we stop? What rule shall we have to set bounds to us, lest the wantonness of our imagination should everywhere destroy the historical and literal sense of Scripture." In response, he answered, "We must nowhere depart from the letter without necessity. With this guide we shall be safe…I think… that philosophy is the interpreter of Scripture in natural things."[74] Burnet's supposition that philosophy was the interpreter of Scripture in natural things upended the approach of Reformation and post-Reformation Reformed orthodoxy. Moses was merely spinning a story. Abandoning Genesis as prescriptive for natural philosophy on origins, Burnet sought hermeneutical justification for doing so and thus reached back to medieval Jewish allegorism. Burnet stated that Maimonides had warned against taking Genesis too literally, suggesting that "if we only attend to the literal sense" readers would be in danger of reading the "narrations concerning Adam…to be but fables."[75]

When critics warned of a slippery slope, Burnet avowed his was a "safe" approach in which reinterpretation of Scripture would take place only where "necessary." However, Burnet's life proved his critics right. In his *Of the State of the Dead* (1720), published posthumously, it became clear that on the basis of his view of "reason, the nature of God, and the nature of things that are on the other side," Burnet's hermeneutic had also led him to reject the eternality of hell, going so far as to say it would be "foolish and unworthy of God."[76]

Newton and Whiston: From Ambiguity to Day-Year Interpretation

During his lifetime, Burnet corresponded with Isaac Newton (1642–1727). Newton also rejected a literal hermeneutic toward the Bible's creation account,

---

72. Burnet, *Archaelogia Philosophica*, 44–46.
73. Burnet, *Archaelogia Philosophica*, 48.
74. Burnet, *Archaelogia Philosophica*, 59.
75. Burnet, *Archaelogia Philosophica*, 85.
76. Thomas Burnet, *Of the State of the Dead and of the Resurrection* (London, 1727), 80–82.

writing that the universe preexisted what occurred in the Mosiac account and that the "distinction of the six days in the Mosaical formation of the world is no physical reality."[77] Newton's interaction with Burnet revealed an approach that was at times decidedly nonliteral and ambiguous toward the Genesis record of creation, though Newton maintained there must be some correspondence of the scriptural account with reality. While stating that Moses' account was neither "philosophical nor feigned," Newton claimed that

> [Moses] described realities in a language artificially adapted to the sense of the vulgar…so when he tells us of the two great lights and stars made the fourth day, I do not think their creation from beginning to end was done the fourth day nor in any one day of the creation nor that Moses mentions their creation as they were physical bodies…but only as they were lights to this earth…. You may make the first day as long as you please…. But be as it will I think [the fourth commandment] given by God at mount Sinai…observed…with a day's alteration by all Christians to this day, should not be grounded on a fiction.[78]

Newton's successor at Cambridge, William Whiston (1667–1752), advocated a modified understanding of the Genesis creation account that openly contrasted with Burnet's.[79] Through his life, Whiston was marked as a freethinking spirit; like Newton, he rejected orthodox Trinitarianism. Whiston further argued that the early church writing *The Apostolic Constitutions* should be added to the canon of Scripture. He left the Church of England under heresy charges to found his own "primitive Baptist" church directed by the *Apostolic Constitutions*.[80]

In his new approach to Genesis, Whiston argued that the first part of the first verse of Genesis referred to an ex nihilo act of creation prior to the six days. This act was followed by creative activity of an unspecified length of time—the works of creation prior to the six days including the formation of sun, moon, stars and planets.[81] Whiston argued that these simply were

---

77. Burnet to Newton, January 13, 1680/81, Keynes ms. 106(A), King's College, Cambridge, U.K.

78. Newton to Burnet, Keynes ms. 106(B), King's College, Cambridge, U.K.

79. William Whiston, *A New Theory of the Earth…* 5th ed. (London, 1737), 1–3.

80. While Whiston had initially intended to pursue ordination in the Church of England, he became a critic of the trinitarian formulation of the Nicene Creed, rejecting the consubstantiality of the Father and the Son—standing as one example of the pervasive influences of varieties of Arian, Socinian, Unitarian, and Deist thought during the latter part of the eighteenth century. A. J. D. Farrer, "William Whiston," *Transactions of the Baptist Historical Society* 4, no. 3 (1914): 145–61.

81. Whiston, *New Theory*, 33–35.

made visible during the six days and posited that these "days" were each a year in length.[82] Like Newton, Whiston also referred to the Mosaic account as primitive and rudimentary.[83] He articulated these positions in his Genesis commentary, which prefaced his larger work of elucidating a new natural philosophy or cosmology.

An "Enlightened" Religious-Philosophical Synthesis on Origins

Burnet, Newton, and Whiston demonstrate that by the late seventeenth century, philosophical and religious challenges to both a literal interpretation of Genesis and its derivative theology were increasing in England and on the European continent. Drawing on sources that included Jewish Kabbalah, indigenous pagan histories, and Greek natural philosophy, these challenges spawned new syncretist views of God, creation, the age of the earth, and the origin of humanity.

To this point, advocates of alternate views had not employed geological and biological interpretations to buttress and popularize their views—that endeavor evolved in the eighteenth and nineteenth centuries. But the theological and religious shifts making inroads into the Protestant church and her educational institutions during this time period set the stage for both the development of and receptivity to significant shifts in natural philosophy on origins that would arise in the next centuries. Those shifts in turn would create increased pressures for the adoption of nonliteral hermeneutic approaches to the Genesis accounts of creation.

Simon Patrick's Interpretive Shift

The new departures from a literal reading of the Genesis account on creation origins gained ground among Anglicans in the late seventeenth and early eighteenth centuries, though a decided majority in England continued to hold the literal approach. In 1694, the devout Anglican Simon Patrick (1626–1707), bishop of Ely, posited that the first day of creation may have been significantly longer than the subsequent five days of God's work of creation, which he said were twenty-four hours long.[84] In doing so, Patrick followed an approach to Genesis 1:1–2 earlier posited by the Dutch Remonstrant Simon Episcopius

---

82. Whiston, *New Theory*, 52–72.

83. Whiston, *New Theory*, 17–18, 26–27.

84. Simon Patrick, *A Commentary on the Historical Books of the Old Testament* (London, 1851), 3.

(1583–1643)—which also bore some similarity to figurative approaches to these verses from medieval and patristic times.[85]

Patrick's interpretive shift was more modest than that of Burnet, Newton, or Whiston, as he held to a literal interpretation of the text on the creation of Adam and Eve although he accepted a modified approach to the first verses of Genesis 1. In commenting on Genesis 2:5, Patrick noted criticism of pre-Adamite theory, stating, "from hence some collect there were no Preadamites (people before Adam), for then Moses could not have said, 'There was no man to till the earth.'"[86] Maintaining a literal interpretation of the creation of Adam and Eve on a sixth day of ordinary duration, he commented on the creation of Eve from Adam's rib, stating, "[This] was as easy for the Divine power to do, as to make the man himself out of the earth."[87]

Woodward, Science, and a Literal Genesis

The year after Patrick's commentary was published, John Woodward (1665–1728), a professor of physics at Gresham College in London and a great collector of fossils, published *An Essay Toward a Natural History of the Earth* (1695).[88] In light of discussions among natural philosophers, Woodward sought to assess whether natural evidence, including the diverse and widespread presence of fossils, was coherent with the Reformation and post-Reformation literal interpretation of Genesis. Having mulled the wide distribution of fossils over the face of the earth, Woodward posited that the great catastrophe of the flood had profoundly affected the surface of the earth and served as the mechanism for the vast majority of fossilization of once-living creatures.

He explained that his quest was impartial and sound as it was based in his own scrutiny—a consideration of Moses as a historian in comparison with the present condition of nature: "I freely bring what he has related to the test, comparing it with things as they now stand, and finding his account to be punctually true, I fairly declare what I find; wherein I do him but simply right,

---

85. There is some indication for a lineage of the gap approach to Genesis 1:1–2 propounded by Simon Patrick as traceable through Simon Episcopius and the Amsterdam rabbi Manasseh ben Israel—whose circle of relationships included Isaac La Peyrère and disciples of the German mystic Jakob Böhme (1575–1624). Böhme in turn was influenced by the writings of the occultist Philip von Hohenheim—or "Paracelsus" (1493–1541)—another proponent of pre-Adamite theory who was also intrigued by Greek natural philosophy.

86. Patrick, *Commentary*, 10.

87. Patrick, *Commentary*, 14.

88. John Woodward, *An Essay Toward a Natural History of the Earth…With an Account of the Universal Deluge and the Effect It Had Upon the Earth* (London, 1695), 1–148.

and only the same that I would do to a common historian…to Herodotus or Livy, on like occasion."[89] Like many of his contemporaries and in contrast to men like Newton, Burnet, and Whiston, Woodward reaffirmed not only God's "continuing superintendence and agency of providence in the natural world" but also "the fidelity and exactness of the Mosaic narrative of creation, and of the deluge."[90]

Continuities of the Literal Tradition in English Nonconformity

Matthew Henry: "A Signal and Immediate Act of Divine Wisdom and Power"
Literal views of man's creation were even more prominent among the dissenting heirs of English Puritanism than they were among Anglicans. The Presbyterian commentator Matthew Henry (1662–1714) saw Genesis 1:1–5 as speaking of the first day of creation, "which was not only the first day of the world, but the first day of the week."[91] Henry followed the Reformation and post-Reformation Reformed literal interpretation that the work of creation took place in the space of six days.[92] In *Scripture Catechism*, which was an expansion of the Westminster Shorter Catechism, Henry asked: "Did [God] make all in six days? Yes: for in six days the Lord made heaven and earth, Exod. xx.11."[93] Henry's Genesis commentary notes,

> Man was made last of all the creatures…. [His] creation was a more signal and immediate act of divine wisdom and power than that of the other creatures. The narrative of it is introduced with something of solemnity, and a manifest distinction from the rest. Hitherto it had been said "Let there be light"…and "let the earth, or waters, bring forth" such a thing; but now the word of command is turned to a word of consultation, "Let us make man," for whose sake the rest of the creatures were made…. Man was to be a different creature from all that had been hitherto made. Flesh and spirit, heaven and earth, must be put together in him, and he must be allied to both worlds…. Man was made in God's image and after his likeness…. Man was not made in the likeness of any creature that

---

89. Woodward, *Natural History of the Earth*, preface.

90. Woodward, *Natural History of the Earth*, preface.

91. Matthew Henry, *Commentary on the Whole Bible* (Peabody, Mass.: Hendrickson, 1994), 1:3–4.

92. Henry, *Commentary*, 1:1–10. Henry distinguishes between the first six days and all succeeding days in the created order: "after the end of the first six days God ceased from all works of creation…. In his providence…he does not form any new species of creatures." Henry, *Commentary*, 1:10.

93. Matthew Henry, *A Scripture Catechism* in *The Complete Works of Matthew Henry* (Grand Rapids: Baker, 1997), 2:182.

went before him, but in the likeness of the Creator; yet still between God and man there is an infinite distance. Christ is the only express image of God's person, as the Son of his Father, having the same nature.[94]

Henry viewed the account of Genesis 2 as "a more particular account of the creation of man."[95] This detailed narrative of the creation of Adam, his placement in the garden of Eden, and the creation of Eve on the sixth day,

> [is] an account of the origin of both [soul and body] and the putting of both together.... Observe then, the mean origin, and yet the curious structure of the body of man. The matter was despicable. He was made of the dust of the ground, a very unlikely thing to make a man of, but the same infinite power that made the world out of nothing made man, its master-piece, of next to nothing. He was made of the dust.... The Lord God, the great fountain of being and power, formed man. Of the other creatures it is said they were created and made; but of man that he was formed, which denotes a gradual process in the work with great accuracy and exactness.... The soul of man takes its rise from the breath of heaven...it was not made from the earth, as the body was.... It came immediately from God.... It is by it that man is a living soul, that is, a living man; for the soul is the man. The body would be a worthless, useless, loathsome carcass, if the soul did not animate it.[96]

Following a connection made by some of his English Puritan predecessors, Henry posited, "When our Lord Jesus anointed the blind man's eyes with clay perhaps he intimated that it was he who first formed man out of the clay; and when he breathed on his disciples, saying 'receive you the Holy Ghost,' he intimated that it was he who at first breathed into man's nostrils the breath of life. He that made the soul is alone able to new-make it."[97]

Thomas Ridgley: Owning Versus Perverting the Scripture

Minister and theologian Thomas Ridgley (1667–1734), who served an Independent church in London, was another English representative of the continuity of literal Genesis interpretation as he directly engaged proposed alternatives to a literal reading of the Genesis text on creation and human origins.[98] In *A Body of Divinity* (1731), which was organized as an exposition of the Westminster Larger Catechism, Ridgley gave substantial attention to the doctrine

---

94. Henry, *Commentary*, 1:8.
95. Henry, *Commentary*, 1:11.
96. Henry, *Commentary*, 1:12.
97. Henry, *Commentary*, 1:12.
98. Livingstone, *Adam's Ancestors*, 53–54.

of creation. He critiqued those who "give an account of the antiquity of the world…represent[ed] as a great deal more remote than what appears from scripture…who suppose that the antiquity of it exceeds the scripture account by many ages."[99]

He noted that the foundation for objections against the scriptural account of "no more than between five or six thousand years" was "found principally in the writings of those who were altogether unacquainted with the divine word" such as the Egyptians, the Chaldeans, and the Chinese.[100] Interestingly, Ridgley defended a more recent creation not only on the basis of genealogical estimates, but also on the known history of human civilization, stating it was easily comprehended within the parameters of a literal interpretation of scriptural history.

Turning to the Genesis 1 and 2 account of creation itself, Ridgley contrasted an instantaneous creation with one that took place in the "space of six days," defending the latter.[101] He also concluded that the individual creative acts could have occurred in a moment or over a longer period of time, so long as the creative works ascribed to each day together took up no more than "the space of a day" and thus were "agreeable to the express words of Scripture."[102] Following the Westminster Larger Catechism, Ridgley viewed Adam as being created on the sixth day, "his body was formed from the dust of the ground" and Eve "was formed from the rib of the man."[103] Ridgley stated that Adam and Eve "were the first parents of all mankind" noting that the apostle Paul "expressly calls Adam the first man…[which] is very agreeable to the account which Moses gives of his creation on the sixth day from the beginning of time."[104]

Turning from this positive statement on human origins, Ridgley described one of the varied approaches (apparently La Peyrère's) now "propagated and defended by many atheists and deists" rejecting the literal reading of the Genesis account of human origins:

> None who own the divinity of scripture ever questioned the account of Moses respecting the origin of the human race, till a bold writer, about the middle of the last century, published a book, in which he advanced a new and fabulous notion. He says that there was a world of men who lived before Adam was created, and that these were all heathen. He alleges

---

99. Thomas Ridgley, *A Body of Divinity* (New York, 1855), 328.

100. Ridgley, *Body of Divinity*, 328–29.

101. Ridgley, *Body of Divinity*, 332–33.

102. Ridgley, *Body of Divinity*, 333.

103. Ridgley, *Body of Divinity*, 346–47.

104. Ridgley, *Body of Divinity*, 347.

that Moses speaks of their creation as having occurred many ages before Adam,—that he speaks of their creation in the first chapter of Genesis, and of Adam's in the second chapter...whereas Adam is called by the apostle Paul, "the first man," this writer supposes that he is only so styled as to be contradistinguished from Christ, who is called "the second man;" the design being, according to him to compare the person whom he supposes to be the head of the Jewish church, with him who is the Head of the Christian church.... He...perverts that scripture where it is said, "Until the law, sin was in the world" as if the sense of it were, that there was a sinful generation of men in the world, before God erected his church and gave laws to it, when he created Adam as its head and father.[105]

Ridgley contends that the apostle Paul "clearly speaks of sin prevailing in the world before the law was given by Moses" rather than prior to Adam, and that "the historical account of the creation of man in scripture" plainly indicates that the second chapter of Genesis is a focused and detailed expansion of the creation and created context of man.[106] Ridgley's literal hermeneutic was further evidenced as he argued that Scripture indicates "there was no man to till the ground" prior to the creation of Adam, questioning that if there were a world of men prior to Adam, what would be the purpose "for him to be created out of the dust of the ground? He might have been the father of the church, and yet descended, in a natural way, from one that was then in being."[107]

John Gill: "The Hebrew Text is the Surest Rule"
Similarly, the English Baptist theologian John Gill (1696–1771) held to a literal interpretation of early Genesis, including the origins of man, even while engaging alternative approaches. Gill argued that the world

has not, as yet, run out six thousand years, according to the scriptural account...which may be depended on. Indeed, according to the Greek version, the age of the world is carried fourteen or fifteen hundred years higher; but the Hebrew text is the surest rule to go by; as for the accounts of the Egyptians, Chaldeans, and the Chinese, which make the original of their kingdoms and states many thousands of years higher still; these are only vain boasts, and fabulous relations, which have no foundation in true history. The origins of nations...the invention of arts and sciences...

---

105. Ridgley, *Body of Divinity*, 348.
106. Ridgley, *Body of Divinity*, 348.
107. Ridgley, *Body of Divinity*, 348. Ridgley also engages with the argument that the account of both Cain's fear after his murder of Abel and his "building a city" are inexplicable apart from the existence of pre-Adamites. See Ridgley, *Body of Divinity*, 349–50.

with many other things, appear to be within the time the Scripture assigns for the creation…nor does any genuine history give an account of anything more early, nor so early, as the Scriptures do.[108]

Gill stated that the "manner and order of the creation" was

done at once by the mighty power of God…. He gave the word, and every creature started into being in a moment; for though God took six days for the creation of the world and all things in it, to make his works the more observable, and that they might be distinctly considered…yet the work of every day, and every particular work in each day, were done in a moment…without labour and fatigue, only by a word speaking, by an almighty fiat, let it be done, and immediately was done.[109]

This, Gill argued, was also the manner of the creation of Adam and Eve: "In another moment on the [sixth] day he created man after his image, his soul immaterial out of nothing, his body out of the dust of the earth; and in another moment on the same day created the woman out of the rib of man, immediately infusing into her a rational soul as into man, since both were made after the image of God."[110] In his expanded section on the creation of man, Gill further defended a special, temporally immediate creation of man on the sixth day:

Man was made on the sixth and last day of creation, and not before; nor were there any of the same species made before Adam, who is therefore called *the first man Adam:* there have been some who have gone by the name of Preadamites, because they held there were men before Adam…. In the last century Peirerius [Isaac La Peyrère] wrote a book…in favour of the same notion; which has been refuted by learned men over and over…. Why was Adam formed out of the dust of the earth? And Eve from one of his ribs? And these two coupled together, that a race of men might spring from them, if there were men before? But it is certain that Adam was the first man, as he is called; not only with respect to Christ, the second Adam; but because he was the first parent of the human race,

---

108. John Gill, *A Body of Practical Divinity* (Atlanta: Turner Lassetter, 1965), 259.

109. Gill, *Practical Divinity*, 261. In *An Exposition of the Old Testament*, commenting on Genesis 1:5, Gill posits that "in the space of twenty-four hours there was a vicissitude of light and darkness; just as there is now by the like motion either of the sun, or of the earth… both together one natural day, consisting of twenty four hours." He goes on to note William Whiston's suggestion that the six days may have been six years, a view of time he sees as being remarkably similar to that propounded by the Greek natural philosopher Empedocles (c. 490–430 BC). John Gill, *An Exposition of the Old Testament* (London, 1810), 1:5.

110. Gill, *Practical Divinity*, 261.

and the common parent of mankind; and Eve, the mother of all living; that is of all men living.[111]

Scottish Presbyterians and the Genesis Text

To the north in Scotland, strong support for the Reformation and post-Reformation tradition of a literal interpretation of Genesis on creation and human origins continued into the eighteenth century. This is not surprising in view of the Church of Scotland's historic commitment to the Westminster Confession of Faith and Catechisms.

Thomas Boston: "There Was No Man in the World before Adam"
Presbyterian theologian Thomas Boston, known for his defense of the free offer of the gospel of Jesus Christ during the Marrow controversy in the Church of Scotland, articulated the literal approach to the creation account of Genesis 1 and 2 in *An Illustration of the Doctrines of the Christian Religion*. Boston stated that "all things were made of nothing...by the word of God's power...an act of his will commanding them to be."[112] Boston went on,

> Our next business is to show in what space of time the world was created. It was not done in a moment, but in the space of six days, as is clear from the narrative of Moses. It was as easy for God to have done it in one moment as in six days. But this method he took, that we might have that wisdom, goodness, and power that appeared in the work, distinctly before our eyes.... Although God did not make all things in one moment, yet we are to believe, that every particular work was done in a moment, seeing it was done by a word, or an act of the divine will.... No sooner was the divine will intimated, than the thing willed instantly took place.... [God's] goodness appears, in that he first prepared the place before he brought in the inhabitants, first provided the food before the living creatures were made, and adorned and fitted all for the use of man, before he formed him.[113]

---

111. Gill, *Practical Divinity*, 269.

112. Thomas Boston, "Of the Work of Creation," in *An Illustration of the Doctrines of the Christian Religion*, in *The Complete Works of the Late Rev. Thomas Boston*, ed. Samuel M'Millan (London, 1853), 1:172.

113. Boston, *Works*, 1:173. Boston reemphasizes this in his treatise on the fourth commandment where he notes that the "third reason" for this command of God: "the third reason is taken from God's example, who, though he could have perfected the world in a moment, yet, spent six days in it, and but six days, resting the seventh, taking a complacency in the work of his own hand; and this is an example to be imitated by us...[as] a most binding rule." Boston, *Works*, 2:201.

In commenting on the creation of man, Boston noted his acquaintance with Girolamo Zanchi's *Concerning the Works of God in Creation During the Space of Six Days*. He also repeatedly indicated that he held to the Mosaic narrative as an intentionally literal historical revelation by God of His own work. Because "the man's body, as Moses tells us, was formed of the dust of the ground." Boston states, "Hence he was called Adam, which signifies red earth; of which sort of virgin earth man's body seems to have been made. The word rendered dust, signifies not dust simply (says Zanchius), but clay, which is earth and water. This may teach us humility, and repress our pride…especially seeing, as we derived our first being from it, we must return to it again, there to abide till the resurrection day."[114]

Turning from the creation of the body to the soul, he noted,

> Moses gives us this account of it, Gen. ii.7. "The Lord God—breathed into his nostrils the breath of life, and man became a living soul." The Lord inspired him with a living reasonable soul, which presently appeared by his breathing at his nostrils; whereas before he was only a fair lifeless body…. This different account of man's soul and body clearly holds forth, that it was not fetched out of any power in the matter of his body, but was created out of nothing…. Hence the soul is immortal, being a spirit, and dies not with the body…. Men can kill the body, but not the soul… neither does it sleep till the resurrection…. Our Lord told the thief on the cross, that that very day he (that is, his soul) should be with him in paradise, not to sleep, but to be actively employed in [activities] peculiar to the heavenly state.[115]

Undoubtedly aware of pre-Adamite theory, Boston carefully articulated the implications of a literal reading of the Genesis account of human origins. Commenting on the Genesis 1 account of making "male and female," he stated, "Adam was the male, and Eve the female. These were the common parents of mankind, and there was no man in the world before Adam. He is expressly called 'the first man,' 1 Cor. xv. 5, and Eve 'the mother of all living,' Gen. iii. 20. And hence it is said 'God hath made of one blood all nations of men,' Acts xvii. 26."[116] In his expositions of Genesis 1 and 2 on human origins, Boston explained what it meant that man was created "in the image of God" and in a state of innocence—a theme he more extensively expounded in his widely popular *The Fourfold State of Man*. Here he described not only

---

114. Boston, *Works*, 1:178.
115. Boston, *Works*, 1:180.
116. Boston, *Works*, 1:178.

the theological implications of the teaching of Scripture on human origins and the original context of humanity, but also reflected on the sheer goodness of these realities:

> Man had a life of pure delight and unalloyed pleasure, in this state. Rivers of pleasure ran through it. The earth with the produce thereof, was now in its glory; nothing had yet come in to mar the beauty of the creatures.... [Man's] delights were pure, his pleasures refined...wisdom had entered into his heart...knowledge was pleasant to his soul! What delight do some find in their discoveries of the works of nature, by those scraps of knowledge they have gathered!... But how much more exquisite pleasure had Adam while his eyes read the book of God's works.... Above all, his knowledge was of God, and that as his God, and the communion he had with him could not but afford him the most refined and exquisite pleasure in the innermost recesses of the heart.[117]

Fisher and the Erskines: "In What Time Did God Create All Things?"

Historical evidence indicates Scottish Presbyterians after Boston continued to hold a literal hermeneutic toward Genesis 1 and 2. James Fisher (1697–1775), son-in-law of Boston's close friend and colleague Ebenezer Erskine (1680–1754), reflected this view in *The Westminster Assembly's Shorter Catechism Explained*, a volume coauthored with Ebenezer and Ralph Erskine (1685–1752).[118]

In answer to the question of in what time God created all things, Fisher and the Erskine brothers answered, "in the space of six days," citing Exodus 20:11.[119] They then ask whether or not God "could have created all things in a moment of time," to which they responded: "Yes: but he saw it more for his own glory, and the good of mankind, to set them an example of working six days and resting the seventh."[120] Their exposition on the creation of Adam and Eve closely reflected Boston's as they advocated both were products of a

---

117. Thomas Boston, *The Fourfold State of Man* (Edinburgh: Banner of Truth, 2002), 51–52.

118. James Fisher, Ebenezer Erskine, and Ralph Erskine, *The Westminster Assembly's Shorter Catechism Explained* (Philadelphia, 1765), 58–65.

119. Fisher et al., *Shorter Catechism Explained*, 59.

120. The next question addressed by the men in this extended catechism is "on which of the six days, is it reckoned, that the angels were created? It is probable they were created upon the first day, as would seem from Job xxxviii. 4, 7: 'Where were you when I laid the foundations of the earth,—when the morning stars sang together, and all the sons of God shouted for joy?'" Fisher et al., *Shorter Catechism Explained*, 59.

special, temporally immediate creation on the sixth day, distinct and separate from the creation of "the rest of the creatures."[121]

John Brown of Haddington: God Created "In the Most Distinct and Orderly Manner"

John Brown (1722–1787) of Haddington, a leading pastor-theologian of the Associate Synod and a prolific writer, also advocated for a literal understanding of early Genesis. In *A Compendious View of Natural and Revealed Religion*, Brown began the section on "God's Execution of his Decrees in the Work of Creation" by arguing that both general and special revelation show:

> The world did not exist from eternity. The actual infinity of the duration of matter or any other finite being, is altogether inconceivable. The late invention of useful arts;—the short reach of [written] history into past periods of but a few thousand years;—the room on the earth for many more inhabitants, though they have been generally on the increase;—the remaining heights on the surface of it, notwithstanding that they are gradually washed down by the rain, etc., prove that it cannot be eternal. But from Scripture we learn, that it had its beginning little more than 5780 years ago.—Common sense plainly dictates, that the world could not make itself, or be formed by a fortuitous concourse of atoms. But the Scripture informs us, that God, Father, Son, and Holy Ghost, by the word of his power, created all things in six days,—in the most distinct and orderly manner,—all very good in themselves, and marvelously fitted to answer their respective ends and manifold connections.[122]

Brown addressed the created origins of humanity more extensively under the entry "Adam" in his *Dictionary of the Holy Bible*.[123] Here Brown wrote,

> ADAM. This name was divinely imposed on both the original parents of the human race, to import their earthly original, their comeliness, and affectionate conjunction, Gen. v. 2; but it is ordinarily appropriated to the man. On the sixth day of creation, when God had fitted earth for his residence, he formed man's body of the dust of the ground: he breathed into his nostrils the breath of life, and endued him with a rational soul, resembling himself in knowledge, righteousness, and holiness....

---

121. Fisher et al., *Shorter Catechism Explained*, 62.

122. John Brown, *A Compendious View of Natural and Revealed Religion*, in *The Systematic Theology of John Brown of Haddington* (Grand Rapids: Reformation Heritage Books, 2002), 170.

123. John Brown, *A Dictionary of the Holy Bible* (Edinburgh, 1816), 1:21–23. Under the entry "create," Brown reiterates his view of a "young" earth and the fact that "God employed six days in bringing his work of creation to perfection." Brown, *Dictionary*, 1:312–13.

That same day, God constituted him lord of the fish, fowls, cattle, and creeping things, vegetables, and other things on the earth: the fowls, cattle, creeping things, he convened before Adam, as his vassals.... Adam assigning to each its proper name. None of these animals being a fit companion for Adam, God cast him into a deep sleep, took a piece of flesh or a rib from his side…and formed it into the body of a most beautiful woman; her too he endued with a reasonable soul, and brought her to Adam, who received her with the utmost affection as his wife.[124]

While Brown's positing of "a piece of flesh" for a "rib" from Adam's side appeared to be unique, the remainder of his approach reflected the almost monolithic continuity to this point of the literal interpretive tradition in post-Reformation Reformed orthodoxy.

From Europe to the American Colonies

Across the Atlantic in eighteenth-century colonial British America, Reformed thought on the creative context and origins of humanity reflected trends in England and Europe.

Cotton Mather's Failed Publication

Cotton Mather (1663–1728), a Puritan Congregationalist minister in New England and a friend of Church of England bishop Simon Patrick, wrote extensively on Genesis, interacting with the wide range of theories of his day, including those of Burnet, Whiston, and La Peyrère.[125] Like Patrick, Mather was more tentative when engaging the critics of the literal early Genesis hermeneutic than were a number of his Reformed contemporaries. Though clearly appreciative of the literal six-day account of Thomas Pyle (1674 – c. 1756), Mather's own view was at times ambiguous.

Mather received the following request: "It cannot be denied, that the common glosses, in which the Mosaic account of the creation is addressed to our understanding, are full of difficulties. For this cause, you know, learned men have lately used several essays…to rescue the inspired writings of Moses, from the hardships that have been put upon them. Favor me with communicating at least one or two of those essays." He replied, "If I do, you must not expect, that I declare myself, how far I concur, with every point, that shall be offered.

---

124. Brown, *Dictionary*, 1:21–22.
125. Cotton Mather, *Biblia Americana, vol.1, Genesis*, ed. Richard Smolinski (Grand Rapids: Baker, 2010), 79–85.

And I will also leave you, to that same liberty that I take to myself."[126] While Mather did make occasional critical comments when he felt that an essayist, such as Burnet, was simply beyond the pale, he avoided commenting on Whiston's argument that it was "disproportionate" for the creation of the earth to occupy five out of the six days with one day for the creation of the rest of the cosmos, or that too much occupied the sixth day of creation for it to be a literal, ordinary day.[127] Mather was clearly intrigued by the efforts of the natural philosophers of his day and engaged a variety of theories, including Newton's comet theory, regarding the mechanism of the flood. He also revealed a wide cultural interest in indigenous pagan flood accounts, all the while maintaining the universality of the flood.[128]

However, Mather minced no words in opposing pre-Adamite theory. Referring to comments about Cain's fear of being killed by other men for his murder of Abel, Mather said that "the silly and profane Deist cavils, that here must needs be Pre-adamites."[129] Mather further stated that "Adam was a parent of all the world. We read (1. Cor. 15.45) he was the first man; and, (Gen. 2.5) when he was first made, there was no man else. Preadamism is by the Apostle condemned as heresy. Thus our Lord Jesus Christ is the parent of all true believers; they are (Isa. 53.10) His Seed."[130] Despite his steady attempts over nearly three decades, Mather failed to find a publisher prior to his death that would commit to producing his reflections on early Genesis and human origins, which were a part of his massive *Biblia Americana*.[131] Thus, while Mather's thought reflected both accommodation to and criticism of nonliteral trends, this leading New England Puritan failed to exert a significant influence during his lifetime regarding theories of Genesis in British colonial North America.

Jonathan Edwards: Adam "the First Made of All Mankind"

Unlike Mather, Jonathan Edwards (1703–1758), the leading New England Puritan theologian of the next generation, held to the literal hermeneutical tradition common to earlier English Puritanism. In *The "Miscellanies"* Edwards

---

126. Mather, *Biblia Americana*, 337–38.

127. Mather, *Biblia Americana*, 347–48. In his introduction to this volume Richard Smolinski views Mather's "digest of Whiston's *New Theory*" as being what Mather himself "readily concedes." Mather, *Biblia Americana*, 83–84.

128. Mather, *Biblia Americana*, 625–36. Newton supported Whiston's comet theory of the deluge.

129. Mather, *Biblia Americana*, 517.

130. Mather, *Biblia Americana*, 501.

131. This work by Mather remained unpublished until 2010.

spoke of creation as taking place in six days, proposing in postmillennial hope that "the work of redemption is gradually carried on in the world, till the church shall be brought to the most perfect and glorious and happy state on earth, to a state of rest; which will probably be after the expiration of the first six thousand years of the world, which answer to the six days of creation, putting a thousand years for a day."[132] Edwards revealed a fascination with ascertaining typological and even allegorical significance in the unfolding of redemptive history in the Scriptures.[133] However, he did so while maintaining the reality of the literal sense of the creation account. Reflecting on man as created in the image of God, Edwards stated,

> In the first creation of man...his body was formed immediately by God, not in a course of nature or in the way of natural propagation; yet the soul is represented as being in a higher, more direct and immediate manner from God, and so [it is] communicated that God did therein as it were communicate something of himself: "The Lord God formed man" (ie. his body) "of the dust of the ground" (a mean and vile original), "and breathed into his nostrils the breath of life" (whereby something was communicated from an infinitely higher source, even God's own living spirit or divine vital fullness), "and so man became a living soul."[134]

Edwards further addressed the significance of Adam and his origin in relation to the person and work of Christ in The "Miscellanies":

> Adam, in his creation, or in the state wherein he was created, was a remarkable type of Christ. Rom. 5:14, "After the similitude of Adam's transgression, who was the figure of him that was to come." He was so in various respects. He was the first man that was formed of the dust of the earth; so Christ was the first begotten from the dead, or first raised out of the dust.... He was the first made of all mankind; so Christ was the first born of every creature. As he was he out of whom the woman was taken, even from near his heart, bone of his bone, and flesh of his flesh, by his deep sleep; so Christ was he out of whom the church is, as it were, taken, from his transcendent love and by the deep sleep of his death. As Adam was the natural father of all mankind; so Christ is the spiritual father of all in the new creation. Adam was made the federal head of all

---

132. Jonathan Edwards, "Entry 702," in The Works of Jonathan Edwards: Volume 18— The "Miscellanies," 501–832, ed. Ava Chamberlain (New Haven, Conn.: Yale University Press, 2000), 285.

133. Edwards, The "Miscellanies," 283–309.

134. Jonathan Edwards, "The Great Concern of a Watchman for Souls," in The Works of Jonathan Edwards: Volume 25—Sermons and Discourses 1743-1758, ed. Wilson H. Kimnach (New Haven, Conn.: Yale University Press, 2006), 64–65.

his seed; so Christ is the federal head of all his seed…. As Christ was formed immediately out of the womb of a virgin, by the Spirit of God, without the seed of a man; so Adam was immediately formed out of the bowels of his mother earth, which is in Scripture made use of to represent the formation of the body in womb (Ps. 139:15); and it was from the womb of the earth while yet as it were a virgin…in its pure and undefiled state. And this was by the Spirit, as the formation of Christ in the womb of the virgin, for it was that which breathed into him the breath of life. Adam, though made of the mean vile dust of the earth, yet was made in the image of God….

Though made from so vile an original, yet he was crowned with glory and honor, and was set over the works of God's hand…. This was a type of the glorious and exalted state that man is brought into—particularly Jesus Christ the head of man, and they in him as their head.[135]

Edwards further stated that he viewed man as distinct from the animals because he was created uniquely by God as His image-bearer. In *The Freedom of the Will*, Edwards stated that God created man as a "moral agent," and that "herein does very much consist the image of God wherein he made man, by which God distinguished man from the beasts."[136] His writings reflected continuity with previous literal tradition on creation and the origins of Adam and Eve without any indication of divergence.[137]

The Scottish "Enlightenment": Adam, the White Man, and Other Species

Despite the strong tradition among confessional Protestants of a literal interpretation of early Genesis and the creation of man, critics of that literal understanding proliferated through the "Enlightenment" era of the mid to late eighteenth century. Among them was the Scottish philosopher David Hume (1711–1776), who followed La Peyrère and other proponents of pre-Adamite theory, advocating racial inferiority of "the negroes" as another species of men "naturally inferior to the white."[138] Like his friend Hume, philosopher Henry Home, Lord Kames (1696–1782) believed that "natural history, that of man

135. Edwards, *The "Miscellanies,"* 287–88.

136. Jonathan Edwards, *The Freedom of the Will*, in *Works of Jonathan Edwards*, ed. Paul Ramsey (New Haven, Conn.: The Jonathan Edwards Center at Yale University, 1957), 1:166.

137. This is further evidenced in Jonathan Edwards, "A History of the Work of Redemption," in *The Works of Jonathan Edwards: Volume 9—A History of the Work of Redemption*, ed. John F. Wilson (New Haven, Conn.: Yale University Press, 1989), 116–40.

138. David Hume, "Of National Characters," in *The Philosophical Works of David Hume* (Edinburgh, 1825), 3:236.

especially, is of late years much ripened." He argued that Africans, among others, appeared to be other species.[139]

Kames, like many abandoning the literal Genesis understanding of human origins, wrote with some ambiguity. In his *Sketches of the History of Man* (1774, 1778) he initially appeared to hold to a literal approach to Genesis on the origin of man. After arguing against the French philosopher Montesquieu and others who were proponents of variations in humanity due to climate, Kames stated,

> It is thus ascertained beyond any rational doubt, that there are different races or kinds of men, and that these races or kinds are naturally fitted for different climates: whence we have reason to conclude, that originally each kind was placed in its proper climate, whatever changes may have happened in later times by war or commerce.
>
> There is a remarkable fact that confirms the foregoing conjectures. As far back as history goes, or traditions kept alive by history, the earth was inhabited by savages divided into many small tribes, each tribe having a language peculiar to itself. Is it not natural to suppose, that these original tribes were different races of men.... Upon summing up the whole particulars mentioned above, would one hesitate a moment to adopt the following opinion, were there no counter-balancing evidence, namely "That God created many pairs of the human race, differing from each other...that the peculiarities of the original pairs were preserved entire in their descendants...?" But this opinion, however plausible, we are not permitted to adopt; being taught a different lesson by revelation, namely, that God created but a single pair of the human species. We cannot doubt of the authority of Moses.[140]

Then where did the diversity of the human race find its source? Kames argued, "To account for that...mankind must have suffered some terrible convulsion [which] is revealed to us in the history of the Tower of Babel, contained in the 11th chapter of Genesis.... Here light breaks forth in the midst of darkness."[141] Nevertheless, Kames proceeded to argue that the natives of America were separate in origins from the rest of humanity: "I venture still farther; which is to indulge a conjecture, that America has not been peopled from any part of the old world.... Adam and Eve might have been the first parents

---

139. Henry Home, Lord Kames, *Sketches of the History of Man*, 2nd ed. (Edinburgh, 1778), 1:49–50, 55. The use of the term "species" was drawn from the Latin Vulgate translation of Genesis 1. Commonly used English translations of Genesis 1 used the term "kind."

140. Home, *History of Man*, 1:75–77.

141. Home, *History of Man*, 1:77–78.

of all mankind, i.e. of all who at that time existed, without being the first parents of the Americans.... A local creation, if it may be termed so, appear[s] unavoidable...every rational conjecture leans to a separate creation."[142]

Such pre- and co-Adamite theories had by this point long been used to rationalize both conquest and slavery—whether by British merchants or Spanish conquistadors. Rather than one human race in Adam, the "enlightened" posited different human races, with a clear hierarchy of value—much as the medieval Jewish Kabbalists and ancient Greeks had done.

Literal Genesis Rebuttals to Racism

While mistreatment of non-European ethnicities was not limited to proponents of pre- and co-Adamite theory, opponents of such mistreatment during this period were most commonly proponents of the special immediate creation of Adam and Eve as the first parents of all humanity. One such was Ottobah Cugoano (c. 1757–after 1791), an English-African abolitionist. Cugoano was well aware of ethical implications of pre-Adamite and co-Adamite polygenetic theory. Relating the literal understanding of Genesis on human origins to Christian ethics in *Thoughts and Sentiments on the Evil and Wicked Traffic of Slavery* (1787), he declared,

> This will appear evident to all men that believe the scriptures, that every reason necessary is given that they should be believed; and, in this case, that they afford us this information: That all mankind did spring from one original, and that there are no different species among men. For God who made the world, hath made of one blood all the nations of men that dwell on all the face of the earth. Wherefore we may justly infer, as there are no inferior species, but all of one blood and of one nature, that there does not an inferiority subsist, or depend, on their colour, features or form, whereby some men make a pretence [*sic*] to enslave others; and consequently, as they have all one creator, one original, made of one blood, and all brethren descended from one father, it never could be lawful and just for any nation, or people, to oppress and enslave another. And again, as all the present inhabitants of the world sprang from the

---

142. Home, *History of Man*, 3:139–48. For further discussion of pre-Adamite thought through the eighteenth and into the twentieth century, see Livingstone's *Adam's Ancestors*. In reviewing Livingstone's work, Stephen Alter notes that it forwards the argument that "pre-Adamite theory eventually proved useful in the effort to reconcile the Bible with science...the undeniable evidence for the high antiquity of man led a number of biblically-oriented thinkers to embrace what Livingstone calls the 'pre-Adamite safety valve.'" Stephen Alter, Review of *Adam's Ancestors: Race, Religion and the Politics of Human Origins*, by David N. Livingstone, *Fides et Historia* 41, no. 2 (Summer-Fall 2009): 118–20.

family of Noah…there is no doubt, but the difference [of complexion] which we now find, took its rise very rapidly after they became dispersed and settled on the different parts of the globe.[143]

The scriptural replies of men like Cugoano gained little traction among the "enlightened" proponents of a multiracial humanity. As he indicated, to acknowledge them meant acknowledging the truth of a literal Genesis and the authority of Scripture as a whole.

The French "Enlightenment": Scripture as Fable

While proponents of the literal approach to the Genesis account of human origins like Cugoano articulated its cogency and value, the religious and philosophical challenges to that literal interpretation continued to proliferate. This was particularly the case in France, where Roman Catholic hegemony meant the literal interpretive approach to Genesis had been less pervasive historically.[144]

The great critic of Scripture, Voltaire (1694–1778), wrote sarcastically of Adam in his "Philosophical Dictionary" (1764) as "always utterly unknown to the nations."[145] Commenting on the Genesis 1 account of the creation of light prior to the sun, moon, and stars, he declared that "the author [of Genesis] accommodates himself to…popular error…condescend[ing] to the gross and wild ideas of the nation."[146] What others had proposed with greater subtlety and caution, Voltaire declared plainly: "Many ingenious men are of opinion, with the great Newton and the learned Leclerc that the Pentateuch was written by Samuel when the Jews had a little knowledge of reading and writing,

---

143. Ottobah Cugoano, *Thoughts and Sentiments on the Evil and Wicked Traffic of Slavery: The Commerce of the Human Species, Humbly Submitted to the Inhabitants of Great-Britain* (London, 1787), 30–31.

144. Blaise Pascal (1623–1662) is at times claimed as a proponent of a literal interpretation of Genesis among French Roman Catholics in the eighteenth century. In his *Pensées*, Pascal states that "we who see the prophecies fulfilled should believe in the Flood and Creation." Pascal viewed the genealogies of Scripture as a particular testament to its historical veracity and believed the world to be about six thousand years old. He was also explicitly critical of pre-Adamite thought. In relation to Genesis 1, his statement that "the six days which Moses represents for the creation of Adam are only an image of the six ages for creating Christ and the church," may indicate a literal view but presents enough ambiguity in the words "represents" and "are only an image" that it could indicate a figurative approach—particularly if connected to an Augustinian model of an instantaneous creation. Blaise Pascal, *Pensées*, ed. A. J. Krailsheimer (London: Penguin, 1995), 36, 93–94, 196, 334.

145. Voltaire, "Philosophical Dictionary," in *The Works of Voltaire. A Contemporary Version*, trans. William F. Fleming (New York: E. R. DuMont, 1901), vol. 3, "Adam"; vol. 5, "Genesis."

146. Voltaire, "Genesis," in "Philosophical Dictionary," vol. 5.

and that all these histories are imitations of Syrian fables."[147] Voltaire further argued for an ancient creation which throughout its existence remained essentially the same. The latter conception brought conflict with his contemporary George-Louis Leclerc, Comte de Buffon (1707–1788), the director of the Royal Gardens in Paris.[148]

Buffon pursued the creation of a new natural history more thoroughly than his predecessors had. He argued in his *Histoire Naturelle* (1749, 1789) that while Burnet, Whiston, and other natural philosophers attempted to explain the origins of the universe, a new and better attempt was needed: one, as Voltaire suggested, delivered from the constraints of a literal interpretation of Genesis.[149]

Buffon stated that in Whiston's case, "Physics and astronomy occupied his principal attention, he mistook passages of holy writ for physical facts…and so strangely jumbled divinity with human science, that he has given birth to the most extraordinary system that perhaps ever did or will appear."[150] According to Buffon, Whiston's system of natural philosophy suffered the fatal flaw of being too contrived as it attempted to cohere to the Genesis text.

In contrast, Buffon argued that he was merely proposing "probable conjectures" and argued "it is impossible to give demonstrative evidence on this subject…[as] our knowledge in…natural history depends entirely on experience, and is limited to the method of reasoning by induction."[151] Nonetheless, in his few comments on Scripture and early history, he affirmed that he believed that God had created the world, including man, and that there had been a "universal deluge."[152] He argued that "for a succession of ages what we now know to be dry land…was the bottom of an immense ocean."[153]

---

147. Voltaire, "Genesis."

148. The philosopher Jean-Jacques Rousseau (1712–1778) was also involved in these discussions with Buffon, proposing his own theories of human origins and suggesting that the relationship of orangutans and man ought to be further studied. It was particularly Rousseau's radical political writings that led to his books being banned in Geneva; fearing arrest, Rousseau took up David Hume's invitation to join him in England. By 1774, Voltaire and Buffon were reconciled relationally. Jacques Roger, *Buffon: A Life in Natural History*, trans. Sarah Lucille (Ithaca, N.Y.: Cornell University Press, 1997), 346–66; Mary Efrosini Gregory, *Evolutionism in Eighteenth Century French Thought* (New York: Peter Lang, 2008), 157–65.

149. George-Louis Leclerc, Comte de Buffon, *Natural History, General and Particular…*, 2nd ed., trans. William Smellie (London, 1785), 1:2–3.

150. Buffon, *Natural History*, 1:107–8.

151. Buffon, *Natural History*, 1:4.

152. Buffon, *Natural History*, 1:15.

153. Buffon, *Natural History*, 1:15. This view was later popularized by the German mineralogist Abraham Gottlob Werner (1749–1817).

Buffon was intrigued by the effects of natural processes on the earth; setting aside early Genesis and using induction, he argued that these must have been occurring through "operations uniformly repeated" over the "long periods" since "time immemorial." His view harmonized with his appreciation of continuities of Greek natural philosophy.[154] These natural processes, he argued, "alone ought to be the foundation of our reasoning."[155] Bypassing the majority of the content of the early chapters of Genesis, Buffon's quest for a new natural history "unhindered" by the text of Scripture led him to posit views of the ancient age of the earth and the proliferation of plant and animal diversity from a much smaller original group.

Jean-Baptiste Lamarck (1744–1829), Buffon's assistant and successor at the gardens, proposed a more detailed evolutionary hypothesis. Lamarck believed that biological life had originated through spontaneous generation, arguing that natural processes brought about increased complexity. He also posited that creatures had developed adaptations to their environment through the striving of each generation to adapt. Slight, beneficial physical changes caused by striving up to and during the reproductive period of life were then passed on to succeeding generations.[156]

James Hutton: Nature as Creator and a Rising Humanity

In Paris at the time was James Hutton (1726–1797), a well-to-do Scottish student of medicine and chemistry; whether he was at the time in personal contact with Buffon or Lamarck is unknown, though it is quite likely he sat under the teaching of one of Buffon's associates, Guillaume-François Rouelle.[157] Hutton was in Paris in part to avoid potential consequences of his fathering an illegitimate child as a student at the University of Edinburgh—a reality kept secret until after his death.[158] After Paris, Hutton studied further at Leiden, then decided to move to London after completing his studies. Whether or not he had met Buffon in person, Hutton was intrigued by his writings, as well as

---

154. Buffon, *Natural History*, 1:30–34.

155. Buffon, *Natural History*, 1:34.

156. This, Lamarck hypothesized, explained natural phenomena like the long legs and necks of giraffes; the stretching of each generation to reach leaves resulted in succeeding generations with longer legs and longer necks. Lamarck presented his initial foray into the subject in a lecture in 1800 in Paris. He would also affirm a form of uniformitarianism in a later work on geology.

157. Jack Repcheck, *The Man Who Found Time: James Hutton and the Discovery of Earth's Antiquity* (Cambridge, Mass.: Perseus, 2003), 88.

158. Repcheck, *James Hutton*, 88–89.

those of Whiston and Newton. Hutton's much-appreciated mathematics professor at Edinburgh, Colin Maclaurin (1698–1746), was a friend of Newton's and a fellow deist.

Making regular visits to friends in Edinburgh during his years away, Hutton eventually resettled in the city in 1767, actively spending his evenings engaging in the social circle of the Scottish "Enlightenment." This group included William Smellie (1740–1795)—publisher of the first edition of *Encyclopedia Britannica* and also of the English translation of Buffon's work. David Hume was there as well; Hutton and Hume shared a close mutual friend in the chemist Joseph Black (1729–1799).[159]

In *An Investigation of the Principles of Knowledge* (1794), Hutton stated that he desired to investigate "the nature or progress of human understanding" by "scientific analysis" for the "end of knowing ourselves…understanding the purpose of our being or existence, and of seeing the means appointed for our happiness as well as misery."[160] He claimed that while "among the ancients, the learned had their mysteries, true science admits of no mystery."[161] Hutton argued that only those "learned in the science of physics…who understand the nature of things" could "properly undertake" the development of a rational and intelligent metaphysic.[162] "Until we have something fixed and certain in our science…we cannot proceed with success to philosophy of any kind."[163] Thus, his work was addressed to "only the enlightened part of mankind."[164]

Hutton went on to describe the process of "speculation" which led him to these conclusions. Having abandoned the literal interpretation of the Genesis account of the creation of man, Hutton viewed man "as an animal," "in the natural state," but one who had developed a capacity for reasoning beyond the "brutes":

> Man, from the state of a blind agent in which he had first existed, becomes an intelligent being, that is…instead of judging like the animal merely for acting, judges more immediately for the sake of knowing… this intelligent being acts then rationally, from the knowledge which he had acquired in that progress of his mind. Thus nature, which conducts the action of the ignorant animal in perfect wisdom, has done still more

159. Repcheck, *James Hutton*, 128–29.
160. James Hutton, *An Investigation of the Principles of Knowledge, and of the Progress of Reason, from Sense to Science and Philosophy* (Edinburgh, 1794), 1:i.
161. Hutton, *Principles of Knowledge*, 1:ii.
162. Hutton, *Principles of Knowledge*, 1:ii.
163. Hutton, *Principles of Knowledge*, 1:xi.
164. Hutton, *Principles of Knowledge*, 1:iii.

for man, in making him a conscious reasoning being.... Having thus arrived at wisdom, he then corrects occasional folly.[165]

Hutton argued that man in his rise from "brute" or "animal" had invented language and progressed in science—and was now progressing to new heights as the philosopher of science. Through human progress, man had "gained wisdom" and displayed this wisdom "by forming a system of morals."[166] While common man stood in continuity between animal and "the philosopher," through initial, rudimentary science and its increasing development, "man acquires superiority in relation to the brutes…[and] philosophy raises the mind of man above the rest of his species."[167]

Hutton's ultimate goal for his formulation of an "enlightened," holistic approach to knowledge was a bold one and reflected a near complete abandonment of Scripture. He stated, "Moral philosophy has never yet been established in science by having its principles ascertained…. An attempt of this kind will not be unacceptable to philosophers, who consider virtue as a source of happiness to mankind."[168]

Natures' Cycles and Time Immemorial

Like many engaged in philosophical and scientific endeavor, Hutton was fascinated by the structures and formations of the earth. He eagerly collected fossils and roamed the countryside studying rocks, minerals, soils, formations, and strata layers, seeking to better understand their properties and formations and also to develop a theory of the history of the earth that would contribute to his philosophical system. His interests coincided with his one employment commitment during these years: serving on the committee overseeing the construction of the Forth and Clyde Canal (where he worked with Lord Kames) between Edinburgh and Glasgow.

In 1784 and 1785, Hutton presented his theories in two lectures at the Royal Society of Edinburgh, one entitled *Concerning the System of the Earth, Its Duration, Its Stability*.[169] Having taken his philosophy to the field to see if it could be used to interpret the evidence, Hutton eagerly concluded that his system was indeed coherent with reality, publicly proposing that the earth was

---

165. Hutton, *Principles of Knowledge*, 1:xviii–xxix; 503–7.
166. Hutton, *Principles of Knowledge*, 2:453–69; 506–7.
167. Hutton, *Principles of Knowledge*, 1:506–7.
168. Hutton, *Principles of Knowledge*, 1:xxxiv–xxxv.
169. James Hutton, *Abstract of a Dissertation…Concerning the System of the Earth, Its Duration, Its Stability* (Edinburgh, 1785).

ancient beyond all calculation—that all of natural existence had continued in endless cycles from time immemorial. Although Hutton combined his lectures into a written work published in 1795, it was difficult to read; his friend John Playfair (1748–1819), who taught natural philosophy at the University of Edinburgh, took Hutton's notes after his death and spent five years polishing, revising, and adding to them to create *Illustrations of the Huttonian Theory of the Earth* (1802).[170]

Hutton's approach was at first viewed as too speculative and stood in contrast to another, initially more popular theory of the earth which posited that its surface had been significantly altered by a universal flood or ocean.[171] This concept was historically rooted in the Noahic flood, but by Hutton's day had seen a variety of formulations—a number of which had also abandoned the idea of a recent creation. Most popular at this point was Abraham Gottlob Werner's (1749–1817) theory, which posited that an ancient universal ocean through precipitation or deposition formed most of the current surface material and structures of the earth. The growing popularity of Hutton's view became evident when a former student of Werner's, Robert Jameson (1774–1854), professor of natural history at the University of Edinburgh and strong critic of Hutton, came to accede to his approach.[172]

Monboddo's Allegorical Genesis and Wild Men with Tails

A leading exemplar of the approach to Genesis, creation, and human origins advocated by the Enlightenment circle in Edinburgh that included Hutton was James Burnett, Lord Monboddo (1714–1799), judge of the High Court. While criticizing Hume as an "atheist" for his attacks on revealed religion, Monboddo viewed the Genesis account of Adam and Eve as allegorically representing man's early natural state.[173] Having abandoned any commitment to a literal Genesis, he reasoned that orangutans and other apes ought to be considered as part of the lineage and present range of the human species as the "wild man of the woods" in proximity to somewhat more developed "savages."[174]

---

170. John Playfair, *Illustrations of the Huttonian Theory of the Earth* (Edinburgh, 1802), 1–528.

171. Derek Flinn, "James Hutton and Robert Jameson," *Scottish Journal of Geology* 16 (October 1980): 251–58.

172. Repcheck, *James Hutton*, 174–75, 190–91.

173. James Burnett, Lord Monboddo, *Antient Metaphysics: Or the Science of Universals* (Edinburgh, 1779), preface, iv; *Of the Origins and Progress of Language* (Edinburgh, 1774), 1:209–11.

174. Monboddo, *Antient Metaphysics*, 1:297–303.

Monboddo's views shocked the general populace and brought some ridi-cule—particularly as he held that men were born with tails which were secretly cut off by midwives at birth. But others took his thought more seriously, includ-ing Erasmus Darwin (1731–1802), the grandfather of Charles Darwin, who corresponded regularly with members of the Edinburgh societies and noted his indebtedness to Monboddo's writings.[175]

Together these Edinburgh circles of friendship were marked by rejection of the literal tradition of Genesis interpretation, replacing it with a milieu of pre- and co-Adamism, ancient earth theories, and early forms of evolu-tionary theory. For the most part, they were lay academics, not ministers or theologians, though they tended to be parishioners of the moderate end of the Church of Scotland. Most of the men were also members of the Royal Soci-ety of Edinburgh, formed in part from the Edinburgh Philosophical Society. A number were also Freemasons.[176] Hutton's Edinburgh milieu thoroughly reflected his own philosophical and theological precommitments.[177]

Erasmus Darwin: Mythology, the Goddess of Nature, and an Evolving Humanity

While Hutton's abandonment of the literal interpretive tradition of Genesis was reflected in his arguments for a dramatic expansion of the age of the earth, the English physician Erasmus Darwin, also appreciative of the work of "the ingenious Mr. Buffon," sought as well to contribute to the development of an overarching natural theory of life and origins. Endeavoring to poetically muse toward a natural philosophy through a celebration of the "botanic goddess" in *The Botanical Garden* (1791), Darwin encouraged readers to turn not only to contemporary philosophers, but also to aspects of Egyptian, Greek, and Roman natural philosophy and mythology, declaring that "many of the important oper-ations of Nature were shadowed or allegorized in the heathen mythology."[178]

This, however, did not mean that Darwin entirely ignored Genesis. In the preface to *Zoonomia* (1794), he somewhat ambiguously stated that "the great Creator of all things has infinitely diversified the works of his hands, but has at the same time stamped a certain similitude on the features of nature, that

175. Repcheck, *James Hutton*, 129; Erasmus Darwin, *The Temple of Nature, or, The Origin of Society* (Baltimore, 1804), 11; *Zoonomia; Or the Laws of Organic Life*, 2nd ed. (London, 1796), preface, 104–8.

176. Repcheck, *James Hutton*, 142–143.

177. Hutton, *Principles of Knowledge*, vols. 1–3.

178. Erasmus Darwin, *The Botanic Garden* (London, 1825), apology, vii–viii.

demonstrates to us, that the whole is one family of one parent."[179] While this statement could be variously interpreted as suggesting an evolutionary tree of life or as simply referring to a similitude in sovereign design, other references by Darwin indicated he viewed the early chapters of Genesis as figurative, and essentially equal in authority with ancient pagan mythologies of origins. In the annotations to his canto on the "production of life" in *The Temple of Nature* (1804) he argued,

> The nations, which possess Europe and a part of Asia and of Africa appear to have descended from one family; and to have had their origin near the banks of the Mediterranean, as probably in Syria, the site of Paradise, according to the Mosaic history. This seems highly probable from the similarity of the structure of the languages of these nations, and from their early possession of similar religions, customs, and arts, as well as from the most ancient histories extant. The two former of these may be collected from Lord Monboddo's learned work on the Origin of Language, and from Mr. Bryant's curious account of Ancient Mythology....
>
> Other families of mankind, nevertheless, appear to have arisen in other parts of the habitable earth, as the language of the Chinese is said not to resemble those from this part of the world in any respect. And the inhabitants of the South-Sea had neither the use of iron tools, nor of the bow, nor of the wheels, nor of spinning, nor had learned to coagulate milk, or to boil water, though the domestication of fire seems to have been the first great discovery that distinguished mankind from the bestial inhabitants of the forest.[180]

Erasmus Darwin exemplified numerous aspects of a growing nonliteral stream of Genesis interpretation, with his ideas including a progressively developing ancient earth as well as pre-Adamite theory of human origins, now merged with progressive development hinting toward an ape in the human lineage. His writing bore testimony to the conceptual roots of these ideas in both Greek natural philosophy and pagan mythologies, and Darwin's poetic, mythological musings were no anomaly in his circles. They plainly reflected a devastating shift of both interpretation and authority with roots dating back to at least La Peyrère, Burnet, and Whiston—if not much further back through Bruno, Paracelsus, and medieval and patristic writers to Origen. Darwin's figurative approach to Genesis gained its impetus in his belief that mythology, Scripture, and the "testimony of nature" were of equal credence in assisting human reason in the quest for a natural philosophy which explained all

---

179. Darwin, *Zoonomia*, preface.
180. Darwin, *The Temple of Nature*, 11–12.

origins, including those of humanity. The teaching and authority of Scripture were jettisoned for a new syncretism of ancient paganism and philosophy.

Kant's "Mother Earth" and the Call for an Evolutionary Alternative to Genesis

Trends similar to those in France, England, and Scotland were also apparent in Germany. In 1790 Immanuel Kant (1724–1804), having abandoned not only a literal Genesis but also the authority of Scripture as a whole, proclaimed the need for a cogent alternative on origins.

Calling for the "archaeologist of nature" to organize the known creatures of the earth, he further challenged them to trace how "mother earth" gave birth first to "creatures of less purposive form," which in turn "gave birth to others which formed themselves with greater adaptation to their place of birth" through time "until this womb becoming torpid and ossified limited its births to definite species not further modifiable."[181] This, Kant suggested, would be "a daring venture of reason."[182]

Enlightenment Declension and the Literal Tradition

In contrast to the self-proclaimed "enlightened" thought embodied partly in these alternative religious systems and natural philosophies, many people continued to view as essential adherence to a literal understanding of human origins as recorded in Genesis 1 and 2. In fact, from the late sixteenth through the late eighteenth century, the vast majority of post-Reformation Protestant theologians, whether adhering to Reformed or Lutheran orthodoxy, whether on the European continent, Britain, or in colonial settings, continued in the literal hermeneutical stream established by the Reformers in their expositions of Genesis 1 and 2 in relation to the origins of Adam and Eve.

The exceptions to the continuity of the literal hermeneutical stream in the post-Reformation era appeared initially on the fringes of or entirely outside of a confessional Reformed or Lutheran adherence. The new figurative approaches to Genesis and the new views of origins developed and gained traction primarily among "free-thinking" individuals in Roman Catholic contexts, the broad church tradition of the Church of England, or affiliates of the

---

181. Immanuel Kant, *Critique of Judgement*, trans. J. H. Bernard (London: Macmillan, 1914), 338–40.

182. Kant, *Critique of Judgement*, 340.

moderate end of the Church of Scotland.[183] Up to this point, most proponents were nominal Christians at best. Many were openly Socinian, deist, agnostic, or atheist, despite their church affiliations. They chafed at the thought of the immediate power and nearness of God their Creator, his self-revelation to them in Genesis, and in the world around them. Perhaps most of all, they desired an intellectual escape from accountability to God.

A significant, and often overlooked, aspect of the history of nonliteral approaches to Genesis and human origins is that a religious and philosophical shift away from a literal interpretation of Genesis 1 and 2 was taking place long before it began claiming modern science as its ally. Rooted in post-Reformation religious and philosophical challenges by proponents of pre-Adamite theory, the increasing departure from a literal Genesis interpretation corresponded with an increasing separation between special revelation and the exploration and understanding of natural revelation.

Though relatively small through the seventeenth century, by the late eighteenth century, an increasingly significant movement had been born that was rejecting commitment to the Mosaic record as the standard for the evaluation of human narratives of ancient times. This separation and shift was achieved in two key ways: (1) by an outright rejection of the authority of Scripture as the inspired and inerrant Word of God; or (2) by moving away from the literal hermeneutic to adopt alternatives, whether through gap theory or by reclaiming or modifying earlier forms of allegorical or figurative readings.

Concurrent with these shifts, increasing achievements of scientific endeavor, from Copernicus to Newton and Pascal, and the beginnings of the great industrial revolution stirred growing optimism in man's ability to explore, understand, and master the natural order. Tremendous advancements in natural discovery were made through the use of the tools of science. Opposition to these endeavors in the sixteenth century had led individuals like Cardinal Baronius and Galileo Galilei to argue that "the Bible was written to show us how to go to heaven, not how the heavens go."[184] To some, the argument that reason, increasingly to the exclusion of special revelation, was to

---

183. In harmony with this assessment, old-earth geologist Davis Young notes, "With the exception of occasional ideas about Genesis 1 that departed from the rigidly literal interpretation, the almost universal view of the Christian world from its beginnings through the seventeenth century was that the earth is only a few thousand years old." Davis A. Young and Ralph F. Stearley, *The Bible, Rocks and Time* (Downers Grove, Ill.: InterVarsity, 2008), 46. Gregg R. Allison concurs in his chapter on creation in his *Historical Theology: An Introduction to Christian Doctrine* (Grand Rapids: Zondervan, 2011), 254–66.

184. Galileo Galilei, *Nov-antiqua sanctissimorum patrum…* (Strassburg, 1636), 16–17.

guide human exploration and understanding of the earth and human origins seemed to cohere with the concept of the "two books" of special revelation and general revelation.

Misapplication of the legitimacy of the Copernican shift in cosmology merged with the philosophical and religious critiques of the literal interpretation of early Genesis to greatly impact the long-accepted role of special revelation in defining and delineating origins. In addition, an increasing number of natural philosophers and scientists failed to maintain clear distinctions between scientific method and interpretive philosophical constructs in natural philosophy, and yet they continued to refer to the whole of their endeavors as "science."

Intellectuals and academics pushed forward this growing, amorphous, and ever-evolving milieu of ideas that formed a potent and critical challenge to literal interpretation of early Genesis. These new ideas particularly challenged the special, temporally immediate creation of Adam and Eve as the first humans, apart from any ancestry.

5

Adam in the Nineteenth and Early Twentieth Centuries

While a substantial stream of literal interpretation of early Genesis remained, theological and philosophical ideas that included diverse conceptions of earth history and human origins grew significantly beginning in the late eighteenth century and continuing through the nineteenth century. These ideas increasingly moved away from the literal interpretation of the early chapters of Genesis, which had been dominant since the Reformation, and ran parallel to broader trends in European culture and society, including a widening rejection of the authority of Scripture.

The Age of Positive Thinking

The context for these shifts included significant advances in science and technology. A swelling human optimism was fed by remarkable advances in industrial machinery, shipbuilding, and railways; discoveries in medicine; new insights in biology, chemistry, and physics; the exploration of remote corners of the world; and the proliferation of books and articles about these advances. Man placed increasing faith in both the ability to accurately read and understand the book of nature and in great expectations of humanity's incipient progress. Alexander Pope's (1688–1744) poetry exemplified the spirit of this new "modern" age:

> Go, wondrous creature!
> Mount where science guides,
> Go, measure earth, weigh air, and state the tides
> Instruct the planets in what orbs to run;
> Correct old time, and regulate the sun;
>
> Take Nature's path, and mad opinions leave;
> All states can reach it, and all heads conceive;

Obvious her goods, in no extreme they dwell;
There needs but right thinking and meaning well.[1]

By the nineteenth century, French scientist and philosopher Auguste Comte (1798–1857) proposed that humanity had now passed through three stages in history. The first had been the theological stage in which man invented the supernatural to explain how the world functioned. This was followed by the metaphysical stage in which abstract ideas were used to explain why things happen. Now, Comte believed, mankind was entering the third stage: the "positive stage," in which everything would be explained on the basis of scientific laws, and in which it would become clear that the new "religion" of "positivism is the successor of Christianity and surpasses it."[2]

It was in this late Enlightenment academic milieu in Britain and Europe that rejection of a literal Genesis view of creation and human origins became increasingly widespread. Alternative "scientific" theories of natural history and origins were promoted by many; among the most influential were those of Charles Lyell (1797–1875) and Charles Darwin (1809–1882). The senior of the two, Lyell pursued the advancement of James Hutton's theory of old earth uniformitarianism.

In his *Principles of Geology*, Lyell argued that past geological realities ought to be interpreted according to present geological phenomena. By Lyell's calculations, this meant that the earth might be as much as 300 million years old.[3] In England, his writings met with both enthusiasm and critique. His proposed geological history found a receptive audience in the post-Enlightenment intellectual circles where a literal Genesis creation was already mostly passé.

Critics ranged from those who still preferred the Wernerian model of ancient seas to those proposing geological theories in closer congruity with a literal Genesis. The latter included naturalist Philip Henry Gosse (1810–1888), a devout member of the Plymouth Brethren who argued for the coherence of an immediately mature creation (by his argument including the divine creation of fossils) with both a literal Genesis and present geological findings.[4]

---

1. Alexander Pope, "Essay on Man: Epistle II," in *Representative Poetry Online* (Toronto: University of Toronto Libraries, 2013), http://rpo.library.utoronto.ca/poems/essay-man-epistle-ii.

2. Auguste Comte, *A General View of Positivism; Or a Summary Exposition of the System of Thought and Life, adapted to the Great Western Republic Formed of the Five Advanced Nations, The French, Italian, Spanish, British, and German* (London, 1865), 370–75.

3. Charles Lyell, *Principles of Geology…* (London, 1830), vols. 1–3.

4. Philip Henry Gosse, *An Introduction to Zoology* (London, 1844), vols. 1–2; *Omphalos: An Attempt to Untie the Geological Knot* (London, 1857), vi, 54–109, 123–24.

Gosse's argument was derisively referred to by critics taking up the title of one of his works: *Omphalos*, a Greek term meaning "navel"—in reference to his belief that Adam had one.

Another critic of the old earth theory was William Cockburn (1773–1858), who in his *A New System of Geology* aimed to provide an alternative geological hypothesis to that of Lyell; one which was "not greatly improbable…not contrary to Scripture…and…that will account for every fact made known to us by geologists."[5] Cockburn, a Church of England cleric, held to a literal Genesis interpretation. Arguing for creation mature at origin which had also seen significant changes since, he hypothesized that postcreation, both gradual processes and episodes of catastrophism (including the Noahic flood) had contributed to fossilization and present geological structures.[6]

Building on the work of Hutton, Playfair, and others, Lyell's explanations tended to be more thorough and detailed than the geological theories proposed to be in harmony with the literal Genesis interpretation. In fact, Lyell was so convinced that he had outpaced others that he believed his work would "free the science from Moses."[7]

Darwin's Evolutionary Theory

The growing reception of Lyell's work marked a new milestone for ancient earth theory—and acceptance of it meant abandonment of the literal reading of Genesis 1 common to the history of the Christian church. Charles Darwin's synthesis of this ancient earth theory with evolutionary theory would heighten the challenge to a literal interpretation of Genesis on human origins, more fully illustrating the consequences of abandoning the hermeneutic.

Darwin's Religious Origins

Darwin was born into a family living outside the parameters of historic Protestant orthodoxy as the Darwin family manifested a clear tendency toward Unitarianism. Charles, although baptized in the Anglican Church, attended a Unitarian chapel with his mother.[8] His father, like his grandfather Erasmus Darwin, was a medical doctor and a skeptic of many of historic Christianity's claims.

---

5. William Cockburn, *A New System of Geology* (London, 1849), 6.

6. Cockburn, *A New System*, 1–61.

7. Katherine Lyell, *Life, Letters and Journals of Sir Charles Lyell, Bart.* (London, 1881), 1:268–71.

8. Nora Barlow, *The Autobiography of Charles Darwin 1809–1882* (London: Collins, 1958), 49.

In 1825 Charles headed to the University of Edinburgh, which by this point had been deeply influenced by the Scottish Enlightenment movement enthusiastically embraced by Erasmus Darwin. In Edinburgh, Charles met and was mentored by Robert Edmond Grant (1793–1874), an atheist, medical doctor, and natural philosopher who was intrigued by marine biology. Grant was appreciative of Erasmus Darwin's *Zoonomia*, and he engaged in the attempt to construct a new "scientific" philosophy of origins and natural history, arguing for progressive development from a common origin of plant and animal life, with the initial beginnings of life lying in occasions of spontaneous generation.

The young Darwin, however, did not remain in Edinburgh. His father, frustrated with his lack of academic progress in medical studies, decided to shift his trajectory toward a position as an Anglican cleric, which meant transferring to Christ's College, Cambridge.[9] There, Darwin found himself initially intrigued by William Paley's apologetic for Christianity, including its argument for species adaptation as a reflection of intelligent design.[10] For a time, he later reflected, "I…persuaded myself that our Creed must be fully accepted…. It never struck me how illogical it was to say that I believed in what I could not understand and what is in fact unintelligible."[11] At the same time, Darwin noted that his time at Cambridge was "worse than wasted…. I got into a sporting set [with] some dissipated low-minded young men…. We sometimes drank too much…. I ought to feel ashamed of days and evenings thus spent… but…I cannot help but looking back to these times with much pleasure."[12]

The Voyage on the Beagle: Abandoning "The Plain Language of the Text"
Darwin's undefined adherence to "our Creed" proved but a fleeting mood during his Cambridge years. He stated that the remarkable opportunity to join an exploratory journey not long after receiving his degree, decisively put away any thought of a clerical position. He now turned to zealously pursue an attempt to reconstitute his grandfather's poetic musings, reiterated to him in a more scientific form by Grant. Charles was dissatisfied with his grandfather's presentation and articulation of natural origins in *Zoonomia*, "the proportion of speculation being so large to the facts given," but nonetheless acknowledged

9. Barlow, *Darwin*, 56.
10. Not to be confused with the modern intelligent design movement.
11. Barlow, *Darwin*, 57.
12. Barlow, *Darwin*, 60.

that "hearing…such views maintained and praised…favoured my upholding them under a different form in my *Origin of the Species.*"[13]

Intrigued by and enthusiastic for the exploration of the natural world, Darwin set out to develop the concepts of Grant and other early evolutionary thinkers into a more coherent system of natural philosophy.[14] His expeditionary voyage to South America was aboard the *Beagle*, captained by Robert FitzRoy, a supporter of Lyell's work. Darwin took with him his own copy of Lyell's *Principles of Geology*, viewing it as "wonderfully superior" to any other "manner of treating geology."[15] He would later reminisce that his pursuit of a more developed alternative theory of origins was not driven by desire for public acclaim, but by a desire for the esteem of mentors and friends: "I cared in the highest degree for the approbation of such men as Lyell."[16]

The voyage would be notable not only as a period of synthesis of a new evolutionary theory of natural origins, but also for the complete erosion of any remnants of Darwin's fleeting intellectual commitment to Christianity at Cambridge. Darwin noted that several of the officers of the *Beagle* "laughed heartily" at him for citing the Bible on "some point of morality." He continued,

> I had gradually come, by this point in time, to see that the Old Testament from its manifestly false history of the world, with the Tower of Babel, the rainbow as a sign, etc., etc., and from its attributing to God the feelings of a revengeful tyrant, was no more to be trusted than the sacred books of the Hindoos, or the beliefs of any barbarian…. I gradually came to disbelieve in Christianity as a divine revelation…. Disbelief crept over me at a very slow rate, but was at last complete. The rate was so slow that I felt no distress.[17]

Darwin recorded that his departure from a literal Genesis progressed steadily onward to the complete abandonment of the authority of Scripture and moved concurrently with his increasing commitment to advance an alternative natural philosophy of origins and existence.[18] Along with his changed

---

13. In an appendix to *The Autobiography of Charles Darwin*, Barlow argues for a direct connection between Erasmus and Charles Darwin's theories, 149–59.

14. Barlow, *Darwin*, 67–71.

15. Barlow, *Darwin*, 77.

16. Barlow, *Darwin*, 82, 84.

17. Barlow, *Darwin*, 86–87.

18. The same spirit was evident in Darwin's close friend and supporter, Thomas Huxley (1825–1895), who stated, "Not only do I hold it to be proven that the story of the Deluge is a pure fiction; but I have no hesitation in affirming the same thing of the story of the Creation. Between these two lies the story of the creation of man and woman and their fall from primitive innocence, which is even more monstrously improbable than either of the other two,

view of the beginnings of history came a changed view of the end: "I can indeed hardly see how anyone ought to wish Christianity to be true; for if so the plain language of the text seems to show that the men who do not believe, and this would include my Father, Brother and almost all my best friends, will be everlastingly punished. And this is a damnable doctrine."[19]

Creating a New Philosophy of Origins and Life

Darwin's lifetime endeavors as a philosopher and naturalist in pursuit of a natural philosophy of origins were perhaps most cogently expressed in his two key works: *On the Origin of Species* (1859) and *The Descent of Man* (1871).[20] In *On the Origin of Species*, Darwin stated,

> When on board H.M.S. *Beagle*, as a naturalist, I was much struck with certain facts in the distribution of the inhabitants of South America, and in the geological relations of the present to the past inhabitants of that continent. These facts seemed to me to throw some light on the origin of species—that mystery of mysteries, as it has been called…. Although much remains obscure, and will long remain obscure, I can entertain no doubt, after the most deliberate study and dispassionate judgment of which I am capable, that the view which most naturalists entertain, and which I formerly entertained—namely that each species has been inde-pendently created—is erroneous…. I am fully convinced that species are not immutable…. I am convinced that Natural Selection has been the main but not exclusive means of modification.[21]

Hairy Quadrupeds, Savage Men, and that Heroic Little Monkey

In his *The Descent of Man*, Darwin proffered an answer to the quest for the his-torical Adam that would shock many—though it was not without precursors:

---

though, from the nature of the case, it is not so easily capable of direct refutation." Thomas Huxley, "Science and Hebrew Tradition," in *Collected Essays by T. H. Huxley* (New York: D. Appleton and Company, 1903), x, 234.

19. Barlow, *Darwin*, 87–88. This portion of Darwin's memoirs was kept out of publication until the time of the full publication of Darwin's autobiography in the mid-twentieth century. By 1871, Darwin publicly argued that "the idea of a universal and beneficent Creator does not seem to arise in the mind of man, until he has been elevated by long-continued culture." In his later years Darwin once again had more thoughts of God but concluded, "I for one must be content to remain an Agnostic." Barlow, *Darwin*, 94; Charles Darwin, *The Descent of Man and Selection in Relation to Sex* (London, 1871), 2:395.

20. Charles Darwin, *On the Origin of Species by Means of Natural Selection, or the Preser-vation of Favoured Races in the Struggle for Life* (London, 1859); *The Descent of Man*.

21. Charles Darwin, *On the Origin of Species…Third Edition* (London: John Murray, 1861), 1, 6.

The main conclusion arrived at in this work, and now held by many natu-
ralists who are well competent…is that man is descended from some less
highly organized life form. The grounds upon which this conclusion rests
will never be shaken…. [They] are facts which cannot be disputed…. He
who is not content to look, like a savage, at the phenomena of nature as
disconnected, cannot any longer believe that man is the work of a separate act of creation…. All [facts] point in the plainest manner to the
conclusion that man is the co-descendant with other mammals of a common progenitor.

By considering the embryological structure of man…we thus learn
that man is descended from a hairy quadruped, furnished with a tail
and pointed ears, probably arboreal in its habits, and an inhabitant of
the Old World. This creature, if its whole structure had been examined
by a naturalist, would have been classified among the Quadrumana, as
surely would the common and still more ancient progenitor of the Old
and New World monkeys. The Quadrumana and all the higher mammals
are probably derived from an ancient marsupial animal, and this through
a long line of diversified forms, either from some reptile-like or some
amphibian-like creature, and this again from some fish-like animal. In
the dim obscurity of the past we can see that the early progenitor of all
the Vertebrata must have been an aquatic animal.[22]

Darwin's quest for and solution to an alternative origin of man was in
large measure a synthesis of previously existing thought. With Grant and Lyell
as immediate influences, Darwin's synthesis drew on a direct lineage of precursors. His grandfather Erasmus Darwin, James Burnett, Lord Monboddo,
and French Enlightenment philosophers such as Voltaire and Rousseau had
argued for alternative theories of human origins. Monboddo had most explicitly posited monkeys and apes as the ancestors of humans, with Erasmus
Darwin giving applause.

James Hutton had proposed that man had risen from "brute" or "animal."
Others, like Immanuel Kant, had challenged philosophers to create an entirely
new system of the origins of life. All of these in turn had drawn on the prior
thought of Newton, Whiston, and Burnett, who laid foundations by positing
an earth far more ancient than that of biblical record, along with La Peyrère's
theory of the existence of a pre-Adamite humanity of alternative origins.

Near the end of his work in *The Descent of Man*, Darwin stated,

The main conclusion arrived at in this work, namely, that man is
descended from some lowly organised form, will, I regret to think, be

---

22. Darwin, *The Descent of Man*, 2:385–89.

highly distasteful to many. But there can hardly be a doubt that we are descended from barbarians. The astonishment which I felt on first seeing a party of Fuegians on a wild and broken shore will never be forgotten by me, for the reflection at once rushed into my mind—such were our ancestors. These men were absolutely naked and bedaubed with paint, their long hair was tangled, their mouths frothed with excitement, and their expression was wild, startled, and distrustful. They possessed hardly any arts, and like wild animals lived on what they could catch; they had no government, and were merciless to everyone not of their own small tribe. He who has seen a savage in his native land will not feel much shame, if forced to acknowledge that the blood of some more humble creature flows in his veins. For my own part I would as soon be descended from that heroic little monkey, who braved his dreadful enemy…or from that old baboon, who descending from the mountains, carried away in triumph his young comrade from a crowd of astonished dogs—as from a savage who delights to torture his enemies, offers up bloody sacrifices, practices infanticide without remorse, treats his wives like slaves, knows no decency, and is haunted by the grossest superstitions.

Repeating nearly verbatim the wonderment of some of the early European explorers who turned to pre- or co-Adamite theories upon encountering "primitive" peoples, Darwin's abandonment of a literal Genesis left him unable to consider that the condition of such peoples was in part a reflection of generations of fallen life, in spiritual darkness and rebellion against God, and apart from Christ.

Juxtaposing heroic monkeys and apes with brute and savage men—the latter by Darwin's model standing in a less-evolved human condition—he continued: "Man may be excused for feeling some pride at having risen, though not through his own exertions, to the very summit of the organic scale; and the fact of his having thus risen, instead of having been aboriginally placed there, may give him hope for a still higher destiny in the distant future."[23]

Having laid claim to the discovery of a new historical Adam in "that heroic little monkey…or…that old baboon" Darwin pursued a broad consistency: language, morality, and religion were also products of the evolutionary process.[24] Gifted with a keen observation of the existing natural order, particularly in chronicling potential cases of microevolution,[25] Darwin worked

---

23. Darwin, *The Descent of Man*, 2:405.

24. Darwin, *The Descent of Man*, 2:390–96.

25. Microevolution has been a term commonly used by twentieth-century creationists to distinguish from macroevolution, particularly where the latter posits a species-to-species evolutionary fluidity along with universal common ancestry. However, Todd Wood, Kurt Wise,

hard to furnish his vast and holistic theory of origins with "facts," much as Hutton and Lyell sought to do in the realm of geology. While many joined the efforts, others were skeptical, challenging his model and its claimed evidences. In response to critics of his marshaling of evidence toward his theory of human origins, Darwin argued,

> The great break in the organic chain between man and his nearest allies, which cannot be bridged over by any extinct or living species, has often been advanced as a grave objection to the belief that man is descended from some lower form; but this objection will not appear of much weight to those who, convinced by general reasons, believe in the general principle of evolution. Breaks incessantly occur in all parts of the series, some being wide, sharp and defined, others less so in various degrees....
>
> But all these breaks depend merely on the number of related forms which have become extinct. At some future period, not very distant as measured by centuries, the civilised races of man will almost certainly exterminate and replace throughout the world the savage races. At the same time the anthropomorphous apes, as Professor Schaffhausen has remarked, will no doubt be exterminated. The break will then be rendered wider, for it will intervene between man in a more civilised state, as we may hope, than the Caucasian, and some ape as low as a baboon, instead of as at present between the negro or Australian and the gorilla.[26]

In his reply, Darwin elucidated that he had not only conceived a new philosophy of origins, but also a new hierarchy of animal humanity: Caucasians were most advanced, then came the Negroes or Australians, followed by the gorilla and the baboon.[27] Abandoning the plain language of the text of Genesis meant the abandonment of the unity of the human race in the dignity and equality of being created in the image of God.

---

and others have argued that using microevolution in this manner is potentially problematic, particularly when the question is raised regarding the relation between modern categorizations of species and the created kinds recorded in Genesis. Wood and Wise, along with other members of the Creation Biology Society, have adopted "baramins" as a better understanding of created kinds, a categorization that includes an approximation of a species-genus-family, allowing for wider ranges of speciation and transformism while holding to the fixity of "created kinds." This approach is very similar to earlier reflections on "species fixity" by theologians including Herman Bavinck and Charles Hodge. Todd C. Wood, Kurt P. Wise, Roger Sanders, and N. Doran, "A Refined Baramin Concept," in *Occasional Papers of the Biology Study Group* (2003), 3:1–14; Todd C. Wood and Megan J. Murray, *Understanding the Pattern of Life: Origins and Organization of the Species*, ed. Kurt P. Wise (Nashville: Broadman & Holman, 2003), 1–50.
   26. Darwin, "On the Affinities and Genealogy of Man," in *The Descent of Man*, 1:200–201.
   27. Darwin, *The Descent of Man*, 1:200–201.

Popularity and Accommodation

While Darwin took the approach of arguing that the gaps were to be expected, others, like the controversial German evolutionist Ernest Haeckel (1834–1919), made more ambitious proposals. While holding that evidence was not essential to an evolutionary theory of origins, Haeckel nonetheless argued with remarkable specificity that transitional forms in the chain of human evolution would be discovered in the Dutch East Indies, providing detailed descriptions of the nature of the find and providing the name *Pithecanthropus alalus* in advance.[28]

One of his disciples who traveled there, Eugène Dubois (1858–1940), discovered a skullcap, thighbone, and teeth, which he initially gave the name provided by Haeckel, then artistically reconstructed in print and sculpture in full physical form, visually popularizing evolutionary theory of human origins.[29] In time, and after much controversy, the remains were depicted as part of the category of *Homo erectus*.[30]

At the same time, others were discovering, describing, and positing dates for the existence of *Neanderthals* as exemplary of an earlier form of human development. Some, like Darwin's cousin Francis Galton (1822–1911), eagerly sought to use Darwin's theory in explaining heredity in contemporary human populations, as well as seeking to find ways to further advance human evolution through eugenics.[31]

Darwin and Lyell both developed and popularized the models of natural history and human origins of their predecessors. Increasing receptivity, however, did not mean universal or even majority acceptance at this point. As with Lyell, there was significant critique of Darwin—some coming from natural philosophers in the academy (by now increasingly termed "scientists") and at least

---

28. Ernest Haeckel, *History of Creation: Of the Development of the Earth and Its Inhabitants by the Action of Natural Causes. A Popular Exposition of the Doctrine of Evolution in General*, trans. E. R. Lancaster (New York, 1876), 2:263–333, 338–40; Robert J. Richards, "Ernst Haeckel and the Struggles over Evolution and Religion," *Annals of the History and Philosophy of Biology* 10 (2005): 89–115; Ian Tattersall, *The Fossil Trail: How We Know What We Think We Know about Evolution* (Oxford: Oxford University Press, 1995), 32–40; Marvin L. Lubenow, *Bones of Contention: A Creationist Assessment of Human Fossils* (Grand Rapids: Baker, 2007), 86–97.

29. Bert Theunissen, *Eugene DuBois and the Ape-man from Java* (Dordrecht, The Netherlands: Kluwer Academic Publishers, 1989), 26–35, 73–75.

30. Theunissen, *DuBois and the Ape-man*, ix.

31. Francis Galton, also a grandson of Erasmus Darwin, became the editor of the *Eugenics Review* and the president of the *Eugenics Education Society*, spearheading a movement that gained significant following both in England and the European continent, particularly in Germany. In 1910 he completed a never-to-be-published novel presenting a better world shaped by a eugenic religion which guided human breeding programs. Francis Galton, *Inquiries into Human Faculty and its Development* (London: J.M. Dent, 1907), 1–255.

as much, if not more, from within those Protestant churches who maintained a high view of Scripture. Some critique was philosophical, some theological, and some focused on the interpretation or significance of particular present natural realities in relation to the past. Many remained unconvinced that the theories were accurate or capable of retrospective discovery of the origins and early history of creation, including that of man.[32]

Others saw the theories as a brilliant series of new insights into natural history and origins. Lyell and Darwin marked a watershed transition: the nineteenth and early twentieth centuries would be marked by wide-ranging debate and discussions on theories of natural history and origins, including the place of various human and other remains. The bold "new" alternative views of origins challenged the continuity of a literal Genesis understanding of origins, particularly the origin of man.

Protestant Response to New Natural Philosophies

The rise of enthusiasm over the new natural philosophies, their growing sophistication, and the popular blurring of the philosophical constructs and categories of hypothetical models with aspects of genuine growth in scientific knowledge, meant the revival of and increase in the pressures previously felt by Origen, Augustine, Eriugena, Aquinas, La Peyrère, Burnet, Whiston, Le Clerc, and others. Historian Anthony Grafton notes that in the seventeenth century, Isaac La Peyrère was driven in part because he was convinced that "by making Genesis a more reasonable text, he would make it more convincing, and thus the heathen would be more receptive to it and would be more willing to convert to the true religion, Christianity."[33]

While it is dubious that La Peyrère adhered to a genuinely orthodox Christianity, Grafton's comment provides a helpful insight into the development of nonliteral thought on Genesis among the confessional Protestants of the nineteenth century. Just as in previous eras of the church, some theologians adopted alternative hermeneutical approaches to scriptural texts on creation and human origins after they encountered novel, challenging systems of thought.

---

32. Some historians argue that the Darwinian model, albeit in neo-Darwinian forms, came to dominance between 1930 and 1950.

33. Anthony Grafton, *New Worlds, Ancient Texts: The Power of Tradition and the Shock of Discovery* (Cambridge: Belknap Press of Harvard University Press, 1992), 211.

Charles Hodge: "Facts" and the Reinterpretation of Genesis 1

In the United States, Princeton theologian Charles Hodge (1797–1878) exemplified the influence of the increasingly popular transitions and theological implications of natural philosophy while also providing a critical evaluation of them. His tenure as a theologian at Princeton Theological Seminary was culminated by his work, *Systematic Theology* (1871–1873), in which he stated both his awareness of the long-standing Protestant commitment to a literal Genesis interpretation of creation and his openness to the idea that an alternative, replacement interpretation might be needed.

"According to the more obvious interpretation of the first chapter of Genesis," Hodge wrote, "this work [of creation] was accomplished in six days. This therefore has been the common belief of Christians…a belief founded on a given interpretation of the Mosaic record, which interpretation, however, must be controlled not only by the laws of language, but by facts. This is at present an open question."[34]

Hodge went on to state that "again, according to the generally received interpretation of the first chapter of Genesis, the process of creation was completed in six days, whereas geology teaches that it must have been in progress through periods of time which cannot be computed."[35] Hodge was aware that sophisticated interpretations of natural evidence stated as "facts" were better understood as "explanations" of facts.[36]

Yet, in the face of the increasingly popular model of an ancient earth history, and with seemingly little awareness of its religious and philosophical roots, Hodge, like his other Scottish and American Presbyterian contemporaries, proffered two alternative readings of Genesis 1: gap theory and day-age approach. Gap theory held that the first verses of Genesis 1 referred to an ancient period long prior to the six days of creation; the day-age approach explained the days of Genesis 1 as figurative, representing indeterminate ages.

---

34. Charles Hodge, *Systematic Theology* (Grand Rapids: Baker, 1997), 1:557.

35. Hodge, *Systematic Theology*, 1:570.

36. Charles Hodge, "What Is Darwinism?," in *What Is Darwinism? and Other Writings on Science & Religion*, ed. Mark Noll and David Livingstone (Grand Rapids: Baker, 1994), 134. In contrast to the assessments of George Marsden, Mark Noll, and others, David P. Smith argues that Hodge and Warfield have been mischaracterized as standing under the influence of Scottish common sense realism whereas they actually stood closer to Dutch Reformed approaches to epistemological issues. David P. Smith, *B. B. Warfield's Scientifically Constructive Theological Scholarship*—Evangelical Theological Society Monograph Series 10 (Eugene, Ore.: Wipf and Stock, 2011), 95–101.

While admitting that taking the Genesis account "by itself, it would be most natural to understand the word [day] in its ordinary sense," Hodge felt that "if that sense brings the Mosaic account into conflict with facts, and another sense avoids such conflict, then it is obligatory on us to adopt that other."[37] Hodge showed significant appreciation for James Dwight Dana (1813–1895), who argued that a day-age approach suited the "profoundly philosophical" nature of "the record in the Bible" for those living in the new age of science. Hodge, citing Dana, stated "the first thought that strikes the scientific reader [of the Mosaic account of the creation] is the evidence of divinity, not merely in the first verse of the record…but in the whole order of creation. There is so much that the most recent readings of science have for the first time explained…. By proving the record true, science pronounces it divine; for who could have correctly narrated the secrets of eternity but God himself?"[38]

For Dana, the key to this breakthrough of understanding the Genesis narration correctly was "science's" reading of "the whole order of creation"; fallen man had finally risen to read general revelation correctly. The unspoken implication was that through its history to this point, the church had manifestly misunderstood and misread significant aspects of the text of Genesis 1. At the same time, there was little apparent awareness of the exegetical implications such a hermeneutical shift would set in motion. Hodge's focus was in line with Dana's: Dana of Yale, like Guyot of Princeton, belonged to "the first rank of natural scientists; and the friends of the Bible owe them a debt of gratitude for their able vindication of the sacred record" through the day-age interpretive approach.[39]

While Hodge was decidedly sympathetic to the general geological approaches of Hutton and Lyell, he did not hesitate to note that Lyell's "ten editions of his *Principles of Geology*…so differ as to make it hard to believe that it is the work of the same mind…. The change on the part of this eminent geologist, it is to be observed is a mere change of opinion. There was no change of the facts of geology between the publication of the eighth and the tenth edition of his work, neither was there any change in his knowledge of those facts…the whole change is a subjective one."[40]

Hodge went on to use Lyell as an example for a general critique of the "science" of his day: "One year the veteran geologist thinks the facts teach one

37. James Dwight Dana as cited in Hodge, *Systematic Theology*, 1:570–71.
38. Hodge, *Systematic Theology*, 1:572–73.
39. Hodge, *Systematic Theology*, 1:573.
40. Hodge, "What Is Darwinism?," 134.

thing, another year he thinks they teach another. It is now the fact, and it is feared will continue to be a fact, that scientific men give the name of science to their explanations as well as to the facts. Nay, they are often, and naturally, more zealous for their explanation than they are for the facts. The facts are God's and their explanations are their own."[41]

Hodge engaged extensively with contemporary scientific theories and theorists. While holding many of the offerings of "science" with a loose hand, he retained a sympathetic openness toward ancient earth theory, giving acclaim to alternate readings of early Genesis. However, he was decidedly more opposed to significant aspects of the Darwinian model of evolution—arguing that it stood in conflict with species fixity and was essentially atheistic in its denial of biblical teleology.[42] Yet, here also, Hodge did not necessarily call for a wholesale rejection of all forms of evolutionary thought: "There are Christian men who believe in the evolution of one kind of plants and animals out of earlier and simpler forms; but they believe that everything was designed by God, and that it is due to his purpose and power that all the forms of vegetable and animal life are what they are. But this is not the question. What Darwin and the advocates of this theory deny is all design."[43]

Allegorical Days but Not Allegorical Dust
Though allowing for alternative interpretive approaches to Genesis 1 and the possibility of evolutionary development among plants and animals, Hodge remained particularly opposed to suggestions that human origins involved evolutionary processes. He thus retained a decidedly literal approach to the Genesis 1 and 2 texts on the creation of man and argued for the crucial significance of the traditional, literal reading of the Mosaic account of the creation of man. "The facts here recorded, including as they do the creation and probation of man, lie at the foundation of the whole revealed plan of redemption. The whole Bible therefore, rests upon the record here given of the work of creation, and consequently all the evidence which goes to support the divine authority of the Bible, tends to sustain the historical verity of that record."[44]

Later referring to the Genesis 1 and 2 accounts of the creation of man, Hodge argued, "Two things are included in this account; first that man's body was formed by the immediate intervention of God. It did not grow; nor was it

---

41. Hodge, "What Is Darwinism?," 134.
42. Hodge, "What Is Darwinism?," 143, 149–57.
43. Hodge, "What Is Darwinism?," 101.
44. Hodge, *Systematic Theology*, 1:568–69.

formed by any process of development. Secondly, the soul was derived from God. He breathed into man 'the breath of life,' that is, that life which constituted him a man, a living creature bearing the image of God."[45]

Hodge's son and successor at Princeton, Archibald Alexander Hodge (1823–1886), followed in his father's footsteps, holding similar positions on the interpretation of Genesis in relation to creation and human origins.[46] On the creation of man, he stated,

> Man was created immediately by God, and last of the creatures.... The scientific advocates of the hypothesis of organic development have denied that man was created immediately by God, and have held that the higher and more complex living organisms were developed gradually and by successive stages from the lower and more simple...and that man at the proper time came last of all from the last link in the order of being immediately below him. That man on the contrary was immediately created by God, his body out of materials previously created and his soul out of nothing, is rendered certain by the following evidence. (1) The hypothesis of development is a mere dream of unsanctified reason.... (2) The Scriptures expressly affirm the fact of man's immediate creation. Gen. i. 26,27; ii. 7. (3) This truth is rendered obvious, also, by the immense distance which separates man from the nearest of the lower animals; from the incomparable superiority of man in kind as well as degree.[47]

Hodge further argued that God's creation of "one human pair" from which the "entire race in all its varieties has descended by generation, is a fundamental truth of the Christian revelation."[48] He went on to criticize both Lyell and Harvard geologist Louis Agassiz: the former for his pre-Adamite arguments "that man has existed upon the earth thousands of years before Adam," and the latter for arguing for multiple origins for the human race.[49] Both, Hodge averred, stood in direct opposition to the testimony of Genesis and the rest of the Scriptures.[50] Hodge also commended and wrote the introduction to Joseph Smith Van Dyke's *Theism and Evolution* (1886), a work that granted the possibility of a limited form of evolution within species but was

---

45. Hodge, *Systematic Theology*, 2:3. Hodge here provides precedent for what appears to be the use of the term "immediate" in a temporal sense, rather than in the traditional theological sense of referring to an ex nihilo act.

46. Archibald Alexander Hodge, *A Commentary on the Confession of Faith* (Philadelphia, 1869), 118.

47. Hodge, *Commentary on the Confession*, 121–22.

48. Hodge, *Commentary on the Confession*, 122.

49. Hodge, *Commentary on the Confession*, 122–23.

50. Hodge, *Commentary on the Confession*, 123–24.

broadly critical of evolutionary theory and rejected any evolutionary origins for man in particular.[51]

Although the Hodges and other nineteenth-century confessional evangelical Protestants—including the great English Baptist preacher C. H. Spurgeon (1834–1892)[52]—moved away from a consistently literal hermeneutic toward Genesis 1 and 2, adopting either gap or day-age views, they and most of their company retained the historic Christian commitment to a special, temporally immediate creation of Adam and Eve. However, Protestants of the confessional evangelical stream during the late nineteenth and early twentieth centuries were increasingly open to further hermeneutical adjustments. This became evident in both a manifest ambiguity toward the literal understanding of the creation of Adam and Eve and a greater openness to evolutionary accounts of human origins.

Warfield and Human Origins: Allegorical Dust?

B. B. Warfield (1851–1921), professor of theology at Western Theological Seminary[53] and Princeton Theological Seminary, moved beyond his predecessors at Princeton in granting leeway for a special creation of Adam and Eve using evolutionary processes. Like Charles Hodge, Warfield was critical of aspects of the Darwinian approach, but he was decidedly more open in stating that there is "no quarrel with evolution when confined to its own sphere as a suggested account of the method of divine providence."[54]

Interacting extensively with modern thought on natural history and origins, Warfield concluded that God's creation of man as described in Genesis 2:7 need not "therefore exclude the recognition of the interaction of other forces in the process of his formation."[55] The implication was that Genesis 1:26–28 and 2:7 might also be more figurative in nature than the literal hermeneutical tradition had allowed. Fred Zaspel, in *The Theology of B. B. Warfield*, describes Warfield as willing to give a tentative allowance for a creation of man

51. Archibald Alexander Hodge, "Introduction," to *Theism and Evolution* by Joseph S. Van Dyke (New York, 1886), 23–35.

52. Charles Spurgeon, "The Power of the Holy Ghost: A Sermon Delivered on Sabbath Morning, June 17, 1855...at New Park Street Chapel, Southwark," in *Spurgeon's Sermons Volume 1: 1855* (Christian Classics Ethereal Library), http://www.ccel.org/ccel/spurgeon/sermons01.pdf.

53. Now Pittsburgh Theological Seminary.

54. Fred Zaspel, *The Theology of B. B. Warfield* (Wheaton, Ill.: Crossway, 2010), 373.

55. B. B. Warfield, "The Manner and Time of Man's Origin," in *B. B. Warfield, Evolution, Science and Scripture: Selected Writings*, ed. Mark Noll and David Livingstone (Grand Rapids: Baker, 2000), 214.

including evolutionary processes under supernatural direction, combined with direct supernatural intervention, so long as Adam and Eve were the first and only human progenitors. While granting allowance for this, Warfield nevertheless seems to have viewed evolutionary origins for man as improbable.[56]

By this point, there was a growing hermeneutical movement away from a literal understanding of the days and a traditional reading of the Genesis genealogies. In regard to the latter, Warfield stated that "the scriptural data leave us wholly without guidance in estimating the time which elapsed between the creation of the world and the deluge and between the deluge and the call of Abraham." Warfield was aware that this shift "was a result of the manner of looking at things inculcated by the Huttonian geology, that speculation [which] estimated [the] age of the habitable globe in terms of hundreds of millions of years," and from those critical of "tremendously long estimates of the duration…of human life."[57]

He did not, however, seem to be aware that his alternative hermeneutical system effectively removed any compelling scriptural argument against not only these vast time frames, but also the corresponding hypotheses of human origins.[58] It was in the midst of this that he weighed further scientific and theological considerations, coming to conclusions on what he believed were acceptable latitudes on evolution within his paradigm of biblical interpretation. Pursuing a further harmonization of the new science, Genesis 1, and Scripture's genealogies, Warfield stepped beyond his predecessors and allowed for a broader reinterpretation of the Genesis 1 and 2 accounts of creation and human origins than Charles and Archibald Alexander Hodge had accepted. Yet he made his move merely by further applying their shared hermeneutical principles. Having abandoned the temporal immediacy and constraint of an ordinary sixth day and special creation of man, it appeared only logical to grant the possibility that evolutionary processes were involved in human origins, at least under the rubric of mediate creation.

In many respects, Warfield stood as the bellwether of a significant portion of late nineteenth- and early twentieth-century confessional Protestants. Some, such as William G. T. Shedd (1820–1894), were more critical of evolutionary theory; others, such as James Orr (1844–1913), went beyond Warfield's latitude. Warfield criticized Orr for positing a more comprehensive acceptance

---

56. Zaspel, *Theology of B. B. Warfield*, 374–87.

57. B. B. Warfield, "On the Antiquity and Unity of the Human Race," in *Studies in Theology* (Edinburgh: Banner of Truth Trust), 244.

58. Warfield, *Studies in Theology*, 245–46.

of evolutionary theory in relation to human origins.[59] The influence of these men, and others like them at institutions of higher learning, played a significant role in the move away from a literal interpretation of Genesis. Colleges and universities, whether in Britain, the European continent, or the United States, increasingly embraced the new models of origins and increasingly disdained adherence to the historic literal interpretation of Genesis on creation and human origins.

The Southern Baptists: The Struggle to Maintain the Literal Adam
The changes in hermeneutic and views of creation, particularly at influential seminaries like Princeton, impacted the Protestant church as a whole, whether directly or indirectly. James Petigru Boyce (1827–1888), a Southern Baptist theologian and the first president of Southern Baptist Theological Seminary, was educated at Princeton under Charles Hodge and became convinced that the account of Genesis 1 "does not necessarily teach that this work was done in six days."[60] While a leading Baptist theologian, Boyce appeared to make little mention of evolutionary theory, aside from critically noting that it was "vain to say" that parts of the body "have been developed from inferior forms."[61] However, despite his mentor's love for the writings of Turretin, Boyce surprisingly posited that La Peyrère's pre-Adamite theory if "confined to the past existence of other races of men who had passed away when Adam was created,

---

59. James Orr advocated his view in a number of writings, including "The Early Narratives of Genesis," in *The Fundamentals: A Testimony to the Truth*, ed. R. A. Torrey, A. C. Dixon, et al. (Grand Rapids: Baker, 1988), 1:240. B. B. Warfield, in a review of earlier comments made by Orr in his Princeton Stone Lectures "God's Image in Man," had been significantly critical of Orr and may have been partly responsible for Orr's emphasis on "direct creative activity." Warfield stated: "Unless the thing produced is above what the powers intrinsic in the evolving stuff are capable of producing (under whatever Divine guidance), the product is not a product of 'creation' but of 'Providence.' And 'Providence' can never do the work of 'creation.' Dr. Orr fully understands this and argues therefore that the apparition of man implies the intrusion of a new cause, that it is a creation, strictly so called: and this is what makes the note on p. 87 inexplicable. Let man have arisen through the Divine guidance of the evolutionary process, there is no creative act of God, but only a providential activity of God, concerned in his production, unless there has been intruded into the process the action of a cause not intrinsic in the evolving stuff, causing the complex product to be something more than can find its account in the intrinsic forces, however divinely manipulated. Evolution can never, under any circumstances, issue in a product which is specifically new: 'modification' is the utmost that it can achieve,— 'origination' is beyond its tether." B. B. Warfield, "A Review of God's Image in Man…by James Orr," in *B. B. Warfield, Evolution, Science and Scripture*, 233–34.
60. James P. Boyce, *Abstract of Systematic Theology…First Published in 1887* (Cape Coral, Fla.: Founders Press, 2006), 171.
61. Boyce, *Abstract of Systematic Theology*, 40.

or who were at least destroyed before or at the flood, it may be admitted as a possibility...[though] it is not probably true."[62]

Boyce's excursus reflected the reality of the continuities of the nonliteral stream and its direct connections to prior advocates like La Peyrère—evidenced in Boyce's immediate context in the reformulation of La Peyrère's thought in Vanderbilt University professor Alexander Winchell's *Adamites and Pread-amites.*[63] Boyce's comments likely were intended to offer this pre-Adamism as a potential avenue for harmonizing theories of the antiquity of man with the testimony of Scripture.

Going significantly beyond Boyce was his fellow professor, Crawford Howell Toy (1836–1919). Toy became convinced of both Lyell's model of earth history and Darwin's evolutionary theory, and also pursued a broader imple-mentation of higher critical methods that he had encountered in his studies in Germany, effectively raising science over Scripture. This led to a radical abandonment of a literal Genesis interpretation. By 1879, Toy's theological trajectory led to the recommendation that he resign from Southern Baptist Theological Seminary. Soon after, he transitioned to a post at Harvard and began attending the Unitarian First Parish Church in Cambridge. Boyce grieved the separation with this much-loved friend, stating that he hoped and longed for the day when Toy would return to theological orthodoxy.[64]

Other Southern Baptist leaders in the nineteenth and early twentieth cen-turies, such as John L. Dagg (1794–1884), Joseph Walker, Jeremiah B. Jeter (1802–1880), and Edwin C. Dagan (1852–1930), held with significantly greater clarity than Boyce that God had, by a special and temporally immediate act, created Adam and Eve as the first parents of all mankind, apart from any ancestry. While some, like Dagg, cautiously allowed the possibility of an old earth, others, like Walker, vigorously contended for a literal interpretation of Genesis with its six-day time frame of creation and the special creation of Adam and Eve on the sixth day.[65]

---

62. Boyce, *Abstract of Systematic Theology*, 191.

63. Alexander Winchell, *Adamites and Preadamites...* (Syracuse, N.Y., 1878), 1–52. Winchell lost his position at Vanderbilt in 1878 as a result of his views, moving to take a posi-tion at the University of Michigan where he had taught previously.

64. Gregory A. Wills, *Southern Baptist Theological Seminary, 1859–2009* (Oxford: Oxford University Press, 2009), 108–36. I am indebted to Greg Wills for his kind assistance on the his-tory of Genesis interpretation among Southern Baptists.

65. John L. Dagg, *Manual of Theology* (Charleston, S.C.: Southern Baptist Publication Society, 1857), 1:110–15, 141–44. Joseph Walker served as the editor of the Georgia Baptist's *Christian Index* (1857–1860). Jeremiah B. Jeter was the editor of the Virginia Baptist's *Religious*

The Genesis debates continued among Southern Baptists into the twentieth century. In the 1920s, Southern Baptist Seminary president Edgar Y. Mullins (1860–1928), although he opposed the creation of a confessional statement for the Southern Baptist Convention, took the lead in bringing the denomination to adopt one in what he felt would be the least objectionable manner, retaining an allowance for a latitude of beliefs within the convention.[66] A preamble to the confession stated that "[the confession] was not to be used to hamper freedom of thought or investigation in other realms of life."[67] Mullins aimed to present a confession that avoided "any statement on science or evolution."[68] In his own writings, he had expressed some doubts toward but retained an openness to the possibility of theistic evolutionary processes for human origins.[69] Whereas article 3 of the confession stated that "man was created by the special act of God, as recorded in Genesis," Mullins argued at the convention that this precluded evolution, avoiding mention of theistic evolution.[70] While some were appreciative, other Southern Baptists felt the article was inadequate, realizing that it failed to exclude theistic evolution.[71]

C. P. Stealey (1867–1937), after leading a failed attempt to gain an amendment against evolution at the convention, initiated a campaign to prevent evolutionists from teaching in Southern Baptist schools, gaining widespread sympathy. Because of his efforts, in 1926 the Southern Baptist Convention overwhelmingly adopted the following statement: "This convention accepts Genesis as teaching that man was the special creation of God and rejects every theory, evolution or other, which teaches that man originated in, or came by way of a lower animal ancestry."[72]

At the final session of the convention, messengers further adopted "the Tull resolution," which requested that "the faculty, administration, and trustees of…Southern Baptist schools" follow Southwestern Baptist Theological Seminary's lead in abiding by this statement, including requiring all faculty

Herald (1865–1880). Edwin C. Dargan, *The Doctrines of our Faith* (Sunday School Board of the Southern Baptist Convention, 1905), 43–44, 82–85.

66. Wills, *Southern Baptist Theological Seminary*, 291.
67. Wills, *Southern Baptist Theological Seminary*, 293.
68. Wills, *Southern Baptist Theological Seminary*, 294.
69. E. Y. Mullins, *The Christian Religion in Its Doctrinal Expression* (Valley Forge, Pa.: Judson, 1917), 255–57.
70. Wills, *Southern Baptist Theological Seminary*, 295.
71. Wills, *Southern Baptist Theological Seminary*, 295.
72. Z. T. Cody, "The Convention and Evolution," *Baptist Courier* (May 27, 1926): 2–3; cited in Wills, *Southern Baptist Theological Seminary*, 297.

to agree with it.[73] While the passage of the statement and request revealed the potent influence of supporters of the literal Genesis interpretation on human origins among Southern Baptists, efforts to achieve implementation faltered significantly. Historian Greg Wills argues that by the 1940s at Southern Baptist Theological Seminary, "it is unlikely that a faculty candidate who rejected evolution could have gained election to the faculty for most positions."[74]

Protestant Liberalism: The Poetic and Mythical Freedom of the Ancient Near East

While numerous late nineteenth- and early twentieth-century confessional and evangelical Protestants held mixed opinions of the alternative views of origins, more liberal Protestants wholeheartedly embraced theistic evolutionary origins of mankind with little of the hesitancy that seemed to characterize men such as Warfield. In many cases, the hermeneutical approaches and doctrine of Scripture of figures such as Friedrich Schleiermacher (1768–1834), Crawford Toy, Charles Augustus Briggs (1841–1913), and Adolf von Harnack (1851–1930), were so significantly reformulated that Scripture had little, if any, immediate bearing on natural history and human origins. These were now the purview of philosophy and natural science while the Scriptures provided material for a kind of individual experiential or ethical reflection.[75] Liberal Protestants moved beyond gap and day-age interpretations to include forms of ancient Near Eastern cosmological interpretation, as well as "literary" alternatives to literal Genesis interpretations.[76]

Ancient Near Eastern Cosmological Approach

The roots of the ancient Near Eastern cosmological approach lay in the earlier critically comparative approaches to the Scriptures of writers like La Peyrère, Spinoza, and Voltaire, all of whom argued that Genesis must be interpreted in

---

73. Wills, *Southern Baptist Theological Seminary*, 297.

74. Wills, *Southern Baptist Theological Seminary*, 301.

75. Friedrich Schleiermacher, *The Christian Faith in Outline* (Edinburgh: William F. Henderson, 1922), 16–19, 26–27; Charles Augustus Briggs, *Biblical History: A Lecture Delivered at the Opening Term of The Union Theological Seminary...* (New York, 1889), 26–28; Adolf von Harnack, *What is Christianity? Lectures Delivered at the University of Berlin During the Winter Term, 1899–1900*, 2nd ed. (New York: G. P. Putnam's Sons, 1908), 10–16, 23.

76. These shifts occurred partly because of dissatisfaction with the ability of either the gap or day-age interpretations to cohere with the new models of origins and, in some cases, with the perception of their hermeneutical or exegetical inadequacies, leaving those desiring to reconcile ancient earth theory and evolutionary models of origins in search of a more tenable alternative.

the light of the historical narratives produced by other ancient civilizations. This view harmonized with the positivist spirit promoted by Auguste Comte, following his argument that ancient (i.e., religious or theological) descriptions of history and origins were primitive, if not mythical: the products of simpler minds, in contrast to the advanced insights of moderns in the scientific era.

The ancient Near Eastern cosmological approach argued that the narrative of the early chapters of Genesis was thoroughly embedded in the context of an ancient worldview; it was a primitive understanding, but nonetheless beautiful and doxological as the worshipful response of an ancient people to their natural surroundings. Ancient Near Eastern cosmological hermeneutic developed further sophistication after George Smith's translation and publication of *The Chaldean Account of Genesis* in 1876. Smith believed that "time will show the Babylonian traditions of Genesis to be invaluable for the light they will throw on the Pentateuch," presciently noting his finding that "the name Adam is in the creation legends, but only in a general sense as man, not as a proper name."[77]

Another key figure was the German theologian Hermann Gunkel (1862–1932). He also took up the cause of Genesis reinterpretation, becoming an influential exponent of what became known as "form criticism" through *Creation and Chaos in the Primeval Era and Eschaton* (1895).[78] Gunkel argued that Genesis 1 found its origins in Babylonian myth and was adopted and reshaped by ancient Hebrews as they engaged in religious life in their ancient Near Eastern cultural context.[79] For Gunkel and other advocates of this approach, early Genesis was illustrative of a more primitive, "simpler" ancient Near Eastern worldview and represented the development of human religious tradition.

As such, a "correct" understanding of early Genesis required contextual interpretation in the light of other ancient Near Eastern writings—a project elevating archaeologists and historians to a new level as they pursued their

---

77. George Smith, *The Chaldean Account of Genesis* (New York, 1876), preface, 295. The earliest extant fragments of the Epic of Gilgamesh are believed to date between 1100 and 1700 BC; Moses and the exodus are often dated to the period of 1400–1500 BC, leaving open the question of which was written first; the question of historical precedence of the content of the Mosaic narrative is potentially significant. Those committed to the inspiration and inerrancy of the Scriptures as the Word of God ably argue that the Genesis account is by necessity the original and stands as primary, whereas the Sumerian and ensuing accounts (Babylonian, Assyrian) are derivative and secondary. For an introductory discussion, see Noel Weeks, "Background in Biblical Interpretation: Part 1" and "Background in Biblical Interpretation: Part 2," *Reformation 21* (October 2012), http://www.Reformation21.org.

78. Hermann Gunkel, *Creation and Chaos in the Primeval Era and Eschaton* (Grand Rapids: Eerdmans, 2006), 3–111.

79. Gunkel, *Creation and Chaos*, 78–111.

own quest for a historical Adam or abandoned it for a mythical "Adam," and reinterpreted Scripture through the lenses of their reconstructions of ancient Near Eastern history. The result of this hermeneutical process ranged from ideas that early Genesis embodied some divine reflection of either the current state of creation (possibly, though not necessarily including thematic references to its origins) or perhaps represented a purely mythological narrative reflective of the religious concepts and values of an ancient people. On this spectrum of approaches, Genesis 1 and 2 had conveniently little bearing on the details of human origins.

Literary Approach

The continued development of a "literary" approach was also evident from the beginning of the nineteenth century, sharing roots and concepts with the ancient Near Eastern cosmological approach. During the early period of the century, the writings of the German theologian and philosopher Johann Gottfried Herder (1744–1803) embodied this hermeneutical approach. Herder's thought on Genesis was influenced by Spinoza and Rousseau, and he held to an evolutionary view of humanity similar to Rousseau's.

Popularizing his literary approach to the text, Herder called on his readers to "leave the dull classrooms of the Occident and come into the freer atmosphere of the Orient, where this play was performed."[80] He argued that early Genesis presented an ancient poetic literary device intended to communicate conceptual truths for a theology of history and origins but was never intended in its original context to provide a chronological, timed account of God's work of creation.[81] Genesis 1, according to Herder, was a narrative consisting "of poetic expressions of natural feelings which the human being has when confronted with heaven and earth."[82] Having rejected the literal tradition of the text as a God-given, authoritative, perspicuous, and inerrant revelation of origins, Herder and his followers focused on attempting to draw out a new understanding of the literary devices of early Genesis, from which they in turn sought to draw out thematic aspects of meaning.

By the early twentieth century, Herder's approach had entered the mainstream of Dutch Reformed theology through the University of Utrecht

---

80. Johann Gottfried Herder, *Werke* (Frankfurt: Deutscher Klassiker Verlag, 1985), 5:200.

81. Herder, *Werke*, 5:200; Christoph Bultmann, "Creation at the Beginning of History: Johann Gottfried Herder's Interpretation of Genesis 1," *Journal for the Study of the Old Testament* 68 (1995): 23–32; David L. Simmons, "Poetry, Religion and History: Johann Gottfried Herder on Genesis 1–11" (PhD diss., University of Chicago, 2010), 137–66.

82. Bultmann, "Creation at the Beginning," 27.

divinity professor Arie Noordtzij (1871–1944). One of Noordtzij's forebears at the university, J. J. van Oosterzee (1817–1882) had held that "the answer of an unbiased exegesis cannot be doubtful…the sacred narrator [of Genesis]… thought of ordinary days," with the qualification that this did not apply to "the first three days" because the "heavenly luminaries were placed in no ordered relation to our earth."

Noordtzij took a significant step further away from the literal tradition while proposing a form of Herder's literary approach.[83] In 1924 his "literary framework" conclusions, along with his critique of aspects of the Smith-Gunkel ancient Near Eastern cosmological approach, were published as *God's Word and the Testimony of the Ages: The Old Testament in the Light of Oriental Archaeology*.[84] Through the later part of the nineteenth and early twentieth centuries, both the ancient Near Eastern cosmological approach and the literary approach gained popularity and were embraced by some as better accommodating evolutionary models of human origins than did the gap and day-age hermeneutics.[85]

The End of the Literal Tradition?

Some historians sympathetic to old-earth geological and evolutionary models, like Ronald Numbers in *The Creationists*, have argued that these new approaches to the text and origins were rising as the literal approach to early Genesis was effectively disappearing among the educated in the Western church and society during the nineteenth century. These historians feel adherents of a literal Genesis interpretation simply could not answer the intellectual challenges of the old earth and evolutionary theories of Lyell and Darwin.

According to Numbers, a literal hermeneutic for interpreting early Genesis would effectively be recovered only in a new fundamentalist form in twentieth-century America. This recovery, he posits, occurred primarily

---

83. J. J. Van Oosterzee, *Christian Dogmatics: A Text-Book for Academical Instruction and Private Study* (New York, 1874), 1:318–19. Prior to Van Oosterzee, it appears that the mainstream of the Dutch Reformed church held to a literal hermeneutic. See D. Molenaar, *Handleiding voor Mijne Leerlingen* (Amsterdam, 1852), 160–71.

84. Arie Noordtzij, *Gods Woord en Der Eeuwen Getuigenis: Het Oude Testament in Het Licht der Oostersche Opgravingen* (Kampen: J.H. Kok, 1924), 77–118.

85. In Germany, these hermeneutical approaches were eagerly embraced by proponents of evolutionary models of human origins. In the preface to his work, Noordtzij notes his indebtedness to Friedrich Wilhelm von Bissing (1873–1956), a liberal theologian and archaeologist who was a member of the Lutheran state church. Von Bissing was a National Socialist, though critical of what he viewed as some of the excesses of the movement of National Socialism.

through the influence of the Canadian Sixth Day Adventist George McCready Price and led to the popular "indigenous American bizarrity" of creationism.[86] Price's approach to geology certainly provoked intrigue in twentieth-century fundamentalist circles and gained a wider acceptance among confessional and evangelical Protestants. However, more thorough scholarship reveals significant evidence of a strong stream of both nineteenth- and twentieth-century sources that remained firmly in the millennia old tradition of a literal Genesis hermeneutic. Ample evidence exists to indicate significant numbers of theologians, churches, natural philosophers, and scientists who continued to cultivate a literal interpretation of early Genesis.[87]

In addition, these advocates of a literal interpretation consistently and strongly held to the idea of a special, temporally immediate creation of Adam and Eve apart from any evolutionary biological origins. In fact, even some of the nineteenth- and twentieth-century Protestant theologians who acceded to alternative hermeneutical approaches to Genesis continued to believe in a special creation of humans.

Scottish Presbyterians: Engaging Hutton

Early nineteenth-century Scottish Presbyterians provide examples of approaches that both continued in the literal tradition and moved toward modern approaches to Genesis, creation, and human origins. Late Scottish Enlightenment thinkers who had abandoned the idea of a literal Genesis, including James Hutton, John Playfair, and Robert Jameson, continued to exert significant influence, particularly in the Scottish universities.

Some Scottish theologians, such as Thomas Chalmers (1780–1847), and scientists, such as Hugh Miller (1802–1856),[88] were convinced of an old earth and approached Genesis using a gap theory. Their attempts to harmonize

---

86. Abraham Flipse also promotes this argument, applying it to the Netherlands in his article, "The Origins of Creationism in the Netherlands: The Evolution Debate Among Twentieth Century Dutch Neo-Calvinists," *Church History* 81 (March 2012), 1:104–47, as does R. Scott Clark in broader reference to the Reformed tradition in *Recovering the Reformed Confession: Our Theology, Piety, and Practice* (Phillipsburg, N.J.: P&R, 2008), 49. Both rely on the work of Ronald L. Numbers, including *The Creationists: The Evolution of Scientific Creationism* (New York: Knopf, 1992). Numbers's thesis is significantly weakened through his scant attention to what he terms "clerical creationists."

87. In contrast to Ronald Numbers, James Moore, while sympathetic toward those accepting evolutionary models, presents a more accurately nuanced historical account in *The Darwinian Controversies: A Study of the Protestant Struggle to Come to Terms with Darwin in Great Britain and America 1870–1900* (Cambridge: Cambridge University Press, 1979), 193–216.

88. Both later became part of the Free Church of Scotland.

early Genesis with old-earth geological interpretation were similar to those of Anglican Simon Patrick.[89] Other Scots, like John Wilson, more hesitatingly posited that multiple alternatives might be employed in response to old-earth theory: a literal, six-day creation with immediate maturity, the gap theory, or a view of the days as epochs. However, he continued to hold to a recent, special creation of Adam and Eve.[90]

John Dick: The Genesis Text and Hutton's "Monument of Human Presumption"

Other Scots, like United Secession Church divinity professor John Dick (1764–1833) and a number of "scriptural geologists" who belonged to the Church of Scotland, opposed the transition to old-earth interpretations of Genesis and geology and maintained the special, temporally immediate creation of Adam and Eve.[91] Dick was a widely influential theologian; his *Lectures on Theol-*

---

89. Hugh Miller, *The Testimony of the Rocks* (Boston, 1857), 1–502. While Chalmers's writings only briefly allude to his reinterpretation of Genesis, Hugh Miller more extensively cites his argument for the gap theory. Thomas Chalmers, "Natural Theology," in *Selected Works of Thomas Chalmers* (Edinburgh, 1857), 5:146; Miller, *Testimony of the Rocks*, 143.

90. See Wilson's notes as editor to the 1855 edition of Thomas Ridgley's *Body of Divinity*, 337–38; also see John M. Wilson, *The Heavens, the Earth, and the Sea, or, The Hand of God in the Works of Nature* (London, 1860), 211–18. Wilson critically engaged much of the claimed evidence for the antiquity of humanity in the nineteenth century, coming to the conclusion that the "time tunnel, pronounced by the savants to be 100,000 years or more long from the Christian era, may prove no longer at all, than the popularly received 4004 years." John M. Wilson, *Nature, Man and God: A Contribution to the Scientific Teaching of Today* (London, 1885), 371–410.

91. A number of the "scriptural geologists" were Scottish Presbyterian ministers or Anglican clerics with a keen interest in natural science. Others were engaged in scientific vocations, including George Young (1801–1843), whose writings were recognized by contemporary geologists Andrew Ure, who served as a professor of natural philosophy in Glasgow, and John Murray, an avowed Presbyterian who failed to gain the chemistry chair of King's College, London, due to his refusal to join the Church of England. A survey of the movement is provided by Ralph O'Conner in his article "Young Earth Creationists in Early Nineteenth Century Britain? Towards a Reassessment of 'Scriptural Geology,'" *History of Science* 45 (2007): 357–403. Aside from the young earth creationists, there were also scientists like Richard Kirwan (1733–1812), an internationally renowned chemist, geologist, and president of the Royal Irish Academy, who promoted forms of flood geology. While open to an old earth, Kirwan argued that certain geological formations containing fossils were best attributed to a universal Noahic flood. Richard Kirwan, *Geological Essays* (London, 1799), 67, 75, 98. Thomas Hartwell Horne, a Church of England cleric who also worked at the British Museum, defended both a six-day creation and a young earth. Thomas Hartwell Horne, *An Introduction to the Critical Study and Knowledge of the Holy Scriptures*, 5th ed. (London, 1825), 1:163. See also John Rogerson, "What Difference Did Darwin Make?: The Interpretation of Genesis in the Nineteenth Century," in *Reading Genesis After Darwin*, 75–91.

ogy was often found in the personal libraries of Presbyterian ministers both in Scotland and America and was used as a text in Scottish and American seminaries including Princeton and Mercersburg.[92] Engaging the old-earth geology of Hutton and Playfair from the perspective of Scripture, Dick stated,

> We are encountered by the pretended discoveries of modern science; and the observations which have been made upon the structure of the earth, are supposed to contradict the Mosaic account, by proving that it must have been created at a more distant period, if it was created at all.... Some reject the account of Moses entirely, and others conceive that it tells us not of the original creation, but of the changes which took place upon it after.... This is manifestly a subject beyond the reach of our faculties; and geology as sometimes conducted, is a monument of human presumption, which would be truly ridiculous were it not offensive by its impiety. "Where wast thou" said the Almighty to Job, "when I laid the foundation of the earth?"...Our philosophers do not pretend to have been present when the earth was founded; but they profess to shew us how it was made, and that a much longer period was necessary to form its rocks and strata, than the Scriptures assign.... [They] forsake the only safe guide in such high speculations, and follow the faint and deceitful light of reason.
>
> The vanity of the reasoning of modern geologists...and the basis of their theories may be overturned in a very easy way.... Looking at a piece of granite...they point out the characteristics...and say it was formed by the agency of water or fire, carried on through a long process, which it required ages to complete. It is not denied that the substance might have been produced [in this manner], but is it certain? These laws are at present operating...but, if it was not eternal they must have had a commencement. Why may we not suppose that their Author anticipated their operation, and immediately created substances of such texture or composition, as would have resulted from them in the natural order? No geologist can deny that the thing was possible, unless he be an atheist... and if it was possible, his argument from primitive formations against the comparatively modern date of the earth, vanishes into smoke.... We have no occasion to convert each of Moses' days into thousands of years.
>
> God created the heavens and the earth about four thousand years before the Christian era. The materials were produced out of nothing in an instant.... Six days were employed in arranging them in their present form. Some are of the opinion that these were not natural days, but

---

92. William B. Evans describes Dick as a federal theologian with substantial influence in America as a result of his *Lectures on Theology*. William B. Evans, "Imputation and Impartation: The Problem of Union With Christ in Nineteenth Century American Reformed Theology" (PhD diss., Vanderbilt University, 1996), 324–26.

periods of indefinite length.... This opinion is objectionable on the ground that it puts a meaning on the word day, although it is distinctly defined by the evening and the morning, which it bears nowhere else in simple narrative, it remains to be proved that there is any necessity for such interpretation.[93]

In this context of a literal Genesis and young earth, Dick's description of the creation of Adam and Eve retained the interpretation held through the history of Reformed orthodoxy:

> The creation of man took place on the sixth day, and was delayed till that time, that the earth might be prepared for his reception.... The body of man was made from the dust, or of the earth.... It was not made out of nothing, but pre-existing matter; but equal power was necessary to produce, out of that matter, flesh, and blood, and bones. When the body of man was fashioned, "The Lord God," says the sacred historian, "breathed into his nostrils the breath of life; and man became a living soul.".…The words import at least that God caused the air to enter his body, that its several parts might begin their functions, the lungs to respire, the heart to beat.... Although we may not be able to prove that breathing into man the breath of life necessarily implies the communication [of a living principle...distinct from the body]...yet the cause requires us to understand the words in this sense...as we know the nature of man is compound, consisting of a soul as well as a body.[94]

Dick's approach was neither isolated nor the last in the long Christian tradition of upholding a special, temporally immediate creation of Adam and Eve on the sixth day of the creation week.[95]

---

93. John Dick, *Lectures on Theology* (Philadelphia, 1841), 1:382–84.

94. Dick, *Lectures on Theology*, 1:406–9.

95. Dick's approach is closely paralleled in a series of articles on "the Deluge" in *The Religious Examiner*, ed. Samuel Findley, D. D. (Cadiz, Ohio, 1828), 2:3–9, 66–71, 130–32. The articles reveal a significant acquaintance with a variety of old earth and flood models, ranging from those of Newton, Whiston, and Burnet to contemporary approaches, critiquing where these approaches fail to cohere with a literal approach to early Genesis. Findley was an Associate Reformed Presbyterian minister in Washington, Ohio, and an active churchman who from 1827 onward served as publisher of this periodical devoted to the life of the Associate Reformed Church. Others, like William Davidson, an Associate Reformed Presbyterian minister from Hamilton, Ohio, had by the mid-1850s moved to a position that was either ambiguous toward or accepting of a nonliteral approach to aspects of Genesis 1 and 2. William Davidson, "Lecture on Natural Christology Delivered before the Students of the Associate Reformed Theological Seminary, Allegany City, Pa., March 19, 1855," in *The Pulpit and Intelligencer of the Associate Reformed Presbyterian Church*, ed. James Prestley (Cincinnati, 1854), 5:401–60.

Challenging Princeton: Presbyterians and Congregationalists
in the Northern States

Through the nineteenth and early twentieth centuries in the United States, several significant streams continued with the literal interpretation of early Genesis and its special, temporally immediate creation of Adam and Eve. In the northeast, Congregationalist Moses Stuart (1780–1852), Professor of Sacred Literature at Andover Seminary and a gifted Hebraist, ably argued "that the meaning of the words in Genesis simply cannot be determined by reading in the theories of modern science" and challenged alternate hermeneutical approaches on exegetical and philological grounds.[96]

Two brothers, Presbyterian Eleazar Lord (1788–1871) and Congregationalist Daniel Lord (1792–1880), sons of Congregationalist minister Nathan Lord who served as president of Dartmouth College, wrote steadily to advocate the literal interpretive approach to Genesis on creation and human origins. Their commitment was shared by Richard Dickinson (1804–1874), a graduate of Yale College and Princeton Theological Seminary, where he had studied under the new professor Charles Hodge and used John Dick's *Lectures on Theology* as a text.

After serving several congregations as a Presbyterian minister, Dickinson became a professor at Bangor Theological Seminary in Maine in 1836 and was elected in 1858 by the General Assembly of the Presbyterian Church to serve as professor of sacred rhetoric and ecclesiastical history at Western Theological Seminary in Pittsburgh.[97] Preferring John Dick's Genesis approach to that of Charles Hodge, Dickinson argued in his 1851 introduction to Eleazar Lord's *The Epoch of Creation*:

> In some instances…the lovers of science have not been aware of the tendency of their own views; they have been misled by the spirit of theorizing…. In other instances, objections to the Mosaic record have been stated in so plausible a manner, that even some who hold to its credibility have been inclined to force its clear and admitted import into harmony with the positions of [geological theorists]. But if we are to reconcile the theories of geologists with the teachings of Moses we endanger the record as effectually as we should the Gospel itself, by attempting to harmonize its doctrines with the pre-conceptions of the carnal mind; nor could

---

96. John H. Giltner, "Genesis and Geology: The Stuart—Sillman-Hitchcock Debate," *The Journal of Religious Thought* 23 (1966–67): 1:3–13. See also Giltner, *Moses Stuart: The Father of Biblical Science in America* (Atlanta: Scholars Press, 1988), 1–158.

97. Eleazar Lord, *The Epoch of Creation. The Scripture Doctrine Contrasted with the Geological Theory* (New York, 1851), 1–311.

there be an end to such a process, until we found ourselves hand in hand with the enemies of revelation, in demolishing its divine authority.... If we are at liberty to abandon the cosmogony of the Pentateuch, why not, also, the fall of man, the unity of the race?[98]

Writing the same year that B. B. Warfield was born, Dickinson astutely noted that erosion of the literal interpretation of Genesis 1 would come to impact the church's understanding of man's creation and early history. In noting the danger of adopting unwarranted alternative hermeneutical approaches, Dickinson was not rejecting the use of scientific method as a means for increased understanding of the natural order. Rather, he argued that the literal interpretation of early Genesis was cohesively accurate to the text itself—and thus the ancient-earth conclusions posited by geologists and the alternative scriptural hermeneutics developed to accommodate these geological theories could not be accurate: "Reason and revelation are traceable to that same high source. Science proper cannot be divorced from religion. God's works cannot contradict his Word: hence the presumption that any conclusion from a survey of his works which clashes with the intimations of his Word, is untenable, and will yet yield to some more impartial or profound analysis of physical phenomena."[99]

Dickinson argued that the supernatural work of God's creation, as a theological principle, opposed attempts to create a theory of origins solely or primarily from the laws of nature that had themselves come into operation as part of the work of creation. The latter approach was

> as irrelevant in explanation of the Mosaic record, as the argument drawn from universal experience in disparagement of the miracles recorded in Holy Writ.... Though we may see in what way soils are formed, and by what action rocks are worn away, and how what is now land may have been a lake or the ocean, still it does not follow that the act of creation was any less a miracle; nor that those wonderful stratified formations on which so much stress has been laid in support of certain theories, were not the result of causes acting with a rapidity and a force, or which

---

98. Richard W. Dickinson, "Introduction," in *Epoch of Creation*, vi–viii.

99. Dickinson in *Epoch of Creation*, vii–viii. Lord argued, "The theory of remote antiquity is no part of this [geological] science, but is an appendage to it. The theory is merely an inference, a supposition, a conjecture, derived from the construction which the geologist puts on the facts of the science, the phenomena which he observes, and the mode in which he conceives them to have been produced by the ordinary and exclusive operation of natural causes." Lord sought to provide both an internal critique of the geological theory of his day on the fossil record, as well as stating what he viewed as better and more scriptural explanations, including the influence of the Noahic flood, or "universal deluge." Lord, *Epoch of Creation*, 95, 240–51.

with all our boasted knowledge of natural philosophy and chemistry, we can form no adequate conception. To admit the original act of creation, and to attempt to account for it on natural principles, or to prescribe the mode in which the primeval creation was effected, is preposterous in the extreme; and he who so far presumes…exposes himself to the pertinent rebuke: "Where were you when I laid the foundations of the earth? Declare if you have understanding.…" In all our reasonings, this great fact, that in the beginning God created the heaven and the earth in the space of six days, is to be regarded as a starting point, like a first truth in philosophy, or an axiom in geometry.[100]

By His explanation in His Word, God had placed limitations on what were and were not legitimate conclusions to be drawn by human reason in seeking to understand the history of His created order. Dickinson's appreciation for the writings of Eleazar and Daniel Lord was countered by Hodge's negative review in *The Biblical Repertory and Princeton Review*. Dickinson and the Lords' work, along with Hodge's concern to defend his own position, indicated that among both Presbyterians and Congregationalists in the northern states there was a continuing and cogent awareness of an abiding stream of the literal interpretive approach to Genesis.[101] The same was true, perhaps even more strongly, among Southern Presbyterians.

Southern Presbyterians: Genesis Solves a Thousand Inquiries
Robert Louis Dabney (1820–1898), a leading figure among Southern Presbyterians, supported a literal interpretive approach including the special, temporally immediate creation of Adam and Eve. As a theology professor at Union Theological Seminary in Virginia and the University of Texas, Dabney engaged the hermeneutical debate relating to early Genesis and human origins, noting attempts to harmonize the Genesis account with both contemporary geological theory and evolutionary theory. His mildest objection was to varieties of gap or restitution theory, saying they were "tenable" and "least objectionable."[102] Yet, he did not hesitate to describe old-earth geological theory as lacking "any force to rebut [the] testimony" of a literal understanding of

---

100. Dickinson in *Epoch of Creation*, x–xi.
101. Charles Hodge, "Review of *The Epoch of Creation*," *The Biblical Repertory and Princeton Review* 23 (1851): 4:696–98.
102. Robert Louis Dabney, *Lectures in Systematic Theology* (Richmond, Va., 1871), 254.

God's work of creation in Genesis.[103] Dabney was significantly more critical of the analogical day approach to the text:

> The advocates of the symbolic days (as Dr. G. Molloy) attach much importance to their claim that theirs is not an afterthought, suggested by geologic difficulties, but that the exposition was advanced by many of the "Fathers." After listening to their citations, we are constrained to reply that the vague suggestions of the different Fathers do not yield them any support, because they do not adopt their theory of explanation. Third. The sacred writer seems to shut us up to the literal interpretation, by describing the day as composed of its natural parts, "morning and evening." Is the attempt made to break the force of this, by reminding us, that the "evening and the morning" do not make up the whole of the civic day of twenty-four hours; and that the words are different from those just before, and commonly afterwards employed to denote the "day" and the "night," which together make up the natural day? We reply: it is true, morning and evening do not literally fill the twenty-four hours. But these epochs mark the beginnings of the two seasons, day and night, which do fill the twenty-four hours. And it is hard to see what a writer can mean, by naming evening and morning as making a first, or a second "day"; except that he meant us to understand that time which includes just one of each of these successive epochs:—one beginning of night, and one beginning of day. These gentlemen cannot construe the expression at all. The plain reader has no trouble with it. When we have had one evening and one morning, we know we have just one civic day; for the intervening hours have made just that time. Fourth. In Genesis 2:2, 3; Exodus 20:11, God's creating the world and its creatures in six days, and resting the seventh, is given as the ground of His sanctifying the Sabbath day. The latter is the natural day; why not the former? The evasions from this seem peculiarly weak. Fifth. It is freely admitted that the word day is often used in the Greek Scriptures as well as the Hebrew (as in our common speech) for an epoch, a season, a time. But yet, this use is confessedly derivative. The natural day is its literal and primary meaning. Now, it is apprehended that in construing any document, while we are ready to adopt, at the demand of the context, the derived or tropical meaning, we revert to the primary one, when no such demand exists in the context. Last. The attributing of the changes ascribed to each day by Moses, to the slow operation of natural causes, as Miller's theory does, tramples upon the proper scope of the passage, and the meaning of the word "create"; which teach us this very truth especially; that these things were not brought

---

103. Robert Louis Dabney, "Geology and the Bible," in *Discussions* (Edinburgh: Banner of Truth, 1982), 3:127–51; Dabney, *Lectures*, 256–63.

about by natural law at all, but by a supernatural divine exertion, directly opposed thereto. See Gen. 2:5.[104]

He commented that in relation to the origins of man:

The first three chapters of Genesis present a *desideratum* wholly unsupplied by any human writing, in a simple, natural, and yet authentic account of man's origin. The statement that his body was created out of pre-existent matter, and his soul communicated to that body by God, solves a thousand inquiries, which mythology and philosophy are alike incompetent to meet. And from this first father, together with the help-meet formed for him, of the opposite sex, from his side, have proceeded the whole human race, by successive generation. The unity of race in the human family has been much mooted by half-scholars in natural science of our day, and triumphantly defended.[105]

Dabney's commitment to a literal understanding of the creation of Adam and Eve was reflected in his substantial opposition to any form of evolutionary hypothesis for human or other life origins.[106] Describing the special, temporally immediate creation of Adam and Eve on the sixth day as the first parents of humanity, Dabney reflected,

I would merely point out, in passing, the theological importance of this natural fact. If there are men on earth not descended from Adam's race, then their federal connection with him is broken. But more, their inheritance in the *protoevangelium*, that the "seed of the woman shall bruise the serpent's head," is also interrupted. The warrant of the Church to carry the Gospel to that people is lacking; and indeed all the relations of man to man are interrupted as to them. Lastly, the integrity of the Bible as the Word of God is fatally affected; for the unity of the race is implied in all its system, in the whole account of God's dealings with it, in all its histories, and asserted in express terms. Acts 17:26. See Breckinridge's Theol., vol. ch. 3, 1. For additional Scriptures, Gen. 3:20; 7:23; 9:1, 19; 10:32. Unity of race is necessary to relation to the Redeemer.[107]

---

104. Dabney, *Lectures*, 254–55.

105. Dabney, *Lectures*, 292.

106. Dabney, *Lectures*, 38–45; Dabney, "A Caution Against Anti-Christian Science," in *Discussions*, 3:152–72; Dabney, "The Caution Against Anti-Christian Science Criticised By Dr. Woodrow," in *Discussions*, 3:173–216.

107. Dabney, *Lectures*, 292–93. Despite holding to the unity of race for all mankind in Adam, Dabney held that "the relation of master and slave is recognized as lawful in itself, by the infallible law of God…that for the African race, such as it is, in fact, such as Providence has placed it here, this [the master-slave relation] is the best, yea the only tolerable relation." In his writing, he failed to draw a distinction between indentured servitude of debtors and chattel

Dabney's positions, while influential among and shared by many Southern Presbyterians, did not represent all their responses or approaches to early Genesis hermeneutics and human origins.[108] Yet literal hermeneutical commitment ran deep among Southern Presbyterians. Morton Smith notes that "the conflict over evolution in the South took a very different direction from that in the North. Instead of allowing the faculty of the seminaries simply to come to their own opinions of the matter, the Church dealt with it in the courts of the Church."[109]

The Woodrow Controversy and the Literal Creation of Adam

For a time, the Southern Presbyterian church's engagement with hermeneutics and human origins centered on controversy surrounding James Woodrow (1827–1907), professor of "natural science in relation to revealed religion" at Columbia Theological Seminary in Columbia, South Carolina.[110] During the 1860s and 1870s, Woodrow engaged in a running debate with Dabney on Genesis and scientific theories of natural history. This period also saw rising tensions between Woodrow and fellow professor William S. Plumer (1802–1880), leading to the latter's "enforced retirement" and to John L. Girardeau (1825–1898) offering his resignation, though he would be persuaded to remain.[111]

By the early 1880s, ministers and laypeople were raising concerns that evolution was supported at the seminary in Columbia; the board of the institution reassured supporters that it was not.[112] Subsequently, in 1884, Woodrow argued in an address to the board and alumni association for the legitimacy of nonliteral approaches to the text of Genesis and the evolutionary origins of man:

---

slavery by man-stealing; where the Old Testament Scriptures indicated an allowance of the former, it was bound by the principle of the seventh-year freedom of the Jubilee as described in Exodus 21. Dabney, *Discussions*, 3:68–69.

108. J. H. Thornwell, *The Collected Writings of James Henley Thornwell* (Edinburgh: Banner of Truth, 1974), 1:206–36. Thornwell was committed to a special, immediate creation of Adam and Eve apart from any evolutionary ancestry but said relatively little regarding nonliteral hermeneutical approaches to the remainder of Genesis 1 and 2.

109. Morton Smith, "The History of the Creation Doctrine in the American Presbyterian Churches," in *Did God Create in Six Days?*, ed. Joseph A. Pipa Jr. and David W. Hall (Greenville, S.C.: Southern Presbyterian Press, 1999), 15.

110. Smith, "History of the Creation Doctrine," 17.

111. W. Duncan Rankin and Stephen R. Berry, "The Woodrow Evolutionary Controversy," in *Did God Create in Six Days?*, 53–99; T. Watson Street, "The Evolution Controversy in the Southern Presbyterian Church with Attention to the Theological and Ecclesiastical Issues Raised," *The Journal of Presbyterian History* 37, no. 4 (1959): 237.

112. Smith, "History of the Creation Doctrine," 18.

I have now presented…briefly my views…. Terms are not and ought not to be used in the Bible in a scientific sense…. They are used perfectly truthfully when they convey the sense intended; that on these principles all alleged contradictions of natural science by the Bible disappear; that a proper definition of evolution excludes all references to the origin of the forces and laws by which it works, and therefore that it does not and cannot affect belief in God or in religion; that according to not unreasonable interpretations of the Bible, it does not contradict anything there taught so far as regards the earth, the lower animals, and probably man as to his body; that there are as many good grounds for believing evolution is true in these respects; and lastly that the reasons urged against it are of little or no weight.[113]

Controversy ensued in print, with calls rising for the removal of Woodrow from his post at the seminary. The majority of the board responded to Woodrow's statements of belief on the Bible and science as plain, correct, and satisfactory, although they stated they were not necessarily signifying their agreement with his views on evolution. This response raised further concerns and led to significant debates in the controlling synods. John L. Girardeau, professor of theology at Columbia and an advocate of the literal hermeneutic, "argued from the design and nature of the theological seminaries that they must not teach what is contrary to church doctrine," and further argued that evolutionary theory was indeed contrary to church doctrine.[114] In the course of the debate, Girardeau was careful to note that he viewed Woodrow as being in error but not a teacher of heresy.[115] The Synod of South Carolina, in response to the debate, simply enacted the resolution stating, "That in the judgment of this Synod the teaching of evolution in the Theological Seminary at Columbia, except in a purely expository manner, with no intention of inculcating its truth, is hereby disapproved."[116]

Within several months, however, the other four controlling synods of the institution—Georgia, Alabama, South Georgia, and Florida—all condemned Woodrow's teaching and "acted to replace any of their board members who

---

113. James Woodrow, "Address on Evolution," in John B. Adger, *My Life and Times 1810–1899* (Richmond, Va., 1899), 455.

114. Rankin and Berry, "The Woodrow Evolutionary Controversy," 79.

115. R. A. Webb, "The Evolution Controversy," in *The Life Work of John L. Girardeau, Late Professor of the Presbyterian Theological Seminary, Columbia, S.C.*, ed. George A. Blackburn (Columbia, S.C.: State Company, 1916), 236–37.

116. Adger, *My Life and Times*, 526.

had sided with Woodrow with anti-evolutionists."[117] By December of 1884, the new board of trustees had asked Woodrow to resign. He refused, calling for a full trial and refused to meet in person with the board, which then voted to remove him from his position. While the removal caused further controversy in several synods, Woodrow requested that formal charges be brought against him in his presbytery.

However, before the trial procedure could begin, the General Assembly of the Presbyterian Church met in May of 1886 in Augusta, Georgia, and voted 137 to 17 "to condemn evolution and with it Woodrow's views," passing the declaration: "That Adam and Eve were created, body and soul, by immediate acts of Almighty power, thereby preserving a perfect race unity; that Adam's body was directly fashioned by Almighty God, without any natural animal parentage of any kind, out of matter previously created from nothing."[118] The Assembly also voted to direct the controlling synods to dismiss Woodrow from the seminary. In 1888 Woodrow's final appeal was rejected by the General Assembly in Baltimore.[119]

To be sure, there remained Southern Presbyterians who saw no problem with granting a latitude of views on hermeneutical approaches to Genesis. One was Canadian Presbyterian Francis Beattie (1848–1906), who served as a professor at Columbia Theological Seminary (1888–1893), arriving shortly after Woodrow's departure and later moving on to the Presbyterian Theological Seminary in Louisville, Kentucky (1893–1906). He argued in 1896 that both the Genesis description of a six-day creation and the Westminster Confession of Faith on creation left the door open for either the "idea of twenty-four hours, or that of a long period of time."[120] By 1911, Thornton Whaling, a strong supporter of Woodrow and evolutionary theory, was appointed president of Columbia Seminary. But despite the controversies and the growing movement toward theological liberalism during the early twentieth century, a substantial Southern Presbyterian contingent remained committed to a

---

117. Robert Kovitz Gustafson, "A Study in the Life of James Woodrow Emphasizing His Theological and Scientific Views as They Relate to the Evolutionary Controversy" (PhD diss., Union Theological Seminary, Richmond, Va., 1964), 466–67.

118. Gustafson, "Life of James Woodrow," 127; Rankin and Berry, "The Woodrow Evolutionary Controversy," 81.

119. Rankin and Berry, "The Woodrow Evolutionary Controversy," 82.

120. Francis Beattie, *The Presbyterian Standards* (Greenville, S.C.: Southern Presbyterian Press, 1997), 80–81.

literal Genesis hermeneutic and the special, temporally immediate creation of Adam and Eve.[121]

Lutherans in Germany and America

Another strong stream of the literal interpretation of Genesis on creation and human origins continued to be found among Lutherans. In Germany, a key root of American Lutheranism, the literature of previous centuries testified to the pervasive influence of the literal tradition. Although theological liberalism had made significant inroads by the mid-nineteenth century, the literal tradition continued, as was exemplified in the 1861 publication of Carl Friedrich Keil (1807–1888) and Franz Delitzsch's (1813–1890) Genesis commentary, which argued that "If the days of creation are regulated by the recurring interchange of light and darkness, they must be regarded not as periods of time of incalculable duration, of years or thousands of years, but as simple earthly days."[122]

Keil and Delitzsch also interpreted the passages of Genesis 2 on human origins literally, noting that Adam was "formed from dust (not *de limo terrae*, from a clod of the earth)...but the finest material of the earth" and that "into his nostril a breath of life was breathed, by which he became an animated being."[123] At the same time, fearing an errant anthropomorphism—or perhaps charges of the same—they went beyond the text in seeking to explain their position that "we must not understand this in a mechanical sense": "By an act of divine omnipotence man arose from the dust; and in the same moment in which the dust, by virtue of creative omnipotence, shaped itself into a human form, it was pervaded by the divine breath of life, and created a living being, so that we cannot say that the body was earlier than the soul. The dust of the earth is merely the earthly substratum, which was formed by the breath of life from God into an animated, living, self-existent being."[124] Despite movement toward a strange synergistic view of the shaping of the human form, their hermeneutic and resulting exposition still cohered most closely to that of the literal tradition.

---

121. Much of this stream merged into the Presbyterian Church in America at its formation in 1973.

122. C. F. Keil and F. Delitzsch, *Biblical Commentary on the Old Testament: The Pentateuch*, trans. James Martin (Grand Rapids: Eerdmans, 2006), 1:51.

123. Keil and Delitzsch, *The Pentateuch*, 1:78.

124. Keil and Delitzsch, *The Pentateuch*, 1:79.

As time progressed, however, Delitzsch displayed his dissatisfaction with this collaborative commentary and published his own in 1881, revealing that he had joined the majority of German Lutheran theologians who by this point were abandoning parts or all of the literal tradition in favor of alternative hermeneutical approaches to Genesis. Many abandoned an orthodox doctrine of Scripture altogether. Adopting a day-age approach, Delitzsch stated "with respect to the length of the days of creation…days of God are intended.… McDonald, Dawson, and others who are convinced that the days of creation are…not days of twenty-four hours, but aeons, are perfectly right."

He continued to maintain the special creation of man but amended his exposition to state that "the two acts" of the formation of man, and the inbreathing of life "though near each other were not simultaneous": "the body of man was first formed of the moist dust of the ground…and then man became an animated being" through the divine action of breathing into him the breath of life.[125] His new commentary proved that aspects of the literal tradition were ebbing away even among the remnant of conservative Lutherans in Germany.

In contrast to the tides of change sweeping Germany, Lutherans in America proved far more likely to remain committed to the literal tradition—particularly among those bodies known in the twentieth century as the Lutheran Church–Missouri Synod and the Wisconsin Evangelical Lutheran Synod. William Hausmann describes Franz Pieper (1852–1931), professor of theology and president at Concordia Seminary, St. Louis, and president of the Lutheran Synod of Missouri (1899–1911), as a leading figure "expressing the traditional view of the Missouri Synod" on creation. Hausmann says, "Pieper carried forward the argument of Lutheran Orthodoxy concerning the length of the day of creation in opposition to the modern evolutionary view that the six days of creation represented a long or indefinite period of time."[126]

In his major theological work, *Christian Dogmatics*, Pieper opened his section on creation stating that "since no human being observed the creation of the world, we have no other authentic account of the creation than the one given by God Himself in the Scriptures."[127] He argued,

All creatures bear the divine stamp; God's invisible nature, that is, His eternal power and Godhead, are clearly seen from the creation of the

---

125. F. Delitzsch, *A New Commentary on Genesis*, trans. Sophia Taylor (Edinburgh, 1888), 1:84.

126. William Hausmann, *Science and the Bible in Lutheran Theology: From Luther to the Missouri Synod* (Washington, D.C.: University Press of America, 1978), 100.

127. Francis Pieper, *Christian Dogmatics* (St. Louis: Concordia, 1950), 1:467.

world, from the creatures (Rom. 1:20). But our knowledge of the particular circumstances of the creation (e.g., of the time in which creation was completed and of the order of creation) is derived solely from God's revelation in Scripture. Men who presume to correct God's record of the creation through conclusions drawn from the present condition of the world are playing the role of scientific wiseacres, a procedure unworthy of Christians, as well as of men in general.[128]

Pieper viewed attempts to shift the interpretation of the Genesis text on the days of creation to something other than "days of twenty-four hours" as a rejection of the plain reading of the text "for impious reasons (to bring Scripture into agreement with the 'assured results of science'), to six periods of indefinite length."[129] His comments on the creation of the light on the first day reflected the mainstream of Lutheran Reformation and post-Reformation orthodoxy: "According to the clear statement of Scripture there was light before sun, moon, and stars existed. Nobody will object to this as long as he believes in an omnipotent God."[130]

Pieper also engaged with further criticisms of a literal interpretive approach. In discussing the sixth day of creation and the creation of land animals, he said, "If it be asked whether the scavengers, maggots, and the like, and the predatory animals, which are now at war with man, were also created by God on this day, we should answer that (a) these animals are also part of creation, but (b) they had a different sphere of activity. Before the fall there was no decay in nature, nor had the animals risen against man. The poisonous plants either had a different nature before the Fall, or they were not harmful to man in his uncorrupted state. Thus Luther and the dogmaticians."[131]

Turning to the creation of man on the sixth day, Pieper continued:

> Finally, on the sixth day, God created man. The fact that man is the crown of creation, superior to the other creatures, is indicated by the following circumstances: 1) Before He made man, the Triune God held a consultation: "Let us make man" (Gen. 1:26). 2) God did something special when he created man. He did not simply speak, as He did when He created animals: "Let the earth bring forth," but He molded the body of man out of the clay and by a special act breathed into his nostrils the breath of life (Gen. 2:7). 3) The fact that God breathed into man the breath of life indicates that man was given a life principle different from that of the animals,

---

128. Pieper, *Dogmatics*, 467.
129. Pieper, *Dogmatics*, 468.
130. Pieper, *Dogmatics*, 471.
131. Pieper, *Dogmatics*, 474.

namely, a rational and immortal soul.... 4) Of special importance is the creation of man in God's own image...endowed with the knowledge of God and perfect righteousness and holiness.... 5) The installation of man as ruler over the earth and its inhabitants (Gen. 1:26–28).[132]

Pieper explicitly stated,

There were no pre-Adamites, nor were there co-Adamites (contemporaries of Adam), but all men are Adamites, i.e., Adam is the first man and progenitor of mankind. This is no theological problem, but a doctrine revealed clearly in Scripture.... God did not create the woman independently of Adam, by forming her of the dust and breathing into her the breath of life, but built her out of a part of man, a rib....

Genesis 1 and 2 are not two essentially different stories of the creation, but Genesis 2 is plainly seen to be a fuller report of the creation and of the first dwelling place of man. The reason why "Elohim" of Genesis 1 is changed to "Jehovah Elohim" of Genesis 2 is that from here on God's activity pertaining to man is the subject of the story. Hence we have in Genesis 2 the beginning of the history of mankind.[133]

Pieper's leadership at Concordia Seminary in St. Louis and in the Missouri Synod demonstrates that his views were common in a significant constituency of American Lutheranism.

Other Lutheran theologians, such as Theodore Engelder (1865–1949) and Theodore Graebner (1876–1950), similarly argued against nonliteral approaches to Genesis. Graebner stated that "the average evolutionist is—so far as his belief in evolution goes—not a scientist, but a philosopher," noting further that "it is worth remembering, indeed, that the more cautious evolutionists have often shown their own appreciation of the fact that belief in evolution is, after all, a philosophic rather than a scientific matter."[134]

Arguing against theistic evolution in particular, Graebner made the case that "whatever scientists choose to do with theistic evolution, the evangelical Christian cannot accept it as a compromise between agnosticism and faith. Even theistic evolution leaves no room for the Scriptural doctrine regarding the Fall of Man, natural corruption, the reality of sin, and the need of a Redeemer....

---

132. Pieper, *Dogmatics*, 475.

133. Pieper, *Dogmatics*, 477–79.

134. Theodore Graebner, *God and the Cosmos—A Critical Analysis of Atheism, Materialism, and Evolution* (Grand Rapids: Eerdmans, 1932), 180. In 1922 Graebner published a popular version of a series of theological journal articles, written in 1906–1907, that also upheld a literal Genesis interpretation on creation and human origins. Graebner, *Evolution: An Investigation and Criticism* (Milwaukee: Northwestern, 1922), 1–160.

Those who think they might accept 'theistic evolution' or 'Christian evolution' as different from materialistic or Darwinian evolution are deceiving themselves…. No matter how we try to qualify or modify evolution, its basic principle of natural ascent, natural self-improvement, is always there."[135]

Graebner's volume *God and the Cosmos* was published in 1932, the same year the Missouri Synod adopted the following statement:

> We teach that God has created heaven and earth, and that in the manner and in the space of time recorded in the Holy Scriptures, especially Gen. 1 and 2, namely by His almighty creative word, and in six days. We reject every doctrine which denies or limits the work of creation as taught in Scripture. In our days it is denied or limited by those who assert, ostensibly in deference to science that the world came into existence through a process of evolution; that is, that it has, in immense periods of time, developed more or less out of itself. Since no man was present when it pleased God to create the world, we must look for a reliable account of creation, to God's own record, found in God's own book, the Bible. We accept God's own record with full confidence and confess with Luther's Catechism: "I believe that God has made me and all creatures."[136]

Alongside this continued Lutheran commitment to the literal interpretation of Genesis, including the special, immediate creation of Adam and Eve, another significant stream of continued adherence to the literal tradition of the interpretation of Genesis was found among the Dutch Reformed churches.

Standing in the Gap: The Dutch Reformed in America

Many of the Dutch Reformed in America were the heirs of the 1834 and following secessions from the state church in the Netherlands. The largest North American body of Dutch Reformed seceders was the Christian Reformed

---

135. Graebner, *God and the Cosmos*, 189.

136. Lutheran Church–Missouri Synod, "A Brief Statement of the Doctrinal Position of the Evangelical Lutheran Synod of Missouri, Ohio, and Other States," in *Doctrinal Declarations, A Collection of Official Statements on the Doctrinal Position of Various Lutheran Synods in America* (St. Louis: Concordia, 1932), 45. Dissension against a literal interpretation of Genesis would break out at Concordia Seminary in St. Louis in the late 1960s in response to the 1967 redeclaration of the Synod that "Scripture teaches and the Lutheran confessions affirm that God by the almighty power of His Word created all things in six days by a series of creative actions" and "that the Synod rejects and condemns all those world views, philosophical theories, exegetical interpretations which pervert these biblical teachings and thus obscure the gospel." Lutheran Church–Missouri Synod, *Convention Proceedings of the Forty-Seventh Regular Convention of the Lutheran Church–Missouri Synod, New York, N.Y., July 7–14, 1967* (St. Louis: Concordia, 1967), 95; Hausmann, *Science and the Bible in Lutheran Theology*, 92.

Church; by 1876 these churches had founded Calvin Theological Seminary in Grand Rapids, Michigan. Early professors, such as Gerrit Hemkes (1838–1920), who was the second professor (1883–1908) hired at Calvin Theological Seminary, addressed the text of Genesis in ways consistent with a literal hermeneutic. Hemkes's "De vijf Boeken van Moses" (1895) was an address to prepare young gospel ministers for useful and fruitful ministry. In it he took on what he described as the attacks of naturalism, rationalism, and higher criticism on the first five books of the Scriptures, robustly engaging text-critical and historical-cultural theories that challenged the Mosaic authorship of Genesis.[137] Hemkes viewed the historical authenticity and accuracy of the Mosaic account as crucial to knowing God as the "great Creator of all things," and understanding the creation of man, his fall into sin, and God's unfolding plan of redemption in Christ.[138]

Hendrikus Beuker, who served as a professor at Calvin Seminary from 1894 to 1900, similarly argued that the Scriptures "possess real historical credibility."[139] Beuker defended this view by describing the short path of oral tradition from Adam to Moses (Adam's lifespan overlapping with that of Lamech, Noah living to the time of Abraham's birth, and Shem living to the lifetime of Isaac), while also noting the work of the Holy Spirit in inspiring and directing Moses' writing of the Pentateuch in perfect truth.[140]

Geerhardus Vos: "Pure History" versus "Bad Exegesis"
One of the early Calvin Seminary faculty members transitioned to the world of Presbyterianism. Geerhardus Vos, having served as professor at Calvin Theological Seminary from 1888 to 1893, accepted a call to serve as a professor at Princeton Theological Seminary in 1893. There he became a close friend and colleague of B. B. Warfield, despite their differences on how to interpret Genesis. Vos, in keeping with the teaching of his earlier milieu, proved to be a learned and capable proponent of the literal Genesis interpretation. Early evidence of his views comes from the beginning period of his Princeton teaching

---

137. Gerrit Hemkes, "De vijf Boeken van Mozes, Rectorale Rede uitgesproken den 5 den Sept. 1895, door Prof. G.K. Hemkes" (unpublished manuscript, 1895), Heckman Library Archives, Calvin College, 134–35.

138. Hemkes, "De vijf Boeken van Mozes," 134–39.

139. Hendrikus Beuker, "Isagogische Schets der Systematische Theologie in het algemeen ter Inleiding tot de Gereformeerde Dogmatiek in't bijzonder" (lecture, Calvin Theological Seminary, October 1897), 59–60.

140. Beuker, "Systematische Theologie," 59–60.

career: in a series of lectures on natural theology, Vos significantly criticized evolutionary thought on the basis of biblical teleology.[141]

Vos's lectures on systematic theology, initially given at Calvin Theological Seminary and continued during his nearly forty years at Princeton (1893–1932), speak more directly to the interpretation of early Genesis, including texts on human origins. They shatter the common impression among historians that "the Princeton approach" was "that the findings of science should be enlisted to help discover proper interpretations of Scripture," which would require abandoning a literal Genesis interpretation.[142] In his lectures, Vos argued that God's work of creation as an "incomprehensible almighty act" could neither be proved nor distilled from nature itself; special revelation was essential to understanding the origins of the entirety of creation, including man.[143]

At the same time, Vos held that God's work of creation as revealed in Scripture was the foundation for God's self-revelation, for Christian doctrine in its totality.[144] Vos was careful to qualify that this did not mean the revelation of God's work of creation in Genesis was "encyclopedic"; rather than plumbing the depths of every detail of God's activity in creation, God in the Genesis account reveals all that is necessary to redemptive history.[145] In writing the account, Moses' record maintained perfect accuracy through the inspiration of the Holy Spirit.[146]

Vos described three general hermeneutical approaches to the Genesis account of creation: the allegorical approach, the mythical approach, and what he called the historical approach. He viewed the first two approaches as illegitimate and rejected the view, propounded by J. G. Herder in the late eighteenth and early nineteenth centuries and in Vos's day by Arie Noordtzij, that the text was a stylized and poetic account of first things. He also opposed the argument raised by a variety of writers, including Hugh Miller, that the Mosaic account was a "retrospective prophecy" in exalted prose.[147] Vos countered that

---

141. Geerhardus Vos, *Theologie Naturalis* (lecture notes taken by L. J. Veltkamp, September 27, 1898, Grand Rapids, Michigan), Calvin College Hekman Archives, Vos Collection.

142. Noll and Livingstone, *What Is Darwinism?*, 14–15.

143. Vos, *Systematische Theologie van G. Vos, Ph.D., D. D., Compendium* (Grand Rapids, 1900), 43.

144. Vos, *Systematische Theologie*, 43–44.

145. Vos, "Dogmatiek van G. Vos. Ph.D. D. D., Deel I. Theologie" (Grand Rapids, 1910), 161–62.

146. Vos, "Dogmatiek," 163.

147. Vos, "Dogmatiek," 162.

while "prophetic visions always have a symbolic dimension here we have pure history."[148] Critiquing these and other nonliteral approaches he went on:

> Some desire a hyper-scientific exegesis, meeting the demands of the latest tastes and most recent trends. Men seek to drag all sorts of physical, geological, and astronomical theories into the text. Some claim that the entire evolutionary theory lies in the text. That may be apologetic zeal, but it is bad exegesis. Any declaration on Genesis 1 and 2 must have exegetical justification. That science has discovered this or that, or has not found something is not enough to try to discover it in Genesis. The creation account gives pure truth, but in a general form; it serves God's people in earlier centuries, as well as his children in a later age. (Which delivers the reader from the hyper-scientific approach.) This is precisely what makes it such a great work of the Holy Spirit.[149]

Vos went on to counter gap or restitution theory, arguing that while the goal was to try to harmonize Genesis with geological theories, it was beset with problems: "An undetermined time of catastrophic existence of the earth contradicts the purpose of God in making the earth as the place of the habitation of man. Such vast periods of creative idleness are problematic in their coherence with a pantheistic worldview.... This approach fails to free the text from all of the scientific objections, to name only those of biology. Could life have existed on the earth without light?"[150] Even more problematic, Vos noted, was the misconstrual of the "tohu wabohu" required in the gap theorist's engagement with the Hebrew text.[151]

Vos's commitment to a literal interpretation became even more evident in his comments on Genesis 1:5 when he answered the question, "How should [the phrase] 'the evening and the morning were the first day' be understood?" He wrote, "Not as if the first day of creation began with evening, as between the prior darkness and the night there would not have been a sufficient distinction. It is probably not that the later understanding is followed here (a day being from evening to evening), but rather that the days span from morning to morning. The final words of verse 5 provide in succession the two halves of the first day. The first half closed with the evening, the second half with the morning."[152]

The following question was, "Should the word 'day' be understood here in the ordinary sense, or in the sense of a long period of time?" Vos answered,

148. Vos, "Dogmatiek," 162.
149. Vos, "Dogmatiek," 163.
150. Vos, "Dogmatiek," 164.
151. Vos, "Dogmatiek," 164.
152. Vos, "Dogmatiek," 167.

"There is great controversy over this. However, here as well, the meaning of the text should not be based on geological considerations, etc., but should be purely dependent on exegetical considerations."[153]

Vos carefully noted that the day-age view was not merely a present novelty driven by modern science, noting Augustine, medieval theologians, and Charles Hodge had all been reticent to define the nature of the day. He then presented an extensive defense of the creation days as days of ordinary duration. Vos argued that it was difficult at best to construe the days as thousands of years in duration from the text itself:

> The nature of the text requires that each period, or day, is of identical length. Who can actually conceive that in one of these days, if defined as a vast period, nothing else occurred but the separation of light from darkness, over a period of thousands of years? The fact that the ordinary markers of time, the sun and the moon, did not yet exist, does not mean that time did not exist. God had already ordained, from the beginning, that light should alternate with darkness. When later this light was concentrated in the sun and stars, nothing is reported to us as if now, at this point, the day consisted of twenty four hours. There is no report of any change [in the marking of time]. We can only come to one conclusion from the text: that also prior to the creation of the sun, time passed with the same speed, and the light was located as was needed for the transition of day and night within twenty four hours....
>
> To try to argue that these days were "God's days" is incorrect. God does not have days within himself, either in his being or attributes. While God's Sabbath is surely eternal, we cannot say this of the first sabbath, following the six day creation, which is clearly delineated for the sake of man....
>
> While the use of day in Genesis 9:4 is figurative, in Genesis 1 it is not used in a figurative manner. What proponents of this approach need to do is find another place in Scripture where a first, second, third day, etc.—a series of terms equally sharply separated—and yet speaking of eras, exists.[154]

When asked "whether those who held days to be eras should be considered heretics," Vos, having critiqued figurative days as "bad exegesis," replied, "No, the question is not essential in this sense;...it only rises to this level when on principle they raise the so-called results of science to grant precedence to them over the Word of God."[155] Not surprisingly, Vos viewed God's creation of man

---

153. Vos, "Dogmatiek," 168.
154. Vos, "Dogmatiek," 169–70.
155. Vos, "Dogmatiek," 170.

as distinct and separate from the creation of other living creatures and emphasized that both "let us create" and "in our image" were significant delineations
of both the created origin and the nature of man from the rest of creation.[156]
Where the earth "brought forth" animals at God's command, God used the
dust of the earth to make man in an immediate and intimate act of creation,
both as the crown of His creation and as unique in his being—especially his
capacity for communion with God.[157]

Vos also engaged with proponents of evolutionary theory who argued that
death had occurred prior to the fall. Answering the question, "Is it not true that
the human body appears naturally constituted to eat meat?," Vos replied, "Men
cannot assess the original historical condition of man from the present constitution of the human body. Sin brought with it a radical change. Man, in so far
as his present constitution, now stands in the middle, between herbivores and
carnivores."[158] According to Vos, neither philosophy nor science could provide a correct knowledge of the origins or original condition of man any more
than philosophy and science could bring knowledge of salvation. The fall and
curse necessitated God's gracious divine revelation for right understanding of
creation and redemption. One of the final questions Vos responded to in his
lectures on creation was "whether or not God could have created the world
longer ago, or more recently." His answer reflected his dry wit: "Could he have?
Indeed…if he had willed to do so."[159]

William Heyns: "We Are Safest to Remain with the Historic Understanding"
While Vos spent the majority of his teaching years at Princeton, his successors at Calvin continued to display a commitment to the literal interpretive
approach to Genesis well into the twentieth century. William Heyns (1856–
1933), a graduate of the Theological School of Kampen, served as professor at
Calvin Theological Seminary from 1902 to 1926. In his "Historia Sacra" on the
Old Testament, Heyns affirmed Ussher's chronology, stating that it remained
the most commonly held chronology of biblical history.[160] He criticized those
who confidently asserted new hermeneutical approaches, particularly those
who followed German theologian J. G. Herder in viewing the early Genesis

---

156. Vos, "Dogmatiek," 174.
157. Vos, "Dogmatiek," 174.
158. Vos, "Dogmatiek," 176.
159. Vos, "Dogmatiek," 179.
160. William Heyns, "Historia Sacra. Oud Testament" (unpublished manuscript, n.d.), 2.

text as a series of poetic parallels. Heyns argued that when pursued with consistency, these attempts to force a poetic paradigm on the text failed.[161]

Heyns viewed the literal understanding of the Genesis text as being under attack by modern psychology, philosophy, natural sciences, and other religious histories and noted that the claims of not only modern natural sciences but also the religious histories of the ancient Near East present an entirely different account of origins than that of Genesis 1.[162] Turning to the days of creation, Heyns argued that day-age theory did not cohere well with the textual description of evenings and mornings and that sound exegesis required the days to be of equal length.[163] He also countered claims that a gap approach harmonized with the text.[164] In "Bijbelsche Geschiedenis," Heyns contended that while some were arguing "for long ages, rather than twenty four hour days...in order to try to harmonize the results of natural science with Holy Scripture," this did damage to the text: "we are safest to remain with the historic understanding of the days."[165]

From these preliminaries, Heyns turned to a more extensive excursus on the creation of man, providing commentary on both hermeneutical and exegetical matters, along with a general exposition of the content of Genesis 1 and 2 on the creation of man.[166] Heyns expounded a special, immediate creation by God of Adam from the dust of the ground and Eve from Adam's rib and held that man was uniquely created in God's image. He also argued that the Genesis 2 account of the creation of Adam and Eve was an expanded account of the sixth-day creation of man, rather than a record of a separate and distinct later work of creation.[167] The creation of Adam as the first man, Heyns argued, is the foundation for the unity of mankind—a reality displayed in the procreative compatibility of men and women across cultures and societies.[168]

Foppe Ten Hoor: "No Exegetical Ground" For Alternatives

Foppe Ten Hoor (1855–1934), served as a professor at Calvin Theological Seminary from 1900 to 1924, maintaining a hermeneutical approach to Genesis and a

---

161. Heyns, "Oud Testament," 2.
162. Heyns, "Oud Testament," 3.
163. Heyns, "Oud Testament," 4. See also William Heyns, *Manual of Reformed Doctrine* (Grand Rapids: Eerdmans, 1926), 54–60.
164. Heyns, "Oud Testament," 4.
165. Heyns, "Bijbelsche Geschiedenis" (unpublished manuscript, n.d.), Heckman Library Archives, Calvin College, Grand Rapids, Michigan, 5.
166. Heyns, "Bijbelsche Geschiedenis," 4–8.
167. Heyns, "Bijbelsche Geschiedenis," 5–6.
168. Heyns, "Bijbelsche Geschiedenis," 7.

view of man's origins consistent with the work of Heyns and Vos. In his lectures on theology, Ten Hoor argued that creation and evolution were antithetical.[169] Like Vos, he argued that God's work of creation spanned six ordinary days, further stating, "there is no exegetical ground" to posit any greater length of time, and that attempts to do so were not rooted in the teaching of the Scriptures, but the result of trying to "press a geological interpretation on the text."[170] Ten Hoor went on to argue against any attempts to read an evolutionary hypothesis into the text, particularly in relation to the account of the creation of man as expressed in Genesis 1 and 2, viewing the Genesis 2 account as an expansion of the account of the creation of man in Genesis 1. In doing so, he engaged with a variety of philosophical, theological, and hermeneutical approaches, including pre-Adamite theory.[171] For Ten Hoor, sound exegesis entailed a literal understanding of the special creation of Adam and Eve on the sixth day.[172] Ten Hoor addressed these issues further in his lectures and engaged with hermeneutical approaches arguing for a more figurative or allegorical approach to aspects of the creation account in Genesis 1 and 2.[173]

Louis Berkhof: Adam and Eve as the Beginning of Humanity

Like his predecessors at Calvin, Louis Berkhof (1873–1957), rejected any form of theistic evolution, viewing it as philosophically antithetical to the idea of creation ex nihilo. A graduate of Princeton Theological Seminary, where he had studied under Warfield and Vos, Berkhof was firmly committed to a literal interpretation of Genesis. His widely influential *Systematic Theology* did not hesitate to engage issues of science and hermeneutics in relation to creation and human origins.[174] Commenting on the days of Genesis, Berkhof noted the views of contemporary and recent theologians:

> Hodge, Sheldon, Van Oosterzee, and Dabney, some of whom are not entirely averse to [the day-age view], are all agreed that this interpretation of the days is exegetically doubtful, if not impossible. Kuyper and Bavinck hold that, while the first three days may have been of different length, the last three were certainly ordinary days.... Vos...defends the

---

169. Foppe Ten Hoor, "Dogmatiek" (unpublished manuscript, n.d.), 1.
170. Ten Hoor, "Dogmatiek," 4–5.
171. Ten Hoor, "Dogmatiek," 5–6.
172. Foppe Ten Hoor, *Compendium der Gereformeerde Dogmatiek* (Holland, Mich.: A. Ten Hoor, 1919), 46–52.
173. Foppe Ten Hoor, "Lectures on Systematic Theology" (unpublished manuscript, 1895), 2:27–33.
174. Louis Berkhof, *Systematic Theology* (Grand Rapids: Eerdmans, 1996), 150–64.

position that the days were ordinary days. Hepp takes the same position.... Noordtzij...asserts that the Hebrew word *yom* (day) in Gen. 1 cannot possibly designate anything else than an ordinary day, but holds that the writer of Genesis did not attach any importance to the concept "day," but introduces it simply as part of a frame-work for the narrative of creation, not to indicate historical sequence, but to picture the glory of the creatures.... The arguments adduced for it are not very convincing, as Aalders has shown.... According to Dr. Aalders, too, Scripture certainly favors the idea that the days of creation were ordinary days.[175]

Berkhof's conclusion was that the traditional, literal interpretation was most coherent with the text of early Genesis and the broader scriptural context including the rationale for the Sabbath commandment in Exodus.[176] His critique of and conclusion on theistic evolution was blunt: "it is a very dangerous hybrid...a contradiction in terms...in a word, it is a theory that is absolutely subversive of Scripture truth."[177] Turning to the Genesis 1 and 2 account of the creation of man, Berkhof rejected the opinion of "higher criticism...that the writer of Genesis pieced together two creation narratives," arguing that they were rather two vantages on the same event, the first, "the account of the creation of all things in the order in which it occurred, while the second groups things in relation to man...and clearly indicates that everything preceding it served to prepare a fit habitation for man as the king of creation."[178]

In respect to the act of creating man, Berkhof argued that "the work of God in the creation of man was not mediated in any sense of the word. He did make use of pre-existent material in forming the body of man, but even this was excluded in the creation of the soul."[179] Not surprisingly, Berkhof provided a critical assessment of theistic and Darwinian evolutionary models of human origins, concluding by turning to the "scripture testimony to the unity of the human race":

> God created Adam and Eve as the beginning of the human species... the following generations.... Moreover, the subsequent narrative in Genesis clearly shows the following generations...stood in unbroken genetic relation with the first pair, so that the human race constitutes not only a specific unity, a unity in the sense that all men share the same human nature, but also a genetic or genealogical unity. This is also taught by Paul

---

175. Berkhof, *Systematic Theology*, 153–54.
176. Berkhof, *Systematic Theology*, 153–54.
177. Berkhof, *Systematic Theology*, 163.
178. Berkhof, *Systematic Theology*, 181.
179. Berkhof, *Systematic Theology*, 182.

in Acts 17:26, "And God made of one every nation of man to dwell on all the face of the earth."[180]

Van Til and Kuiper at Westminster: "Evolution is Unsatisfactory"
The stream of a literal interpretation of Genesis on creation and human origins, exemplified by Berkhof and others in the Christian Reformed Church and by Vos at Princeton, did not translate as strongly into the context of the early Westminster Theological Seminary. Following in Vos's footsteps, both Cornelius Van Til (1895–1987) and R. B. Kuiper (1886–1966) entered the world of Presbyterianism in the northern United States, teaching at Westminster. Van Til, who served as professor of apologetics and systematic theology, was more muted than Vos or Berkhof and did not engage in debate on the days of Genesis 1. Yet he was significantly critical of evolution.[181]

R. B. Kuiper did not explicitly address the interpretation of the chronology of the Genesis account either, though he was also known for unhesitatingly addressing issues of "Evolution and Creation." In the 1928–1929 Sunday school class he taught at La Grave Avenue Christian Reformed Church in Grand Rapids, Michigan, Kuiper argued that "the theory of evolution is unsatisfactory," stating:

> We simple Christians know more on the following points than do the evolutionists.
>   1. Origin of the Universe. The evolutionists do not know the origin of the universe, they say matter is eternal. We know God called it into being by His omnipotent power.
>   2. How life originated. They cannot answer this but say all life developed from dead matter from spontaneous generation—it just happened. We know it came from God. He is the very essence of life. He put life into the universe. It is the work of the Holy Spirit of God.
>   3. How we account for the radical difference between man and animal. Man is religious and no animals are. Even the most barbarous men have

---

180. Berkhof, *Systematic Theology*, 188.
181. Van Til nonetheless was plain in stating: "On the question of creation I believe that it pleased God 'for the manifestation of the glory of his eternal power, wisdom and goodness, in the beginning, to create, make of nothing, the world, and all things therein, whether visible or invisible, in the space of six days and all very good.' This doctrine of creation fits in with the doctrine of ontological trinity. If God is fully self-contained then there was no sort of half existence and no sort of non-being that had any power against him. There was therefore no impersonal laws of logic that tell God what he can do and there is no sort of stuff that has as much even as refractory power over against God when he decided to create the world." Cornelius Van Til, *The Defense of the Faith*, 4th ed. (Phillipsburg, N.J.: P&R, 2008), 247.

some religion but it cannot be found among the animals. There is a wide gulf between man and animal and no missing link will be found as there is none. Man was made in God's image…[the] Bible teaches reproduction after kind, Genesis 1:21–25. We should cling to the Bible instead of Evolution, because when the latter is accepted, Christianity is rejected…. God is our Creator, our Sovereign…. Evolution is undermining all morality and religion.[182]

In a series of lectures on Reformed theology, Kuiper further stated: "The Bible…emphatically contradicts the popular evolutionary teaching of the day by declaring that God performed separate acts of creation, for instance in the origination of plants, animals, and man; that God made every living being after its kind; and that man was created in the image of God."[183]

The Reformed in the Netherlands: Debating the Days

More approaches to interpreting Genesis were seen in the early twentieth century in the Netherlands than were evident among the American Christian Reformed, though there continued to be a stream committed to the literal interpretive approach. In the mainline state church, *Nederlands Hervormde Kerk*, Arie Noordtzij argued for a literary framework. In the Dutch Reformed seceder church, the *Gereformeerde Kerken*, theologians including Abraham Kuyper (1837–1920), Herman Bavinck (1854–1921), Klaas Schilder (1890–1952), and Gerhard Charles Aalders (1880–1961) allowed for alternate durations of at least the first three days of Genesis 1, moving a step away from the literal hermeneutic of their predecessors.[184]

Kuyper qualified this support by explicitly rejecting that these days could be "ages" or "thousands of years" in length and continued to hold that Scripture taught the creation took place no more than six thousand to eight thousand years ago.[185] Aalders was also adamant that the days were "actual days" and

---

182. R. B. Kuiper, "Outlines of Topics discussed by Rev. R. B. Kuiper at the meetings of the Advanced Bible Class of the La Grave Avenue Christian Reformed Church, Grand Rapids, Michigan, Season 1928–1929" (unpublished manuscript, 1928–1929).

183. R. B. Kuiper, "The Reformed System of Theology" (unpublished manuscript, n.d.).

184. See H. E. Gravemeijer, *Leesboek over de Gereformeerde Geloofsleer* (Groningen: R. Boerma, 1892), 668–81.

185. Abraham Kuyper, "Locus De Creatione," in *Dictaat Dogmatiek* (1891), 3:50–64; *Evolutie. Rede bij de overdracht van het rectoraat aan de Vrije Universiteit op 20 October 1899 gehouden* (Amsterdam: Höveker & Wormser, 1899), 7. An English translation of Kuyper's essay on evolution is found in James D. Bratt, ed., *Abraham Kuyper: A Centennial Reader* (Grand Rapids: Eerdmans, 1998), 403–40. Max Rogland argues that Kuyper was essentially agnostic on the length of the first three days of creation. However, a more complete explanation is that

not "ages," though like Kuyper he refused to quantify them as twenty-four hours in length.[186] Kuyper and Aalders qualified their broader interpretation of the days of creation in part because of the substantial criticism they faced from defenders of the literal interpretation in the Netherlands, who did not believe the text warranted any such hypotheses.[187] In the *Gereformeerde Kerken*, pastor–theologian J. G. Feenstra (1888–1966), while appreciative of much of Aalder's work, responded,

> Now many in our day want to see the days of creation as extraordinary days, which may have lasted for longer than 24 hours. Prof. Aalders writes, that they may have been longer, or also possibly shorter than our days are. We, however, hold to the days as being the same as our days. On exegetical grounds we cannot conclude otherwise. Even if someone wants to argue from the first three days, they have no proof. Who says, that the first three days, prior to the sun, were of a differing duration? We do not conclude from the unknown, but from the known. We conclude from the last three days to the first three days. And when we consider, that in Genesis 1:14 precise distinction is made between seasons and days and years, who gives us the right to view the creation days as anything other than ordinary days?[188]

"A Slippery Slope": Allegory to Myth

In *De Wekker*, the *Christelijke Gereformeerde Kerken*'s periodical, J. J. van der Schuit (1882–1966), professor of theology at the Theological School at Apeldoorn, criticized the Genesis interpretations of Aalders, Kuyper, and others,

---

while Kuyper left open the possibility that the first three days may have been "considerably longer than our natural days of twenty four hours," at the same time he limits this time period to be too short to be compatible with old earth theory. The second quote selected by Rogland, while leaving a comparative ambiguity with Kuyper's earlier allowance, in context reads more strongly as disallowing the "right to specify another period" other than simply "the first day." This approach is reflective of and coherent with Kuyper's understanding of the relationship of Scripture and worldview. Abraham Kuyper, *Van de Voleinding* (Kampen: Kok, 1929), 1:23; Max Rogland, "*Ad Litteram*: Some Dutch Reformed Theologians on the Creation Days," *Westminster Theological Journal* 63 (Fall 2001): 213.

186. Gerhard Charles Aalders, *De Goddelijke Openbaring in de Eerste Drie Hoofdstukken van Genesis* (Kampen: Kok, 1932), 229–63; Aalders, *Genesis* (Grand Rapids: Zondervan, 1981), 50–97; Rogland, "Dutch Reformed Theologians on the Creation Days," 216–17.

187. Rogland cites G. H. Kersten, a leading pastor-theologian of the *Gereformeerde Gemeeten* as critical of Aalders as well as Klaas Schilder on the issue of the duration of the days. Rogland, "Dutch Reformed Theologians on the Creation Days," 225.

188. J. G. Feenstra, *Onze Geloofsbelijdenis*, 4th ed. (Kampen: Kok, 1966), 110. Feenstra authored numerous theological and practical works and served on the board of the Theological School at Kampen while engaged in pastoral ministry.

stating that "there are Reformed theologians who think that Gen 1 allows them to give free play to their ingenuity, and then in Gen 2 to pick up the strict line of history again."[189] He further argued that theologians like Barth and Brunner were "more honest in their attitude towards this issue than the [Reformed advocates of nonliteral days], who think they can stand for the majesty of the Word of God…while at the same time they set their feet upon a slippery slope."[190] Citing Brunner's statements that "cosmologically and historically the Biblical Worldview has worn out" and "we know that the world has not been created a few thousand years ago…[but] millions of years," van der Schuit saw him as promoting a matured and consistent form of the teaching of Reformed advocates of alternatives to the literal interpretive tradition on Genesis 1.[191] He argued that

> Brunner's quote is very much in line with what professor Aalders teaches…only Brunner dares to face the consequence of his standpoint and therefore writes:
>
> > "We know that the history of our earth, although counting millions of years, is one of the most recent facts in the universe. There is a well-operating hypothesis, which teaches that the lineage of the human race can be traced back as far as the animal kingdom; we know that there has never been a paradise with Adam and Eve and the snake, we know that the greatest part of the pre-history of the Old Testament is not history but mythology, and that there is no uninterrupted series of witnesses from Adam and Noah up till Christ. Yes, even more, even the account of New Testament history has undergone profound changes."[192]

The faculty of the Theological School at Apeldoorn were not alone in voicing concern over the implications of adopting alternative hermeneutics for the early chapters of Genesis. Other theologians in the denomination, including G. Wisse (1873–1957), held strongly to the literal tradition, understanding that

---

189. J. J. van der Schuit, "Het Bijbelsch Wereldbeeld," *De Wekker* no. 9 (June 30, 1933). The *Christelijke Gereformeerde Kerken* (CGK) was an early seceder denomination in the Netherlands that saw the departure of numerous congregations into a union with Kuyper's *Doleantie*, merging into the *Gereformeerde Kerken* (GK); however, this was followed by a return to the CGK of a significant number of congregations that found the GK other than they expected and so exited the union. The CGK retained a close connection with the Christian Reformed Church and Calvin Theological Seminary and shared in retaining a literal interpretive approach to Genesis 1 and 2.

190. Van der Schuit, "Het Bijbelsch Wereldbeeld."

191. Van der Schuit, "Het Bijbelsch Wereldbeeld."

192. Van der Schuit, "Het Bijbelsch Wereldbeeld."

"on the sixth day God created man as the crown of his creation."[193] Over time, somewhat in contrast to Kuyper and Aalders and possibly reflecting his theological affinities to the milieu of the *Christelijke Gereformeerde Kerken* and the Christian Reformed Church in America,[194] Herman Bavinck appeared progressively more conservative in his reading of Genesis 1 and remained steadily critical toward geological claims of the earth's antiquity.[195]

Kuyper, Bavinck, and Aalders: "We Must Maintain Man Was Immediately Created"

Despite their shift of interpretation of the days, Kuyper, Bavinck, and Aalders exemplified an approach to Genesis on human origins that remained significantly different from that of men such as Warfield, Orr, or Boyce, and contrasted even more significantly with those of American theologians enamored by contemporary German theology. These Dutch theologians were more significantly critical of evolutionary theory and explicitly held to a special, temporally immediate creation of Adam and Eve apart from any evolutionary processes.

The more conservative position of these Dutch theologians compared to some of their Presbyterian counterparts may have been influenced somewhat by witnessing the theological trajectory of their German Protestant neighbors, including views of human origins and history and the concurrent rise of National Socialism.[196] Profoundly concerned by the theological, philosophical, societal, and political implications of evolutionary thought in early twentieth-century Europe, Kuyper stated,

> Man is and remains created after God's image. Animal nature has not determined our humanity; just the opposite, the entire lower cosmos is paradigmatically determined by the central position of man.... Since the Evolution-theory...destroys the object and kills the subject among the two indispensable terms for all real Religion—God and man—Religion can do nothing other than...irrevocably condemn the system of Evolution by virtue of the law governing its own life.

---

193. G. Wisse, *Gereformeerde Geloofsleer*, 3rd ed. (Kampen: J. H. Bos, 1911), 39–43.

194. At this point, the CRC was effectively a blend of *Gereformeerde* and *Christelijke Gereformeerde* immigrants to America.

195. Herman Bavinck, *In the Beginning: Foundations of Creation Theology* (Grand Rapids: Baker, 1999), 132–33; Rogland, "Dutch Reformed Theologians on the Creation Days," 225–27.

196. Kuyper, "Locus De Creatione," 3:50–64; Abraham Kuyper, "Evolution," in *Abraham Kuyper: A Centennial Reader*, ed. James D. Bratt (Grand Rapids: Eerdmans, 1998), 403–40; Bavinck, *Our Reasonable Faith: A Survey of Christian Doctrine* (Grand Rapids: Baker, 1977), 184–220; Flipse, "Creationism in the Netherlands," 108–14; Jerry Bergman, *Hitler and the Nazi Darwinian Worldview* (Kitchener, Ontario, Canada: Joshua Press, 2012), 1–327.

To hesitate here would betray one's own convictions. Evolution is a newly conceived system, a newly established theory, a newly formed dogma, a newly emerged faith. Embracing and dominating all of life, it is diametrically opposed to the Christian faith and can erect its temple only upon the ruins of our Christian Confession. No satisfaction with or appreciation of the beauty or riches cast into our laps by the studies it has stimulated may let us be at peace for even a moment with this system as system.... We must not merely defend ourselves against it but attack it.[197]

Bavinck's response to claims for the creation of man via evolutionary processes was similar:

There is no advantage for people to say that it is better to be a highly developed animal than a fallen human. The theory of the animal ancestry of humans violates the image of God in man and degrades the human into an image of the orangutan and chimpanzee. From the standpoint of evolution humanity as the image of God cannot be maintained. The theory of evolution forces us to return to creation as Scripture presents it to us.... In connection with the theory of the origin of man the doctrine of evolution also tends to conflict with Scripture in regard to the age, the unity, and the original abode of the human race.[198]

In *Our Reasonable Faith*, Bavinck further emphasized,

We must, on the basis of Holy Scripture, maintain that [man] was immediately created in the image of God in true knowledge, righteousness and holiness: he was not at first a small, innocent child that had to develop into maturity; he was not a being who, mature in body, was spiritually without any content...and still less was he originally an animal being, gradually evolved out of animal existence, who now at long last by virtue of struggle and effort had become man. Such a representation is in irreconcilable conflict with the representation of Scripture and sound reason.[199]

Bavinck believed this was of crucial significance. Not only was the special, immediate creation of Adam and Eve apart from evolutionary origins the only sure foundation "for the solidarity of the human race," but also for "original sin, the atonement in Christ, the universality of the kingdom of God, the catholicity of the church, and the love of neighbor."[200] With Bavinck, Kuyper, and Aalders representing the "left end" of the spectrum of Genesis interpre-

---

197. Kuyper, "Evolution," 439.
198. Bavinck, *In the Beginning*, 147.
199. Bavinck, *Our Reasonable Faith*, 219–20.
200. Herman Bavinck, *Reformed Dogmatics Volume 2: God and Creation* (Grand Rapids: Baker, 2004), 526.

tation among the confessionally committed Dutch Reformed streams of the early twentieth century, there was a significant breadth of commitment in the Netherlands to a special, temporally immediate creation of Adam and Eve.

Nonetheless, there was also evidence of further hermeneutical shift: J. G. Geelkerken (1879–1960), a student of Kuyper and Bavinck and a graduate of the Free University of Amsterdam serving as a minister in the *Gereformeerde Kerk*, proposed a figurative reading not only of the days of creation but also of the Tree of Life and the serpent in the garden.[201] Schilder and others supported the action of the Synod of Assen in disciplining Geelkerken, while they also defended the Synod's avoidance of hermeneutical matters in relation to Genesis 1. This point was duly noted as inconsistent by advocates of the literal tradition, much to the ire of Schilder, which led to a lengthy exchange between Schilder and J. L. Jaspers, another minister who advocated the literal interpretive tradition in the *Gereformeerde Kerk*.[202]

Valentine Hepp: "Their Dome of Heaven Crashes Down"
Bavinck's successor at the Free University of Amsterdam, Valentine Hepp (1879–1950), also held to the special, immediate creation of Adam and Eve on the basis of a literal reading of Genesis 2 and 3. However, in contrast to Bavinck, Hepp explicitly and holistically returned the theological course at the Free University to favor a literal interpretation of Genesis—much as Vos had done in his theological lectures at Princeton. Invited, likely through Vos, to Princeton Theological Seminary to deliver the Stone Lectures in 1930, Hepp boldly criticized ancient earth theory in his lecture "Calvinism and Geology":

> Today we have arrived at the view that Scripture is silent concerning the absolute age of the earth, and even concerning the absolute age of man. The indications of Scripture are so clear, however, that the Christian who reveres it, cannot and may not take part in the paleontological and geological hunt after millions. The Scripture excludes the possibility of the human race being two hundred thousand years old.... It is not true that the data of the natural sciences demand such high numbers; the

---

201. Rogland, "Dutch Reformed Theologians on the Creation Days," 217–19. Rogland notes that this was, in part, what precipitated the debates over Genesis 1. The Synod, while addressing Geelkerken's openness to alternative hermeneutical approaches on Genesis 2 and 3, remained silent on Genesis 1. Rogland is strongly sympathetic to Schilder's arguments in defense of the Synod against critics, noting that a nonliteral interpretation of the days, even where it still posited a correspondence to historical realities in time and space, logically opened the way for a wider figurative interpretation of early Genesis.

202. Rogland, "Dutch Reformed Theologians on the Creation Days," 217–19.

evolutionistic principle demands this. It is the antithesis against faith in creation that drives to these excesses.[203]

Hepp asked, "Should not all Christians from all lands unite to oppose this?" He answered, "They should have, certainly!" Giving a fiery assessment of why this "did not happen," Hepp asserted,

> A large body of Christian scholars hoisted the white flag. They were afraid lest they be called unscientific when they did not yield to the demands of geology and paleontology: Give us room for our evolutionistic ideas. And so they began to apply the thumbscrew method to Scripture.... They did not call it a thumbscrew method. No, it was called an attempt at reconciliation.... Those went furthest who construed a separate kind of exegesis for the story of creation in order to please unbelief. This exegesis was not to be allegorical, poetical, or mythological, but what it really was, they did not say. It amounts to this, that the hexaemeron of Genesis 1 does not necessarily have to be taken up literally. Rather, one must see in it the narration of six logically differentiated moments in the creative work of God, six divine ideas becoming real through the *formatio*. It would not be possible, according to them, to determine anything from Genesis concerning the length of time used in the preparation of the earth.... In appearance the authority of Scripture is saved, in reality it is undermined.[204]

Hepp noted that the day-age theory was not "exegetically deserving of approbation to change the days of Genesis into millions of years [as] those days only had one evening and one morning" and cited the modernist exegetes of previous decades as concurring that "the writer of Genesis undoubtedly meant an ordinary day when he wrote of creation-days."[205] Hepp's appreciation of "the modernist exegetes" was limited to this point as he had devoted much of his previous lecture, "Calvinism and the Astronomical Conception of the Universe," to rebut those who followed a modernist impulse to reinterpret

---

203. Valentine Hepp, *Calvinism and the Philosophy of Nature* (Grand Rapids: Eerdmans, 1930), 200–201. Hepp, whom Van Til deeply respected, served at the Free University with Herman Dooyeweerd and Dirk Hendrik Vollenhoven. He came into conflict with them over increasing concern that their philosophical-theological approach was "deformational" rather than "reformational"—undermining both the doctrine of Scripture and departing from a fidelity to the Reformed confessions. J. Glenn Friesen, "The Investigation of Dooyeweerd and Vollenhoven by the Curators of the Free University," http://www.members.shaw.ca/hermandooyeweerd /Curators.pdf.

204. Hepp, *Calvinism and the Philosophy of Nature*, 201.

205. Hepp, *Calvinism and the Philosophy of Nature*, 215.

Genesis cosmology as a primitive worldview by use of Babylonian concepts.[206] In the lecture, he critiqued the school of ancient Near Eastern contextual interpretation for "taking all texts, whether from historical, poetical, prophetical or apocalyptic books...in the same way"—taking everything the Scriptures say about the universe and interpreting it according to Babylonian conceptions.[207] After duly noting the results of reading Longfellow's "The Light of Stars" literally, Hepp stated,

> If they confine themselves to the historical books [of Scripture], to which the literal method must be applied, they cannot even find enough fragments for a construction of a[n ancient Near Eastern] biblical world-image. Their dome of heaven crashes down, for the firmament in Genesis 1 only brings separation. We cannot think here of a permanent partition, for God also made separation between light and darkness, between sea and land. Their one refuge is the Septuagint and the Vulgate, in which the word firmament is translated by...*firmamentum*. But these translations were made under the influence of the Hellenistic image. The Hebrew *raquia'* does not contain this meaning of firmness.
>
> But there is more that needs to be said. They do believe that the Babylonian conception of the universe influenced the writers of the Bible, but they cannot prove it. To begin with there is no such thing as a Babylonian conception of the universe. There are only Babylonian conceptions. Yes, but,—so they excuse themselves—these Bible writers did not use a definite Babylonian world-image, but a cross-section of several. If that be true, then we must conclude that these writers had reached a higher degree of astronomical development than the astronomers of Babylon, so that they were able to view all the world-images and to accept only that which was common to all. But so they jump from the frying pan into the fire, for in spite of themselves, they would be ascribing twentieth century knowledge to these writers.[208]

Where many modernists regarded the Genesis creation narrative as a primitive account thus bearing an ordinary-day understanding, Hepp concluded that "we who think of the writer as an instrument of...the Holy Spirit, cannot conclude anything else, but that he recorded an infallible truth here."[209]

---

206. Hepp, "Calvinism and the Astronomical Conception of the Universe," in *Calvinism and the Philosophy of Nature*, 141–81.

207. Hepp, *Calvinism and the Philosophy of Nature*, 158.

208. Hepp, *Calvinism and the Philosophy of Nature*, 162–63.

209. Hepp, *Calvinism and the Philosophy of Nature*, 215. Noting his own commitment to the literal interpretation's view of six ordinary days, Hepp surmised that "the length of those days was not determined by the sun, but by the rotation of the earth on its axis."

Hepp's hermeneutical commitment to the traditional literal interpretation of Genesis 1 and 2 included advocating the special creation of Adam and Eve on the sixth day, from the earth and Adam's rib, respectively, apart from any ancestry. Hepp questioned:

> Can it be considered in agreement with the Scriptures to say that Adam, the first human, was identical to the Heidelberger of geology, who, were he to be met alive anywhere would be considered by everyone to be a degenerate type? Can it be said of this one that he was created in true knowledge, righteousness, and holiness? Is not the idea that the so-called homo sapiens developed after thousands of years...excluded because the Scripture establishes the truth that the first child was born after the fall? Besides this, there is the no less complicated problem of death...in a state of affairs without sin such injurious causes cannot be supposed.... Paul... ascribes this vanity, this transitoriness to the "bondage of corruption" which has come over all of creation because of the sin of man.... Above all, it may not be forgotten that, even as Adam and Eve were not created as children, but as mature persons, so the earth, at the end of the sixth day, was not in a primitive state, but in a completed state.[210]

Whereas Hepp exemplified an intelligent, albeit strident, voice for the literal interpretation within those of the *Gereformeerde Kerken*, the literal approach was more pervasive in other Dutch Reformed streams, such as the *Gereformeerde Kerken (Vrijgemaakt)*, the *Christelijke Gereformeerde*, and the *Gereformeerde Gemeenten*.[211]

---

210. Hepp, *Calvinism and the Philosophy of Nature*, 211–13.
211. Flipse, "Creationism in the Netherlands," 136–46.

6

The Quest for Adam:
From the 1950s to the Present

In postwar North America there was significant growth and development in what would become a burgeoning "creation science" movement. Propelled by earlier hypotheses, including those of Harry Rimmer (1890–1952) and George McCready Price (1870–1963),[1] the movement gained further influence through the endeavors of John Whitcomb (b. 1924) and Henry Morris (1918–2006)—particularly from their publication of *The Genesis Flood*.[2] The growth of the "creation science" movement corresponded with the development of creation science organizations and publications; together, these ensured continuing scientific efforts aimed at countering the claims of old-earth and evolutionary thought, either through critique or the development of young-earth alternatives.[3]

Many proponents of the literal hermeneutical tradition significantly appreciated this resurgence of sympathetic scientific efforts. At the same time, others appreciated the effort but were ambivalent regarding the results of the varied creation science enterprises. They saw scientific endeavor on origins as potentially helpful, but nonetheless innately human and fallible in contrast to a divine and inerrant text.

---

1. Ronald L. Numbers, *The Creationists: The Evolution of Scientific Creationism* (New York: Knopf, 1992), 54–101. Rimmer, a Presbyterian, held to a gap theory approach to Genesis, with a subsequent six-day creation and was an ardent opponent of evolutionary theory. Harry Rimmer, *Modern Science and the Genesis Record* (Grand Rapids: Eerdmans, 1954); *The Harmony of Science and Scripture* (Grand Rapids: Eerdmans, 1954). Following in the footsteps of nineteenth-century and earlier scientific theorists who held to the literal Genesis tradition on creation, McCready Price, a Seventh-day Adventist, proposed a variety of hypotheses interpreting geological strata and fossil remains within the context of a young earth, six-day creation, and a universal catastrophic flood. George McCready Price, *Outlines of Modern Christianity and Modern Science* (Oakland, Calif.: Pacific, 1902); *Genesis Vindicated* (Washington: Review and Herald Publishing, 1941).

2. John Whitcomb and Henry Morris, *The Genesis Flood* (Philadelphia: Presbyterian and Reformed, 1961), 1–518.

3. Numbers, *The Creationists*, 101–339.

Through the twentieth century, vast amounts of materials were published in the debates over Genesis interpretation, scientific interpretation, and human origins. Despite the increasing volume of publications, the hermeneutical field on Genesis 1 and 2 interpretation remained largely unchanged from the mid-twentieth century onward. Ancient earth geological models, rooted in the endeavors of Hutton and Lyell, and evolutionary models both posited immense, or maybe infinite past time. These models continued to propel theologians toward nonliteral interpretations of some or all of the Genesis creation account. As in the previous century, a nonliteral approach to the Genesis 1 and 2 text—and beyond—continued to expand steadily where nonliteral alternative hermeneutics were adopted. There were also occasional reversals of this trend.

Lutherans in America: "Scripture Interprets Scripture"

Although Lutheranism in Germany was in profound and broad theological decline by the mid-twentieth century, Missouri Synod Lutherans in North America presented a more vital example of historic Lutheran theology. Strong support for the literal hermeneutic tradition continued in the Missouri Synod, following the early twentieth-century commitments of Lutheran leaders such as Pieper, Engelder, and Graebner, and demonstrated in the Synod's 1932 reaffirmation of a six-day creation. The denominational preference for the literal view of both the days and the special, immediate creation of Adam and Eve apart from evolutionary origins was reaffirmed in 1947 and 1967.

Alfred Rehwinkel (1887–1979) was one theologian defending the literal-historical understanding of Genesis 1 and 2, arguing that the Hebrew text indicated a sequence of ordinary days. Walter Roehrs (1901–1996), another professor at Concordia in St. Louis, noted that Exodus 20:9–11 and Exodus 31:12–17 refer to the six days of creation, establishing "a parallel between the normal work days of man and the days of the week of creation." He deduced that "if Scripture interprets Scripture, then these verses should be regarded as God's own commentary on what He says in Genesis: the days in the creation account must be taken as literally as the days that elapse between Sabbaths."[4]

---

4. William Hausmann, *Science and the Bible in Lutheran Theology: From Luther to the Missouri Synod* (Washington, D.C.: University Press of America, 1978), 101; Walter Roehrs, "The Creation Account of Genesis," *Concordia Theological Monthly* 36, no. 5 (May 1965): 320.

Commitment and Challenges to Literal Tradition in the Missouri Synod
In 1959 the Missouri Synod published a series of creationist essays reflecting their commitment to the literal tradition.[5] This continuing commitment among North American Lutherans provided fertile and welcome ground for the developing creation science movement, and a significant Lutheran contingent took part in the development of creation science organizations.[6]

Within the Lutheran Church–Missouri Synod, however, there was also challenge to the literal tradition, which was led by Walter Wegner and promoted by others, including Harold Roellig (1930–2008), Ralph Gehrke (1919–2011), and Carl Krekeler (1920–2012). These men sought to challenge both common understanding of a literal Genesis as a confessionally required belief and to promote alternative hermeneutical approaches.[7]

Walter Keller, a Missouri Synod Lutheran serving as chairman of the theology department at the independent Valparaiso University in Indiana, stood with the challengers, arguing that "the distinction between the Law and the Gospel…releases me from the burden of having to say that Adam and Eve must have been historical."[8] Following in the stream of earlier literary approaches, Wegner proposed that previous generations had errantly viewed as literal what were literary or poetic elements of the text of Genesis, such as "days."

Historian William Hausmann describes these views as "a complete break with the older tradition in the Missouri Synod" and the establishment of a new tradition.[9] Both Harold Roellig and Norman Habel would seek to advance a nonliteral hermeneutic into Genesis 2 and 3, with Habel arguing that while Genesis 1 was not myth, it, along with Genesis 2 and 3, were "symbolic religious history." Roellig came to the conclusion that Genesis 2 and 3 were "parables."[10] The debate played out in the pages of *Concordia Theological Monthly* and created significant outcry within the denomination, leading in part to the 1967 Synod statement on the special creation and historical reality of Adam and Eve, which was further amplified at the Missouri Synod convention in New Orleans in 1973:

---

5. Paul Zimmerman, ed., *Darwin, Evolution, and Creation* (St. Louis: Concordia, 1959), 1–231.

6. Numbers, *The Creationists*, 301.

7. Hausmann, *Science and the Bible in Lutheran Theology*, 102; Walter Wegner, "Creation and Salvation, A Study of Genesis 1 and 2," *Concordia Theological Monthly* 37, no. 8 (September 1966): 528–29.

8. Harold Lindsell, *The Battle for the Bible* (Grand Rapids: Zondervan, 1976), 80.

9. Hausmann, *Science and the Bible in Lutheran Theology*, 104.

10. Hausmann, *Science and the Bible in Lutheran Theology*, 107–9.

We believe, teach, and confess that God by the almighty power of His Word, created all things: We also believe that man as the principal creation of God, was specially created in the image of God, that is, in a state of righteousness, innocence, and blessedness. We affirm that Adam and Eve were real, historical beings, the first two people in the world, and that their fall was a historical occurrence which brought sin into the world so that "since the fall of Adam all men who are propagated according to nature are born in sin.... We confess that man's fall necessitated the gracious redemptive work of Jesus Christ and that fallen man's only hope for salvation lies in Jesus Christ, his Redeemer and Lord."

The shifts at Concordia in St. Louis occurred simultaneously with other changes within the denomination connected to a broader battle over scriptural inerrancy. Fueling a movement of conservative resurgence, these issues led to the dismissal and replacement of the president and the majority of the faculty at Concordia Theological Seminary in 1974, along with the creation of a new theological journal—further reaffirming a strong commitment to the continuing literal tradition on Genesis and human origins.[11] This stance was exemplified most recently in a 2004 Lutheran Missouri Synod resolution "to commend preaching and teaching creation," requiring all Lutheran Church–Missouri Synod institutions "to teach creation from the Biblical perspective." The resolution further stated,

That no educational agency or institution of The Lutheran Church–Missouri Synod tolerate any teaching that contradicts the special, immediate, and miraculous creation by God, Father, Son, and Holy Spirit, as an explanation for the origin of the universe; and be it further

That the Synod's educational agencies and institutions properly distinguish between micro and macro evolution and affirm the scriptural revelation that God has created all species "according to their kinds"; and be it finally

That the Lutheran Church–Missouri Synod, in convention, remind its pastors and teachers to increase emphasis to the doctrine of God as the Creator and Author of Life in their preaching and teaching.[12]

---

11. The dismissed seminary president John H. Tietjen promptly moved to create a "seminary-in-exile" gaining "the support of the Association of Theological Schools on the grounds that academic liberty was at stake." Lindsell, *Battle for the Bible*, 84.

12. Matthew Becker, an opponent of the resolution, cites the vote in favor of the Synodical resolution as being 787 to 206. Becker further relates, "When the current president of the LCMS, Dr. Gerald Kieschnick, was elected to that office in 2001, he stated the following as a part of his acceptance speech: 'As I assume the office of presidency of the Synod, you, the members

Recent publications by the Missouri Synod's Concordia Publishing House further indicate this literal Genesis tradition has continued to the present.[13]

The Literal Tradition and Alternatives in Other Synods
The literal tradition also continues to be in evidence in other streams of North American Lutheranism. The Wisconsin Evangelical Lutheran Synod has held steadily to the literal understanding of Genesis 1 and 2, including human origins, to the present day and requires this commitment of its ministers.[14] By contrast, other Lutheran synods, particularly those that merged to form the Evangelical Lutheran Church in America in 1988, have been open to alternate hermeneutical approaches not only to Genesis 1 but also to increasingly wider areas of Scripture.[15] Yet, even within these bodies, there has remained a legacy of literal tradition voices.

H. C. Leupold (1891–1972), professor of Old Testament exegesis at Capital University Seminary (now Evangelical Lutheran Seminary) in Columbus, Ohio, pursued a detailed exegetical argument for a literal understanding of the text of Genesis 1 and 2. Leupold argued that the modifiers of "evening and morning" indicated the passage of ordinary days: "the evening, of course merges into night, and the night terminates with morning. But by the time the morning is reached, the first day is concluded, as the account says succinctly, 'the first day,' and everything is in readiness for the second day's task…'evening' marks the conclusion of the day, and 'morning' marks the conclusion of the night."[16]

---

of the Synod, deserve to know my beliefs:…I believe the world was created in six 24-hour days less than 10,000 years ago.'" Gerald B. Kieschnick, "President-Elect Acceptance Speech," in *2001 LCMS Convention Proceedings* (St. Louis: Concordia, 2001), 114. "When Dr. Kieschnick made this specific comment about the creation of the earth, he was interrupted with resounding applause by the majority of the more than one thousand delegates to this convention of the LCMS. The perspective expressed here by Dr. Kieschnick may well represent the dominant view within the contemporary LCMS." Matthew Becker, "The Scandal of the LCMS Mind: Creationism, Science and Creation in Biblical-Theological Perspective," *The Daystar Journal* (Summer 2005), http://thedaystarjournal.com/the-scandal-of-the-lcms-mind/.

13. See Joel D. Heck, *In the Beginning, God: Creation from God's Perspective* (St. Louis: Concordia, 2011), 1–80.

14. The Lutheran Church–Missouri Synod numbers some four million members (baptized and confirmed); the smaller and more conservative Wisconsin Evangelical Lutheran Synod has nearly seven hundred thousand members, approximately twice the size of the Presbyterian Church in America (PCA).

15. The movement to form the Evangelical Lutheran Church in America was led in part by more liberal figures departing the Lutheran Church–Missouri Synod with John H. Tietjen playing a key role in its development.

16. H. C. Leupold, *Exposition of Genesis* (Grand Rapids: Baker, 1950), 58.

Leupold also stated that "if it be claimed that some works can with difficulty be compressed within twenty-four hours, like those of the third day or the sixth, that claim can well be described as a purely subjective opinion.... He that desires to reason it out as possible can assemble fully as many arguments as he who holds the opposite opinion."[17] Turning to Genesis 2, Leupold discusses whether Genesis 2:4–6 presents a problem for a literal six-day reading of the text and follows an exposition of Genesis 2:7 as narrating the special, immediate creation of Adam on the sixth day.[18]

More recently, Terence Fretheim, Old Testament professor at Luther Seminary, has argued for a literal reading of the days as being sequential and ordinary in length, albeit concluding that resulting scientific challenges are best answered through "accommodation": "namely, that God, in working with the author, accommodated the telling of the story of creation to the knowledge of the times."[19] Fretheim's colleague, Old Testament professor Mark Hillmer, argued that evolution was used in the process of creation; he views Genesis 1 as a "marvelous metaphor of the world's origin" fully compatible with the concept that "the human being evolved like the animals."[20]

The Dutch Reformed: From Poetic Allegory to the Abandonment of Adam

Initially, the Dutch Reformed stream of the Christian Reformed Church was strongly committed to the literal hermeneutic on early Genesis, including human origins. But significant changes occurred from the postwar period into the twenty-first century. Early traces of nonliteral approaches to Genesis on creation and human origins could be seen within the Christian Reformed Church in North America by 1957, when Eerdmans published an English translation of *Is There a Conflict Between Genesis 1 and Natural Science?* by Nicholas Herman Ridderbos.[21]

---

17. Leupold, *Genesis*, 58.

18. Leupold, *Genesis*, 111–15.

19. Terence Fretheim, "Were the Days of Creation Twenty-Four Hours Long?," in *The Genesis Debate: Persistent Questions about Creation and the Flood*, ed. Ronald F. Youngblood (Grand Rapids: Baker, 1990), 33.

20. Mark Hillmer, "Was Evolution Used in the Process of Creation?," in *The Genesis Debate*, 97. In the same volume (pp. 148–65), H. Wade Seaford argued in favor of the existence of pre-Adamites, tracing the lineage of his argument to La Peyrère.

21. Nicholas Herman Ridderbos, *Is There a Conflict Between Genesis 1 and Natural Science?* (Grand Rapids: Eerdmans, 1957), 4. Nicholas Herman Ridderbos is not to be confused with his better-known brother, the New Testament theologian, Herman Nicholas Ridderbos.

Although much of the Dutch Reformed stream in North America served as a bastion of the literal Genesis tradition in the 1950s, that tradition was increasingly disappearing in Europe, and the movements there would eventually prove influential in North America. Unlike the Missouri Synod Lutherans, who were theologically severed from their German counterparts, teaching coming out of the Netherlands deeply influenced the American Dutch Reformed. Ridderbos's work provided a window to ongoing developments and debate.

Nicholas Herman Ridderbos: "No More Than a Mode of Presentation"
Nicholas Herman Ridderbos (1910–1981), a member of the *Gereformeerde Kerk*, served as professor of Old Testament at the Free University of Amsterdam as Aalder's successor. Just as Arie Noordtzij had moved a significant hermeneutical step beyond his predecessor J. J. van Oosterzee a generation earlier in the mainline *Nederlands Hervormde Kerk*, Ridderbos also moved beyond both his immediate predecessor, Aalders, and his father, Professor Jan Ridderbos (1879–1960).[22] Where his father and Aalders rejected describing the first three days of creation as of ordinary duration, Ridderbos appreciatively proposed Noordtzij's literary framework approach. He stated,

> One who reads Genesis 1 without prepossession or suspicion is almost bound to receive the impression that the author's intent is to say that the creation took place in six ordinary days. But we cannot stop here. He is bound also to receive the impression that the author means to say that the earth was created first, and afterwards the sun, moon, stars, etc.... It is open to doubt whether that impression would be correct.... We must seriously ask ourselves whether it is possible to understand [the writer's] meaning at first glance.... Does the author mean to say that God completed creation in six days, or does he make use of an anthropomorphic mode of presentation?... One must take seriously that the account of creation is no more than a mode of presentation.[23]

Ridderbos's conclusion was that "in adopting the frame-work hypothesis we no longer have these difficulties."[24] Yet, Ridderbos was still tentative on what latitudes this approach might give to the proposals of modern scientific theories

---

22. Jan Ridderbos, the father of Herman and Nicholas Ridderbos, served as a professor of Old Testament at the Theological School of the GK at Kampen, and expounded his view of Genesis 1–3 in *Het Verloren Paradijs: Een woord met het oog op de aangaande Genesis 2 and 3 gerezen vragen* (Kampen: Kok, 1925), 1–48. Jan Ridderbos sympathized with Kuyper and Bavinck on Genesis 1 and vigorously defended Genesis 2 and 3 as historical narrative.
23. Ridderbos, *Is There a Conflict?*, 29–30.
24. Ridderbos, *Is There a Conflict?*, 44.

of origins. His adoption of Noordtzij's hermeneutic had removed constraints of order and time from the creation account, and he further noted that Genesis 2:7 was "surely [an] anthropomorphic expression."[25] On human origins and conclusions in the field of natural science, Ridderbos somewhat ambiguously noted that "Genesis 1:26ff. tells us of the unique position of man and gives us basically the correct insight into the distinction between man and animal." He stated, "These verses teach us, particularly when read in the light of Scripture as a whole, that the human race has one ancestral head."[26]

Ridderbos concluded his work by noting the "profound...complex problems...thrown up by historical anthropology.... Natural science has posited that the human race has existed several hundreds of thousands of years.... This cannot easily be squared with the content of Genesis. It is a matter of great urgency that Calvinists devote more attention to problems of historical anthropology than they have done until now."[27] In a footnote, he commended to his readers the "important work" being done on human origins by the theistic evolutionist Jan Lever.[28]

Lever to Kuitert: Teaching Models and an Errant Scripture

Jan Lever (1922–2010), biology professor at the Free University in Amsterdam, advocated the idea that man was formed through providentially directed evolutionary biological processes.[29] He further posited that Adam was a teaching model rather than a specific historical individual: something he believed the biblical writers were likely unaware of, due to the constraints of their understanding.[30] Lever argued that his position was not unorthodox because, he averred, his views stood in harmony with those of Kuyper, who while opposed to "evolutionism" never indicated that he was opposed to a supernaturally directed evolution of man.[31]

---

25. Ridderbos, *Is There a Conflict?*, 30.
26. Ridderbos, *Is There a Conflict?*, 68–69.
27. Ridderbos, *Is There a Conflict?*, 70–71.
28. Ridderbos, *Is There a Conflict?*, 71.
29. Jan Lever, "De Oorsprong van de Mens," *Geloof en Wetenschap* 53 (1955): 133–67; *Creation and Evolution*, trans. Peter G. Berkhout (Grand Rapids: Grand Rapids International Publishers, 1958), 1–232.
30. Jan Lever, *Waar blijven we?* (Kampen: Kampen-Wageningen, 1969), 19–24, 28, 44, 61; Rob P. W. Visser, "Dutch Calvinists and Darwin," in *Nature and Science in the Abrahamic Religions: 1700-Present*, ed. Jitse M. van der Meer and Scott Mandelbrote (Leiden: Brill, 2008), 1:308–11; J. P. Versteeg, *Adam in the New Testament*, trans. Richard B. Gaffin Jr. (Phillipsburg, N.J.: P&R, 2012), 63–64.
31. Lever, *Creation and Evolution*, 226–31.

Where Kuyper's writings expressed ambiguity, Lever's did not. Echoing the Enlightenment thought and higher criticism of previous generations, he summed up his assessment of the relationship of Scripture to reality: "Genesis deals with that reality which we can investigate scientifically. But Genesis does this in such a way…that we may not consider the language that is used as scientific concepts…as scientifically qualified language…. The Bible usually tells us that something has happened, but not how it happened…. We can never derive from Scripture exact physical, astronomical and biological knowledge, and thus also not exact historical knowledge. The Bible simply is not for that purpose."[32]

Within the theology department at the Free University, the hermeneutical shift was correspondingly moving significantly beyond that of founding figures like Kuyper and Bavinck. Professor G. C. Berkouwer (1903–1996), who took up the teaching post previously held by Valentine Hepp, proved drastically different from Hepp in his theological and hermeneutical convictions. Over time, Berkouwer came to argue that Scripture's writings were constrained to the "level of knowledge" of the biblical writers at any given point in time, claiming as evidence that biblical writers held the sun revolved around the earth.[33] God, Berkhouwer came to conclude, uses "a fallible book to convey a divine message."[34]

In *Man: The Image of God*, Berkouwer paid little attention to the matter of human origins, and limited reference arose in relation to his discussion of the origin of the soul. Assessing the 1950 Roman Catholic encyclical *Humani Generis*, Berkouwer concluded that although "the evolution of man's body from existing organic life would not endanger the doctrine of original sin, polygenism appears to do so."[35] Berkouwer stated that in Protestantism, by contrast, "The dilemma of monogenism or polygenism…played no role in the controversy between creationism and traducianism."[36] Berkouwer's chief other reference to human origins was found in *Holy Scripture*, where he stated "the purpose of Scripture is not to orient us concerning the composition of the cosmos in its created parts, nor to inform us scientifically about the 'composition of man.'"[37] These passing references, particularly when set against the backdrop

---

32. Lever, *Creation and Evolution*, 21.

33. G. C. Berkouwer, *De Heilige Schrift* (Kampen: Kok, 1967), 2:93.

34. G. C. Berkouwer, *The Holy Scripture* (Grand Rapids: Eerdmans, 1975), 145, 147–48, 205–12, 360–61; Henry Krabbendam, "B. B. Warfield vs. G. C. Berkouwer on Scripture," in *Inerrancy*, ed. Norman Geisler (Grand Rapids: Zondervan, 1980), 438.

35. Berkouwer, *Man: The Image of God* (Grand Rapids: Eerdmans, 1962), 282–83.

36. Berkouwer, *Man: The Image of God*, 283.

37. Berkouwer, *Holy Scripture*, 245.

of his general silence on creation and human origins in an era of controversy, presented a marked departure from previous Reformed systematic treatments of the doctrine of man. While Berkouwer had at one point planned to produce a volume on creation, he never executed the project.

Berkouwer's successor at the Free University, H. M. Kuitert, filled the gap, moving another step further away from the literal tradition. Accepting evolutionary theory as wholesale fact, Kuitert held that Scripture was produced by writers who were bound by fallible ancient Near Eastern historical contexts. Thus, Kuitert rejected Adam and Eve as historical persons and also disregarded paradise and the fall into sin as historical realities. He stated,

> It has become impossible in our time, in the light of all sorts of scientific data…to insist on what we called the literal-historical interpretation of the first chapters of Genesis. Whatever these chapters of the Bible intend to tell us…they did not intend to teach us that the world is 6,000 years old, and that in this young and complete world an original, human created couple lived alone in the Garden of Eden. It must be possible for orthodox Protestants to abandon this concept…. Faith does not demand that we…insist that the original human couple of Genesis is a literal and historical pair of people.[38]

Much like Crawford Toy among the Southern Baptists a century earlier, Kuitert eventually moved to deny the divinity of Christ, adopting a Unitarian position.[39]

Defending Adam, Avoiding Genesis

Although the *Gereformeerde Kerk* synod made no attempt to discipline or defrock him, Kuitert's views engendered significant controversy in the wider Dutch Reformed community. They especially created outrage in the more conservative Reformed denominations in the Netherlands, like the *Gereformeerde Kerk (Vrijgemaakt)* and the *Christelijke Gereformeerde Kerken*. J. P. Versteeg (1938–1987), professor at the Theological University of the *Christelijke Gereformeerde Kerken* in Apeldoorn substantially challenged Kuitert on the basis of the New Testament, providing a compelling rebuttal that Adam was necessarily a historical figure.

But Versteeg's response, on behalf of the Theological University, was also striking because it revealed an area of faculty silence. The Apeldoorn faculty

---

38. H. M. Kuitert, *Do You Understand What You Read?*, trans. Lewis B. Smedes (Grand Rapids: Eerdmans, 1970), 101.

39. H. M. Kuitert, *Jesus: The Legacy of Christianity*, trans. John Bowden (London: SCM, 1999), 1–285.

produced no exegetical reference to or discussion of Genesis 1 and 2 in relation to the historicity of Adam and the nature of his origin in response to Kuitert.[40] Perhaps even more remarkable was what appeared to be a tacit allowance for an evolutionary origin for a historical Adam: "If an evolutionary view leaves no place for Adam as an historical person and has a place for Adam only as a teaching model, that has direct consequences so far as its view of Christ is concerned.... As the first historical man and head of humanity, Adam is not mentioned merely in passing in the New Testament."[41] No discussion was offered as to whether it was problematic to believe in a model including a historical Adam of evolutionary origins.

The Apeldoorn faculty's response appeared to reflect a hesitancy to pursue a detailed engagement with the Genesis text—indicative of a significant transition within the *Christelijke Gereformeerde Kerken* from previous generations. Where Versteeg, helpfully and somewhat apologetically, focused solely on a New Testament defense of the historical Adam, the context in which he did so was illuminating. Versteeg's colleague, Old Testament professor B. J. Oosterhoff (1915–1996), held that the *Gereformeerde Kerk* Synod of Assen in the Geelkerken case was correct in avoiding issues of the interpretation of Genesis 1 but had erred in mandating a literal reading of Genesis 2 and 3. Oosterhoff held that Genesis 2 and 3 were written in "the form of symbolic-prophetic language," though they were about historical facts.[42] He concluded that Genesis 2:7 "did not precisely state how God formed man...[and as such] science may seek to learn how this occurred."[43] While Oosterhoff's views were protested within the denomination, no actions were taken against the professor. This was the context in which Kuitert's views received only a New Testament critique.

Appreciation, But Not Commitment

Others within the *Christelijke Gereformeerde Kerken*, including J. van Genderen and W. H. Velema, had also moved beyond their denominational predecessors and more conservative precursors in the broader Reformed community, such

---

40. Versteeg noted in his preface that the essay was a New Testament contribution to the seventy-fifth-anniversary anthology for the Theological University of Apeldoorn, and that "for this reason attention has been limited to the data of the New Testament." Versteeg, *Adam in the New Testament*, vii.

41. Versteeg, *Adam in the New Testament*, 67.

42. B. J. Oosterhoff, *Hoe lezen wij Genesis 2 en 3? Een hermeneutische studie* (Kampen: Kok, 1972), 101–7, 219–29, 238–40.

43. Oosterhoff, *Hoe lezen wij Genesis 2 en 3?*, 221.

as Bavinck and Hepp. On one hand, van Genderen and Velema argued that a "created evolution of things could never represent a stumbling block to those who believe in Scripture," stating "we should not make an issue" over "varying opinions" on the nature of the days.[44] On the other hand, they were critical of gap or restitution theory as "purely speculative" and framework theory "as only forming a framework invented by the author." Ridderbos himself realized that "plenty of problems remain."[45] Velema and van Genderen concluded,

> The theory that appeals most to those who start out from the reliability of the Bible is *creationism*, for it recognizes God as Creator of heaven and earth and strives to work scientifically with the *creation model*. Its key ingredients are:
> 1. That the earth is relatively young, perhaps no older than ten thousand to fifteen thousand years, and at any rate not millions or billions of years.
> 2. That geological strata were formed under catastrophic conditions.
> 3. That the main forms of life emerged independently of each other and at approximately the same time.[46]

Consistent with their approach of sympathy for the literal Genesis tradition while avoiding exclusive commitment to it, van Genderen and Velema described the creation of man as "the pinnacle of what God accomplishes in the six days of creation," with Adam being "formed from the dust of the earth." At the same time, they skirted the issue of possible evolutionary origins for Adam.[47] The faculty of the *Christelijke Gereformeerde* seminary was open to and largely presenting sympathy for a six-day literal understanding of Genesis and a special, sixth-day creation of Adam and Eve. Along with the *Gereformeerde Kerk (Vrijgemaakt)* and the *Gereformeerde Gemeenten*, the *Christelijke Gereformeerde* maintained a strong, influential commitment to the literal tradition.

The CRC and Calvin College: Leaving the Literal Tradition, Losing Adam

For the Christian Reformed Church (CRC) in North America, shifts in commitment were evident at both Calvin Theological Seminary and Calvin College. The generation of seminary faculty who exemplified Berkhof's commitments

---

44. J. van Genderen and W. H. Velema, *Concise Reformed Dogmatics*, trans. G. Bilkes and E. M. van der Maas (Phillipsburg, N.J.: P&R, 2008), 274.

45. Van Genderen and Velema, *Dogmatics*, 270.

46. Van Genderen and Velema note, "the term 'creationism' is variously employed…we follow the definition used by W. J. Ouweneel and many other creationists, and not the interpretation given to it by J. Lever." Van Genderen and Velema, *Dogmatics*, 275.

47. Van Genderen and Velema, *Dogmatics*, 246–76.

had largely passed from the scene by the late 1950s. The denomination and its boards moved to allow a greater latitude on approaches to Genesis—a shift most plainly evident at Calvin College during subsequent decades. Where his father, Westminster Theological Seminary professor E. J. Young, had adopted a hermeneutical approach allowing for the initial days as figurative, Calvin College geology professor Davis Young rejected a literal view of the creation days and became a vigorous proponent of both an old earth and an evolutionary view of human origins.

Initially adopting a day-age approach to the text, he later abandoned this view as inherently flawed. Young came to argue that the mainstream conclusions of old-earth geology, evolutionary theory, and modern interpretations of early human history failed to cohere not only with a literal reading of Genesis 1, but also with a literal reading of Genesis 2–4:

> It would seem that trying to preserve the traditional confessional idea of the biological descent of the entire human race from Adam and Eve forces us to adopt positions which require the abandonment of aspects of literal historicity of the early chapters of Genesis. Either we need to interpret the text so that Adam is not the father of Cain or we need to explain why the culture of Genesis 4 really does not include the elements therein mentioned.... Is Genesis 2–4 perhaps adapting ancient Near Eastern conceptions about the beginnings of humanity and culture in order to make theological points about the relationship of God and humans and about the historical event of the fall without necessarily endorsing all the details? This avenue needs to be examined more thoroughly by evangelicals. I suspect that it will prove to be fruitful.[48]

Davis Young's colleague at Calvin College, Howard Van Till, also argued for an alternative to the literal tradition on early Genesis in his work *The Fourth Day*.[49] Drawing partly on the work of Meredith Kline and using G. C. Berkouwer's formulation of the doctrine of Scripture, Van Till posited that it was simply not the intention of early Genesis to speak to matters of scientific reality; thus, evolutionary theory posed no problems of incompatibility with

---

48. Davis Young, "The Antiquity and the Unity of the Human Race Revisited," *Christian Scholar's Review* 24, no. 4 (May 1995): 380–96. More recently, Young has argued that Calvin would have approved of his approach in *John Calvin and the Natural World* (Lanham, Md.: University Press of America, 2007), 1–260; and critiqued the work of geologists holding to young earth and universal flood models in his work with Ralph Stearley, *The Bible, Rocks, and Time: Geological Evidence for the Age of the Earth* (Downers Grove, Ill.: IVP Academic, 2008), 1–510.

49. Howard Van Till, *The Fourth Day* (Grand Rapids: Eerdmans, 1987), 1–286.

Christianity.[50] Whereas the CRC synod criticized Van Till's hermeneutic and protested Young's position, the board of Calvin College allowed both men to continue teaching, and the synod took no further action.[51] Van Till, Young, and others continued a steady stream of publication arguing against a literal Genesis interpretation and proposing a synthesis of ancient Near Eastern cosmological interpretation and literary approaches, so that "Genesis 1:1–2:3 presents a storied rather than a historiographical account of creation."[52]

Within two decades, Davis Young's call for "fruitful" alternatives in reading Genesis would be amplified in the pages of *The Banner*, with CRC minister Edwin Walhout arguing that "we need to take seriously in our theology the theory of evolution" in revisiting not only Genesis 1 and the doctrine of creation, but also the fall, original sin, salvation, and God's purpose in history as "areas [in which] we might need to reconsider our traditional theological understanding."[53] While Walhout's call resulted in some anemic and ineffective protest within the CRC, in reality it simply echoed what had already been put in print by the CRC denominational publishing house in prior years.

The book *Origins: Christian Perspectives on Creation, Evolution, and Intelligent Design*, by Calvin College professors Loren and Deborah Haarsma, argued that evolutionary origins for Adam and Eve were as much if not more compatible with scriptural theology than the literal tradition of a special, immediate creation. In surveying a number of possibilities on human origins in relation to the testimony of Scripture, the Haarsmas argued that viewing Adam and Eve as "recent representatives" of all humanity, including

---

50. Van Till, 6–10, 78ff. In 2006, Russell Moore reported that Van Till had abandoned Christianity for "freethought" or agnostic secular humanism, sharing his "journey" with the Freethought Association of Western Michigan. Russell Moore, "A Theistic Evolutionist Turns Off the Light," http://www.russellmoore.com/2006/07/26/a-theistic-evolutionist-turns-off-the-light/.

51. This reality, argues historian Robert Swierenga, was a key ingredient precipitating the departure of many congregations from the Christian Reformed Church, leading to the formation of the United Reformed Church. Robert P. Swierenga, "Burn the Wooden Shoes: Modernity and Division in the Christian Reformed Church in North America" (paper presented at University of Stellenbosch Conference, South Africa, International Society for the Study of Reformed Communities, June 2000), http://www.swierenga.com/Africa_pap.html.

52. Howard Van Till, Robert E. Snow, John H. Stek, and Davis A. Young, *Portraits of Creation: Biblical and Scientific Perspectives on the World's Formation* (Grand Rapids: Eerdmans, 1990), 238.

53. Walhout concluded his article referring to a 1991 Synod Committee on Creation and Science report regarding human origins by stating, "Neither we nor the church is presently in a position to state authoritatively that Scripture speaks definitively on this issue." Edwin Walhout, "Tomorrow's Theology," *The Banner* (May 3, 2013), http://www.thebanner.org/features/2013/05/tomorrow-s-theology.

contemporaries, was a legitimate possibility; in doing so, they drew on an interpretation of Romans 5 rooted in that of Isaac La Peyrère.[54] The emphasis was that even if one was "not satisfied with any of these scenarios," as the Haarsmas professed of themselves, they all fell within the latitude of Christian freedom: "you can make your own decision."[55] They concluded,

> To some Christians these are vital questions, while to others they are secondary. Some argue that a clear historical first sin, committed by Adam and Eve as our ancestors, is essential to our understanding of Christian theology. Others agree with Lutheran theologian George Murphy: "The Christian claim is that a savior is needed because all people are sinners. It is that simple. *Why* all people are sinners is an important question, but an answer to it is not required in order to recognize the need for salvation. None of the gospels uses the story in Genesis 3 to speak of Christ's significance. In Romans, Paul develops an indictment of the human race as sinful and then presents Christ as God's solution to this problem in chapters 1–3 before mentioning Adam's sin in chapter 5."[56]

Others within Calvin College, such as religion professor Daniel Harlow, argued similarly.[57] The marked trajectory of hermeneutical shift on early Genesis, with its attendant implications for human origins and wider theology within the Christian Reformed Church, was concurrent with a wider theological deterioration in the denomination.

Continuities of the Literal Tradition among the Dutch Reformed

Those who had departed the Christian Reformed Church during the 1990s to form the United Reformed Churches represented a substantially stronger commitment to the literal tradition on Genesis and human origins—albeit more so in Canada and the Midwest than in places like California. The differences were plainly reflected in the commitments of Mid-America Reformed Seminary, which stated, "we hold firmly to the special creation work of God,

---

54. Deborah B. Haarsma and Loren D. Haarsma, *Origins: Christian Perspectives on Creation, Evolution, and Intelligent Design* (Grand Rapids: Faith Alive Christian Resources, 2011), 256–61.

55. Haarsma and Haarsma, *Origins*, 270.

56. Haarsma and Haarsma, *Origins*, 269.

57. Daniel Harlow, "After Adam: Reading Genesis in an Age of Evolutionary Science," *Perspectives on Science and Christian Faith* 62, no. 3 (September 2010): 179–95.

performed in the space of six consecutive, real days" further noting this as a "divine work of non-evolutionary creation."[58]

In contrast, Westminster Seminary California, the other key seminary of influence in the United Reformed Churches, was strongly influenced by criticism of the literal tradition in the teaching of Old Testament professors Meredith Kline and Mark Futato. Along with Michael Horton, R. Scott Clark, and Robert Godfrey, Kline and Futato were committed to nonliteral hermeneutical approaches to Genesis 1 and parts of Genesis 2.[59]

While the United Reformed Churches contained a substantial stream committed to the literal tradition, a more uniform commitment to the literal tradition was found in other Dutch Reformed denominations and their seminaries. The Canadian and American Reformed Churches and the Canadian Reformed Theological Seminary in Hamilton, Canada; the Protestant Reformed Churches and Seminary; as well as the Heritage Reformed Churches and Free Reformed Churches, with their jointly governed Puritan Reformed Theological Seminary in Grand Rapids, Michigan, all continued to support the literal tradition on Genesis and human origins.

The Presbyterians: John Murray, J. G. Vos, and a Literal Genesis

European transitions in Genesis hermeneutic were influential beyond Dutch Reformed circles in North America. At Westminster Theological Seminary in Philadelphia, a school with Dutch Reformed influences and a significant constituency from the Orthodox Presbyterian Church (OPC) and Presbyterian Church in America (PCA), discussion on creation rose to a new prominence in the late 1950s. It was presaged when John Murray's (1898–1978) presented an argument challenging B. B. Warfield's approach to origins.

Warfield had interpreted Calvin on creation in a way that potentially allowed for harmonization with a theistic approach to evolutionary theory. Murray's assessment of Reformation views and particularly Calvin's understanding of "immediate and mediate creation," presented evidence and analysis to the contrary.[60] Murray stated that to create "is not only to make something

---

58. "What the Faculty of Mid-America Reformed Seminary Teaches Regarding the Days of Creation," Adopted by the Board of Trustees, October 19–20, 2000, http://www.midamerica .edu/about/docstandards.htm.

59. The teaching of these faculty members at Westminster Seminary California is discussed in greater detail later in this chapter.

60. John Murray, "Calvin's Doctrine of Creation," *Westminster Theological Journal* 17, no. 1 (November 1954): 21–43.

out of nothing but also to produce something out of unapt material beyond the powers of nature." He approvingly cited the Leiden Synopsis of 1625, stating:

> The omnipotence of…God [is] demonstrated in the things created by him in a twofold manner: either immediately, insofar as he produced the nature of certain things immediately out of nothing, such as the earth, the water, the angels, and the souls of our first parents; or mediately, insofar as he formed some things out of unformed preexisting material, such as the plants of the earth, the body of Adam, and the brute beasts. Hence we define the creation of the world as the external action of God omnipotent, incommunicable to creatures, by which of himself and his most free will, moved by no other, he created the heaven and earth out of nothing at the beginning of time, and fashioned certain things which he willed to form out of that primary material, by his arrangement, in the space of six days, in order that he might make known…especially to rational beings, the glory of his great wisdom, power and goodness, and invite them to the celebration of his name.[61]

Murray noted that in much post-Reformation thought, "the formation of man's body is called creation not because origination of essence in any way entered into the action of God in this case but only because the immediate and omnipotent power of God was alone adequate to form a human body out of so unfit and unapt an entity as dust of the ground."[62] Coming to the conclusion that Calvin's views were not compatible with Warfield's allowance for an evolutionary interpretation of "mediate creation," Murray concluded that the term "mediate" in relation to creation was unhelpful, since in modern context, the use of "mediate" tended toward a misapplication to the agency of God, rather than indicating the supernatural use of materials in themselves "unfit and unapt" to what God created from them. In concurrence with the publication of this position in a journal article, Murray argued in his essay on "The Origin of Man," that the Genesis text persuasively negated on exegetical grounds the possibility that Adam was alive prior to the moment of becoming "a living soul"—thus negating the possibility that man could in any respect be "regarded as animate by evolutionary process."[63]

Even more explicit than Murray in his commitment to the literal tradition on Genesis and human origins was J. G. Vos (1903–1983), son of Geerhardus

---

61. Murray, "Calvin's Doctrine of Creation," 22–23.

62. Murray, "Calvin's Doctrine of Creation," 25.

63. John Murray, "The Origin of Man," in *Collected Writings of John Murray* (Carlisle, Penn.: Banner of Truth, 1977), 2:3–13. See also John Murray, *The Epistle to the Romans* (Grand Rapids: Eerdmans, 1968), 178–81.

Vos and graduate of Princeton University, Princeton Theological Seminary, and Westminster Theological Seminary. J. G. Vos had served as a missionary in China until he was expelled by the invading Japanese in 1942. From 1954 to 1975 he served as professor of Bible and theology at Geneva College in Beaver Falls, Pennsylvania. Following in his father's footsteps, Vos held that "Genesis gives the origin of the universe, the origin of life, the origin of the human race…the origin of the chosen covenant people through whom Christ should come into the world to redeem men to God…the origin of marriage and the family, the origin of the Sabbath."[64] Also like his father, Vos held:

> The most natural interpretation [of the days] is that they are literal days…. The repeatedly used expression "and there was evening and there was morning" strongly favors the view that the days were literal 24-hour days…. According to the view that the days were long periods of time, the terms "morning" and "evening" are merely figures of speech for "end of a period" and "beginning of a period," but such usage would be contrary to the simplicity of language used in the early chapters of Genesis…. Another argument consists in the consideration that the fifth, sixth, and seventh days must have been ordinary days of 24 hours each because they were determined by the sun, just as days are today. If these last three days were ordinary days, then the presumption is that the previous four days were also days of 24 hours each. Although neither view is without its difficulties, it would seem that on the whole the literal interpretation is to be preferred.[65]

Vos argued that the "language used in Genesis 1," including the temporal boundaries set by ordinary days, "requires the acceptance of creation and the rejection of evolution."[66] It was this hermeneutical and exegetical context that framed his understanding of the creation of man:

> In [chapter 2] verse 7 we have a definite account of the creation of man…. Man's body was formed by God out of "the dust of the ground," that is, the substances existing in the soil or in nature. Thus, in the creation of man's body, God used material already in existence. This does not imply, however, that man is descended from animals that existed before him…. Some evolutionists have held that only man's body was developed by evolution from a brute ancestry, while his soul was directly created by God. Some Roman Catholic scholars have favored this view.

---

64. J. G. Vos, *Genesis* (Pittsburgh: Crown & Covenant, 2006), 6.
65. Vos, *Genesis*, 21–23.
66. Vos, *Genesis*, 26.

We believe, on the contrary, that man's body was specially created by God and not derived from a brute ancestry. The expression "the dust of the ground" cannot mean living animals nourished by plants that originally came out of the ground. The record does not say that any of the other creatures were formed of "the dust of the ground"; rather, it uses such language as, "Let the waters bring forth…" (1:20), and "Let the earth bring forth…" (1:24). But of man it says, "The Lord God formed man out of the dust of the ground." Genesis 3:19 also shows that "the dust of the ground" does not mean living animals; there, God tells Adam "thou [shalt] return unto the ground; for out of it wast thou taken; for dust thou art, and unto dust shalt thou return." If "the dust of the ground" in 2:7 means living animals from which man was descended, then the terms "dust" and "ground" in 3:19 must imply that Adam would return to a former animal state…. Another Scripture text…is I Corinthians 15:39…[which] implies that the flesh of man is different from that of the beasts…. We conclude, then, that "the dust of the ground" in 2:7 means inorganic material substance that already existed and was used by God to form the physical body of man.[67]

Vos's hermeneutic approach to Genesis 1 and 2 was nuanced in relation to some of the aspects of evolutionary theory with relevance to human origins. Rejecting the popular conception of evolutionary models proposing "crossing the boundary lines between species," Vos qualified this, stating that the "'kinds' spoken of in Genesis are the true natural species…. When we say that God created definite kinds of plants and animals, we do not mean that everything called a species by modern scientists was specially created by God…. Each kind created by God may have contained within itself the power to produce many varieties, some of which may be classified as 'species' by scientists. The words 'after its kind' imply that there is a God-ordained barrier between true natural species."[68]

Vos argued that evolution, defined as a natural process crossing the boundaries of kinds, even under divine superintendence, "means rejecting or diluting the supernatural element in the Bible." He warned that "those who reduce the supernatural element in Genesis tend to do the same all along the line…. The tendency is to seek consistency by giving up more and more of the supernatural."[69]

---

67. Vos, *Genesis*, 42–43.
68. Vos, *Genesis*, 25.
69. Vos, *Genesis*, 26.

Like Murray, Vos held that the statement, God "breathed into his nostrils the breath of life; and man became a living soul," described "the creation of the spiritual part of man…out of nothing" and that "it was the creation of the spirit or soul that made man alive: He 'became a living soul,' that is, a living being."[70] Vos explains, "The Hebrew words for 'a living soul' in 2:7 are identical to the words translated 'living creature' in 1:24. But of man alone is it said that God 'breathed into his nostrils the breath of life.' Clearly, the principle of life that man received from God was different from that received by the animals. From other parts of the Bible we know that man has a soul that can never die. Compare Ecclesiastes 3:21: 'Who knoweth the spirit of man that goeth upward, and the spirit of the beast that goeth downward to the earth?'"[71]

However, for Vos it was not merely the soul that reflected the image of God in man:

> As God is a pure Spirit, having no body or form, a physical resemblance to God cannot be meant [by the "image" and "likeness" of God]. Yet there is a sense in which man resembles God. Alone of all the creatures, man was created in the image of God…. Because he possesses the image of God, man is like God and different from the animals.
>
> Orthodox theology holds that the image of God consists of knowledge, righteousness, and holiness. Man resembles God, then, in the possession of a rational nature and in the possession of a moral nature. [He]…can think and reason…is capable of distinguishing between right and wrong…[and] possesses personality and character. When man was created by God…he was then capable of perfectly reflecting the glory of God…. As created, man was to have dominion over all other creatures in this world. This also marks man as the bearer of the image of God. In a limited and subordinate sense man was to be ruler of the world. He was to be God's representative in ruling the creatures.[72]

Vos held that human origins, in the context of supernatural creation, the act of God's special creation of man, and man's placement in the garden of Eden, all very good, presented a stark contrast to much contemporary thought. He noted,

> It is a common idea at the present day that the original state of mankind was a state of savagery, from which human civilization has slowly developed. This idea, however, is quite contrary to the account of early mankind given in the Bible. According to the biblical record, mankind originated in a state of simple civilization and of moral uprightness. From

---

70. Vos, *Genesis*, 43.
71. Vos, *Genesis*, 43–44.
72. Vos, *Genesis* 29.

this original condition, the great majority of the human race degenerated to the condition of crime, violence, and lawlessness that existed just before the Flood.... The savage and primitive peoples that have existed in ancient and modern times are to be explained as products of retrogression...they...have deteriorated from the original civilization and moral uprightness of mankind. The head-hunters of Borneo are not really "primitive people"; they are really people far advanced in their degeneration. Evolutionists take for granted that man originally was a savage and has gradually developed into a gentleman; the truth is that man originally was a gentleman, and rapidly degenerated into a savage in many parts of the world.[73]

Meredith Kline: "Because It Had Not Rained"

During the late 1950s at Westminster Theological Seminary, in spite of the literal tradition tenor of John Murray's 1954 argument in the *Westminster Theological Journal* and the teaching of alumnus J. G. Vos at Geneva College, Old Testament professor Meredith Kline (1922–2007) followed the English language publication of N. H. Ridderbos's book with the article, "Because It Had Not Rained" in the *Westminster Theological Journal*.[74] In his article, Kline presented the literary hypothesis as a new hermeneutical alternative for the English-speaking world, noting that while "traditional interpretations [of Genesis] continue to be dominant in orthodox circles, there also continues to be debate, and its flames have recently been vigorously fanned by the bellows of dissenters."[75]

Kline aimed to vindicate his suggestion for an alternative hermeneutic by challenging the literal Genesis tradition. He argued that "the traditionalist interpreter...will be compelled at one point or another to assume that God in his providential preservation of the world during the 'six days' did not operate through secondary means in the way which men now daily observe and analyze as natural law."[76] What Kline believed was necessary to the traditional view, he also believed was contradicted by Genesis 2:5. He argued that the passage's reference to the lack of the ordinary providence of rain and consequent provision of a "mist to water the ground" (2:6), along with what he interpreted as a reference in 2:5 to the original creation of vegetation, created a profound

---

73. Vos, *Genesis*, 44–45.
74. Meredith Kline, "Because It Had Not Rained," *Westminster Theological Journal* 20, no. 2 (May 1958): 146–57.
75. Kline, "Because It Had Not Rained," 146.
76. Kline, "Because It Had Not Rained," 148.

problem for the literal view. Kline further stated that there could not have been light prior to the creation of luminaries on the fourth day. Together, he said, these stood as "a decisive word" against a literal interpretation of Genesis 1.[77]

Kline's case that Genesis 2:5 entailed a rejection of the literal Genesis tradition on Genesis 1 and 2 was built on three key assumptions. The first was that the reference in Genesis 2:5 to the nonexistence of "shrubs" and produce-bearing vegetation that required cultivation by and for man, implied an all-encompassing reference to global vegetation, and thus to the need for the original act of creation of vegetation.[78] Kline's argument operated on a second assumption: that the literal hermeneutical tradition held that God's creation of vegetation on the third day must have covered the entirety of the global land surface and included the existence of all varieties of plant life in every geographical location.[79] His third assumption was that God's supernatural separation of dry land from the waters (on the second day, for those who held to the literal tradition) had not actually created any areas of truly dry land within the span of an ordinary day.[80] Kline argued that at least some of the process of forming dry land must have taken place according to ordinary providence, hence involving a longer period of time than an ordinary day.[81] Despite his claim that this allowed for a delineation between supernatural acts and ordinary providence, Kline's insistence on a longer period failed to further clarify the delineation between what was a supernatural act and what was ordinary providence in the formation of dry land.

With his exegetical discourse resting on these assumptions, Kline presented what he felt was the Genesis 2:5–6 conundrum for a literal interpretation. He did so with little reference to the majority stream's literal hermeneutical tradition, which held that the immediate narrative context of Genesis 2:5 indicated this was a sixth-day transformation of a somewhat empty and dry geographical region into a garden planted (Gen. 2:8) with specific kinds of vegetation for man.[82] He also failed to recognize the cogent ground in the text for truly dry land regions prior to the sixth day.

---

77. Kline, "Because It Had Not Rained," 148.

78. Kline, "Because It Had Not Rained," 150, 153.

79. Kline, "Because It Had Not Rained," 149.

80. Kline, "Because It Had Not Rained," 150–52.

81. The Mosaic account of the Red Sea crossing by the Israelites uses the same Hebrew term for dry land as is used in Genesis 1. This should provide a hermeneutical parallel, and, by Kline's standard, perhaps raise the question of the duration of the night of Exodus 14:21 in which the path through the sea was made dry.

82. A minority stream of the literal hermeneutical tradition has argued that Genesis 2:5 and following indicate that particular kinds of vegetation were created for the first time on the

E. J. Young: Sequential Figurative Days and a Literal Adam

At the same time that Kline was beginning to propound the literary framework approach, another Westminster Theological Seminary professor, E. J. Young (1907–1968), began to advocate the approach of Kuyper, Aalders, and Bavinck, arguing that the first three days of creation were likely not ordinary days, though the latter three were. Engaging with Noordtzij and Ridderbos, Young argued in direct contrast to Kline that the text of Genesis 1 necessitated a chronological sequence, regardless of the length of the first days.[83]

Young also engaged with ancient Near Eastern literature, arguing that the documents and references of ancient Babylonia were "the garbled version of the truth that finally trickled down to the Babylonians" through the line of Cain.[84] This stood in contrast to what had been passed down "among the Sethites [where] the truth…that God spoke to Adam…would have been handed down from generation to generation."[85] Young concluded,

> It may be that Moses had access to written documents which were at his disposal. It may also be that he was acquainted with oral tradition. If, however, we approach this question Scripturally we will be compelled to the conclusion that the author of Genesis one was a holy man who was

---

sixth day, rather than the verse indicating that God "planted a garden" (Gen. 2:8) using already existing forms of vegetation, which then also bear fruit. James B. Jordan further modifies this view that this verse refers to forms of vegetation created after the fall in *Creation in Six Days: A Defense of the Traditional Reading of Genesis One* (Moscow, Idaho: Canon, 1999), 14, 52–55. Another possibility is described by R. Kent Hughes, who derives his view from the Jewish commentator Cassuto: "The noes in these verses tell us why the earth was untended: There was 'no bush'—'no small plant'—no 'rain'—and 'no man to work the ground.' Significantly, day three of creation, which described the earth's production of vegetation, did not include the Hebrew words for 'bush' and 'small plant.' This is because, as Cassuto explains, 'these species did not exist, or were not found in the form known to us, until after Adam's transgression, and it was in consequence of his fall that they came into the world or received their present form.' 'The plants of the field' were those that would grow under Adam's cultivation. And the bushes? Cassuto equates them with weeds." R. Kent Hughes, *Genesis: Beginning & Blessing* (Wheaton, Ill.: Crossway, 2004), 51; Umberto Cassuto, *A Commentary on the Book of Genesis* (Jerusalem: Magnes Press, 1989), 7. Victor P. Hamilton makes a similar case to that of Hughes and Cassuto in *The New International Commentary on the Old Testament—The Book of Genesis: Chapters 1–17* (Grand Rapids: Eerdmans, 1991), 153–54.

83. E. J. Young, "The Days of Genesis—I," *Westminster Theological Journal* 25, no. 1 (November 1962): 1–34; "The Days of Genesis—II," *Westminster Theological Journal* 25, no. 2 (May 1963): 143–71. See also Young's earlier article, "The Interpretation of Genesis 1:2," *Westminster Theological Journal* 23 (November 1960–May 1961): 151–78. See also E. J. Young, *Studies in Genesis One* (Grand Rapids: Baker, 1973), 1–105; and *In the Beginning* (Carlisle, Penn.: Banner of Truth, 1976), 5–79.

84. Young, "The Days of Genesis—II," 154.

85. Young, "The Interpretation of Genesis 1:2," 162–63.

borne by the Holy Spirit. That is to say, God, in his providence, prepared by training and education the particular man whom he desired to write the first chapter of the Bible, and when that man set to the work of writing he was superintended by the Spirit of God with the result that what he wrote was what the Spirit of God intended him to write…. The resultant writing, therefore, was Scripture, trustworthy Scripture, indeed, infallible Scripture.[86]

Young, holding to a literal interpretation of the latter creation days, also argued that it was not "possible to hold to the Bible and to theistic evolution at the same time…. If you accept the Bible you cannot accept the evolution of the body of the woman. The best you can do is to hold that the body of the first man evolved from something lower than man, and, personally, I do not think that you can even do that. It is a stretching of things in order to meet up with the claims of science."[87] However, Kline rejected Young's exegetical counterarguments on the chronological sequence of the creation days and his approach to ancient Near Eastern contexts, and continued to popularize in his teaching what he had initially presented in his 1958 article.

Kline's Synthesis

In 1970, Kline's commentary on Genesis was published, in which he presented a brief exposition of the creation narrative following the scheme of Noordtzij and Ridderbos.[88] In 1996, he published an expanded explanation in "Space and Time in the Genesis Cosmogony," presenting the literary framework approach in greater detail, again according to Noordtzij's model, though once again without reference to him.[89]

Kline argued that the creation week was a literary structure, and like Noordtzij, claimed that there was a poetic parallelism between the first three figurative days and the second three figurative days.[90] Drawing on ancient Near Eastern studies, he argued for a "two register cosmogony" as both a prevailing scriptural pattern and a hermeneutical key to the realization that references to

---

86. Young, "The Interpretation of Genesis 1:2," 163.

87. Young, *In the Beginning*, 52–53.

88. Meredith Kline, "Genesis," in *The New Bible Commentary*, 3rd rev. ed., ed. Donald Guthrie (Downers Grove, Ill.: InterVarsity, 1970), 81–84.

89. Meredith Kline, "Space and Time in the Genesis Cosmogony," *Perspectives on Science and the Christian Faith* 48, no. 1 (March 1996): 2–15.

90. Cf. Arie Noordtzij, *Gods Woord en Der Eeuwen Getuigenis: Het Oude Testament in Het Licht der Oostersche Opgravingen* (Kampen: J. H. Kok, 1924), 79–80; Ridderbos, *Is There a Conflict?*, 11; Kline, "Space and Time in the Genesis Cosmogony," 2–15.

space and time in Genesis 1 regarding the "lower register" of the visible world, "do not mark the passage of time" but are poetically analogical or figurative in nature.[91] This coincided with his earlier suggestion that in terms of chronology both "day one" and "day four" were at the beginning.[92]

While far more complex, Kline's formulation of the literary framework both borrowed aspects of ancient Near Eastern cosmological approaches and turned them on their head. The result was a hermeneutical approach that conceived of early Genesis as highly sophisticated, complex, and figurative literature, rather than the primitive, anthropomorphic conception of the creation of the universe espoused in the ancient Near Eastern cosmological approach. At the same time, the literary framework went beyond some of the forms of the ancient Near Eastern cosmological approach in removing any meaningful correspondence to chronology.

Where the ancient Near Eastern cosmological approach allowed for but did not require removing a correspondence between time and chronological order from the creation account, Kline's statement of the literary framework removed both time and chronological order from the Genesis 1–2 creation narrative. Also, apart from his claim to figurative days and his use of ancient Near Eastern cues, other aspects of Kline's structural and stylistic reflections in reality did not depart from the literal tradition, but had long been noted within it. From the patristic era through the dominantly literal tradition in the Reformation and post-Reformation eras, proponents of the literal tradition, like Luther, had noted arguments for a poetic or exalted prose beauty in the language and structure of Genesis 1. They, however, had done so without negating the literal interpretation of the chronology of the text.

A Framework of Options: The Literal Adam, or Not

Kline and others celebrated the fact that the literary framework hermeneutic did "not allow [the] binding [of] the conscience of the Church to one particular view of the age of the universe" as it removed "false expectations" from the text. They were somewhat more muted on their hermeneutic's consequent removal of other expectations from the text.[93] In a footnote, Kline quietly reflected on the breadth of the implications of his hermeneutical shift, stating, "In this article I have advocated an interpretation of biblical cosmogony

---

91. Kline, "Space and Time in the Genesis Cosmogony," 2–15.

92. Kline, "Genesis," 82–83.

93. Lee Irons and Meredith Kline, "The Framework View" in *The G3N3SIS Debate* (Mission Viejo, Calif.: Cruxpress, 2001), 217–18.

according to which Scripture is open to the current scientific view of a very old universe and, in that respect, does not discountenance the theory of the evolutionary origin of man."[94]

By removing the time and chronological order of six ordinary days, the literary framework hypothesis did not require a special, temporally immediate creation of Adam and Eve. And, like the ancient Near Eastern cosmological approach, it provided a plausible rationale on the ground of its hermeneutic to exegete Genesis 2:7 as anthropomorphic to the extent of allowing evolutionary biological origins for Adam. Despite this, Kline did not personally adopt an evolutionary model of human origins.

However, where some of his disciples entirely rejected evolutionary theory, others influenced by Kline's thought, such as Michael Horton and Bruce Waltke, demonstrated a marked openness to evolutionary ancestry for Adam.[95] From his first article in 1954 where he indicated his personal belief that God produced "Adam's body out of existent dust," through his 1996 article where he negated the possibility of a "pre-human" life of Adam, Kline remained committed to a special creation of Adam and Eve apart from any evolutionary process.[96]

In defending his rejection of evolutionary origins for Adam, Kline drew on an exegetical argument of the literal tradition, as propounded by John Murray: "I…deem commitment to the authority of scriptural teaching to involve the acceptance of Adam as an historical individual, the covenantal head and ancestral fount of the rest of mankind, and the recognition that it was the one and same divine act that constituted him the first man, Adam the son of God (Luke 3:38), that also imparted to him life (Gen. 2:7)."[97]

While Kline held to this view, he never provided a textual and contextual exegetical rationale for this reading of Genesis 2:7 in relation to his literary framework; possibly because he believed such a rationale could no longer be constructed from Genesis 1 and 2. Michael Horton, Kline's colleague in later years at Westminster Seminary California, viewed Genesis 2:7 differently, arguing that an "instantaneous creation of Adam and Eve is not explicitly required by the text or its subsequent interpretation."[98]

The growing promotion of alternative hermeneutical approaches within institutions and publications serving the milieu of more conservative

---

94. Kline, "Space and Time in the Genesis Cosmogony," 15.

95. Michael Horton, *Lord and Servant: A Covenant Christology* (Louisville: Westminster John Knox, 2005), 118–19.

96. Kline, "Because It Had Not Rained," 146.

97. Kline, "Space and Time in the Genesis Cosmogony," 15.

98. Horton, *Lord and Servant*, 119.

Presbyterian denominations led to increasing concern, most pervasively among confessional Presbyterians in the southern United States who were committed to the literal tradition. The latter viewed the multiplying hermeneutical approaches as an incipient threat to both scriptural doctrine and the doctrine of Scripture; others viewed them as a beneficial rapprochement in the church's witness in Western culture. Through the 1990s, tensions between and within denominations increased.

The Orthodox Presbyterian Church and the Gray Case

Within the Orthodox Presbyterian Church (OPC), Calvin College biology professor Terry Gray, a ruling elder in a local OPC congregation, proposed that both the increasingly accepted hermeneutical alternatives to the literal tradition and what he viewed as the realities of the record of natural history should allow for the possibility that Adam and Eve were created through a process involving primate ancestors.[99] Disagreeing with John Murray's literal reading of Genesis 2:7, Gray argued that the "dust of the ground" was "a nontechnical term" that simply referred to "the physical-chemical constituency of the human body" and that the verse did not address the process by which God formed man.[100]

Gray's views were mainstream in his context at Calvin; colleagues including Davis Young and Howard Van Till had argued similarly, and their views stood within the contemporary latitude of the Christian Reformed Church. When initial complaints were brought against Gray, his OPC session held that the charges were unwarranted, claiming that Gray's position stood in harmony with the Westminster Confession of Faith and Catechisms.[101] Charges against Gray were then brought to the Presbytery, which ruled against Gray, and the church session subsequently acted to suspend him.

Gray appealed to the Presbytery, which denied his appeal; he then appealed to the 1994 OPC General Assembly. A significant majority of the assembly

99. Terry Gray, "A Letter to the Committee of Five in Response to the First Draft of the Charges, March 14, 1994," *Documents Related to the Evolution Trial in the OPC at The American Scientific Affiliation*, http://www.asa3.org/gray/evolution_trial/response_to_PMWcharges.html.

100. Terry Gray, "Excerpts from the Minutes of the 63rd General Assembly of the Orthodox Presbyterian Church," *Documents Related to the Evolution Trial in the OPC at The American Scientific Affiliation*, http://www.asa3.org/gray/evolution_trial/general_assembly_actions.html#anchor8409563.

101. Terry Gray, "Being an Evolutionist in a Confessionally Reformed Church," *An Evangelical Dialogue on Evolution*, http://evanevodialogue.blogspot.com/2010/03/being-evolutionary-creationist-in.html.

voted to deny the appeal, sustaining charges against Gray who remained suspended from his office of elder.[102] Some in the OPC were dismayed by the decision, including Lee Irons, a student of Meredith Kline at Westminster Seminary California, who would soon become a leading proponent with Kline of the literary framework hypothesis.[103]

The New Geneva Study Bible

An example showing how hermeneutical latitude was becoming more widely distilled among the more conservative Presbyterian bodies was found in the 1995 publication of the *New Geneva Study Bible*. The editorial team was led by R. C. Sproul and included a significant number of faculty members from a wide variety of institutions.[104] While the work was a significant contribution to a popular, scriptural understanding of Reformed theology, the study notes on Genesis undertook what no previous Bible with Reformed study notes had done—it gave brief reference to the literal tradition as one option among a variety of legitimate alternatives, extensively proposing the literary framework hypothesis.[105]

---

102. The decision was protested by a minority of delegates to the Assembly including Donald J. Duff, Roger L. Gibbons, Jack J. Peterson, A. M. Laurie, Theodore J. Georgian, William I. Crawford Jr., Stephen L. Phillips, and Douglas A. Felch, who served as Gray's counsel through the process. Gray states, "I remained in that state [of suspension] until January 1998 when I was restored after recanting of my views. My recantation was not a denial of primate ancestry, but rather an admission that I did not know how to hold my views about human evolution together with the uniqueness of Adam as taught in the Confessions and in Scripture. This small step back from my previous assertion was satisfactory to the church elders. I did not violate my conscience in this and continue to this day to have no firm idea about how to put all the pieces together." Gray, "Being an Evolutionist in a Confessionally Reformed Church."

103. Lee Irons, "The Bruce Waltke Affair and the Westminster Confession," *The Upper Register*, http://upper-register.typepad.com/blog/2010/04/the-bruce-waltke-affair.html.

104. The volume has been more recently republished as the *Reformation Study Bible*. Old Testament contributors included Bruce Waltke, Meredith Kline, J. Alan Groves, Tremper Longman III, Mark Futato, and numerous others holding to nonliteral approaches to Genesis 1. In 2006 R. C. Sproul published a statement that he had moved away from the framework hypothesis to the traditional, literal, six-day position; six years later he clarified that he did not view this as synonymous with either a young earth or a very old earth, and that "there has to be room for some flexibility" on the interpretation of Genesis 1. R. C. Sproul, *Truths We Confess: A Layman's Guide to the Westminster Confession of Faith, Volume I: The Triune God* (Phillipsburg, N.J.: P&R, 2006), 127–28; Tim Challies, "An Interview with R. C. Sproul," *Challies.com*, http://www.challies.com/interviews/an-interview-with-rc-sproul#more.

105. See "1:3–31" and "first day," in *New Geneva Study Bible*, ed. R. C. Sproul (Nashville: Thomas Nelson, 1995), 7.

Though an ancient Near Eastern cosmological approach to the text was not explicitly mentioned as one of the alternatives, a number of the notes on Genesis 1 reflected that view, arguing that the term firmament "suggests something flat and hard," and positing that the "great sea creatures" referred to "the sea dragons associated with ancient mythology."[106] Though reflecting the late twentieth-century multiplication of hermeneutical approaches to the text of Genesis 1 and 2, the note on "living being" nonetheless maintained a literal approach to Genesis 2:7, calling readers to understand that the text "does not say 'a living being became man'—man is not formed from preexistent life. Man is differentiated from the animals by bearing the image of God, and he shows his authority over the animals by naming them."[107]

The Genesis 1 study notes produced by the editorial committee of the *New Geneva Study Bible* were indicative of hermeneutical trends, coupled with a remaining reserve toward evolutionary origins for Adam. Undoubtedly, this was due in part to the awareness of a fierce commitment to a special, temporally immediate creation of Adam and Eve, which was part and parcel of a commitment to the literal tradition among the majority of the members of smaller bodies of confessional Presbyterians, like the OPC and PCA, coming out of mainline Presbyterianism. Whereas it was not uncommon for proponents of alternative hermeneutics to be open to evolutionary origins for humanity, that idea was usually precluded by commitment to the literal tradition.

Futato and "the Theological Context of Canaanite Religion"

At Westminster Theological Seminary (Philadelphia), where some, like Kline, had adopted the framework hypothesis, subsequent generations of faculty, particularly in the Old Testament department, moved to champion a more diverse blend of hermeneutical alternatives increasingly distanced from the literal tradition. Enthusiasm for ancient Near Eastern cosmological approaches to Genesis grew under the presidency of Samuel Logan through faculty members including Tremper Longman III and Alan Groves.

Other seminaries were also adopting these approaches to Genesis, including Westminster Seminary California, where Kline was followed by Mark Futato; and the Reformed Theological Seminary campus in Orlando, Florida.

---

106. "Firmament" and "great sea creatures," in *New Geneva Study Bible*, 7–8.
107. "Living being," in *New Geneva Study Bible*, 10.

That campus was particularly influenced by Bruce Waltke, along with Futato, who would transition to the seminary in 1999.[108]

Futato argued that the interpretation of early Genesis required an understanding of the "immediate and broader literary contexts, as well as the geographical context of the Ancient Near East, and the theological context of Canaanite religion."[109] As a proponent of a literary framework approach, Futato, like Kline, argued that Genesis 2:5 was the crucial indicator that the wider pericope was topical rather than chronological. Rejecting a day-age approach by arguing that the writer presents the days as "ordinary solar days," Futato simultaneously argued that these apparently chronological aspects were "accidental," functioning as a stylistic, literary device.[110]

Futato concluded that Genesis 2:5 in reality indicated that "it had rained," but that the text stated what it did "as a polemic against Canaanite Baalism," which he believed stood "at the heart of OT covenant theology."[111] As a result, his reading of the Genesis text was as sophisticated literary apologetic, done in a manner and arriving at results remarkably congruent with other ancient Near Eastern cosmological approaches to the text. Like Kline, Futato rejected evolutionary origins although his hermeneutical approach and implications for Genesis 1 and 2 provided no compelling reason to do so.

A Literal Resurgence?

While Westminster Seminary California was becoming nearly synonymous with commitment to the literary framework approach, Greenville Presbyterian Theological Seminary (GPTS) in Greenville, South Carolina, affirmed an exclusive commitment to the literal hermeneutical tradition on Genesis 1 and 2.[112] Board and faculty members at Greenville viewed the literal tradition as accurate to the text of Genesis 1 and 2 and believed alternative hermeneutical

---

108. "Mark Futato, Facing Charges, Renounces Jurisdiction of the PCA," *Presbyterian and Reformed News*, http://www.presbyteriannews.org/volumes/v5/2/Futato.html.

109. Mark Futato, "Because It Had Rained: A Study of Genesis 2:5–7 with Implications for Genesis 2:4–25 and Genesis 1:1–2:3," *Westminster Theological Journal* 60, no. 1 (Spring 1998): 1–21.

110. Mark Futato, "Because It Had Rained," 1; Lee Irons, "The Framework Interpretation: An Exegetical Summary," *The Upper Register: Papers and MP3s by Lee Irons*, http://www.upper-register.com/papers/framework_interpretation_print.html.

111. Futato, "Because It Had Rained," 2, 19.

112. The position represented a shift for systematic theology professor Morton Smith, who had earlier held, "We do not have enough information to settle [the question of the days] definitively." Morton Smith, *Systematic Theology* (Greenville, S.C.: Greenville Seminary Press, 1994), 1:187.

approaches eroded exegetical grounds for the special, immediate creation of Adam and Eve on the sixth day.

Led by a new president and professor of theology, Joseph A. Pipa Jr., who had previously served at Westminster Seminary California, they engaged the alternative hermeneutical approaches and promoted adherence and return to the literal hermeneutical tradition.

"In the Space of Six Days"

In 1999, GPTS held a spring theology conference and provided a platform for proponents of both the literal Genesis tradition and alternative approaches to speak and engage in discussion and debate. The conference papers, subsequently published as *Did God Create in Six Days?*, created significant consternation among Presbyterian proponents of alternative views.[113] This was not due to the engagement with figurative views on the basis of exegesis and theology, nor the positive defense of the literal-day interpretation through exegetical analysis of Genesis 1–2 and the wider context of Scripture.[114]

Rather, the consternation was due to the argument, presented at the conference and then published, that the alternative approaches stood contrary to the Westminster Confession of Faith and Catechisms, due to their rejection of God's creation as taking place "in the space of six days." Ministers and elders within Presbyterian denominations like the PCA were required to subscribe to the Westminster Confession of Faith and Catechisms, and proponents of figurative views wanted their approaches to be considered as acceptably within the purview of these confessional standards.

The GPTS conference, along with the PCA's formation of a committee to study creation the previous year, prompted a flurry of responses, particularly within the pages of the *Westminster Theological Journal*. There, a succession of writers did their best to make a case from church history that the Confession's phrase "in the space of six days" could reflect a wide variety of meanings and that alternative hermeneutical approaches to Genesis stood within the mainstream of historic Christianity.[115]

---

113. Joseph A. Pipa Jr. and David W. Hall, eds. *Did God Create in Six Days?* (Greenville, S.C.: Southern Presbyterian Press, 1999), 1–339.

114. Joseph Pipa Jr., "From Chaos to Cosmos: A Critique of the Non-Literal Interpretations of Genesis 1:1–2:3"; Morton Smith, "The Theological Significance of the Doctrine of Creation"; Benjamin Shaw, "The Literal Day Interpretation"; and Sid Dyer, "The New Testament Doctrine of Creation," in *Did God Create in Six Days?*, 153–265.

115. Robert Letham, "'In the Space of Six Days': The Days of Creation from Origen to the Westminster Assembly," *Westminster Theological Journal* 61, no. 2 (1999): 149–74; William S.

PCA Study Committee: "No More or Less Explicit than Scripture Itself"
The 1998 PCA General Assembly's study committee on creation had been tasked to provide a review of hermeneutical approaches on Genesis 1 and 2, their consequences in relation to evolutionary theory, and their acceptability in relation to the confessional standards of the denomination. The committee report presented to the PCA General Assembly in 2000 outlined what it termed "the calendar day interpretation," the "day-age interpretation," "the framework interpretation," and "the analogical days interpretation."[116] Reflecting a diverse milieu, including a strong Southern Presbyterian legacy of commitment to the literal tradition, the report included a defense of the literal tradition, defenses of alternative hermeneutic views, and critical notes on each, as well as notes on aspects of evolutionary and old-earth theory.

In relation to the statement of the Westminster Confession of Faith and Catechisms that God's work of creation took place "in the space of six days," the PCA report stated, "The interpretation of this phrase has received more attention in the last three years than in the previous three-hundred-fifty. No doubt, more light will be shed on the phrase as research continues…. To some of us, the evidence leads to the conclusion that the Assembly meant 'six calendar days.' To others of us, the evidence is not strong enough to conclude that the Assembly wished to exclude any other view than the instantaneous view of Augustine."[117]

A third position on the implication of the doctrinal standards reflected the previous two:

> [This] position held by some members of the Committee is that although there is evidence that certain individual members of the Westminster Assembly held to a creation week of six calendar days…the confessional language…is substantially equivalent to Scripture, and…the clear expressed intention of the Westminster Assembly is thus to be no more or less explicit than Scripture itself.
>
> Under this analysis…if a candidate were to take exception to the language "in the space of six days" then he would be deemed to have taken

---

Barker, "The Westminster Assembly on the Days of Creation: A Reply to David W. Hall," *Westminster Theological Journal* 62, no. 1 (Spring 2000): 1–16; Max Rogland, "*Ad Litteram*: Some Dutch Reformed Theologians on the Creation Days," *Westminster Theological Journal* 63, no. 2 (Fall 2001): 211–35; J. V. Fesko, "The Days of Creation and Confession Subscription in the OPC," *Westminster Theological Journal* 63, no. 2 (2001): 235–49.

116. Presbyterian Church of America, *Report of the Creation Study Committee to the 28th General Assembly of the Presbyterian Church in America* (printed by author, 2000), 2302–91.

117. Presbyterian Church of America, *Report of the Creation Study Committee*, 2357.

an exception to the language of Scripture itself, such as Exodus 20:11: "[f]or in six days the LORD made the heavens and the earth, the sea, and all that is in them...." If an examining court allows latitude in the interpretation of Genesis 1 and related passages regarding the length of creation days, that same latitude should be allowed for the candidate's interpretation of the phrase "in the space of six days" contained in the Standards, and no exception should be noted. If, on the other hand, an examining court does not grant latitude in the interpretation of Genesis 1 and related passages, no exception should be allowed, because the PCA obviously does not permit exception to the language of Scripture.[118]

The committee's report, as received by the General Assembly, acknowledged and reflected a latitude of hermeneutical views and promoted a revisionist interpretation of the Westminster Confession and Catechisms' declaration that creation took place "in" or "within the space of six days." At the same time, it maintained the literal tradition on the accounts of the creation of man in Genesis 1 and 2, stating that these Scripture passages taught "the special creation of Adam and Eve as actual human beings, the parents of all humanity (hence they are not the products of evolution from lower forms of life)."[119] In receiving the report, the Assembly "affirmed that such diversity as covered in this report is acceptable as long as the full historicity of the creation account is accepted."[120]

OPC Study Committee: Exhorting Spirit of Unity

The OPC followed suit by creating a committee of its own, with perhaps more influential proponents of alternative approaches, to formulate its *Report of the Committee to Study the Views of Creation*, received by the OPC General Assembly in 2004.[121] In it, the committee presented the literal interpretive tradition as one legitimate option among others, including literary framework, day-age, and analogical interpretations. They did so while exhorting a spirit of unity and without binding presbyteries or congregations to which approach they might accept or reject in examining men for ordained service.

---

118. Presbyterian Church of America, *Report of the Creation Study Committee*, 2361.

119. Presbyterian Church of America, *Report of the Creation Study Committee*, 2302.

120. Presbyterian Church of America, *Report of the Creation Study Committee*, 2302.

121. Orthodox Presbyterian Church, *Report of the Committee to Study the Views of Creation to the 71st General Assembly of the Orthodox Presbyterian Church* (printed by author, 2004), 1601–1740. Committee member Leonard J. Coppes provided extensive commentary and critique for the report on two of the more popular alternative hermeneutical approaches (literary framework and analogical) from the vantage of the literal tradition, along with significant appendices on hermeneutics and ancient Near Eastern sources and contexts as supportive of the literal tradition.

In receiving the report, the General Assembly affirmed the "priority of Scripture in the relationship between special and general revelation."[122] The Terry Gray case of a decade earlier provided a circumscribing judicial precedent within the OPC for the interpretation of Genesis 2:7 according to the literal tradition.[123] Within both the PCA and OPC there were presbyteries and local church sessions that retained a strong commitment to the literal tradition, while others supported a latitude of hermeneutical approaches.

As time went on, both denominations would see an increase of openness among ministers, elders, and laity toward a figurative interpretation of human origins compatible with theistic evolution. This interpretation, however, would remain a minority position which was out of accord with denominational commitments.

A Literal Genesis, a Literal Adam: Presbyterianism in the South

Reformed Theological Seminary, an independent institution with significant ties to the PCA, revealed diverging polarities across its multiple campuses. In Orlando, Florida, Waltke and later Futato criticized the literal tradition and championed nonliteral approaches; meanwhile in Jackson, Mississippi, Ligon Duncan, Duncan Rankin, and others supported the literal tradition while Miles Van Pelt advocated the framework hypothesis.

Ligon Duncan would emerge as a leading proponent of the literal understanding, contributing to its ongoing exegetical defense.[124] His contribution, with David Hall, to *The G3N3SIS Debate*, elucidated grounds for the literal reading of Genesis, and provided responses to the day-age and framework views. Duncan and Hall paid substantial attention to the testimony of Scripture for "normal creation days," concluding that "the uniform testimony of Scripture attests to divine creation out of nothing by God's word in the space of six normal days. There simply is no contrary evidence *within* the canonical Scriptures. It requires the imposition of extrabiblical concepts to reinterpret the texts in other ways."[125]

---

122. Orthodox Presbyterian Church, *Report of the Committee to Study the Views of Creation*, preface.

123. Orthodox Presbyterian Church, *Report of the Committee to Study the Views of Creation*, 1664.

124. J. Ligon Duncan and David W. Hall, "The 24-Hour View," in *Three Views on the Days of Creation: The G3N3SIS Debate*, ed. David G. Hagopian (Mission Viejo, Calif.: Cruxpress, 2001), 21–66, 95–122, 165–78, 257–68.

125. Duncan and Hall, "The 24-Hour View," 25–47.

Duncan and Hall addressed the common objections to the text raised by supporters of nonliteral approaches to the text, arguing,

> We should not grant natural revelation (which is always filtered by the interpreter) a status equal to, or greater than, special revelation as it has been interpreted by the community of the faithful and circumscribed by the analogy of faith.
>
> While there is certainly a "light of nature"—and Protestant theology has embraced a range of understandings about the role of natural revelation—the evangelical tradition has not assigned the same epistemological authority to natural revelation as to special revelation rightly interpreted. When forced to choose between conflicting sources of authority, we join the chorus begun by the apostle Paul, "Let God be true, and every man a liar" (Rom. 3:4).[126]

Their position on the relationship of special and general revelation stood in the mainstream of Reformation and post-Reformation Protestant orthodoxy, particularly in regard to how it could be applied to interpret the first chapters of Genesis.

While only brief references to human origins were made in the volume, Duncan and Hall's literal hermeneutic clearly required a special, temporally immediate creation of Adam and Eve within the parameters of a sixth day of ordinary duration. As they noted, it did so in contrast to the nonliteral approaches: "A framework hermeneutic forces us into an ongoing theological discussion about other potentially 'figurative' elements in Genesis protology (Adam and Eve, the lifespans of Genesis 5, the *nephilim* of Genesis 6, the table of nations in Genesis 10, Babel, etc.). In the end, this [non-literal] approach seriously endangers our ability to honestly claim that we hold to the historicity of Scripture."[127]

The Charlotte Campus

Among the Reformed Theological Seminary campuses, the Charlotte campus had perhaps the strongest literal tradition, other than what was seen in Jackson, as evidenced in the teaching and writings of faculty members including Richard Belcher, John Currid, Douglas Kelly, and Michael Kruger.[128] Each of

---

126. Duncan and Hall, "The 24-Hour View," 58–59.

127. Duncan and Hall, "The 24-Hour View," 264.

128. Richard Belcher, "From Genesis to Joshua," *Reformed Sermons by Third Millennium Ministries*, http://reformedsermons.org/series.asp/srs/Genesis%20to%20Joshua; "Did Adam and Eve Really Exist: A Review," *Reformation 21* (October 2012), http://www.reformation21.org /articles/did-adam-and-eve-really-exist-a-review.php; John Currid, "Genesis 1 and Other

the four engaged with alternative hermeneutical approaches, providing posi-tive defenses of the literal tradition.

Kelly did so extensively in his book *Creation and Change: Genesis 1.1–2.4 in the Light of Changing Scientific Paradigms*. Weaving together reflections on science, philosophy, theology, and exegesis, Kelly argued that the literal tradition of Genesis interpretation was most sound and accurate. Both the Old Testament, and the New, he said, "[assume] the chronological, historical veracity of chapters 1 and 2 of Genesis…. With one accord they clearly assume a plain, historical/chronological reading…a 'literal' rather than a 'literary' reading, so to speak."[129]

While Kelly's work focused on the first creation account of Genesis 1:1–2:4, he noted that "Genesis 2 gives us fuller information about the creation of male and female, but what little Genesis 1 tells us about their origins agrees totally with the expanded account of Genesis 2."[130] Kelly also noted what he viewed as a significant implication of God's revelation that "he saw everything that he had made, and behold, it was very good":

> The absence of evil, killing and death is confirmed by the concluding words of Genesis 1, summarizing the remarkable work of the sixth day of creation…. In light of this goodness pervading the freshly created order, the evolutionary theory which necessitates evil, in the form of compe-tition, struggle, killing and death as the means of the upward advance of the creatures *from the very beginning* of life on earth is ruled out by clear revelation of God Himself. Although not the subject of this brief volume…Genesis 3 and the rest of the Scriptures (particularly Romans 5, 6 and 1 Corinthians 15) teach with one voice that evil and death entered the universe only after Adam sinned. The entire significance of the aton-ing work of Christ as the Last Adam, lies in his reversal of the sin of the First Adam, which caused all the disorders that result in death.

Ancient Near Eastern Creation Accounts," in *Against the Gods* (Wheaton, Ill.: Crossway, 2013), 1–153; *A Study Commentary on Genesis* (Darlington, UK: Evangelical Press, 2003), 1:1–109; "Genesis 1–11: The Creation, the Fall, the Promise," Parts 1–6, chapel messages given at RTS Jackson, http://www.rts.edu/Site/RTSNearYou/Jackson/Chapel/currid_creation.aspx; Douglas Kelly, *Creation and Change: Genesis 1.1–2.4 in the Light of Changing Scientific Paradigms* (Fearn, Scotland: Christian Focus, 1997), 1–240; Michael J. Kruger, "An Understanding of Genesis 2:5," *CEN Technical Journal* 11, no. 1 (1997): 106–10. For a helpful critical review of Currid's method in engaging literature on the ancient Near East in *Against the Gods*, see David Graves, "Review of *Against the Gods*," *Reformation 21*, November 2013, http://www.reformation21.org/shelf-life /against-the-gods.php. By the time of publication this source had been removed from the Internet.

129. Kelly, *Creation and Change*, 95–114.
130. Kelly, *Creation and Change*, 201.

While secular evolutionists can easily ignore the biblical testimony on this vital point, theistic evolutionists have a much harder time coping with what God says, for it is plainly contradictory to their paradigm of origins.... There are many things in the Scripture "hard to be understood" (cf. 2 Peter 3:16), but this is not one of them. Nothing could be more clear than the fact that the original created order was a place of holy beauty and peace, but then that..."by one man sin entered into the world, and death by sin."... The "incoherence" of the theistic evolutionary thesis...places evil and death in the created order *before* man's choice to sin against the Creator.[131]

Robert Reymond's New Systematic Theology

Faculty at Reformed and Greenville Presbyterian seminaries who were robustly defending the literal tradition, were joined by Robert Reymond (1932–2013) from Knox Theological Seminary in Fort Lauderdale. Reymond advocated the literal tradition in his teaching and more widely through his *A New Systematic Theology of the Christian Faith*.[132] Addressing the hermeneutic and exegesis of Genesis 1, he reflected,

I can discern no reason, either from Scripture or from the human sciences, for departing from the view that the days of Genesis were ordinary twenty-four-hour days. The following points favor this view:

1. The word "day" (*yôm*) in the singular, dual and plural, occurs some 2,225 times in the Old Testament with the overwhelming preponderance of these occurrences designating the ordinary daily cycle. Normally, the preponderate meaning of a term should be maintained unless contextual considerations force one to another view...no such contextual demand exists in Genesis 1.

2. The recurring phrase, "and the evening and the morning [taken together] constituted day one, etc." (1:5, 8, 13, 19, 23, 31), suggests as much. The qualifying words, "evening and morning" attached here to each of these recurring statements occur together outside of Genesis in 37 verses (e.g., Exod. 18:13; 27:21). In each instance these words are employed to describe an ordinary day.

3. In the hundreds of other cases in the Old Testament where *yôm* stands in conjunction with an ordinal number (first, second, third,

---

131. Kelly, *Creation and Change*, 202–5.

132. Robert Reymond, *A New Systematic Theology of the Christian Faith*, 2nd ed., rev. (Nashville: Thomas Nelson, 2001), 383–96, 415–27.

etc.) e.g., Exodus 12:15; 24:16; Leviticus 12:3, it never means anything other than a normal, literal day.

4. With the creation of the sun "to rule the day" and the moon "to rule the night" occurring on the fourth day (Gen. 1:16–18), days four through six would almost certainly have been ordinary days. This would suggest that the seventh would also have been an ordinary day. All this would suggest in turn, if we may assume that the earth was turning on its axis at that time, that days one through three would have been ordinary days as well.

5. If we follow the *analogia Scripturae* principle of hermeneutics enunciated in the Westminster Confession of Faith...that "the infallible rule of interpretation of Scripture is the Scripture itself: and therefore, when there is a question about the true and full sense of any Scripture (which is not manifold, but one), it must be searched and known by other places that speak more clearly" (I/ix), then the "ordinary day" view has the most to commend it since Moses grounds the commandment regarding seventh-day Sabbath observance in the fact of the divine Exemplar's activity: "In six days the Lord made the heavens and the earth, the sea and all that is in them, but he rested on the seventh day. Therefore the Lord blessed the Sabbath day and made it holy" (Exod. 20:11; see also 31:15–17).

6. In the 608 occurrences of the plural "days" (*yāmîm*) in the Old Testament (see Exod. 20:11), their referents are always ordinary days. Ages are never expressed by the word *yāmîm*.

7. Finally, had Moses intended to express the idea of seven "ages" in Genesis 1 he could have employed the term *'ôlām*, which means "age" or "period of indefinite duration."[133]

In keeping with his exegetical commitment to a literal interpretation of the days in Genesis 1, Reymond also upheld a special, direct creation of Adam and Eve on the sixth day:

After God had made all other creatures, He created man, male and female.... Man is a *creature* of God, indeed the crowning work of God's creative activity; uniquely the "image of God" with whom God has entered into covenant.... The Bible definitively teaches the creation of man by a direct act of God. There is not a hint that he is the product of either naturalistic or theistic evolution.... Man's creation occurs as the

133. Reymond, *New Systematic Theology*, 392–94.

last major event of the sixth day of the creation week.... The creation of man receives special attention in Genesis 2:5–25, which is *not* a "second account" of creation differing in many details from the account in Genesis 1, but a more detailed account of God's creative activities on day six of Genesis 1.... Man is distinguished from the animals in a very special way in Genesis 2. Not only is he made their ruler in the Genesis 1 narrative, but also *into man's nostrils alone* does God breathe the "breath of life."[134]

As evident at a number of seminary campuses, continued support for the literal tradition on Genesis 1 and 2 among Presbyterians appeared indebted, at least in part, to a historically strong commitment among Southern Presbyterians.[135]

Westminster Theological Seminary: From Allegory to Myth

During the 1990s, writings of proponents of alternative approaches appeared in the pages of the *Westminster Theological Journal*, pushing back against a revived awareness of the implications of the Westminster Confession and Catechisms for hermeneutics and early Genesis. At the same time, some of the faculty at Westminster Theological Seminary (Philadelphia) were moving further away from a literal interpretation of early Genesis.

A decade earlier, Old Testament professor J. Alan Groves had commended the use of form criticism as proposed by George W. Coats, who categorized the early chapters of Genesis as "primeval saga."[136] By the 1990s, faculty members Tremper Longman III and Ray Dillard argued that the first chapters of Genesis "[do] not allow us to be dogmatic over such questions as the length of time and order of God's creative process.... The theme of Genesis 1 and 2 is not how God created, but that God created."[137] In assessing the genre of Genesis, they rejected deeming it mythological, but like Groves, manifested an appreciation for Coats as well as Gunkel. Stating that defining early Genesis as "saga" was not "inherently antagonistic toward a historical intention in the text," they implied a legitimacy for the approach, so long as a commitment to a "historical nucleus"

134. Reymond, *New Systematic Theology*, 415–17.

135. One mid-twentieth-century example was found in Manford George Gutzke (1896–1993), professor of English Bible at Columbia Theological Seminary in Decatur, Georgia, between 1940 and 1967. While Gutzke's understanding of the emanation of light from the sun appeared to reveal a lack of scientific understanding, his hermeneutical approach, exegesis, and exposition of Genesis 1 and 2 were thoroughly congruent with the literal tradition. Manford George Gutzke, *Plain Talk on Genesis* (Grand Rapids: Zondervan, 1975), 19–31.

136. J. Alan Groves, "Review of *Genesis: With an Introduction to Narrative Literature* by George W. Coats," *Westminster Theological Journal* 46, no. 2 (1984): 400–402.

137. Tremper Longman III and Ray Dillard, *An Introduction to the Old Testament* (Grand Rapids: Zondervan, 1994), 51–52.

was preserved.[138] The statement bore a remarkable similarity to Protestant liberals' "kernel theory" approach to the whole of the Scriptures. Yet Longman and Dillard stood in harmony with the more common approaches of day-age, analogical days, and the framework hypothesis, which similarly shed aspects of the historical literal tradition while retaining a core commitment that God had created in some manner in the past. Longman would later argue that Genesis 1 did not necessitate a creation ex nihilo, nor, he argued, should "interpreters press the text in ways that it does not intend to be read in order to argue against modern scientific conclusions on the origins of human beings."[139]

Peter Enns: "There Is No 'Adam' To Be Found"
Peter Enns, who had been a student at Westminster under Groves and Longman, returned there fresh from a Harvard PhD to teach Old Testament studies in 1994. As a new professor, he entered an academic and institutional milieu substantially critical of the literal tradition and supportive of alternative approaches to Genesis 1 and 2. As such, he stood as an heir to the literary framework, analogical days, and ancient Near Eastern cosmological approaches, all of which opened both Genesis 1 and 2 to evolutionary models of origins, according to their leading proponents, including scholars such as Meredith Kline and Michael Horton. Intellectually nurtured in this setting, Peter Enns took a logical step forward, taking up Calvin College professor Davis Young's challenge by seeking a more consistent Genesis interpretation that would accommodate evolutionary models of origins and ancient Near Eastern worldviews.[140]

At points, like higher critics from the late nineteenth and early twentieth centuries, Enns appeared to conclude that the authorial understanding of the text of early Genesis was approximate or equivalent to that of the literal hermeneutical tradition. But he went on to aver that this understanding was merely reflective of the author's primitive conceptual context—which modern man had advanced far beyond. In fact, Enns believed, scientific results indicated an evolutionary chain of origins that left no place for a special, immediate creation of an Adam and Eve.[141] Enns asserted that the same was true in the

---

138. Longman and Dillard, *Introduction to the Old Testament*, 49.

139. Tremper Longman III, *How to Read Genesis* (Downers Grove, Ill.: InterVarsity, 2005), 102–3, 106–7.

140. Peter Enns, *The Evolution of Adam: What the Bible Does and Doesn't Say about Human Origins* (Grand Rapids: Baker, 2012), xvii–xviii.

141. Enns, *The Evolution of Adam*, 42, 57, 122; xiv–xv.

New Testament era: Paul understood "Adam as a historical person" due to his context, but was in error.[142]

Settling to adopt a mytho-poetic form of the ancient Near Eastern cosmological approach to the text, Enns denied not only a special, temporally immediate creation of Adam apart from evolutionary biological origins, but also the existence of Adam as a historical individual from whom all humanity was descended.[143] Enns's quest for the historical Adam ended with a clear conclusion: "there is no 'Adam' to be found."[144]

His deduction was remarkably similar to that found at Princeton Theological Seminary at the time. Having seen its last significant proponents of a literal hermeneutic on early Genesis in Geerhardus Vos and the guest lectures of Valentine Hepp, by the late twentieth century, Princeton had long moved well beyond the teaching of B. B. Warfield on human origins. In the late 1990s, Princeton's theology of origins was represented by J. Wentzel van Huyssteen, who declared the Genesis account of creation "myth," and advocated human evolutionary biological origins, including the evolution of religious awareness among early humans, through the development of "symbolizing minds."[145]

Enns's hermeneutical shift had been evident in his earlier work, *Inspiration and Incarnation: Evangelicals and the Problem of the Old Testament*, where he had argued, like Howard Van Till and G. C. Berkouwer, that the Scriptures were so thoroughly a product of their human authors that at times they reflected a view of reality that did not accurately cohere to existing reality. Enns continued application of this theme in *The Evolution of Adam*.[146] His attempt to reconcile the negation of the historical Adam as the father of all humanity with Romans 5 bore distinct similarities to the arguments of La Peyrère, and Enns acknowledged appreciation for other precursors of his thought, including Spinoza and Gunkel.[147] He had now moved to a position of plain agreement with Gunkel that "Genesis contains legends."[148]

---

142. Enns, *The Evolution of Adam*, 121–22.

143. Enns, *The Evolution of Adam*, 9–76.

144. Enns, *The Evolution of Adam*, 138.

145. J. Wentzel van Huyssteen, "Human Origins and Religious Awareness" (Presentation from Nobel Conference, Gustavus Adolphus College, 2008), http://www.youtube.com/watch?v=7QQXfiPtR0M.

146. Peter Enns, *Inspiration and Incarnation: Evangelicals and the Problem of the Old Testament* (Grand Rapids: Baker, 2005), 1–197.

147. Enns, *The Evolution of Adam*, 17–18, 23.

148. Peter Enns, "Reading Genesis: Let's Be Adult about This, Shall We," *Patheos* (September 10, 2012), http://www.patheos.com/blogs/peterenns/2012/09/reading-genesis-lets-be-adult-about-this-shall-we/.

Enns's movement displayed an inherent fluidity within nonliteral approaches to Genesis 1 and 2. To be sure, most evangelical allegorists (proponents of day-age, literary framework, and analogical days) avoided the claim of a primitive, errant authorial conception of reality evident in Enns's adoption of the category of myth, yet his approach was otherwise strikingly similar to—and arguably derivative from—theirs. Both claimed a core of theological and historical meaning communicated through figurative language. Enns's step forward in the treatment of the Genesis account brought him, and his seminary teaching, into complete continuity with nineteenth- and early twentieth-century theological liberalism.

In that era, F. C. Bauer and David Strauss, arguing that they could not accept the miracles of Jesus in light of science, posited that the language was not to be taken literally, but symbolically. Enns was doing the same with Genesis and Adam. While many were reticent to recognize it, he provided yet another example of the now-often-repeated history of institutional and generational "slippery slope" among proponents and heirs of nonliteral hermeneutics in Genesis interpretation.

Recovering the Inerrancy and Priority of Scripture at Westminster

While some Reformed theologians, including Bruce Waltke and Tremper Longman III, voiced their appreciation for Enns's work, many others were critical.[149] Enns's postulations created a backlash among significant elements of the supporting constituency of Westminster and brought divisive controversy within the seminary. While a majority of the faculty sided with Enns, the board of the institution voted by a slim margin to dismiss him.

Following Enns's departure, a series of faculty and board resignations at Westminster opened the way for a more conservative regrouping of the seminary. The changes reaffirmed commitment to inerrancy—with a somewhat more critical view toward ancient Near Eastern cosmological approaches to Genesis and a substantially unified defense of the historicity of Adam and Eve. Richard B. Gaffin Jr. was instrumental in the reprinting of Versteeg's *Adam in the New Testament*, with its exegetical and theological argument from the New Testament for a historical Adam. The publication included a foreword by Gaffin that provided a significant theological analysis and critique of Enns's views

---

149. A number of theologians, including G. K. Beale, Paul Helm, Hans Madueme, Scott Oliphint, Richard Gaffin, Lane Tipton, John Frame, and William B. Evans, wrote responses to Enns's *Inspiration and Incarnation* and *The Evolution of Adam*. The responses ranged from Internet articles to full-length monographs.

and their implications, including footnotes providing theological critique of those who would replace a special, temporally immediate creation of Adam and Eve with evolutionary origins.[150]

Gregory Beale, who had written several critiques of Enns's writings, was hired as a New Testament professor. Beale's *The Erosion of Inerrancy in Evangelicalism* was a direct rebuttal to Enns's writings, particularly in relation to ancient Near Eastern cosmology. Primarily on the basis of his use of Old and New Testament texts, Beale argued that the Scriptures often described the cosmos using temple analogies. Beale's answer about how this intersected with the context of ancient Near Eastern cosmology differed markedly from that of Enns:

> As noted, we should not think that Israel's temple was like those of her pagan neighbors because she merely copied the religious traditions around her. Rather, the likeness of the Israelite temple to pagan temples should be viewed, at least, from two perspectives. First, the similarity is intended at times to be a protest statement that, while the pagan nations think that they have cornered the market on divine revelation from their gods who dwell in their temples, their gods are, in fact, false and their temples purely idolatrous institutions—the den of demons (Deut. 32:17; Ps. 106:37; 1 Cor. 10:19–20).
>
> From another angle, it is appropriate to ask whether anything in ancient pagan religion and its institutions resembled the truth about the true God and his designs for humanity. Certainly, pagan nations had not received any special revelation to draw them into saving relation with the true God. Nevertheless, just as the image of God is not erased but distorted in unbelieving humanity, it is plausible to suggest that some of the affinities in ancient pagan beliefs and religions to that of Israel's may be due to the fact that they are garbled, shadowy representations about the being of the biblical God and of his design for his dwelling place.[151]

---

150. Richard B. Gaffin Jr., "Translator's Foreword," to *Adam in the New Testament*, by J. P. Versteeg (Phillipsburg, N.J.: P&R, 2012), ix–xxv. See also Richard B. Gaffin Jr., "'All Mankind Descending from Him…'?," *New Horizons* 33, no. 3 (March 2012): 3–5.

151. Gregory K. Beale, *The Erosion of Inerrancy in Evangelicalism: Responding to New Challenges to Biblical Authority* (Wheaton, Ill.: Crossway, 2008), 175. The last sentence of Beale's statement here could be stated more strongly, with scriptural warrant. It is not merely "plausible to suggest" but reality that these "garbled, shadowy representations" are actually driven by defiance against God, and intended to deceive (cf. Rom. 1:18–23; 2 Cor. 4:4; Eph. 2:1–3). Beale's volume drew on his *The Temple and the Church's Mission: A Biblical Theology of the Dwelling Place of God* (Downers Grove, Ill.: InterVarsity, 2004), 1–458.

While Scripture's priority over ancient Near Eastern narrative was being recovered, its priority over scientific narratives of origins would not yet be at Westminster—though there would be a distinct shift in tone toward the literal tradition. A few years after Beale's engagement with Enns, Vern Poythress, also a New Testament professor at Westminster (Philadelphia), produced a slim primer on Christian interpretations of Genesis 1. It provided more sympathetic attention to the literal tradition, termed "young earth creationism," along with an appreciative note toward the analogical-day approach propounded by C. John Collins.[152] For the first time since the publications of John Murray and E. J. Young in the 1950s and early 1960s, there was print evidence from Westminster of appreciation for the literal hermeneutic tradition on Genesis and creation.

Making History, and Critiquing the Literary Framework

The first decade of the twenty-first century at Westminster Seminary California would see the publication of Robert Godfrey's *God's Pattern for Creation*, presenting a modified form of the literary framework approach, and Scott Clark's *Recovering the Reformed Confession*.[153] In his work, Clark was decidedly not advocating a recovery of a confessional subscription to the post-Reformation understanding of "in the space of six days."

Instead, relying on Ronald Numbers's weak historiography in *The Creationists*, he argued that "Numbers has shown that one of the primary sources of the creationist movement is not orthodox Reformed theology but the Seventh Day Adventist movement, the distinguishing beliefs of which have little in common with the Reformed confession. From the middle of the nineteenth century through the middle of the twentieth century, virtually none of the leading Reformed theologians held or taught that Scripture teaches that God created the world in six twenty-four-hour periods."[154]

---

152. Vern S. Poythress, *Christian Interpretations of Genesis 1* (Phillipsburg, N.J.: P&R, 2013), 31–32. See also Vern Poythress, "Evaluating the Claims of Scientists," *New Horizons* 33, no. 3 (March 2012): 6–7; "Adam Versus Claims from Genetics," *Westminster Theological Journal* 75, no. 1 (Spring 2013): 65–82. In the latter, Poythress cautions against accepting popular evolutionary hypotheses, noting a number of problematic assumptions and implications. Poythress argues for a special creation of Adam in the image of God; however, he does so allowing for possible "gradualism"—a creative process not necessarily one taking place within the confines of an ordinary day.

153. Robert W. Godfrey, *God's Pattern of Creation: A Covenantal Reading of Genesis 1* (Phillipsburg, N.J.: P&R, 2003), 1–141.

154. R. Scott Clark, *Recovering the Reformed Confession: Our Theology, Piety, and Practice* (Phillipsburg, N.J.: P&R, 2008), 49. A more sound historical approach would have been

Not only did he claim Reformed orthodoxy was not a primary source of the literal Genesis tradition, but Clark further argued that the Westminster Standards did not propound creation as taking place "in" or "within the space of six days" of ordinary duration, but were "ambiguous."[155] Seeking to solidify his argument, Clark contended that even if members of the Westminster Assembly were committed to a six-ordinary-day view, it was because of scriptural misinterpretation equivalent to that of post-Reformation Reformed orthodox theologians who held to geocentrism.[156]

While the literary framework continued to dominate at Westminster Seminary California, it would receive significant further critical attention in the writings of Paulin Bédard, a minister in the Reformed Church of Quebec and proponent of the literal tradition. Bédard's *In Six Days God Created: Refuting the Framework and Figurative Views of the Days of Creation* engaged the exegetical critiques by Kline, Futato, Godfrey, and others against the literal interpretation of Genesis 1, and in turn critiqued their case for a literary framework approach to the text.[157]

Biologos, Waltke, and Theistic Evolution

Tensions over the quest for the historical Adam among Presbyterians reached another flashpoint during this period. At Reformed Theological Seminary (RTS), Orlando, Bruce Waltke, a venerable Old Testament professor and proponent of the literary framework hypothesis and theistic evolution, became embroiled in controversy.[158] In 2005, Waltke had endorsed the approach of

---

for Clark to argue that although the evidence exhaustively indicated the *Westminster Confession* did mean "in the space of six [ordinary] days," the understanding of seventeenth-century Reformed orthodoxy on this, like on geocentrism, was wrong. However, the challenge of this approach was that the language of the confession drew directly on Scripture, making ecclesiastical exceptions and revisions difficult for proponents of figurative views.

155. Clark, *Recovering the Reformed Confession*, 49.

156. Clark, *Recovering the Reformed Confession*, 49–61.

157. Paulin Bédard, *In Six Days God Created: Refuting the Framework and Figurative Views of the Days of Creation* ([Maitland, Fla.]: Xulon Press, 2013), 1–252.

158. Bruce Waltke and Cathi J. Fredricks, *Genesis: A Commentary* (Grand Rapids: Zondervan, 2001), 1–90. Waltke would state that "from the viewpoint of modern historiography, internal evidence within the Pentateuch supports the narrator's inferred claim to represent what really happened"; however, in relation to Genesis 1–2, he argued that the genre of the Genesis account was "an artistic, literary representation of creation intended to fortify God's covenant with creation. It represents truths about origins in anthropomorphic language." He further argued that "Genesis 1 is concerned with ultimate cause, not proximation.... Genesis is prescriptive, answering the questions of who and why and what ought to be, whereas the purpose of science is to be descriptive, answering the questions of what and how" (pp. 75–76).

Enns's book *Inspiration and Incarnation*. The flashpoint, however, came in March 2010, after Waltke stated in an online video at the Biologos Foundation:

> If the data is overwhelmingly in favor of evolution, to deny that reality will make us a cult…some odd group that is not really interacting with the world. And rightly so, because we are not using our gifts and trusting God's Providence that brought us to this point of our awareness…. To deny the reality would be to deny the truth of God in the world and would be to deny truth. So I think it would be our spiritual death if we stopped loving God with all of our minds and thinking about it, I think it's our spiritual death.[159]

Waltke's host, the Biologos Foundation, was supported by significant funding from the Templeton Foundation and dedicated to advancing the acceptance of theistic evolution in the evangelical church. It is a vocal proponent of alternative hermeneutic approaches and evolutionary biological models. Both Waltke and Enns had previously contributed articles to its website.[160] Others within Presbyterian circles warmly supported the Biologos effort—particularly the widely popular Tim Keller and Redeemer Presbyterian Church in New York City. Keller had hosted meetings and contributed to the Biologos effort by writing a proposal for a theistic evolutionary model of human origins.[161]

Though Waltke's latitude on Genesis hermeneutics and human origins had previously been accepted within RTS, the seminary at this point was troubled by his critical public statement against the literal tradition and those opposed

---

159. Justin Taylor, "On Theistic Evolution and Professor Waltke's Resignation," *The Gospel Coalition* (April 9, 2010), http://thegospelcoalition.org/blogs/justintaylor/2010/04/09/on-theistic-evolution-and-professor-waltkes-resignation/.

160. Bruce Waltke, "Barriers to Accepting the Possibility of Creation by an Evolutionary Process I: Concerns of the Typical Evangelical Theologian" (paper presented at the Biologos Theology of Celebration conference, Redeemer Presbyterian Church, November 2009), http://biologos.org/blog/barriers-to-accepting-creation-by-an-evolutionary-process. In an appended letter to the paper, Waltke stated, "The paper is one of several to be presented to a conference that has been organized by Francis S. Collins, Alister McGrath, Os Guinness, Tim Keller and Darrel Falk. The purpose of the meeting and papers is to bring together a group of evangelical leaders who will think together about the apparent gulf that currently exists between science and faith, and how the Church can best narrow that gulf without diminishing our shared commitment to the evangelical Christian faith."

161. Timothy Keller, "Creation, Evolution, and Christian Laypeople, Part 6: A Model," *Biologos Foundation* (March 30, 2012), http://biologos.org/blog/creation-evolution-and-christian-laypeople-part-6. Proffering Derek Kidner's model of theistic evolution for Adam and special creation of Eve in his article, Keller refers in an interview to his position as "not quite" theistic evolution, going on to state, "If you believe in an old earth you have to believe in evolution of some sort." Eric Metaxas and Timothy Keller, "Fireside Chat" (interview from New Canaan Society 2012 Washington Weekend), http://vimeo.com/42020632.

to theistic evolutionary models. Eventually, Waltke resigned and moved to Knox Theological Seminary.[162] As events unfolded, a statement sympathetic to Waltke's position was published on the Biologos website.[163]

Covenant Theological Seminary: From Figurative Days to a Figurative Adam

Among confessional Presbyterian institutions in the United States, the other major seminary was Covenant Theological Seminary in St. Louis, the denominational seminary of the Presbyterian Church in America. Like many of the other Presbyterian seminaries, Covenant had previously allowed for a substantial latitude of views on the interpretation of Genesis 1 and 2, as evident in the teaching of R. Laird Harris (1911–2008) and Francis Schaeffer (1912–1984). Harris favored a day-age approach to Genesis 1, while Schaeffer viewed the length of days as undefined; both maintained a literal understanding of the creation of Adam and Eve.[164] Robert Reymond had encouraged the maintenance of the literal tradition on Genesis 1 and 2; his departure from the seminary in 1990 reflected the changing milieu at the institution.[165]

C. John Collins: An Analogical Approach

Following Harris and Reymond, C. John Collins, professor of Old Testament studies, became the new voice at Covenant on Genesis, hermeneutics, and human origins. Collins popularized the "analogical" hermeneutic, presenting

---

162. Knox Theological Seminary had seen significant recent change, including the resignations of board members R. C. Sproul and Richard Phillips and the faculty resignation of Robert Reymond, who had previously served for many years as a professor at Covenant Theological Seminary. The resignations were not centered on issues regarding Genesis and human origins; however, the departures meant the loss of three influential voices at the seminary who were committed to the special creation of Adam and Eve, as understood by the literal approach to Genesis 2:7 and following.

163. Bruce Waltke, "Why Must the Church Come to Accept Evolution?," *Biologos Foundation* (March 24, 2010), http://biologos.org/blog/why-must-the-church-come-to-accept-evolution. In the midst of the controversy, Waltke's video statement with Biologos was removed, though the transcript remained.

164. R. Laird Harris, "The Length of the Creative Days in Genesis 1," in *Did God Create in Six Days?*, ed. Joseph A. Pipa Jr. and David W. Hall (Greenville, S.C.: Southern Presbyterian Press, 1999), 101–11; *Man—God's Eternal Creation: Old Testament Teaching on Man and His Culture* (Chicago: Moody, 1971), 15–17, 66–71; Francis A. Schaeffer, *Genesis in Space and Time* (Downers Grove, Ill.: InterVarsity, 1972), 39, 52.

165. Robert Reymond, "Does Genesis 1:1–3 Teach Creation Out of Nothing?," in *Scientific Studies in Special Creation*, ed. Walter E. Lammerts (Nutley, N.J.: Presbyterian and Reformed, 1971), 9–21.

the six days of the creation week as bearing all the markers held by the literal tradition, but arguing that as a whole it was a God-given analogy. The fulcrum for his argument was that "God's Sabbath is not an 'ordinary day,'" rather this "is part of an anthropomorphic presentation of God.... The days are God's work days, which need not to be identical to ours: they are instead analogous."[166] Thus, Collins viewed the days as "broadly consecutive" yet "of unspecified relation to time"—a position markedly similar to the day-age approach, but without the requirement of an exact chronological sequence of ages correspondent with the days.[167] Beyond this, Collins argued that the terms "let there be" and "made" (cf. Gen. 1:3, 6, 14–17; Ex. 20:11) were not necessarily describing "ontological origination," the beginning of existence.[168]

Collins claimed that such an approach was actually a "literal" approach to the text and should not be construed as "non-literal."[169] However, the result was more figurative than the day-age approach of his predecessors at Covenant and remarkably similar in effect to the literary framework hypothesis, albeit without all of the latter's hermeneutical complexities, of which Collins was critical.[170] Collins's claim that at a number of points the text did not clearly or necessarily speak to "ontological origination" was a step beyond previous day-age formulations. It also went beyond the typical claims made by proponents of the framework hypothesis. At the time of his lecture at Greenville Presbyterian Theological Seminary in 1999, Collins went on to argue that while his view was compatible with old earth theory, it was "definitely not compatible with naturalistic theories of origins (or theistic evolutionary ones for that matter) because of its stance on God's action."[171]

---

166. C. John Collins, "Reading Genesis 1:1–2:3 as an Act of Communication: Discourse Analysis and Literal Interpretation," in *Did God Create in Six Days?*, 139. R. Kent Hughes argued similarly for an "analogical" approach in *Genesis: Beginning and Blessing* (Wheaton, Ill.: Crossway, 2004), 26–27.

167. Collins, "Reading Genesis 1:1–2:3," 146.

168. Collins, "Reading Genesis 1:1–2:3," 135.

169. Collins, "Reading Genesis 1:1–2:3," 131–32. Longman argues similarly stating, "I do not use a 'figurative hermeneutic.'... I use a historical-grammatical interpretive method that, when appropriate, identifies figurative language and interprets appropriately." Tremper Longman III, "Responses to Chapter Two," in *Reading Genesis 1–2: An Evangelical Conversation*, ed. J. Daryl Charles (Peabody, Mass.: Hendrickson, 2013), 66. Both Collins's and Longman's self-definition as holding to "literal" or "historical-grammatical" approaches on Genesis 1–2 stand in contrast to the Reformation and post-Reformation uses of "literal," versus "allegorical" or "figurative" in relation to this passage; as such I would argue they are a redefinition of the historic use of the terms in relation to Genesis interpretation.

170. Collins, "Reading Genesis 1:1–2:3," 143, 149.

171. Collins, "Reading Genesis 1:1–2:3," 144.

Collins published more articles and a book defending a historical Adam and Eve in the midst of and after the Enns controversy.[172] In these, he argued against reading Genesis with the understanding that "the author intended to relay 'straight history,' with a minimum of figurative language."[173] Instead, Collins argued that the reader ought rather to believe that "the author was talking about what he thought were actual events, using literary and rhetorical techniques to shape the reader's attitudes towards those events."[174] Where the literal tradition held these two points in harmony, Collins set the latter in opposition to the former.

Appropriately critical of Enns's description of Genesis as "myth" and "an ancient, premodern, prescientific way of addressing questions of ultimate origins and meaning in the form of stories," Collins proposed that the text of early Genesis was a "historical account."[175] Yet Collins's definition of a "historical account" once again differed from that commonly held by literal tradition proponents. Taking a cue from ancient Near Eastern writings including Mesopotamian origin and flood stories, Collins claimed that these "provide the context against which Genesis 1–11 are to be set, [and] provide us with clues on how to read this kind of literature."[176] He further stated, "These [ancient Near Eastern] stories include divine action, symbolism, and imaginative elements; the purpose of the stories is to lay the foundation for a worldview, without being taken in a 'literalistic' fashion. We should nevertheless see the story as having what we might call an 'historical core,' though we must be careful in discerning what it is."[177]

---

172. These include the following: "Adam and Eve as Historical People, and Why It Matters," *Perspectives on Science and the Christian Faith* 62, no. 3 (September 2010): 147–65; "Adam and Eve in the Old Testament," *The Southern Baptist Journal of Theology* 15, no. 1 (2011): 4–25; *Did Adam and Eve Really Exist?: Who They Were and Why You Should Care* (Wheaton, Ill.: Crossway, 2011), 1–192.

173. Collins, *Did Adam and Eve Really Exist?*, 16.

174. Collins, *Did Adam and Eve Really Exist?*, 16.

175. Collins, *Did Adam and Eve Really Exist?*, 29, 34.

176. Collins, *Did Adam and Eve Really Exist?*, 35.

177. Collins, *Did Adam and Eve Really Exist?*, 35. In his contribution to a more recent volume, Collins argues that the "overarching pattern from Mesopotamia provides a literary and ideological context into which Genesis 1–11 speaks, and it is reasonable to conclude that it does so as a whole…. Further it appears that the Mesopotamians aimed to accomplish their purpose by founding their stories on what they thought were actual events, albeit told with a great deal of imagery and symbolism. Thus it is reasonable to take Gen 1–11 as having a similar purpose in Israel, expecting similar attention to history without undue literalism." Collins, "Reading Genesis 1–2 with the Grain: Analogical Days," in *Reading Genesis 1–2: An Evangelical Conversation*, ed., J. Daryl Charles (Peabody, Mass.: Hendrickson, 2013), 77.

Collins's suggestion that the intent in the early chapters of Genesis was to convey a "historical core" that was communicated in the midst of and through rhetorical and figurative elements, rested on two key assumptions: (1) that ancient Near Eastern religious-cosmological concepts were contextually formative to the writing of Genesis; and (2) that Mesopotamian myths were not taken in a "literalistic" fashion by ancient Mesopotamians—views extensively popularized by Wheaton College professor John Walton.[178] Neither assumption, however, had a foundation of documentary evidence but were at best historiographical and linguistic theory.

Not only was there no hard evidence to indicate that ancient Mesopotamians read their narratives the way Collins and Walton did, there was also no evidence the divinely inspired human author of Genesis did. However, this lack had not deterred previous creative theorizing toward alternate interpretations of the early chapters of Genesis—even centuries prior—as evidenced by La Peyrère's, Spinoza's, and Voltaire's pursuit of similar arguments in the early Enlightenment era.[179] Collins's analogical hermeneutic, self-described as resting on his ancient Near Eastern literary hypothesis, stood within the milieu of figurative approaches to Genesis 1 and 2, rather than within the literal tradition—despite some effort to claim the contrary. The argument that the Genesis narrative, as a "historical account," intended to convey a "historical core" resembled that of those who served as Peter Enns's Old Testament teachers at Westminster (Philadelphia).

---

178. John H. Walton, *The Lost World of Genesis One: Ancient Cosmology and the Origins Debate* (Downers Grove, Ill.: InterVarsity, 2009), 1–191; John H. Walton, *Genesis 1 As Ancient Cosmology* (Winona Lake, Ind.: Eisenbrauns, 2011), 1–214.

179. This is one of the weaknesses of the historiographical conclusions made by a number of past and present Old Testament scholars intrigued by ancient Near Eastern history. It seems that a more compelling case can be made to the contrary—with the potential of significant contribution toward a more scripturally grounded understanding of ancient Near Eastern belief. As an initial observation, both ancient Egyptian and ancient Greek mythology appears to have been taken quite "literally" in its early context. Ancient Egyptians invested heavily in detailed preparations for the afterlife, with precise attention to a literalistic reading of their texts. In ancient Greek contexts, it was not until significantly later centuries that particular schools of Greek philosophy came to view the narratives of the Greek pantheon as embarrassingly barbaric and crude, opting for more figurative approaches. The latter transition influenced the development of early Christian nonliteral hermeneutics on Genesis, as exemplified by Clement and Origen in Alexandria. Beyond these issues, contemporary contextual approaches often fail to distinguish between the fallible and incomplete sources of the ancient Near East, with no promise of the aid of the Holy Spirit, versus the infallible and fully sufficient source of the Holy Scriptures, with God's promise of the aid of the Holy Spirit to illuminate the believer.

Collins's hermeneutical approach was also reflected in his conception of the legitimate boundaries of latitude in relation to human origins, which he referred to as the "freedoms and limitations" consistent with his theological argument for a historical Adam.[180] While he had previously stated his "personal" commitment to a special creation of Adam from the soil, Collins now pursued what he felt were the maximal bounds of Christian orthodoxy in relation to his conception of the historicity of Adam and Eve, in part as a counterargument against Enns, as well as Daniel Harlow and others.[181] Engaging the suggestions of a variety of proponents of alternative views of human origins, he argued that the following requirements marked the bounds of "sound thinking":

(1) the image of God in man "could not be the outcome of natural processes alone";

(2) "we should see Adam and Eve at the headwaters of the human race";

(3) "the 'fall,' in whatever form it took, was both historical and moral, and occurred at the beginning of the human race";

(4) "if someone should decide that there were, in fact, more human beings than just Adam and Eve at the beginning of mankind, then, in order to maintain good sense, he should envision these humans as a single tribe. Adam would then be the chieftain of this tribe (preferably produced before the others), and Eve would be his wife. This tribe 'fell' under the leadership of Adam and Eve. This follows from the notion of solidarity in a representative. Some may call this a form of 'polygenesis,' but this is quite distinct from the more conventional, and unacceptable kind."[182]

While maintaining the necessity of an actual Adam and Eve in history, Collins did so in a manner allowing for evolutionary biological processes in

---

180. C. John Collins, "Replies to Reviews of *Did Adam and Eve Really Exist?*," *Journal of Creation Theology and Science Series B: Life Sciences* no. 2 (2012): 43–47.

181. Collins, *Did Adam and Eve Really Exist?*, 9. Writing in *The Southern Baptist Journal of Theology*, Collins would provide a more muted version of his argument for latitude on the origins of Adam and Eve, briefly stating in passing that the Genesis "style of telling the story may leave room for discussion on the exact details of the process by which God formed Adam's body, and how long ago." Collins, "Adam and Eve in the Old Testament," 14. In a blog exchange with Kevin DeYoung, Collins stated, "My understanding of Adam and Eve (at least my preference) is pretty much what you describe as the ordinary one…but yes, I am saying 'it could be different and still be biblical.'" Kevin DeYoung, "Adam and Eve Follow-Up: A Dialogue with Jack Collins," *DeYoung, Restless, and Reformed* (July 28, 2011), http://thegospelcoalition.org /blogs/kevindeyoung/2011/07/28/adam-and-eve-follow-up-a-dialogue-with-jack-collins/.

182. Collins, "Adam and Eve as Historical People, and Why It Matters," 156; *Did Adam and Eve Really Exist?*, 120–21.

their origins, as long as there was some form of supernatural intervention in "refurbishing an existing hominid."[183] The other key boundary was that Adam was "preferably" the first human produced, with Eve as his wife, while allowing for a separate production of their contemporaries—so long as they were a tribe which "fell" under the leadership of Adam and Eve.

Referring specifically to Derek Kidner's partly evolutionary model of human origins, Collins argued that it was "worthy of consideration" so long as one imagined "Adam as chieftain, or 'king,' whose task it is not simply to *rule* a people but more importantly to *represent* them."[184] Engaging with C. S. Lewis's theistic evolutionary proposal, Collins suggested that to make it acceptable, "we should make it more like Kidner's…with Adam as the chieftain and Eve as his queen."[185] In the face of recent proposals from parts of the scientific community regarding human evolution and DNA, Collins concluded: "Nothing requires us to abandon monogenesis altogether for some form of polygenesis; rather a modified monogenesis, which keeps Adam and Eve, can do the job."[186]

Collins concluded that despite the fact that there were "many uncertainties" with his modifications, one could nonetheless hold to these views and at the same time "hold fast to the Biblical story line with full confidence."[187] In response to a query by a reviewer on the potential implications of his proposal, Collins responded, "I should note that I share his discomfort with the prospect that 'early humans committed bestiality, had half human, half animal offspring, and that offspring mated with other humans to such an extent that modern humans carry around perhaps as much as 4% animal genes,' and hope that it is not so."[188]

Where Collins had stated a decade earlier that his analogical approach was incompatible with theistic evolution, he was now, though still committed to the same hermeneutic, unable or unwilling to discount the possibility of hominid-human hybrids; he supported the "evolved chieftain of a tribe" model as an option coherent with the teaching of Scripture. His description of boundaries for what he described as "the traditional view" of Adam and

---

183. Collins, *Did Adam and Eve Really Exist?*, 124–25.

184. In this theory, Adam was a hominid, becoming human through divine intervention, which Kidner held likely occurred to a wider group of hominids around the same time. Derek Kidner, *Genesis: An Introduction and Commentary* (Downers Grove, Ill.: InterVarsity, 1967), 26–32. Collins, *Did Adam and Eve Really Exist?*, 125.

185. Collins, *Did Adam and Eve Really Exist?*, 130.

186. Collins, *Did Adam and Eve Really Exist?*, 130.

187. Collins, *Did Adam and Eve Really Exist?*, 131.

188. Collins, "Replies to Reviews of *Did Adam and Eve Really Exist?*," 44.

Eve did not in fact cohere with the literal tradition, but rather reflected a hybrid lineage of its own.[189] The tradition behind his claim for the potential legitimacy of hominid precursors, the possibility of human-hominid hybrids, as well as human contemporaries to Adam and Eve, included Jewish Kabbalists, early Socinians like Jacob Palaeologus, and Enlightenment figures such as Burnett, Monboddo, and Erasmus Darwin. Collins's argument for the sufficiency of a representative Adamic leadership of contemporaries, rather than the necessity of physical descent for all humanity from Adam, was remarkably similar to La Peyrère's.

Regarding his personal flexibility toward these options in light of contemporary DNA hypotheses, Collins stated, "If genetics eventually forces reconsideration...[I] could perhaps reconceive of Adam and Eve as the king and queen of a larger population."[190] Collins's quest for the historical Adam left a wide array of potential Adams. Both his analogical hermeneutic and ensuing latitude on human origins proved influential among students; his views also received the support of Covenant Theological Seminary president Bryan Chapell.[191]

---

189. Collins, *Did Adam and Eve Really Exist?*, 133.

190. Richard N. Ostling, "The Search for the Historical Adam," *Christianity Today* 55, no. 6 (June 2011): 27. Collins's statement resembled a previous response from Bryan Estelle, Old Testament professor at Westminster Seminary in California, to tensions regarding theistic evolution. Estelle had claimed, "Creationism is the best thing that could have happened to Darwinism, the caricature of religion that seemed to justify Darwinist contempt for the whole of religion." He stated that he held to the literal understanding of Genesis 2:7 but that it was not within the preacher's domain to evaluate science, further noting his belief that "it may come to be, based on further reflection on the dust metaphor from the standpoint of analysis of how the metaphor functioned in the Bible and ancient Near East that our understanding of Gen. 2:7 may grow with rereading. But I do not see presently how it can take away from Murray's point touching on the issues at hand." Bryan Estelle, "Preachers in Lab Coats and Scientists in Geneva Gowns," *Ordained Servant Online* (November 2010), http://www.opc.org/os.html?article_id=220&cur_iss.

191. Chapell suggested in a panel discussion that the boundary line for a biblical anthropology was what occurred "within the garden"; a potential implication of Chapell's delineation was that it granted allowance that Adam's origins "outside the garden" might indeed include something beyond a literal creation from the dust of the earth. Bryan Chapell and R. Albert Mohler, "Are Adam and Eve Historical Figures?" (Panel discussion, Gospel Coalition National Conference, April 9, 2013), http://thegospelcoalition.org/resources/entry/are_adam_and_eve_historical_figures_-_panel_discussion_albert_mohler_bryan_chapell. By the time of publication this source had been removed from the Internet.

Responses to Collins

Richard Belcher, Old Testament professor at Reformed Theological Seminary in Charlotte and a proponent of the literal tradition, was one of the first Presbyterians to respond in print. He noted,

> The way Collins defines the traditional view is problematic because he omits from the discussion the very text that is at the heart of the debate. He explicitly says that how God created Adam in Genesis 2 is outside the purview of his analysis and that the origin of the material for Adam's body is not going to be addressed (p.13). In other words, he bypasses an exegesis of Genesis 2:7, the main text that should be at the center of this discussion.... The traditional view, however, should include not just the historicity of Adam and Eve and the immediate special creation of Adam and Eve, but also the traditional understanding of Genesis 2:7, which is that God took soil from the ground and made Adam from it.[192]

While Collins continued propounding what he believed were the maximal bounds of orthodoxy in relation to human origins, his colleague at Covenant, systematics professor Michael Williams, published an article in which he defined "the image of God" in relation to human origins and nature in a manner congruent with an anthropological monism, and lending itself to coherence with theistic evolution. Williams had argued that "as to our origin and the stuff from which we are made, the human is no different from any member of the animal kingdom.... The uniqueness of the human predicated in the fact that this creature is made in the image of God (Gen. 1:26) *does not identify a distinction* between human and animal life so much as it calls the human to a unique role within creation."[193]

---

192. Richard Belcher, "Did Adam and Eve Really Exist? A Review," Reformation 21, February 2012. http://www.reformation21.org/articles/did-adam-and-eve-really-exist-a-review.php.

193. Emphasis added. Michael Williams, "Man and Beast," *Presbyterion* 34, no. 1 (Spring 2008): 15. Louis Berkhof notes, "Calvin...states that the image of God extends to everything in which the nature of man surpasses that of all other species of animals.... By this term is denoted the integrity with which Adam was endued when his intellect was clear, his affections subordinated to reason, all his senses duly regulated, and when he truly ascribed all his excellence to the admirable gifts of his Maker.... The primary seat of the divine image was in the mind and the heart, or in the soul and its powers, there was no part even of the body in which some rays of glory did not shine." Berkhof goes on to state, "the Socinians and early Arminians taught that the image of God consisted only in man's dominion over the lower creation." *Systematic Theology* (Grand Rapids: Eerdmans, 1996), 202–3. The Westminster Confession of Faith (4.2) states, "God...created man, male and female, with reasonable and immortal souls, endued with knowledge, righteousness, and true holiness, after His own image; having the law of God written on their hearts, and power to fulfil it." Williams gave little to no attention to these aspects of the image of God in man.

While no public criticism occurred, several years later, Williams revisited the topic in the same journal, elucidating a somewhat improved approach in his "First Calling: The *Imago Dei* and the Order of Creation":

> Here is what we absolutely must not miss about the creation of human beings: we are creatures of the sixth day.... The second chapter of Genesis is explicit here. The man was fashioned—by God's own hand—of the dust of the ground (v.7). Adam is sculpted from clay. He is by God's design and personal handiwork, an earthling.... We are rooted in God's creation no less than are the animals, for like them, the earth is our home and we are ever dependent upon our Creator.... Yet Genesis 1 *does declare a difference* between the human and the nonhuman creature.... Here is what distinguishes us from the animal kingdom. Human beings have been made after the image of God.... Of all of God's creatures it is the human alone who has been created in such a way that Genesis can say that we have been made in God's own image.[194]

Williams's second article stood in substantial contradiction to his first. It appeared to be an anomaly in the Genesis commentary coming from Covenant Theological Seminary on human origins, particularly as it was substantively more consistent with the literal tradition than his first. However, he appeared to veer in an opposite direction, now bringing the strikingly anthropomorphic language of the more poetic genres of Job and the Psalms—"by God's own hand"—into the Genesis text.

Presbyterian Responses to the Quest for Adam

More significant than the writings of individuals were the ecclesiastical actions resulting from the controversies over Genesis interpretation and human origins. In 2012, the Associate Reformed Presbyterian Church, the oldest American Presbyterian denomination, exemplified its movement from

---

194. Emphasis added. Michael D. Williams, "First Calling: The *Imago Dei* and the Order of Creation—Part I," *Presbyterion* 39, no. 1 (Spring 2013): 30–44. Williams, in defining what the image of God in man refers to, still appears to lean toward seeing it as primarily in reference to "role." He somewhat circumscribes this with commentary on Anthony Hoekema's statement that "the image of God consists of more than mere functioning; it concerns not only what man does but what he is," along with Herman Bavinck's statement that "a human being does not *bear* or *have* the image of God but that he or she *is* the image of God," settling for the idea that man is neither "bare copy or a copying, image as noun or verb" but rather fits the analogy of a photocopier. He still fails to engage the rich language and understanding of the Westminster Confession and Catechisms, along with the breadth of Reformation and post-Reformation understanding of the image of God and human origins. Williams, "First Calling," 42–43.

a mainline to a more confessionally evangelical direction by overwhelmingly passing a synodical teaching statement declaring:

1) We affirm that Adam and Eve were special, unique direct creations of God, created in His image, with Adam being formed from the dust of the ground and Eve being made from his side; as such, they were real human beings and the first man and woman;

2) We affirm that the account of the creation of Adam and Eve as found in Genesis 1 and 2 is history;

3) We deny any teaching that claims that the account of creation of Adam and Eve, as found in Genesis 1 and 2, is mythology;

4) We deny any theory that teaches that Adam and Eve descended from other biological life forms and that such a theory can be reasonably reconciled with either the Standards of the Associate Reformed Presbyterian Church or Holy Scripture.[195]

By contrast, within the much younger and larger Presbyterian Church in America, efforts at its General Assembly to present a similar teaching statement in response to the ongoing controversy failed. This failure appeared to be due to a convergence of those in two broad camps. Some argued that the confessional standards of the Westminster Confession of Faith and Catechisms provided sufficient clarity on the topic—positing that if there were concerns, they ought to be pursued through the means of church discipline. Other delegates held that belief in evolutionary biological processes in human origins, as circumscribed by Collins, Keller, or others, was harmonious with Scripture and represented a legitimate latitude of ecclesiastical theology.[196]

---

195. Associate Reformed Presbyterian Church, *Minutes of the General Synod of the Associate Reformed Presbyterian Church 2012* (printed by author, 2012), 503–5. Of the several hundred delegates, three voted in opposition.

196. Don K. Clements, "At the PCA General Assembly: Commissioners Vote on Controversial Overtures," *The Aquila Report* (June 21, 2012), http://theaquilareport.com/from-the-pca-general-assembly-commissioners-vote-on-controversial-overtures/. Reflecting on the vote, Timothy R. LeCroy, a minister in the PCA, stated: "Though I am personally against theistic evolution, I do not believe that *in thesi* statements are the answer to the problem. I do believe that holding to the special creation of Adam is essential to preserve several of our fundamental doctrines (one of which being original sin), but I am not of the opinion that the best way to handle these issues is to beat our brothers into submission. Let us do the hard work to discuss these issues with our brothers and persuade them of the rightness of our view. There are certainly boundaries that cannot be crossed, but I do not believe that passing *in thesi* statements for the purposes of forming blunt weapons to be used in such battles is the way to go." Timothy R. LeCroy, "Thoughts on the 40th PCA GA, Part Two: *in thesi* Statement on the Creation

Through the latter half of the twentieth century and into the early twenty-first century, it was abundantly clear that alternative hermeneutical approaches toward the early chapters of Genesis had gained significant support among more conservative Presbyterians. Concurrently, a proliferation of possible end-points had developed in the quest for the historical Adam. The new "Adams" were significantly unlike the Adam of Genesis as understood in the literal tradition. At the same time, there continued to be a stream of commitment to—and even recovery of—the enduring literal tradition on Genesis and human origins.

Baptists and the Quest for Adam

Whereas Presbyterians appeared to be dividing into increasingly divergent streams regarding human origins and Genesis interpretation, Baptists in the latter part of the twentieth century displayed a remarkable and influential return to the literal interpretive tradition on Genesis 1 and 2, including human origins. [197] This return came despite the fact that the mid-twentieth century gave little evidence that this would ever be the case; in fact, it appeared that some of the most influential Baptist writers were leading in the opposite direction, while institutions like Southern Baptist Theological Seminary tended to be characterized by distance and suspicion toward proponents of the literal tradition.

Bernard Ramm: "No Clear, Precise Rule to Tell What Is Cultural"

Bernard Ramm (1916–1992), who taught at the Bible Institute of Los Angeles, Bethel College and Seminary, Baylor College, and the American Baptist Seminary of the West, opened the 1950s with a broadside against the literal tradition on Genesis 1 and 2. In his preface to *The Christian View of Science and Scripture*, Ramm stated that in researching the book, he had "discovered that there were two traditions in Bible and science both stemming from the developments of the nineteenth century." [198] Viewing the literal tradition as one of these developments, he described it variously as "the ignoble tradition which

---

of Adam," *Vita pastoralis* (June 25, 2012), http://pastortimlecroy.wordpress.com/2012/06/25/thoughts-on-the-40th-pca-ga-part-two-in-thesi-statement-on-the-creation-of-adam/.

197. While realizing there are differences in history and at times ecclesiastical structure between Baptist and nondenominational churches (the latter including independent churches, Bible churches, and others), I have referred under this heading to those who would not usually be termed Baptists but are committed to credo-baptism and church polities fitting within the spectrum of Baptist churches.

198. Bernard Ramm, *The Christian View of Science and Scripture* (Grand Rapids: Eerdmans, 1954), preface. Ramm's statement would be echoed by later critics of the literal tradition,

has taken a most unwholesome attitude toward science," "unfortunately...the major tradition in evangelicalism in the twentieth century," and "a narrow evangelical Biblicism and...Plymouth Brethren theology [which] buried the noble tradition."[199] Ramm's "wish [was] to call evangelicalism back to the noble tradition of the closing years of the nineteenth century," exemplified in the writings of men including J. W. Dawson, Hugh Miller, James Orr, and Asa Gray.[200]

Ramm's hermeneutical approach was predicated on the assumption that "the language of the Bible in relation to natural things is *popular, prescientific, and non-postulational*."[201] He further stated that the Bible used "the terminology of the culture prevailing at the time the various books were written... [and] the Spirit of God [speaks] through these terms so that (i) the terms are not themselves made infallible science, and that (ii) the theological content is in no wise endangered."[202]

The implications of Ramm's commitment to these postulations soon became evident as he stated, "The truth of God...under the cultural partakes of the binding character of inspiration, not the cultural vehicle," while averring that some passages of Scripture were "clearly didactic, theological, and hence, transcultural."[203] Ramm seemed to have some sense of the difficulty he had entered by formulating a deeply compromised doctrine of Scripture as he reflected on the work of the classicist:

> There is no clear, precise rule for the classicist to tell what is cultural and what is transcultural. That is an art, and a skill developed from his learning. Similarly the Biblical theologian (i) knowing that some of the Bible is in terms of the prevailing culture [i.e., fallible and not partaking of the binding character of inspiration], and (ii) that some of it is evidently transcultural, and (iii) also knowing from research much of the culture surrounding the Old and New Testaments, is able to formulate his Biblical theology, and to see what is transcultural under the mode of the cultural.[204]

Ramm's hermeneutical approach to Genesis 1 and 2 was further outlined in his chapter on geology. Rejecting what he termed the "naïve-literal view,"

---

including Ronald Numbers and R. Scott Clark. Both would argue that the modern roots of the literal tradition lay in Seventh-day Adventism in the North American context.

199. Ramm, *Science and Scripture*, preface.
200. Ramm, *Science and Scripture*, preface.
201. Ramm, *Science and Scripture*, 76.
202. Ramm, *Science and Scripture*, 76.
203. Ramm, *Science and Scripture*, 77.
204. Ramm, *Science and Scripture*, 80.

along with gap theory and day-age approaches, Ramm argued that Scripture and geology were best harmonized through "(i) the pictorial-day theory of Genesis' days, (ii) the moderate theory of concordism, and (iii) progressive creationism," with the latter being "the belief that Nature is permeated with divine activity but not in any pantheistic sense."[205]

Gaps in the fossil record, according to Ramm, were indicators that "from time to time [over the course of millions of years] the great creative acts, *de novo*, took place. The complexity of animal forms increased. Finally, when every river had cut its intended course, when every mountain was in its proposed place, when every animal was on the earth according to blueprint, then he whom all creation anticipated is made, MAN, in whom alone is the breath of God. This is not theistic evolution which calls for creation from within with no acts *de novo*. It is progressive creationism."[206]

Later, in discussing biology, Ramm made it clear that he did not view evolutionary theory as fact, but rather as a probability statement: "No one has seen evolution at work over the hundreds of thousands of years of geologic time. What we have is a vast collection of data of almost every conceivable sort... [which] is organized by the theory of evolution, a generalization of the broadest possible type."[207] Ramm concluded, "The theory of progressive creationism is that interpretation of life which the author advocates and which he thinks is a much more comprehensive theory than the theory of evolution."[208] Thus, Ramm had not necessarily abandoned a special, temporally immediate creation of Adam and Eve at this point. In his chapter on anthropology, however, while defending the need for the unity of the human race and at one point stating that pre-Adamite theory "has its vexing problems," Ramm turned to Emil Brunner's theory in which "there was no historical Adam nor historical Fall...

205. Ramm, *Science and Scripture*, 229, 227.

206. Ramm, *Science and Scripture*, 228.

207. Ramm, *Science and Scripture*, 268.

208. Ramm, *Science and Scripture*, 271. Like a number of those holding to the literal tradition on Genesis 1 and 2, Ramm allowed for a limited form of "evolution" within created kinds. He described this as where a "root-species may give rise to several species by horizontal radiation, through the process of the unraveling of gene potentialities or recombination...the gaps in the geological [fossil] record are gaps because vertical progress takes place only by creation." While critical of evolution, Ramm left open the possibility that through "responsible scholarship," a form of theistic evolution might in time be determined to cohere with Christianity. Ramm, *Science and Scripture*, 272, 292. Ramm's model of progressive creationism would be adopted and developed by others including Fazale Rana and Hugh Ross, who would postulate the existence of human-like pre-Adamites who became extinct. Fazale Rana with Hugh Ross, *Who Was Adam?: A Creation Model Approach to the Origin of Man* (Colorado Springs: NavPress, 2005), 1–299.

[and] man became truly man at that point in his evolution when he became self-reflective."[209] Ramm noted with appreciation Brunner's stance that

> there must have been an act of God in making some pre-human a human. Who that pre-human was, and when man fell into sin, is all lost in the vast stretches of prehistory and are irrecoverable to the theologian. But none of this alters the Biblical essentials about man and sin. To Christian theology Adam represents the unity of the human race.... The record of the Fall means that sin and imperfection are universal in humanity.... This sort of theology is new in non-evangelical circles, and one hopes that it might be the harbinger of a great revival of evangelical theology. On the debit side of the ledger there is a certain disquietude with Brunner's exegesis.... We wonder if he has not paid too great an attention to criticism, and forced the Bible into an unnatural position.

After considering authors like James Orr and George Mivart, who had adopted a figurative approach to the language of Genesis 2 and allowed for a theistic evolutionary process for human origins, Ramm concluded: "Many evangelical scholars would feel apprehensive over taking too many liberties with the interpretation of the text.... We may take theistic evolution as the solution to our problem of the origin of man.... We must await more information from science and exegesis before we can propound a pointed theory of the harmony of Genesis and anthropology."[210]

While he began with what seemed to be a nonevolutionary form of special creation, Ramm's quest for the historical Adam ended with an uncertain array of potential Adams, ranging from the Adam of the literal tradition to an evolving hominid which became self-conscious, and thus human, through an act of God. As Meredith Kline noted, the flames of debate in Baptist circles and beyond were being "vigorously fanned by the bellows of dissenters" to the literal tradition on Genesis and human origins.[211]

Ralph Elliot's "Parabolic and Symbolic" Genesis

Not long after Ramm's publication, further controversy roiled the Baptist community: Ralph H. Elliot, formerly an Old Testament professor at Southern Baptist Theological Seminary, published *The Message of Genesis* (1961) with Broadman Press, a publishing house owned by the Southern Baptist

---

209. Ramm, *Science and Scripture*, 319.
210. Ramm, *Science and Scripture*, 321–28.
211. Kline, "Because It Had Not Rained," 2:146.

Convention.[212] In it, Elliot categorized the first eleven chapters of Genesis as "parabolic and symbolic" literature. His hermeneutical approach to Genesis led to his dismissal from Midwestern Baptist Theological Seminary the following year—an episode indicative of ongoing struggles within the Southern Baptist Convention.[213]

Whitcomb and Morris: Literal Genesis and Creation Science

The same year that Elliot's work appeared, John Whitcomb and Henry Morris published *The Genesis Flood*.[214] Focusing on an attempt to correlate geological data with the universal Noahic flood, the authors sought to use scientific models in order to defend a young-earth position, viewing this as a means to promote the literal hermeneutic tradition on Genesis. The book quickly gained a wide audience, and Morris and others involved with him at the Institute for Creation Research kept up a steady stream of publications promoting a young earth via flood geology.

Morris's most substantial foray into the realm of hermeneutics and exegesis came a little more than a decade later, with his publication of "a scientific and devotional commentary on the book of beginnings."[215] In keeping with the literal tradition, Morris viewed Genesis 2:7 as God's special creation of man from the dust of the ground, though he moved beyond the text to infer that "in modern terminology," this referred to "the basic chemical elements: nitrogen, oxygen, calcium, etc."[216] Where the text of Genesis 2:7 stated God "breathed into his nostrils the breath of life," Morris argued that though this might seem "anthropomorphic," "such a notion is quite inadequate."[217] He stated,

---

212. Gregory A. Wills, *Southern Baptist Seminary, 1859–2009* (Oxford: Oxford University Press, 2009), 406–7; Ralph H. Elliot, *The Message of Genesis* (Nashville: Broadman, 1961), 1–209.

213. James Leo Garrett, E. Glenn Hinson, and James E. Tull, *Are Southern Baptists "Evangelicals"?* (Macon, Ga.: Mercer University Press, 1983), 112–17. Several decades later, Ralph Elliot published his account of the events as *The Genesis Controversy and Continuity in Southern Baptist Chaos: A Eulogy for a Great Tradition* (Macon, Ga.: Mercer University Press, 1992), 1–178.

214. Morris was a Baptist with a PhD in hydraulic engineering who taught at a number of universities prior to establishing the Institute for Creation Research. Whitcomb belonged to the Fellowship of Grace Brethren Churches and served as a professor of theology and Old Testament at Grace Theological Seminary, where he had also received his ThD; he was dismissed from his position after controversy in 1990.

215. Henry M. Morris, *The Genesis Record: A Scientific and Devotional Commentary on the Book of Beginnings* (Grand Rapids: Baker, 1976), 1–716.

216. Morris, *The Genesis Record*, 85.

217. Morris, *The Genesis Record*, 85. In his second work devoted to the exposition of Scripture on creation and the flood, Morris continued to promote the literal tradition; however,

Man's body...completely formed, equipped with nostrils, lungs, and the entire breathing apparatus...was lifeless. It must be energized. The breathing mechanism must be activated, the heart must start to pump.... But life can come only from life, and the living God is the only self-existent Being, so it must ultimately come from Him. Especially to stress the unique relationship of human life to the divine life, this Scripture verse tells us that God Himself directly imparted life and breath to man...only to man.... God directly (rather than at a distance, as it were, by His spoken Word) "breathed" in the "breath of life." At this point, man became a "living soul."[218]

Although Morris's exposition was fully congruent with the literal tradition on this point, he took a somewhat unconventional or at least ambiguous turn when he argued not only that "the 'soul' is the *nephesh* also shared by animals (Genesis 1:24), and refers to the consciousness principle, the realm of mind and emotions," but also that "the soul was created on the fifth day."[219] Morris went on to distinguish between the human and animal "soul" by stating, "Just as man's body was tremendously more complex and capable than those of animals, so man's soul was of much higher order than the animal soul, requiring God's direct energizing for its activation."[220]

Morris provided some clarification as he concluded: "Not only did man receive his soul directly from God rather than from an animal ancestry, but Adam was the first man. There was no 'pre-Adamite man,' as some have suggested."[221] While an ardent promoter of a literal approach, Morris's language regarding God's "energizing" and "activation" of the soul of man was not common in the literal tradition. His distinction between man and animal and description of the soul also raised questions about his understanding of the nature of man's creation in the image of God. However, Morris's ongoing writings on creation, the flood, and science—a fruit of his Genesis commitments—proved significant in the advancement of a growing creation science movement and in a wider resurgence of a literal hermeneutic on human origins.

---

he not only repeated previous inferences but now also adopted decidedly anthropomorphic language not found in the text of Genesis: "Adam's body was carefully and lovingly formed directly by God's own hands (not, like the animals, merely by the divine spoken Word) out of the 'dust of the ground,' the basic elements of earth matter from which all physical systems had been made (Gen. 2:7)." Henry Morris, *Biblical Creationism: What Each Book of the Bible Teaches about Creation and the Flood* (Grand Rapids: Baker, 1993), 24–25.

218. Morris, *The Genesis Record*, 86.
219. Morris, *The Genesis Record*, 86.
220. Morris, *The Genesis Record*, 86.
221. Morris, *The Genesis Record*, 86.

Carl F. H. Henry: "A Factual Record of God's Creation of the Universe"

A contemporary to Ramm, Elliot, and Morris, Carl F. H. Henry (1913–2003), served as professor of theology at Northern Baptist Theological Seminary, professor and dean at Fuller Seminary, and editor of *Christianity Today*— providing influential leadership among Baptists and other evangelicals. Henry opened his discussion of creation in *God, Revelation, and Authority*, noting that "what Genesis teaches about man and the world as a divine creation differs remarkably from the other ancient views of origins."[222]

In contrast to Ramm, Henry's concern over an errant comparative religious approach between Genesis and the historical remnants of ancient Near Eastern cultural contexts was plain: "The tendency of *Religiongeschichte* scholars to minimize the differences between Genesis and so-called nonbiblical 'creation' accounts found in other religions of the Near East must not be allowed to obscure very real and important dissimilarities.... The Genesis creation account confronts and challenges [them]."[223]

Henry further noted that he viewed ancient Near Eastern traditions as derivative and distorted, while the Genesis account, as the Word of God, was normative:

> Interestingly enough even the ancient polytheistic traditions often single out a supreme Creator-God who has precedence.... Even amid their alterations these corrupted traditions of the primal creation preserve a kind of witness to the transcendent creation of the universe by an act of personal divine power.... At the center of the scriptural creation narrative, as at the center of the entire Bible, stands the living God.... The living God creates voluntarily according to his sovereign pleasure.... The universe is a wholly contingent reality.[224]

Turning from the position and nature of Scripture in relation to ancient Near Eastern accounts, Henry directly engaged Ramm. While at first proffering some positive gleanings, he critically concluded:

> By imposing the grid of empirical science on the Genesis account Ramm abstracts certain elements from the narrative as a whole that unlike other elements are to be regarded as factually significant. But this method of interpretation necessarily suspends what is or is not to be considered factual upon the changing theories of science; it provides no firm basis,

---

222. Carl F. H. Henry, *God, Revelation, and Authority* (Waco, Tex.: Word Books, 1983), 6:109.
223. Henry, *God, Revelation, and Authority*, 6:109.
224. Henry, *God, Revelation, and Authority*, 6:110–11.

moreover, for excluding the factual significance of other elements. And it offers no consistent hermeneutical procedure for selecting from the data of Scripture, or for interpreting Scripture where it adduces once-for-all phenomena whose miraculous or nonmiraculous nature empirical science is not competent to decide. Ramm's harmonizing of Scripture with geology by correlating the pictorial-day theory, moderate concordism and progressive evolution seems more a wedding of convenience than an orderly claim that the creation account makes upon its readers.[225]

Unimpressed with Ramm's formulations, Henry stated, "Nothing in the Genesis account encouraged subsequent biblical writers to accept it as other than a factual record of God's creation of the universe."[226] He viewed the genre of the Genesis creation account as "straightforward prose," rather than being "cast in poetic form." Going on to carefully qualify, Henry noted that "this is not to say, however, that if any facets of the biblical account and of man's fall are to be retained as literal, it follows that all elements must be interpreted literally."[227]

Henry's warrant for applying this general principle to the text of Genesis 1 and 2 mistakenly included conflating a literal interpretation of the text with an anthropomorphic inference potentially, but not necessarily, drawn from the text of Genesis: "God's 'speaking' or 'saying' does not involve laryngeal utterance, for example."[228] He further argued, "In any event man was not present before the sixth day to 'hear' the voice and Word of God in creation."[229] What Henry exactly meant by the latter was unclear—was it that there was no sound, or merely no one to hear? However, it was clear that he intended by it to provide a foundation for a hermeneutic that allowed for a literal understanding of some aspects of the text and a figurative understanding of others.[230] Thus, he

---

225. Henry, *God, Revelation, and Authority*, 6:115.
226. Henry, *God, Revelation, and Authority*, 6:116.
227. Henry, *God, Revelation, and Authority*, 6:116.
228. Henry, *God, Revelation, and Authority*, 6:116.
229. Henry, *God, Revelation, and Authority*, 6:116.
230. The absence of human ears (i.e., the absence of man prior to his creation) does not mean the necessary negation of audible divine speech, nor does the nature of God preclude audible divine speech. Several factors testify to the opposite, the first being the creation itself: if God, who is sovereign, immaterial Spirit, can create physical reality, certainly there is no reason to believe He cannot or did not speak audibly. God the Father spoke audibly at the baptism of His incarnate Son, saying, "This is My beloved Son, in whom I am well pleased" (Matt. 3:17); another divine speech event occurs at the transfiguration (Matt. 17:5–6), with the apostle Peter stating, "We heard this voice which came from heaven when we were with Him" (2 Peter 1:17–18). These audible divine speech events, recorded in the New Testament, are not typically considered as figurative due to concerns over anthropomorphism—in fact to do so would call into question the testimony of the Gospel writers and Peter. Henry might

could state: "A sovereign immaterial Spirit, though lacking a creaturely larynx, can moreover make himself 'heard' not only by Adam in the garden but also 'overheard' by the inspired writer to whom he subsequently discloses the sacred account of creation, fall and redemption."[231]

Figurative Days and a Literal Adam, with Literal Origins
Henry's presuppositions as to the nature of the Genesis text became evident in his further assessment of hermeneutical approaches to the text. He noted that "nothing in the text suggests that the writer has expressly in view the extensive geological timespans that modern science identifies as evolutionary aeons." However, he argued that the text did present a sequential description of creative activity.[232] Critical of the literary framework approach, Henry stated, "Its removal of temporal sequence from Genesis 1 seems to do less than full justice to the creation account…[even] distinctions retained by the theory imply certain sequences."[233] Surveying the history of Genesis exegesis, Henry asserted:

> When historico-grammatical exegesis of the Genesis record was accommodated to scientific perspectives a significant and ominous turn took place in fixing the meaning of the biblical text; what may be called scientifico-concept exegesis gradually replaced historico-grammatical interpretation. The literal meaning that later biblical writers attached to

---

have made a stronger case using the example: "[God] breathed into his nostrils the breath of life" from Genesis 2:7; yet, even here the description of this divine intimate care and personal activity in giving life to his creature does not require more than the "breath" initiated by God being what caused Adam to become alive. Just as God can create a physical universe without "hands" and audible sound without a "larynx," so God can initiate a life-giving breath without the physical realities necessary for a human to do so. The seventh day where God "rested" and was "refreshed" (Gen. 2:2–3; Ex. 23:12) is similar. The understanding common to the literal tradition—that this refers to the fact that God ceases from His creative work, having completed it, and delights in it—does not require a weary God. Nor does it require a figurative interpretation; rather, it requires a God who actually condescends to do this in a way that sets the pattern for the man and woman He has created in His image. He was not tired, and yet He rested from all His work. There are clear instances in Genesis where God does anthropomorphize Himself: walking with Adam in the garden (Gen. 3:8) and walking to visit and eat with Abraham (Gen. 18). Commentators going back as far as Theophilus of Antioch view these as occasions in which the preincarnate Christ makes himself visibly manifest in human form; some within the literal tradition also apply this to Genesis 2 on the basis of Colossians 1:16. Other parts of Scripture do make reference to God using figurative language, whether anthropomorphic, or otherwise. Theophilus of Antioch, "Apology," in *Anti-Nicene Fathers* (Grand Rapids: Eerdmans, 1989), 2:103.

231. Henry, *God, Revelation, and Authority*, 6:116.
232. Henry, *God, Revelation, and Authority*, 6:134.
233. Henry, *God, Revelation, and Authority*, 6:134.

the Genesis account was dismissed as a matter of culture accommodation, while allegory and metaphor gained a larger role in expounding the creation narrative. Reluctant on the one hand to break completely with the biblical importance of cosmic and human beginnings, and equally reluctant, on the other, to dispute the scientific view of the origins of the earth and man, more and more clergymen professed to discern an evolutionary hypothesis in the scriptural record.... Scientific theory was allowed to define the way in which the Genesis creation account is to be understood, the relational significance of Genesis came to mean simply that the sovereign living God originated the evolutionary process...and that he achieves his ends by means of that process.[234]

Henry expresses both appreciation for and criticisms of aspects of a wide variety of approaches to the understanding of creation without clearly stating his own position. James Garrett views Henry as having "concluded that he could accept 'a modified theory of evolution as long as no animal species is regarded as the progenitor of man,' the idea of 'an ancient earth,' and a non-literal interpretation of six twenty-four hour days in Genesis 1, but he insisted on a historical Adam and Eve."[235]

Henry was emphatic on the latter, describing the creation of man as a "timeless tenet of evangelical theism": "The First Adam or man is a creation supernaturally made in the image of God, an historical being divinely fashioned from the dust of earth and rationally, morally, spiritually, genetically and culturally different from any prior species of life.... Man is not merely an animal or even a product of animal ancestry; man is a special divine creation made in the image of God who fashioned him from dust and enlivened him for a distinctive role in relation to God, the cosmos, and his fellowman."[236]

James Leo Garrett: Searching for Adam

Where Henry's approach stood in substantial opposition to Ramm's and Elliot's, James Leo Garrett, professor of theology at Southwestern Baptist Theological Seminary, wrote with significant appreciation for and indebtedness to Ramm.[237] In *Systematic Theology*, first published in 1990, Garrett criticized the literal tradition on Genesis, citing it as "the two-track view of religion and

---

234. Henry, *God, Revelation, and Authority*, 6:139.
235. James Leo Garrett, *Baptist Theology: A Four Century Study* (Macon, Ga.: Mercer University Press, 2009), 519; and *Systematic Theology: Biblical, Historical & Evangelical* (Grand Rapids: Eerdmans, 1990), 1:314, 408.
236. Henry, *God, Revelation, and Authority*, 6:227.
237. Garrett, *Baptist Theology*, 520–24.

science [which] by its definition throws the question [of fossils and faith]…out of court."[238]

He was generally appreciative of a variety of alternative hermeneutics and defended Ramm's pictorial-day theory. Regarding the possibility of evolution, Garrett was most sympathetic toward "progressive creation," which he viewed as offering "more promise than the other major options," particularly if it allowed for "micro-evolution" or "intra-kind" development.[239] Garrett's conclusion on hermeneutical approaches to the general account of creation was, "It should be quite evident that we have not obtained final answers."[240]

Turning to the question of human origins, Garrett criticized those he saw as rejecting "all anthropological and geological evidence and holding to the recent origin of mankind."[241] While appreciative of the solution provided by pre-Adamism, Garrett noted objections raised against it on the basis of: Genesis 2:5 ("and *there was* no man to work the ground"); Genesis 2:20 ("but for Adam there was not found a helper comparable to him"); and Genesis 3:20 ("she [Eve] was the mother of all the living").[242] He tentatively suggested the solution provided by individuals like Brunner, who argued that the text of Genesis did not speak to "the antiquity of humankind," a subject that "must be left entirely to the sciences."[243] Garrett aptly noted, however, that "the more one finds a historical dimension to Genesis 1–3 the more unsatisfying" this view.[244]

The final option Garret gave was "direct divine creation of Adam and Eve at a time conformable with anthropological data."[245] To Garrett, each of these latter approaches manifested "genuine difficulties," with the result that "it is fitting to be cautious as to any final statement of the question."[246] Thus, Garrett concluded his quest for the historical Adam with a lingering uncertainty.

Southern Baptist Theological Seminary: Genesis and Recovery

While there remained a strong popular stream of Baptist commitment to the literal tradition on Genesis, including human origins, in many respects a recovery of the literal interpretive tradition in the academy, particularly

---

238. Garrett, *Systematic Theology*, 1:312.
239. Garrett, *Systematic Theology*, 1:317.
240. Garrett, *Systematic Theology*, 1:319.
241. Garrett, *Systematic Theology*, 1:408–9.
242. Garrett, *Systematic Theology*, 1:410.
243. Garrett, *Systematic Theology*, 1:410.
244. Garrett, *Systematic Theology*, 1:410.
245. Garrett, *Systematic Theology*, 1:410.
246. Garrett, *Systematic Theology*, 1:410–11.

within leading Southern Baptist Convention institutions, seemed unlikely. The milieu on Genesis among influential Baptist theologians could largely be summarized as occupying a Ramm-to-Henry continuum. In fact, through the 1980s, the Convention's flagship Southern Baptist Theological Seminary appeared to be on a trajectory toward increasing openness to aspects of liberal Protestantism. Despite maintaining an ethos of broad evangelicalism, the school espoused a multiplicity of approaches to the early chapters of Genesis and warm appreciation for evolutionary models of human origins.

During the same time period, conservative Southern Baptists, who were increasingly voicing concern over what they viewed as the theological and spiritual deterioration of Southern Baptist Theological Seminary, began to pursue change. However, as historian Gregory Wills notes, conservatives in position to influence the seminary "in many instances" found their concerns about theological error were easily dismissed "because of the clumsy way in which they stated their charges."[247]

Roy L. Honeycutt: "Different Kinds of Truth"

The response of the seminary, under the leadership of President Roy L. Honeycutt, to conservative complaints only widened the divide. Wills states, "When Honeycutt's report came before the full board of trustees, the new conservative trustees believed that Honeycutt's report was a whitewash. They were deeply dissatisfied that he characterized faculty beliefs as sound and orthodox. They believed that Honeycutt had evaded discussion of some errors and had recast others implausibly as scripturally valid."[248]

Among the wide range of issues under debate, one came to the fore when committee member Adrian Rogers pressed Honeycutt as to whether the Bible was "truth without mixture of error."[249] According to Wills, Honeycutt's eventual response was that "it was necessary 'to distinguish between different kinds of truth.'"[250] Taking Genesis 1–11, "Honeycutt suggested [they] did not reveal historical truth but nevertheless revealed 'ultimate truth,' or 'theological truth.' Honeycutt explained that the biblical references to Adam and Eve were symbolic and represented the experience of every human. He said that the faculty believed that 'Genesis created a description of your experience and my experience...that Adam is you, that you have a garden, that you are the

---

247. Wills, *Southern Baptist Theological Seminary*, 452.
248. Wills, *Southern Baptist Theological Seminary*, 452.
249. Wills, *Southern Baptist Theological Seminary*, 450.
250. Wills, *Southern Baptist Theological Seminary*, 450.

first man.' He told Rogers that most of the faculty probably saw 'Adam and Eve as a representative of man.'"[251] The exchange between Rogers and Honeycutt continued, Wills writes, as "Rogers explained that such beliefs—denying the historicity of a literal Adam and Eve…angered the Southern Baptists who supported the seminary with their money. He asked also for an explanation of faculty support for abortion rights, of rejection of Peter's authorship of the letters of 1 and 2 Peter, and of statements suggesting that persons could be saved apart from conscious faith in the gospel of Jesus Christ."[252]

The exchanges and concerns indicated a wider conservative resurgence within the Southern Baptist Convention that was marked by a consistent determination to pursue reformation. Honeycutt and the rest of the seminary leadership made adjustments in public relations in the face of increased pressure, such as adopting and promoting *The Glorieta Statement*, but Honeycutt told the faculty that he "had no intention 'to compromise consciously.'"[253] Through these actions, Honeycutt and the faculty sought to avoid implementing a requirement for all faculty members to affirm that "the Bible is inerrant in all matters including science, philosophy, cosmology, etc."[254]

Meanwhile, within the Southern Baptist Convention, conservatives increasingly gained majorities, electing individuals to key positions, which began to impact the membership of the Board of Trustees of Southern Seminary. By 1990, the situation reached a tipping point. A conservative majority was seated on the board and began to implement a requirement of scriptural inerrancy among faculty members—a key point of which was the belief "in [the] direct creation of mankind and therefore…that Adam and Eve were real persons."[255]

R. Albert Mohler: Encouraging Recovery of the Literal Tradition

Having for some years slowed the transition toward a conservative evangelicalism, Honeycutt announced his retirement in 1992, and R. Albert Mohler was elected president of the Southern Baptist Theological Seminary in 1993. With the support of the seminary's trustees, Mohler moved to implement a meaningful adherence to the seminary's historic Abstract of Principles, along with other faculty requirements, leading to major transitions in faculty between

---

251. Wills, *Southern Baptist Theological Seminary*, 450.
252. Wills, *Southern Baptist Theological Seminary*, 451.
253. The statement appeared to affirm inerrancy but gave interpretive leeway on what the term meant. Wills, *Southern Baptist Theological Seminary*, 468.
254. Wills, *Southern Baptist Theological Seminary*, 469.
255. Wills, *Southern Baptist Theological Seminary*, 491.

1994 and 1997. These changes brought the seminary to a firmly conservative evangelical position.

Mohler was personally committed to the literal tradition on Genesis 1 and 2, including human origins. As a seminary president and theologian, his public articulation of a literal interpretation of Genesis 1–2, along with a vast shift in faculty members from a previous moderate-to-liberal ethos to conservative evangelical, brought with them a significantly wider resurgence of appreciation for the literal tradition. This resurgence affected seminarians heading for ministry in the denomination and was also more widely felt. Not only were Adam and Eve once again viewed at Southern as real historical persons, but a high regard was also given for the literal tradition when engaging with issues of their origins and Genesis hermeneutics.[256]

In 2001, the seminary devoted an issue of *The Southern Baptist Journal of Theology* to the topic of Genesis. In it Paul House, writing on "Creation in Old Testament Theology," and Russell Fuller, writing on "Interpreting Genesis 1–11," exemplified a favorable regard for the literal tradition. Fuller in particular emphasized the need to interpret Genesis 1–3 "as straightforward historical narrative according to the 'plain sense' of the text" while at the same time noting the appropriateness of seeing christological and typological aspects of the text in relation to the whole of Scripture.[257]

A decade later, in 2011, the seminary devoted an issue of *The Southern Baptist Journal of Theology* to the topic of Genesis and human origins. All of the articles in this edition of the journal, with the exception of John Collins's guest piece, "Adam and Eve in the Old Testament," were fully congruent with the literal tradition.[258] In his introduction to the issue, editor Stephen Wellum stated,

> Unfortunately…in recent years a growing number of evangelicals are now adopting the approach of "liberal" theology and re-interpreting Scripture in light of the perceived "facts" of science. In so doing, the Adam of the Bible is either being denied outright as an historical figure or reinterpreted

---

256. See, for example, Gregg R. Allison, *Historical Theology: An Introduction to Christian Doctrine* (Grand Rapids: Zondervan, 2011), 254–76, 321–41.

257. Russell Fuller, "Interpreting Genesis 1–11," *The Southern Baptist Journal of Theology* 5, no. 3 (Fall 2001): 18–27.

258. "Debating Adam," *The Southern Baptist Journal of Theology* 15, no. 1 (Spring 2011): 1–107. In his article, Collins largely demurs from engaging in discussion of matters of the origins of Adam and Eve, though he gives some muted criticism of the literal approach, stating, "We have plenty of reasons from the text to be careful about reading it too literalistically; and at the same time we have reasons to accept a historical core." Collins goes on to state, "The style of telling the story may leave room for discussion on the exact details of the process by which God formed Adam's body, and how long ago." Collins, "Adam and Eve in the Old Testament," 14.

as a symbol for Israel, or something along these lines. Along with this denial is a re-interpretation of the fall. Instead of grounding the human problem in space-time history, Genesis 3 is treated as a symbolic representation of the human problem. But as Augustine noted many years ago: If Adam had not sinned in history the Son of Man would not have come. Ultimately, what is at stake is the grounding for the gospel itself.

In light of these recent debates, we are devoting this issue of *SBJT* to this crucial topic. We are seeking to stake a claim that to deny an historic Adam and fall and go the way of recent evangelicals is not only unnecessary, it is unbiblical in the strongest of terms. In the end, it will lead to a denial of other parts of Scripture, and ultimately it will undercut the glorious gospel of our Lord Jesus Christ.[259]

Only a few months after publication of the special issue, Mohler responded to rising challenges against both the historicity of Adam and Eve and their special creation apart from evolutionary origins as "the first parents of all humanity" that were coming from Biologos writers such as Darrel Falk, Kathryn Applegate, Dennis Venema, and Karl Giberson. He wrote,

> The implications for biblical authority are clear, as is the fact that if these arguments hold sway, we will have to come up with an entirely new story of the Gospel metanarrative and the Bible's storyline. The denial of an historical Adam and Eve as the first parents of all humanity and the solitary first human pair severs the link between Adam and Christ which is so crucial to the gospel. If we do not know how the story of the Gospel begins, then we do not know what that story means. Make no mistake: a false start to the story produces a false grasp of the Gospel.[260]

Two years later, at a Gospel Coalition conference panel shared with Bryan Chapell, Mohler again defended not only the historical existence of an Adam and Eve, but also the historicity of the Adam and Eve as understood by the literal tradition on Genesis—including matters of their origins and attendant hermeneutical issues for both Genesis 1 and 2.[261]

---

259. Stephen Wellum, "Editorial: Debating the Historicity of Adam: Does It Matter?," *The Southern Baptist Journal of Theology* 15, no 1 (Spring 2011): 3.

260. R. Albert Mohler, "False Start? The Controversy Over Adam and Eve Heats Up," *AlbertMohler.com*, (August 22, 2011), www.albertmohler.com/2011/08/22/false-start-the -controversy-over-adam-and-eve-heats-up/. See also Mohler, "Adam and Eve: Clarifying Again What Is At Stake," *AlbertMohler.com* (August 31, 2011), www.albertmohler.com /2011/08/31/adam-and-eve-clarifying-again-what-is-at-stake/.

261. Chapell and Mohler, "Are Adam and Eve Historical Figures?"

Sailhamer: A New Nonliteral, Literary Alternative

While support for the literal tradition was reappearing at Southern Baptist Theological Seminary, alternative hermeneutical approaches to Genesis 1 and 2 continued to multiply in Baptist circles and beyond. John Sailhamer, who served as Old Testament professor at Trinity Evangelical Divinity School, Southeastern Baptist Theological Seminary, and Golden Gate Baptist Theological Seminary, led development of one of these alternatives.

In an early publication on Genesis, "Exegetical Notes: Genesis 1:1–2:4a," Sailhamer asked, "How do we go about finding what the biblical writers were teaching in their carefully wrought narratives?"[262] He answered by emphasizing "the viewpoint of the author who recounts the event," which was, according to Sailhamer, most influenced by "the overall framework" or "literary context" of the presentation.[263] Taking Genesis 1:1–2:4a as a "unit of historical narrative," he argued that the "repetition of the phrase 'evening and morning' which divides the passage into a 7-day scheme...forms a period of one work week concluding with a rest day."[264] Rather than concluding that this was "the course of the historical event itself," and actually God's creation of the first work week and day of rest, Sailhamer concluded: "Already in this simple structure there is the tilting of the account that betrays the interests of the author: creation is viewed in terms of *man's* own work week."[265]

Sailhamer noted a number of potential typological inferences of the Genesis 1:1–2:4a text as set in the context of the Pentateuch, taking up the concept, also held by Kline, that the covenant relationship established at Sinai and more broadly reflected throughout the Pentateuch "[is] clothed in the metaphor of the ancient Near Eastern monarch: God the Great King, grants to his obedient vassal prince the right to dwell in his land and promises protection from their enemies."[266]

The converse of Sailhamer's hypothesis was that God in His creative and covenanting activity was the primary and normative universal reality, from the beginning of history onward and that in their cultures ancient Near Eastern kings were seeking to assert themselves as godlike in rebellion against Him, suppressing and distorting His truth in unrighteousness. This possible interpretation was not mentioned. Sailhamer did not appear to consider the possibility that Genesis was original and that ancient Near Eastern myth was

---

262. John Sailhamer, "Exegetical Notes: Genesis 1:1–2:4a," *Trinity Journal* 5 (1984): 73–82.
263. Sailhamer, "Exegetical Notes," 74.
264. Sailhamer, "Exegetical Notes," 74.
265. Sailhamer, "Exegetical Notes," 74.
266. Sailhamer, "Exegetical Notes," 75.

a derivative distortion. The weight of Sailhamer's interpretive approach in this article appeared to rest on the human author, a biblical theology of the Pentateuch, and ancient Near Eastern contexts.

In his subsequent commentary on Genesis, Sailhamer pursued a similar approach to the text. While in the body of his writing he gave no exposition of Genesis 1:4–5, in a footnote he stated his disagreement with Cassuto's interpretation "that there was only one day, for the second had not yet been created" and sought to argue that the writer may have had another "first day" in view in relation to Genesis 1:1.[267] Coming to the fourth day of creation, Sailhamer made no mention of the literal tradition's common understanding that the light of the previous days was a supernatural act of divine creation prior to the existence of the sun, moon, and stars. Rather, arguing for a modified version of the medieval Jewish commentator Rashi, he stated that "the narrative assumes that the heavenly lights have been created already 'in the beginning.'"[268] While Sailhamer's approach differed from the literal tradition at these points, his approach to Genesis 2 was coherent with the literal tradition:

> What the author had stated as a simple fact in chapter 1 (man, male and female, was created in God's likeness) is explained and developed throughout the narrative of chapter 2.... The first point the author is intent on making is that man, though a special creature made in God's image, was nevertheless a creature like the other creatures God had made...he was made "of the dust of the ground."... The notion that man's origin might somehow be connected with that of the divine is deliberately excluded by this narrative. Man's origin is of the dust of the ground.... In Creation man arose out of the dust, but in the Fall he returned to the dust.[269]

Sailhamer offered no comment on the second part of verse 7, including "and the man became a living being," a phrase key to the literal tradition on the origin of man. At this point, Sailhamer allowed readers with a range of views on human origins to read his exposition according to their own view.

---

267. John Sailhamer, "Genesis," in *The Expositor's Bible Commentary* (Grand Rapids: Zondervan, 1990), 2:27–28.

268. Sailhamer, "Genesis," 33–34. Sailhamer equates Keil's and Calvin's view of the fourth day as "similar to that of Rashi," despite the significant difference that the former do not state that the sun, moon, and stars preexisted the fourth day.

269. Sailhamer, "Genesis," 41.

"Historical Creationism": God's Organization of the Promised Land of Israel
In following years, Sailhamer further developed his approach to Genesis, proposing a hermeneutical approach he termed "historical creationism."[270] Focusing on Genesis 1:1 in particular, Sailhamer argued that "the beginning" in this verse spoke "of an indeterminate period of time, not a single moment of time…. According to the text [God] may have created the world over a rather lengthy period."[271] He saw verse 1 as allowing the author "to say that God had created everything, without going into the details."[272]

Sailhamer believed this was key to unlocking the Genesis and science problem; practically, the result was significantly similar to the older gap theory approach. However, there were also differences—the implications of which were unaddressed. Where Genesis 1:1 spoke to the "long period of time" in which "God created the whole universe," Sailhamer went on to argue that Genesis 1:2–2:4a were the account of six literal days which followed "after that period of time."[273] In them, "the author called unique attention to the labors God expended in preparing the [promised] land"—focusing on the beginnings of Israel's history.[274]

This approach raised numerous challenges in exegeting the text. The first was why Sailhamer had translated as "land" what was historically translated as "earth." He claimed that because the semantic range of the Hebrew term extended "only to what we see of the earth around us, what is within our horizons," it was best understood as "land," despite the fact that elsewhere in Genesis (18:25) it referred "to earth in a global sense."[275] Sailhamer went on to argue that, "viewed from the perspective of the Hebrew text, the phrase 'formless and void' means simply 'uninhabitable land'…the 'wasteland' is about to become 'the promised land.'"[276] When it came to the actual creative work of the six days, Sailhamer was initially ambiguous. In relation to the six days, he stated both that "the scope and focus…seems to be the whole universe" and that "Genesis 1 is an account of God's preparation of the promised land."[277] Sailhamer's ambiguity was resolved

---

270. John Sailhamer, *Genesis Unbound: A Provocative New Look at the Creation Account* (Sisters, Ore.: Multnomah, 1996), 1–257.
271. Sailhamer, *Genesis Unbound*, 38.
272. Sailhamer, *Genesis Unbound*, 38.
273. Sailhamer, *Genesis Unbound*, 44.
274. Sailhamer, *Genesis Unbound*, 50–59.
275. Sailhamer, *Genesis Unbound*, 48.
276. Sailhamer, *Genesis Unbound*, 64.
277. Sailhamer, *Genesis Unbound*, 89, 91.

in successive chapters where he elucidated that he believed the "literal six days" narrated the shaping of the geography of the Promised Land of Israel.[278]

According of Sailhamer, the account of the first day simply referred to the sunrise of an already existent sun; the second day God "created" clouds over the land; the third day He removed waters from the surface of the Promised Land into the Sea of Galilee, Dead Sea, and Mediterranean Sea and furnished the region with fruit trees—all vegetation having already been created "in the beginning"; the fourth day, God simply declared or announced the purpose of the sun, moon, and stars. The fifth day God "populated the promised land with the creatures that were created 'in the beginning.'… God spoke, and frogs, fish, and birds came from somewhere and filled the skies and waters of the land. There is no need to suppose that these creatures did not already exist as a result of God's work of creation 'in the beginning.'"[279]

Where "the use of the word *bara*" or "created" was found in the text subsequent to 1:1, Sailhamer argued that it did not speak to an act of original creation but was a literary device intended to turn "the reader's attention back to the comprehensive statement about creation in 1:1."[280] It was only in the *bara* of Genesis 1:1 that God briefly and with minimal context, "without going into the details," revealed His work of original creation of all things.

---

278. Sailhamer claimed that he had a precursor in the English Puritan John Lightfoot. However, this seems questionable when one turns to examine Lightfoot's writing. While at times adding inferences to his exposition with little (or no) exegetical warrant, Lightfoot clearly viewed the days of the creation week of Genesis 1 as devoted to a sequential material and functional creation of the entirety of the universe, simply viewing the creation of Eden as a culminating subset of this work: "verse 3. Twelve houres did the heavens thus move in darkeness, and then God commanded and there appeared light to this upper Horizon, namely to that where Eden should be planted [for to that place especially is the story calculated], and there it did shine twelve other houres, declining with degrees to the other Hemisphere, where it inlightened twelve houres also…. verse 9. In the new created ayre the Lord thundered and rebuked the waters…the earth instantly brought forth trees and plants…. And now was Eden planted with all bodies of trees fit for meat and delight, which by the time Adam is created are laden with leaves and fruit…. verse 25. Beasts wild and tame created, and all manner of creeping things, and the World furnished with them from about Eden as well as with[in]." John Lightfoot, *A Few New Observations upon the Book of Genesis*, in *The Whole Works of the Rev. John Lightfoot, D. D.*, ed. John Rogers Pitman (London, 1822), 2–4. A subsequent reference by Sailhamer to Johann Heidegger's view of the location of the garden of Eden (Heidegger being a proponent of the literal tradition, like Lightfoot) had little if any supportive relevance for Sailhamer's hermeneutic. Sailhamer, *Genesis Unbound*, 216, 221.

279. Sailhamer, *Genesis Unbound*, 141.

280. Sailhamer, *Genesis Unbound*, 138.

Removal of "Details" Also Removes Barriers

With the days of Genesis 1 now descriptive of God's organization, arrangement, and filling of the Promised Land, or garden of Eden, Sailhamer's hermeneutical approach created a new set of problems. In removing "the details" of how and when God created all things, his approach not only allowed for a potentially vast timescale but also removed exegetical barriers to a special creation of a pre-Adamite humanity or a theistic evolutionary origin for humanity. This was especially due to his explanation that the use of the word *bara* in Genesis 1, along with the use of "made," did not actually refer to God doing anything aside from further shaping and arranging what existed or "making a proclamation" about it.[281]

If Sailhamer were consistent, the sixth-day "creation" of man also pointed backward to God's creation of man, male and female, "in the beginning"—and did not necessarily refer to Adam and Eve. Where Sailhamer's hermeneutic held that the "create" and "made/make" in Genesis 1:2–2:4a were not to be understood as they had been in the literal tradition, God's "forming" of Adam and "making" of Eve in Genesis 2 could arguably also continue in the same pattern. The additional fact that Genesis 2:8 indicated that Adam was created outside of the garden of Eden and afterward placed within it, meant that Adam's origins "from the dust" could lie in an obscure distant past—long prior to the sixth day of shaping and arranging the garden of Eden.

However, although his hermeneutic and possible exegetical results demonstrated a lack of support for key aspects of the traditional literal understanding of human origins, Sailhamer was critical of evolutionary theory and personally maintained a special creation of Adam and Eve. In his exposition of Genesis 2:7, Sailhamer stated that "God fashioned his body and breathed into his nostrils the breath of life. The narrative is quite clear that human beings have no biological antecedents."[282]

Several years after publishing his book, Sailhamer wrote the article, "Creation, Genesis 1–11, and the Canon," in which he sought to evaluate early Genesis more substantively in the context of the Pentateuch.[283] Once again he paid particular attention to the opening phrase of Genesis 1:1, appreciatively citing Gunkel and noting that this passage apparently functioned as a

---

281. Sailhamer, *Genesis Unbound*, 134.
282. Sailhamer, *Genesis Unbound*, 152.
283. John Sailhamer, "Creation, Genesis 1–11, and the Canon," *Bulletin for Biblical Research* 10, no. 1 (2000): 89–106.

title "at the head of the Pentateuch."[284] Drawing on the thought of Gerhard von Rad (1903–1971) and Ludwig Köhler (1880–1956), Sailhamer argued that "Genesis 1–11 is already focused on Israel's own history.... Genesis 1–11 is not an answer to how the world began...rather [it is] an answer to the question of Israel's history."[285]

He sympathized with Franz Delitzsch's argument "that Genesis 1–11 does not intend to tell us that the world had a beginning." Rather, it was "prophecy turned backwards," an "eschatological event."[286] While many exegetes in the literal tradition had noted the significance of Genesis 1–11 to both Israel's history and the themes of biblical eschatology, Sailhamer, in keeping with his previous work, appeared to emphasize these elements as a replacement for the literal tradition's view that early Genesis provided a chronological, six-day narration of how God created the world.[287]

John Walton: An Enlightenment and Ancient Near East Remix

John Walton, Old Testament professor at Wheaton College, proffered an approach similar to Sailhamer's, albeit drawing more heavily on ancient Near Eastern studies and arriving at somewhat different conclusions. Like Collins, Sailhamer, and others, Walton claimed that his view was also "a literal reading."[288] However, in his view, the correct reading of the early chapters of Genesis required the ability to enter the ancient Near Eastern cultural context surrounding the writer.[289]

Walton stated, "We can't interpret the literature without understanding the culture, and we can't understand the culture without interpreting the literature.... *The key then is to be found in the literature from the rest of the ancient world.*"[290] While his approach appeared intriguingly new to some, it was not. Walton's principles of comparative religious approach continued a lineage going back through the Enlightenment era to Harriot and La Peyrère.

---

284. Sailhamer, "Creation, Genesis 1–11, and the Canon," 95.

285. Sailhamer, "Creation, Genesis 1–11, and the Canon," 91.

286. Sailhamer, "Creation, Genesis 1–11, and the Canon," 91–92.

287. Sailhamer's most recent work is his substantial *The Meaning of the Pentateuch: Revelation, Composition and Interpretation* (Downers Grove, Ill.: IVP Academic, 2009), 1–632. In it he seeks to use both literary analysis and biblical theology to advance understanding of the Pentateuch.

288. Walton, *Lost World of Genesis One*, 169.

289. Walton, *Lost World of Genesis One*, 10. See also Walton, "Creation in Genesis 1:1–2:3 and the Ancient Near East: Order out of Disorder after *Chaoskampf*," *Calvin Theological Journal* 43 (2008): 48–63.

290. Emphasis added. Walton, *Lost World of Genesis One*, 10.

His initial focus was engagement with a range of extant ancient Near Eastern literature—from Egyptian to Sumerian and Akkadian, the latter partly mediated through Assyrian and neo-Babylonian contexts. Walton averred that he was not stating that "Genesis 'borrowed' from Gudea or any other piece of ancient Near Eastern literature.... Instead, the Israelites *shared* with the rest of the ancient world certain basic concepts about temples, rest, and cosmos that are naturally reflected in an account such as Genesis 1."[291]

In Walton's approach, Genesis 1, in "light" of surrounding cultural realities, ought to be understood as a "cosmic temple inauguration"—which Walton acknowledged was "far different from what has been traditionally understood about the passage."[292] Like Sailhamer, Walton appeared to view only Genesis 1:1 as speaking to material origins. The remainder of Genesis 1 offered "no clear information about material origins," but was rather "an account of functional origins," based on Walton's assumption that ancient Near Eastern literature in general was not concerned with "material origins" but rather with "functional origins."[293]

Declaration Instead of Creation

According to Walton, the formless void, or emptiness of the earth in Genesis 1:2, referred to a lack of assigned functions. Rather than creating physical entities in Genesis 1:3 and following, God was simply assigning functions to what already existed. Each successive day, God assigned functions, and the "recurring comment that 'it is good' refer[red] to functionality (relative to people)."[294] God, whether actually or didactically, was setting up the functions of the cosmic temple, "for the benefit of humanity, with God dwelling in relationship with his creatures."[295]

While typological reflections on the creation and God's temple, as revealed in Scripture, had long been the purview of the literal tradition, what exactly Walton meant by claiming a previous lack of assigned functions is unclear, particularly in light of his assumption that all the material entities mentioned in the text preexisted their reception of assigned functions. This idea stood in contrast with the literal tradition which held that the material entities received functionality when they were created. In response to the question, "What

---

291. Walton, *Genesis 1 As Ancient Cosmology*, 183.
292. Walton, *Lost World of Genesis One*, 161.
293. Walton, *Lost World of Genesis One*, 162.
294. Walton, *Lost World of Genesis One*, 162.
295. Walton, *Lost World of Genesis One*, 162.

would people have seen if they were there as eyewitnesses (i.e. what 'really happened') on these days?," Walton somewhat evasively replied:

> We overrate eyewitnesses in our culture. The Bible is much more interested in understanding what God did rather than what an eyewitness would see. For example, an eyewitness would have seen the waters of the Red Sea part, but would have no physical evidence that God did it. Genesis 1 is an account of creation intended to convey realities about the origins of the cosmos and God's role in it and his purpose for it. Most importantly it is designed to help the reader understand that the cosmos should be understood as a temple that God has set up as he dwells in their midst. The perspective of an eyewitness would be inadequate and too limited to be of any good. Genesis 1 is not intended to be an eyewitness account.[296]

Despite his avoidance of the question, Walton appeared to be left with three alternatives: (1) a complete material creation in a state of dysfunctional chaos prior to the first day; (2) a bizarrely suspended nonfunctional, yet complete material creation prior to the point in time of Genesis 1:3; or (3) an already existent creation, including existing functionality ("God assigned functions"), meaning that God "announced functions" that were already existent, so that He, as recorded by the writer of Genesis, was merely describing existing reality, including existing functionality, in a figurative and theological manner. The latter appeared most likely, particularly as an ensuing publication by Walton described "dust" and "rib" to be "archetypal affirmations about the nature of humanity…the focus is on all womankind and mankind."[297]

Evolution, and Adam as Failed Savior of Mankind

The result of Walton's ancient Near Eastern cosmological hermeneutic was a decided openness to theistic evolution:

> If Genesis 1 is not an account of material origins, then it offers no mechanism for material origins, and we may safely look to science to consider what it suggests for such mechanisms. We may find the theories proposed by scientists to be convincing or not, but we cannot on the basis of Genesis 1 object to any mechanisms they offer…. Accepting at least some of the components of biological evolution as representing the handiwork of God, we could propose a mechanism for material origins designated *teleological evolution* meaning that evolutionary processes may well describe

---

296. Walton, *Lost World of Genesis One*, 170.
297. Walton, "Human Origins and the Bible," *Zygon* 47, no. 4 (December 2012): 889.

some aspects of origins (noting that human origins need to be discussed separately), even though much controversy still exists about how evolutionary changes took place.[298]

On a world lecture tour funded by Biologos to promote his hermeneutic, Walton said that he personally believed in the historicity of Adam and Eve although the organization was noncommittal on that point. At the same time, critically reflecting on those who would answer questions of "material origins" from the Genesis text, he noted:

> The discussion of creation in the apocryphal book of Ben Sira (2nd century BC) offers one of the earliest interpretations that we have of the early chapters of Genesis. Of course, it is already in the Hellenistic period and therefore not reflecting an ancient Near Eastern context. Chapter 16:26–27 says, "When the Lord created his works from the beginning, and, in making them, determined their boundaries, he arranged his works in an eternal order." Chapter 17 has a long discussion of God creating humans that is entirely functional in focus. It is interesting to see this perspective in the Hellenistic period.[299]

Consistent with his "functional" approach, Walton sought to avoid attempts toward exegetical reflection on the "material origins" of humanity. However, an evolutionary genetic model received an appreciative nod as he cited fellow Biologos lecturer Dennis Venema's argument that "a history is unmistakably evident when we compare the human genome to the genomes of other species.... Genetic markers provide persuasive evidence for genetic dependence and continuity."[300]

Walton went on to state, whether through a "functional" inference or by "safely look[ing] to science," that "Adam was created mortal (and with pain and suffering—after all, 'good' does not mean 'perfect'), but he was given the hope for life through the tree and (more importantly) through relationship with God in his presence. This means that Adam did not *bring* death, pain, and suffering to an immortal humanity—he simply failed to acquire life for

---

298. Walton, *Lost World of Genesis One*, 163–64. See also John Walton, "Human Origins and the Bible," 875–89.

299. John Walton, "Reflections on Reading Genesis 1–3: John Walton's World Tour, Part 2," *Biologos Foundation* (September 18, 2013), http://biologos.org/blog/john-waltons-world-tour-part-2.

300. John Walton, "Reflections on Reading Genesis 1–3: John Walton's World Tour, Part 3," *Biologos Foundation* (September 18, 2013), http://biologos.org/blog/john-waltons-world-tour-part-3.

them (forfeited access to the tree of life; the need for the tree of life indicated their mortality)."[301]

Walton's quest for the historical Adam ended with an Adam who likely had at least partial evolutionary biological origins: one who was "created" mortal and who failed to be a savior for humanity. This novel view is radically different not only from the historic literal interpretation of Genesis, but also from historic Christian belief as a whole. Like his hermeneutical predecessors, Walton's forward momentum of a nonliteral approach to Genesis unravels biblical Christianity.

Defending the Adam of Genesis

A number of well-known Baptist theologians, while not maintaining the traditional literal approach to Genesis 1, nonetheless maintained the special creation of Adam and Eve, as described in Genesis 1 and 2, apart from any evolutionary origins. For example, John Piper became a prominent supporter of Sailhamer's approach, similarly maintaining a special creation of Adam and Eve according to the literal tradition: "I think we should preach that he created Adam and Eve directly, that he made them of the dust of the ground, and he took out of man a woman. I think we should teach that. I know there are people who don't, who think it's all imagery for evolution or whatever."[302]

Gordon Lewis and Bruce Demarest, sympathetic to the day-age approach, were similarly representative of those holding to an alternative approach to Genesis while maintaining a literal view of human origins. They were also more exegetical than many others, turning to Genesis 2:7 and arguing:

> The play on the Hebrew words for "man" and "ground" indicates that Adam's origin is earthly; God created him from substances found in the earth's crust. The verse continues that the Lord God "breathed into his nostrils the breath of life," which means that Adam's material body received life—breath by a direct creative act of God. The final phrase... affirms simply that Adam became a living creature.... Although the process of Adam's formation is not specified, the language conveys the idea of a special creation from inorganic matter, rather than a development

---

301. Walton, "Reflections on Reading Genesis, Part 2."

302. John Piper, "What Should We Teach About Creation?," *Desiring God* (June 1, 2010), http://www.desiringgod.org/resource-library/ask-pastor-john/what-should-we-teach-about -creation; Matt Perman, "Science, the Bible, and the Promised Land: An Analysis of John Sailhamer's *Genesis Unbound*," *Desiring God* (January 1, 1998), http://www.desiringgod.org /resource-library/articles/science-the-bible-and-the-promised-land.

from some extant organic form.... The fact that God fashioned Eve from Adam's side appears to be a fatal blow to the theistic evolutionary claim that humanity was genetically derived from a nonhuman ancestor.[303]

Wayne Grudem, though critical of aspects of the literal tradition in his *Systematic Theology* and *Bible Doctrine*, was similarly supportive of a special, temporally immediate creation of Adam and Eve and objected to those who would posit theistic evolutionary origins for humanity. He did so, however, without direct reference to the text of Genesis 2.[304] Millard Erikson, a proponent of the day-age approach, like Lewis and Demarest, also held to the special creation of Adam and Eve apart from evolutionary origins.[305] Others, ranging from Norman Geisler to Mark Driscoll, similarly hold to the literal tradition on the origins of humanity.[306]

Alongside the significant resurgence of appreciation for the literal tradition on human origins at the Southern Baptist Theological Seminary, there are also the influential voices of John MacArthur and the faculty at the Master's College and Seminary in California.[307] Both institutions hold "that man was directly and immediately created by God in his image and likeness."[308] As a preacher, theologian, and college and seminary president, MacArthur remains an influential proponent of the special creation of Adam and Eve apart from any evolutionary ancestry, as reflected in his *The Battle for the Beginning*:

303. Gordon R. Lewis and Bruce Demarest, *Integrative Theology* (Grand Rapids: Zondervan, 1990), 29–30.

304. Wayne Grudem, *Systematic Theology* (Grand Rapids: Zondervan, 1994), 277–79, 291–92, 461–62; and *Bible Doctrine: Essential Teachings of the Christian Faith* (Grand Rapids: Zondervan, 1999), 133–35.

305. Millard J. Erikson, "The Origin of Humanity," in *Christian Theology*, 3rd ed. (Grand Rapids: Baker, 2013), 438–56.

306. Norman Geisler, *Systematic Theology* (Minneapolis: Bethany House, 2003), 2:449–73; Mark Driscoll and Gary Breshears, *Doctrine: What Christians Should Believe* (Wheaton, Ill.: Crossway, 2010), 92–93; Driscoll, "Answers to Common Questions About Creation," *Resurgence: A Ministry of Mars Hill* (July 3, 2007), http://theresurgence.com/2006/07/03/answers-to-common-questions-about-creation. In late 2014, Driscoll resigned from Mars Hill.

307. Richard Mayhue, "Editorial: Scripture on Creation," *Master's Seminary Journal* 23, no. 1 (Spring 2012): 1–6; Trevor Craigen, "Review of Keith Miller, ed., *Perspectives on An Evolving Creation*," *Master's Seminary Journal* 18, no. 1 (Spring 2007): 130–32; Trevor Craigen, "Review of Robert W. Godfrey, *God's Pattern for Creation: A Covenantal Reading of Genesis 1*," *Master's Seminary Journal* 15, no. 1 (2004): 117–18; John MacArthur, "Creation: Believe It or Not," *Master's Seminary Journal* 13, no. 1 (Spring 2002): 5–32.

308. "The Distinctives," *The Master's College website*, http://www.masters.edu/abouttmc/doctrine.aspx.

Creation, Evolution and the Bible, and *The MacArthur Bible Commentary*.[309] In addition, some Baptist seminaries and colleges maintain an exclusive commitment to the literal tradition on Genesis and human origins; one of the largest among those institutions is Liberty University.[310]

Even though alternative approaches advocated by Sailhamer, Walton, and others have attracted a good deal of attention, a proportionally large stream in the Baptist tradition has remained fully committed to the literal tradition of Genesis interpretation through the late twentieth century and into the twenty-first century. Placed on a spectrum with other streams of Protestant Christianity, conservative evangelical Baptists seem somewhat more substantially aligned with the literal tradition than their Presbyterian counterparts but less so than their conservative Lutheran counterparts.

The Literal Tradition and Alternatives Today

Across Christianity there remains today, as in previous eras, a strong commitment to the millennia-old literal approach toward early Genesis, which includes the special, temporally immediate creation of Adam and Eve as the first humans, apart from any ancestry or immediate contemporaries. This approach survives despite the best efforts of both a secularized society and those within the church who hold alternative views. A recent Biologos Foundation survey (2012) indicated that even after some two hundred years of substantial challenges, fifty-four percent of all American pastors, including mainline Protestants, lean toward a literal understanding of creation and human origins. That number rises to sixty-eight percent among those identifying as evangelical. Proportionately more pastors ages twenty-eight to forty-six either leaned to or were committed to a literal interpretation than did those between the ages of forty-seven and sixty-five, indicating a recent increase in

---

309. John MacArthur, *The Battle for the Beginning: Creation, Evolution and the Bible* (Nashville: Thomas Nelson, 2001), 1–237; and *The MacArthur Bible Commentary* (Nashville: Thomas Nelson, 2005), 4–15.

310. At Capital Bible Seminary in Washington, D.C., both Todd Beall and James Mook have written on Genesis, hermeneutics, and human origins from the perspective of the literal tradition. See, for example, Todd Beall, "Reading Genesis 1–2: A Literal Approach," in *Reading Genesis 1–2: An Evangelical Conversation*, ed. J. Daryl Charles (Peabody, Mass.: Hendrickson, 2013), 44–59; James Mook, "The Church Fathers in Genesis, the Flood, and the Age of the Earth," in *Coming to Grips with Genesis: Biblical Authority and the Age of the Earth*, ed. Terry Mortenson and Thane H. Ury (Green Forest, Ariz.: Master Books, 2008), 23–51. "Who We Are: Doctrinal Statement," *Liberty University* website, http://www.liberty.edu/aboutliberty/.

commitment to the literal tradition or the aging of those committed to alternative approaches.[311]

The literal hermeneutical tradition and its view of human origins remains substantial within Lutheran churches.[312] For the Dutch Reformed, this is true in the Netherlands,[313] North America,[314] Australia, and New Zealand. Substantial continuities of the literal hermeneutical approach also exist in the Presbyterian churches, both in Canada and in the United States.[315] In the United Kingdom, there is a significant commitment to the literal tradition among the Evangelical Presbyterian Church of England and Wales, as well as lesser commitments in Scotland among a variety of Presbyterian bodies. Confessional Presbyterian and Reformed denominations in Australia and New Zealand have also maintained a fairly significant stream of commitment to the literal tradition on creation and human origins. A German Reformed body, the Reformed Church in the United States, is exclusively committed to the literal hermeneutical tradition.

Perhaps most significant in terms of influence among North American evangelicals, the literal tradition has seen a resurgence in the largest conservative evangelical denomination in the United States, the Southern Baptist Convention. This revival has resulted in part from a significant theological recovery at the Southern Baptist Theological Seminary, but many Baptist churches and Baptistic nondenominational churches in North America have remained committed to the literal tradition through their histories. Globally, many in the Baptist stream continue a strong adherence to the literal tradition, though this is less true in Europe than in other regions.

Despite these streams of strong continuance in the literal tradition, a substantial effort to harmonize Scripture with science led to a proliferation of

311. Biologos Editorial Team, "A Survey of Clergy and their Views on Origins"; "More from our Survey," *Biologos Foundation* (May 2013), http://biologos.org/blog/a-survey-of-clergy-and-their-views-on-origins.

312. This is true for the Lutheran Church–Missouri Synod and the Wisconsin Evangelical Lutheran Synod.

313. In the *Christelijke Gereformeerde, Gereformeerde Kerken Vrijgemaakte, Herstelde Hervormde, Gereformeerde Gemeenten,* and minorities in the *Gereformeerde Kerk* and the *Protestantse Kerk van Nederland*.

314. This is substantially the case within the United Reformed, Free Reformed, Canadian Reformed, Protestant Reformed, Heritage Reformed, and Netherlands Reformed churches, while more of a minority in the Christian Reformed Church and Reformed Church in America.

315. The strand is more substantial in the Presbyterian Church in America and the Associate Reformed Presbyterian Church and perhaps less so in the Orthodox Presbyterian Church and the Evangelical Presbyterian Church.

alternative hermeneutic approaches beginning around the mid-nineteenth century and continuing to the present. With the hermeneutical alternatives have come attendant varieties of approach to the quest for the historical Adam.

Many conservative evangelical denominations, institutions, and local churches have granted at least some latitude to alternative hermeneutical approaches since the nineteenth century. However, there remains a substantial reluctance to abandon adherence to the literal understanding of the creation of Adam and Eve—a reluctance that continues to be challenged from within the evangelical community. By contrast, within most mainline, liberal Protestant bodies in North America,[316] alternative hermeneutical approaches to the text of Genesis 1 and 2 and alternative views of human origins are accepted as ordinary, if not normative.

Hermeneutics and the Quest for the Historical Adam

The history of Genesis interpretation in relation to the understanding of human origins is incredibly valuable, providing a wealth of rich commentary and reflection on the grandeur and humility of man's beginning. We see believers across the centuries filled with wonder and worship toward God, the Creator of the heavens and the earth, and everything that dwells in them. There is also the great encouragement in the fact that the history of Christian interpretation of Genesis across the millennia reveals a wide uniformity of understanding of human beginnings.

The Genesis 1 and 2 account of a special, direct creation of Adam and Eve as the first man and woman, without any ancestry, has seen very few exceptions in the history of Christianity. Alternatives to that account include only one or two in the patristic and medieval eras, a scattered fringe during the post-Reformation and Enlightenment eras, and more in the post-Darwinian era of the last 150 years. In each case, the pressure to take up an alternative interpretation of human origins has come from sources external to Scripture and Christian theology.

The history of the understanding of Genesis, hermeneutics, and human origins among the pastors and teachers Christ has given to His church provides opportunity for insightful questions and analysis. Among them is whether—and if so, how and to what degree—the development and proliferation of modern alternative hermeneutical approaches to Genesis 1 and 2 are

---

316. These include the Episcopalian Church, the United Methodist Church, the Evangelical Lutheran Church, the Presbyterian Church (USA), the Reformed Church of America, the United Church of Christ, and the American Baptist churches.

connected to the present quest for the historical Adam. To begin to answer the question, we must first note that none of the alternative hermeneutical approaches (gap or restitution theory, day-age, literary-framework, analogical, ancient Near Eastern cosmological, or even the mythopoeic) *necessitate* the rejection of the traditional literal interpretation of the creation of Adam and Eve. Equally important, it should also be noted that most contemporary alternative approaches do not inherently *require* the Adam and Eve who originate and exist as described in the literal tradition. This is a profoundly significant shift.

The history of Genesis hermeneutics indicates that the older, once popular, hermeneutical alternative of gap or restitution theory, followed by the "first days of indefinite length" approach, established a principle of hermeneutical adjustment which opened the way for greater hermeneutical and exegetical adjustments. Initially, many of the proponents of these views held to a literal understanding of the creation of Adam and Eve as the first and sole human pair without any evolutionary origins. However, among these alternative views, the gap or restitution theory and Sailhamer's more recent hermeneutical approach allow for the existence of a pre-Adamite humanity.

Whereas the older hermeneutical alternatives to the literal tradition usually required further internal adjustments to abandon a literal understanding of human origins, contemporary and popular alternative approaches—such as the literary framework, day-age, pictorial days, analogical, ancient Near Eastern cosmological, and mythopoeic—are fully open to an Adam and Eve created through a divine use of evolutionary biological processes. Many leading proponents of these views openly acknowledge this openness, which is possible because the hermeneutical approaches remove exegetical barriers of time, chronology, and a literal-sense, grammatical-historical exegesis of words and syntax from parts or all of the text. When these alternative interpretations are used to examine aspects of even a part of the Genesis text, it is difficult and perhaps impossible to not apply the same hermeneutical and exegetical principles to the whole of the passage.

As a result, although many proponents of these alternative approaches have sought to retain the historical Adam and Eve and remained committed to their special creation apart from any evolutionary origins, others use the principles of the alternative approaches to posit their choice of a range of "Adams and Eves" with varying degrees of evolutionary origins. Some move to the outright rejection of the historical existence of an Adam and Eve. The fluid freedom, blank spaces of new figurative obscurity, or simple lack of information created by the alternative hermeneutical approaches are filled at the whim of the interpreter with either "the God of the gaps" or "the science of the gaps."

The result is an evangelical Protestant hermeneutical field on early Genesis and human origins that bears some similarity to the late medieval era, when William Tyndale lamented, "For Origen and the doctors of his time drew all the Scripture into allegories: whose ensample they that came afterward followed so long, till they at last forgot the order and process of the text, supposing that the scripture served but to feign allegories upon; insomuch that twenty doctors expound one text twenty ways, as children make descant upon plainsong."[317]

Along with the troubling loss of a perspicuous early Genesis is the perhaps even more troubling reality that the history of hermeneutics on Genesis and human origins, particularly in the last two centuries, reveals a repeated pattern toward an erosion of scriptural inerrancy, sufficiency, and historic Christian theology. Despite naysayers, the history of Genesis hermeneutics across the centuries does provide numerous examples of sequential changes: if these changes do not indicate a "slippery slope," they certainly indicate consecutive slides. In the history of each of the "schools" of alternative approaches and the institutions and denominations that grant latitude to them, there is an unbroken pattern of progressive movement, initially away from the literal tradition on Genesis 1, then away from the Adam and Eve of the literal tradition toward an evolved Adam, and then to no recognizable or existing Adam and Eve at all. There have been exceptions to—and reversals of—this trend, but they are rare.

There are close parallels between the nineteenth-century quest for the historical Jesus and the present quest for the historical Adam. Reinterpreting historical narrative as figurative, in response to philosophy or science, brings us into a close proximity to the adoption of the category of myth, with its rejection of an inerrant, infallible Scripture, and attendant rejection of the authority of Scripture—and of God himself. To ignore this, or merely accept it out of hand, is a sign of blinded naiveté rather than intellectual wisdom and is done at the church's peril.

Yet there are further questions we need to engage, consider, and decisively answer in harmony with the truth of the Word of God, as summarized in historic and orthodox Christian confession. Why does it matter how and when

---

317. William Tyndale, "The Four Senses of the Scripture," in *Works of William Tyndale* (Edinburgh: Banner of Truth, 2010), 1:307.

Adam and Eve were created, or whether they existed at all as specific, historical individuals? What difference does it make how we or others resolve the quest for the historical Adam? The remainder of this volume offers a beginning in engaging, considering, and answering these questions.

7

What Difference Does It Make?

Through the first eighteen centuries of Christian church history, commitment to a literal understanding of human origins was nearly monolithic among exegetes and theologians. This included the patristic and medieval clergy who held to the now-obsolete alternative hermeneutical stream exemplified in Origen and Augustine. Nearly the entirety of Christendom held to an Adam and Eve who were the first human pair, without ancestry or contemporaries at their point of origin. Almost every Christian theologian, whether in the Roman Empire, the Eastern or Western church, Roman Catholicism or Reformation Protestantism—even most through the Enlightenment era—understood Adam and Eve as literally created in the manner described in Genesis 2:7 and Genesis 2:21–22.

Darwin's nineteenth-century synthesis of a minor stream of thought into a more cogent evolutionary theory, along with a growing, enthusiastic audience primed by Hutton and Lyell, proved vastly influential in Western thought. The next century, with its massive cultural shift in natural philosophy on origins, bore witness not only to the erosion, but also to the resilience of the literal interpretation of Genesis on human origins. Despite a wide acceptance of evolutionary thought on human origins in mainline Protestant and post-Christian sectors of Western society, the vast majority of evangelical and confessional Protestants remain committed to the Adam and Eve of Genesis as understood by the literal tradition. In fact, despite some ebb and flow in the past century, there remains a substantial commitment to the literal understanding of the entire Genesis 1–2 creation narrative—not only because of the weight of long historical tradition, but also because of close coherence with the text.

The history of Genesis hermeneutics makes it clear that it is possible to hold to hermeneutical alternatives to the literal tradition on Genesis 1 and 2 and still maintain support for the special, temporally immediate creation of

Adam and Eve of the literal tradition. At the same time, a significant number of proponents of hermeneutical alternatives to the literal tradition on Genesis 1 and 2 have pursued greater degrees of compatibility with mainstream scientific thought, moving to either a noncommittal ambivalence on human origins or an adoption of evolutionary models of origins.

But, even if the latter trend is plainly evident, why should we care? What is at stake when the quest for the historical Adam arrives at proposals to abandon the millennia-old tradition of a literal interpretation of early Genesis on human origins? Does it matter how and when Adam and Eve were created, or whether they existed at all as specific, historical individuals? What difference does it make how we, or others, resolve the quest for the historical Adam?

Theistic Evolution and Finding Adam

Comparing the theological implications of human origins according to the literal tradition versus alternative models can be challenging because of the diversity and fluidity of views that posit Adam and Eve were created at least in part via evolutionary biological processes (EBP). At times, even individual proponents will suggest varying dates and hypotheses for what they believe may have occurred—because any certitude is unverifiable. Even with these challenges, a basic taxonomy proves helpful here. While individuals can easily float between these or other variations, models involving EBP in the origins of Adam and Eve can presently be organized into three general categories, which are detailed below.

EBP1: Origins by Theistic Evolution with Divine Impartation of Soul

Through theistic evolution (ape-hominid-human) under ordinary providence, humanity comes into existence, receiving the image of God by a sovereign direct act of imparting "soul"; this modifies them from hominid to humans bearing "the image of God." This modification possibly occurred during the Neolithic period (ten thousand to fifteen thousand years ago) with one pair of hominids. The imparting of a soul is an act of special creation causing a distinct delineation between humans and hominids. The latter die out in time.[1]

---

1. Gregg Davidson, author of *When Faith and Science Collide* (Oxford, Miss.: Malius, 2009), stands as a proponent of this view. With Ken Wolgemuth, Davidson argues, "There is no difference between Adam specially created by God from the dust, and Adam as a hominid adopted by God and given a soul." "The PCA Creation Study Committee a Dozen Years Later: What Does Science Say Now?" (seminar, Presbyterian Church General Assembly, Louisville, Kentucky, June 20, 2012).

Proponents of this view or of close variants include C. S. Lewis, Derek Kidner, Tim Keller, Gregg Davidson, and Francis Collins. Varieties of this view fall within C. John Collins's range of legitimate Christian views.

EBP2: Origins by Theistic Evolution with Divine Relationship

Through theistic evolution (ape-hominid-human) under ordinary providence, at some point, possibly Neolithic (ten thousand to fifteen thousand years ago), humanity receives or "seals" the "image of God" by coming into special relationship with God, via a Neolithic pair gaining "God-consciousness" or "spiritual life." The change is primarily the gaining of a new relational dimension, in contrast to the ontological transformation or "addition" to man that occurs in EBP1. In EBP2, everything aside from the new awareness of and relationship with God is a result of evolutionary biological processes. Depending on the proponent of this view, this event may be described as humanity receiving the "image of God" by a sovereign direct act of "image bestowal" (or its completion) in the establishment of a covenant relationship between God and humanity, via this pair.

The pair, sometimes described as being specially "adopted" by God, act representatively or federally for all other (including previous) humans, all of whom are already "body and soul" beings by virtue of evolutionary processes. Some further argue that "soul" describes human cognition, not a distinct, separable entity from the body.[2] Denis Alexander names a form of this "*Homo divinus* Model." Varieties of this view also fall within C. John Collins's range of legitimate Christian views.

EBP3: Origins by Theistic Evolution with Divine Revelation

Through theistic evolution (ape-hominid-human) under ordinary providence, God reveals Himself to a large group of early humans possibly around 150,000 years ago; the biblical Adam and Eve are understood as literary figures, symbolic of the group. Adam did not exist historically in any sense. Some who hold to this model posit that God may have revealed Himself later, perhaps fifty thousand years ago, or during the Neolithic period (ten thousand to fifteen thousand years ago), and that there was merely a form of basic religion

---

2. Bearing some similarity to the first two of these models—though perhaps most closely resembling the second—is the old-earth creation model where God through an act of special immediate creation formed humans about 150,000 years ago, apart from any evolutionary origins, but then selected a pair of them (Adam and Eve) about ten thousand years ago to represent all humanity.

prior. Issues relating to "soul" and "image of God" in this view tend to parallel those of EBP2.

Denis Alexander describes a form of this as the "Retelling Model." Peter Enns, Daniel Harlow, and Dennis Lamoureaux are presently proponents of this view. At a Discovery Institute Conference at Westminster Theological Seminary in Philadelphia, Lamoureaux offered a viewpoint that appeared to be a hybrid of EBP1 and EBP3.

Naïveté and Agnosticism

While these three general models reflect the three main streams of approach, many scientists and theologians who hold to the creation of Adam and Eve in part or whole via EBP are agnostic or tentative about the options.[3] Some, like Denis Alexander, view EBP2 and EBP3 as legitimate models while admitting that "no-one is naïve enough to think that such models are completely satisfying."[4] There is an evident willingness to embrace ambiguity on the origin and existence of Adam and to live with unsatisfying theological models that challenge the historic theological consensus. There is little to no willingness to live with scientific models that challenge the scientific models of origins accepted in the contemporary mainstream. The wider commitments and priorities are clear.

Internal Challenges for Theistic Evolutionary Models

Within and related to the three EBP models are several challenges which are readily acknowledged by their proponents.

Formation of Eve from Adam's Rib

One challenge for these varied models comes from the Genesis 2 account of the creation of Eve, which distinctly notes her formation from the rib of Adam. In most cases in the EBP models, this mention of Adam's rib is understood similarly to "the dust" (Genesis 2:7)—as a literary device or symbol. However, some proponents of EBP1–2 read Genesis 2:21–22 according to the

---

3. See for example, Deborah B. Haarsma and Loren D. Haarsma, *Origins: Christian Perspectives on Creation, Evolution, and Intelligent Design* (Grand Rapids: Faith Alive Christian Resources, 2011).

4. Denis Alexander, "How Does a BioLogos Model Need to Address the Theological Issues Associated with an Adam Who Was Not the Sole Genetic Progenitor of Humankind?," *The BioLogos Foundation*, http://biologos.org/resources/essay/how-does-a-biologos-model-need -to-address-the-theological-issues.

literal tradition's understanding of the creation of Eve from Adam even while the reference to Adam being "formed of the dust of the ground" is viewed as figurative language allowing for evolutionary ancestry.[5]

Agrarianism, Urbanity, and the First Humans
The EBP1 and EBP2 models (and old-earth models that place the creation of humanity at 150,000 years ago) are also challenged by the fact that the narrative of Genesis 1–4 indicates that Adam and Eve and their children engaged in farming activities and built towns or cities. The biblical record indicates an agrarian and settled lifestyle, which according to the dominant evolutionary models of human origins could only have been during the Neolithic period, at the earliest some ten thousand to fifteen thousand years ago. European Neanderthals (*Homo neanderthalis*), considered in evolutionary models to have existed for 350,000 years or more, have been found buried in ways that indicate religiosity. According to consensus evolutionary models, *Homo sapiens* have existed for around 150,000 years. If one posits that Adam and Eve were Neolithic while holding to current evolutionary models, then not all humanity is descended from Adam, because some peoples, like the Australian Aboriginals are posited as having been in Australia for at least forty thousand years.

According to evolutionary models, there is significant ground to believe religiosity existed prior to the Neolithic period. But it is also problematic to posit Adam and Eve as being two million years old or even 135,000 years old prior to the birth of Cain and Abel, who were very clearly their sons, while their activity would require them to be Neolithic.

Added to this challenge is another significant problem: human morphology has great antiquity in evolutionary time scales. It remains remarkably consistent across vast time and classifications. Neanderthals go back nearly a half a million years and show no significant morphological distinction from modern humans: they had a larger brain, had the ability to speak, had musical instruments, and buried their dead in human burial postures, including with trinkets and dogs. *Homo erectus*, in the evolutionary timescale, go back about two million years and should not be excluded from human classification. They are classified in the same genus, are postcranially indistinguishable from humans, have cerebral design consistent with modern humans, and have a cranial capacity that does not preclude human intelligence. Arguably the "hominid" to "human"

---

5. Tim Keller, in his essay "Creation, Evolution, and Christian Laypeople," proposes Derek Kidner's variant of this model as one of the most viable current alternatives. Derek Kidner, *Genesis: An Introduction and Commentary* (Downers Grove, Ill.: InterVarsity, 1967), 28.

distinction is more conjecture than reality. Attempting to add "creation" theological distinctions at any given point in time within the *Homo erectus* to *Homo sapiens* span is effectively arbitrary. This challenge has led a number of theologians and scientists more recently to shift to variants of EBP3.[6]

A Human Pair?

A third challenge to the first two EBP models is the issue of whether there was an actual initial "human" pair at the point of "becoming fully human." Recent arguments from the field of genetics, which posit that there were never less than ten thousand to one hundred thousand hominids or humans, have pushed some proponents of EBP1–2 to accept the concept of a group rather than an initial pair, again moving them toward an EBP3 position.

Comparing the Consequences: Literal Origins versus EBP Models

Having described the various EBP models and noting some of the internal challenges they face, it remains to be seen what theological implications may arise from the varied views on human origins. Are there any theological implications, real or potential, to abandoning the literal tradition in the quest for the historical Adam? Are there any shifts or changes from the stream of Protestant orthodoxy today manifested in conservative evangelical and confessional churches? To understand what difference this makes, we now turn to ten areas of doctrine that are connected to the historic, literal view of the special, temporally immediate creation of Adam and Eve. In each case, problematic areas of doctrinal implication arise due to the various nonliteral views associated with EBP1–3.[7] The comparative analysis is only an initial attempt, which will hopefully spur further, more substantive engagement with the issues.

---

6. This internal difficulty was noted by Davis Young in "The Antiquity and Unity of the Human Race Revisited," where he challenged that "a satisfactory solution to these issues will require close attention to the literary character of Genesis 2–4." Subsequent writers have echoed or taken up the challenge. See, for example, Daniel Harlow, "After Adam: Reading Genesis in an Age of Evolutionary Science," *Perspectives on Science and Christian Faith* 62, no. 3 (September 2010): 179–95; Alexander, "BioLogos Model"; Peter Enns, *The Evolution of Adam: What the Bible Does and Doesn't Say about Human Origins* (Grand Rapids: Baker, 2012).

7. This is done within the framework of an evangelical, confessional Reformed theology, giving an initial, summary evaluation of key biblical doctrines associated with the text of the early chapters of Genesis in relation to human origins.

Scripture and Hermeneutics

The literal tradition's approach to the early chapters of Genesis by necessity entails a literal Adam and Eve, created the sixth day. As the historical survey in this volume has shown, numerous theologians have provided strong exegetical arguments for the understanding that the Genesis 1 and 2 account does indeed present the creation of Adam and Eve, as the first humans, specially created on the sixth day apart from any ancestry.[8]

In doing so, the literal tradition does not negate the literary beauty and structure of the passage, but it enables rich reflection on the narrative and the unfolding themes of biblical theology, in harmony with the rest of the Scriptures.[9] It harmonizes fully with broader biblical themes relevant to the garden, Temple, Promised Land, person and work of Christ, and eschatology. The cohesiveness of the literal reading of early Genesis with the rest of Scripture is also readily evident when comparing Old and New Testament references to creation, such as Mark's account of the creation ordinance of marriage (Mark 10:6–9), Luke's genealogy beginning with Adam (Luke 3:23–38), the account of the blood of the prophets shed "from the foundation of the world…from the blood of Abel to the blood of Zechariah" (Luke 11:50–51), the Romans explanation of the fall (Rom. 5:12–14), and the Pauline accounts of the creation of Adam and Eve in relation to marriage (1 Cor. 11:8–9; 1 Tim. 2:11–14). First Corinthians 15:42–49 also stands in unity with a literal understanding of early Genesis in stating, among other things, that "the first man *was* of the earth, *made* of dust" (1 Cor. 15:47).

The reading of the grammatical-historical hermeneutic of the literal tradition on the early chapters of Genesis also harmonizes fully with other scriptural accounts of the miraculous and supernatural, God's acting above and beyond the natural, intervening in the ordinary processes and principles of the created order which He created, sustains, and rules. The exegetical and expository results of the literal hermeneutic in the creation account stand consistent with God's supernatural actions, including the testimony to the resurrection of Christ and the prophesy of His coming return on the day of judgment and glory. The literal tradition is also historically connected to a

---

8. See, for example, John Murray, "The Origin of Man," in *Collected Writings of John Murray* (Edinburgh: Banner of Truth, 1977), 2: 3–13; and Andrew Kulikovsky, *Creation, Fall, Restoration: A Biblical Theology of Creation* (Fearn, U.K.: Christian Focus, 2009), 182–86.

9. Richard Phillips, Nick Batzig, and Kenneth Kang-Hui, "The Historical Adam," *Reformed Forum*, Friday, January 27, 2012, reformedforum.org/podcasts/ctc212/.

high view of the authority and perspicuity of Scripture as the interpreter of creational and human existence, connecting with a significant view of the noetic effects of sin in man's inability in a fallen condition to appropriately assess creational and human existence by general revelation.

In assessing the juncture between hermeneutics and views of human origins, it must also be noted that the creation of Adam and Eve apart from any evolutionary biological processes can be—and is—posited by some who advocate alternative hermeneutical approaches to the remainder of Genesis 1 and 2. The transition to a more literal hermeneutic, often at the end of Genesis 2:3 or shortly thereafter, is at least partly due to an awareness of the increasing theological difficulties encountered if alternative hermeneutical approaches are consistently applied to the text in the expanded account of the creation of Adam and Eve in Genesis 2.

Many proponents of framework and analogical hypotheses, in advocating alternative hermeneutics and choosing where to "draw the line" between figurative and literal, do so to loosen the text of Genesis 1 from at least the literal reading's temporal chronology. Doing so allows for either instants of supernatural creation and "in-kind" evolutionary development occurring within the general parameters of an evolutionary timescale or for acts of creation by theistic evolutionary processes. All options posit at least animal death prior to the fall, and leave a nearly 2-million year history of (likewise dying) creatures assigned to the classification *Homo*—prior to what is posited to be the appearance of Adam (whether at ten thousand to fifteen thousand years, or up to 150,000 years). Even where a line of hermeneutical transition to a more literal approach is drawn at Genesis 2:3, the more detailed account of Adam and Eve in Genesis 2:7 and following effectively remains subsumed under the loosening effect of the hermeneutical approach to Genesis 1.

On the positive side, this approach largely preserves Christianity's historic doctrine of man, but at the same time it weakens or outright nullifies a primary exegetical ground (a sixth day of ordinary duration) for the special, temporally immediate creation of Adam and Eve apart from evolutionary origins. It also establishes reasonable hermeneutical grounds for those seeking to apply a more figurative reading to Genesis 2:3 and following (God's formation of the man from the dust, etc.). A strong exegetical case for a special, temporally immediate creation of Adam and Eve apart from evolutionary origins in keeping with their contextual hermeneutic has not yet been made by proponents of framework hypothesis or analogical days, nor have they provided substantive warrant for a transition to a literal reading in Genesis 2.[10]

The EBP models for human origins all adopt nonliteral hermeneutical approaches (whether framework hypothesis, analogical, or other) from Genesis 1:1 at least up to Genesis 2:7. The challenge for the proponents of EBP models is where to draw the line in terms of hermeneutic transition and why. The more theologically conservative EBP proponents who hold to EBP1 or EBP2, such as Tim Keller and Terry Gray, often argue that as long as there is "an historical Adam and Eve" (e.g., a Neolithic pair) who mark a special point of transition in terms of now being in the image of God, whether their origins were in part via EBP is irrelevant to maintaining an orthodox theology.[11] Theologians such as C. John Collins in his recent book, *Did Adam and Eve Really Exist?*, and his article, "Adam and Eve in the Old Testament," make an extensive theological and exegetical case for the existence of an Adam and Eve but do so avoiding any exegetical comment on Genesis 2:7 or prior, granting latitude for the possibility of at least a partial EBP.[12]

Collins's latitude leaves an ad hoc "Adam" whose origins lie in obscurity.[13] Articles in a recent issue of *New Horizons*, the church periodical of the Orthodox Presbyterian Church, address the issue of the historicity of Adam and Eve in a similar manner, arguing theologically and exegetically from other parts of Scripture for the existence of an Adam and Eve, rather than turning to the Genesis 1 and 2 accounts.[14] While the latter case presents a common evangelical pattern, it may in some circumstances reflect a reticence to engage Genesis

---

10. As Davis Young notes in "The Antiquity and the Unity of the Human Race Revisited," a more consistent approach (where a framework hypothesis, analogical, or other nonliteral hermeneutic is adopted in light of the mainstream consensus on origins in the scientific community) is to revisit the literary character of the whole of Genesis 2–4. *Christian Scholar's Review* 24, no. 4 (May 1995): 380–96.

11. Keller, "Creation, Evolution, and Christian Laypeople"; Terry Gray, letter to Rev. Thomas E. Tyson, editor of *New Horizons*, February 15, 1993, www.asa3.0rg/gray/evolution_trial/NHevolution.html.

12. C. John Collins, *Did Adam and Eve Really Exist? Who They Were and Why You Should Care* (Wheaton, Ill.: Crossway, 2011); and C. John Collins, "Adam and Eve in the Old Testament," *Southern Baptist Journal of Theology* 15, no. 1 (2011): 4–25. See also Richard Belcher's helpful critique in "Did Adam and Eve Really Exist? A Review," Reformation 21, February 2012, http://www.reformation21.org/articles/did-adam-and-eve-really-exist-a-review.php.

13. Peter Enns, "Still in the Weeds on Human Origins: A Review of C. John Collins' *Did Adam and Eve Really Exist?*," *Perspectives: A Journal of Reformed Thought* (December 2011), http://www.rca.org/Page.aspx?pid=7796.

14. Danny E. Olinger, ed., "Adam: Man or Myth?," special issue, *New Horizons* (March 2012) contains articles on the topic by Richard B. Gaffin, Vern S. Poythress, and Brian Estelle, along with a book review by Olinger.

hermeneutics directly rather than a rejection of an Adam and Eve created as described by the literal tradition.

Maintaining the existence of "a" historical Adam and Eve, without definitive commentary on their origins, can restrain some of the theologically problematic issues of harmonization with the broader testimony of Scripture. However, implicitly or explicitly granting a latitude of options on human origins leaves a standing tension that promotes—and in many cases logically requires—reinterpretive reengagement with passages such as Romans 5 and 1 Corinthians 15:47. This issue is duly noted not only by proponents of the literal tradition, but also by proponents of EBP3, who point out remaining problems from the other side, pressing for a fuller coherence with contemporary evolutionary theory on human origins.[15]

Proponents of EBP3 contrast themselves with proponents of EBP1-2 by arguing for a greater consistency in applying alternative hermeneutics, moving them forward through the text to provide a greater consistency with evolutionary models of origins.[16] In doing so, they bring forward an approach which, while it effectively "harmonizes" Scripture with a mainstream evolutionary consensus, also effectively negates the reality of any historical detail or particularity in the early chapters of Genesis. Most significantly, EBP3 asserts that Adam and Eve did not exist as historical individuals.

While some proponents of EBP3 initially argued for a broadening of the scope of the hermeneutical shift into Genesis 2–4, others now posit it must apply to at least chapter 11.[17] By logical implication, this affects New Testament hermeneutics. The challenge of what to do with New Testament writers

---

15. Davis Young states, "If the data in Genesis 4 are correlated with the cultural setting of the Neolithic Revolution in the ancient Near East about 8000 to 7500 B.C., then the biblical representation of Adam as Cain's immediate father suggests that Adam and Eve lived only about ten thousand years ago. The fossil record of anatomically modern humans, however, extends at least one hundred thousand years before the present. There are at least three solutions to this dilemma. All three alternative solutions pose difficult exegetical or theological challenges that result in either a refinement of the doctrine of original sin or a significant departure from traditional historical readings of Genesis 2–4." "The Antiquity and the Unity of the Human Race Revisited," *Christian Scholar's Review* 24, no. 4 (May 1995): 380. Young fails to address the fact that mainstream anthropology universally agrees that the genus *Homo* extends nearly two million years back.

16. This places the defenders of EBP1-2, or those who believe that issues of origins are irrelevant so long as there is a "historical Adam and Eve" in an awkward position of having to rationalize an inconsistent hermeneutic along with inconsistency with the consensus of the scientific community. The arguments for their delineation of hermeneutical approaches rest on theological and exegetical cues from texts external to the early chapters of Genesis.

17. Harlow, "After Adam."

such as Luke and Paul is in many ways similar to the challenge of the early Genesis chapters. Where the Genesis text is reinterpreted and contextualized to ancient Near Eastern culture, the New Testament texts are contextualized to Greco-Roman and Jewish Second Temple culture. In both cases, the writers are posited as being understandably and unwittingly localized within their culture and time, accounting for any fallible references to scientific realities, including belief in an Adam and Eve who are specially and temporally immediately created by God without ancestry.

The EBP models are connected to a high view of natural human ability and reason in the exploration and understanding of present and past realities. They also display a significant acceptance of contemporary natural philosophy viewed as "science" on origins. At times, this appears to correlate with a belief in human ability to autonomously read general revelation and special revelation—undermining a historic doctrine of Scripture and introducing a significantly problematic principle for hermeneutics. Geerhardus Vos's assessment appears prescient here. When asked "whether those who held days to be eras should be considered heretics," Vos, having noted their poor interpretation of the Word, replied, "No, the question is not essential in this sense.... It only rises to this level when on principle they raise the so-called results of science to grant precedence to them over the Word of God."[18]

The EBP models give significant indication that science, on principle, has been granted precedence over Genesis 1–2. One evidence of this is found in the ongoing efforts to engage in further reinterpretation of Genesis, as well as New Testament passages like Romans 5.[19] There is good ground to view this as significantly abandoning biblical orthodoxy. Even more blatant, however, are those, like Peter Enns, who choose to place Genesis 1–2 in the category of myth. Most complete in pursuing accommodation with evolutionary theory, the hermeneutic of myth, in its claim for an errant biblical text, rejects the authority and inerrancy of Scripture. Where the doctrine of Scripture is lost, a loss of biblical Christianity is sure to follow.[20]

---

18. Geerhardus Vos, "Dogmatiek van G. Vos. Ph.D. D.D., Deel I. Theologie" (unpublished manuscript), Heckman Library Archives, Calvin College, Grand Rapids, Michigan, 1910, 170.

19. Harlow, "After Adam," 182–95.

20. Peter Enns, *Inspiration and Incarnation: Evangelicals and the Problem of the Old Testament* (Grand Rapids: Baker, 2012), 53–55; J. Gresham Machen, *Christianity and Liberalism* (Grand Rapids: Eerdmans, 1992), 69–79.

Man and the Ethics of Human Life

The literal tradition's approach to the Genesis 1 and 2 account of the creation of Adam and Eve harmonizes well with historic Christian understanding of the doctrine of man. While there have been many debates through church history regarding the nature of the image of God in man and the nature of the soul, the literal approach provides clear foundation and rationale for the image of God in man and his "reasonable and immortal soul."[21] Man is a special creation, distinct and separate from the rest of creation, not only by virtue of relationship with God, but also because he is a radically distinct, new act of creation by God, making him a "living being" (Gen. 2:7).[22]

Genesis 1:30 states that the beasts, birds, and creeping things have "the breath of life." While there is a shared physical reality here between humanity and animals, the activity of Genesis 1:26–28 and Genesis 2:7 and following indicates a significant creational differentiation between humanity and animals. Animals were formed or "brought forth" by the creative spoken word of God. But there is a uniqueness in both the decision to "Let Us make man in Our image, according to Our likeness" and the recounting of God's creating man in His own image by forming Adam out of the dust (see 1 Cor. 15:45–49). The latter, bearing similarity to the intimate activity of a potter working with clay (see Isa. 64:8), is a description immediately followed in the Genesis 2 narrative by the action of breathing "into his nostrils the breath of life" as the culminating activity in the creation of Adam as a "living being."[23]

---

21. Westminster Larger Catechism, Q&A 17.

22. Most translations take the Hebrew (*nepesh*) and translate it as "soul" or "being." The English Standard Version translates it as "creature," which I believe is a weaker choice in this context. Wayne Grudem, gen. ed., *English Standard Version* (Wheaton, Ill.: Crossway, 2001). While it is rightly noted by a number of commentators and Hebraists that the text is not indicating the imparting of a soul into an as of yet lifeless body, the text is indicating that God here uniquely "breathed into his nostrils the breath of life," which at that moment made Adam "a living soul." I differ here from Bruce Waltke's application of the semantic uses and range of *nepesh* to Genesis 2:7 in his entry, "napash/nepesh" in *Theological Wordbook of the Old Testament* (Chicago: Moody, 1980), 2:590, and instead follow John Calvin's comments on Genesis 2:7 in his *Commentary on the Book of Genesis*, 112. Keil and Delitzsch also provide helpful commentary on the textual and theological issues in *Biblical Commentary on the Old Testament: The Pentateuch*, trans. James Martin (Grand Rapids, Eerdmans, 2006), 78–80.

23. John Murray argues similarly to Keil and Delitzsch but interestingly cites the Hebrew term for "living soul" as "living creature" in Genesis 2:7 and notes that it is similar to that used in the creation accounts of other creatures in Genesis 1. Murray argues that the content of Genesis 2:7, including the moment and circumstance of becoming a "living creature" rules out the possibility that any part of Adam, including his body, could have been a living creature prior to that point. Murray, "Origins of Man," 2:3–13.

God places Adam into a garden cultured and cultivated as a crowning beauty of vegetation and abundant fruitfulness. The emphasis is on God's special, direct, intimate creative activity—using materials normally incapable of producing human life. This text, along with the rest of Scripture, affirms the uniqueness of humanity as an intentionally separate, unique creation of God, in His image. Where each animal is created "according to its kind" (Gen. 1:25), God states, "Let Us make man in Our image, according to Our likeness" (Gen. 1:26). This is further emphasized in the creation mandate in Genesis 1:28–30 as God places man as a steward over the rest of creation.

Connected with the reality of the temporally immediate creation of Adam and Eve in a mature state apart from evolutionary origins is the reality that they were fully human, fully God's image-bearers from the moment of receiving life. This stands in harmony with the wider doctrine of man in Scripture in relation to ethics of life: Adam and Eve's offspring are seen as coming into living existence at the point of conception (see Gen. 4:1, 17), a point clearly reiterated in the Mosaic law (Ex. 21:22–25).

The EBP models, while diverse, all posit an inherent and essential connection of humanity in origin to animals and the rest of creation. In the cases of EBP1–2 models, this may be modified by any or all of the following factors: (1) the special creation of Eve; (2) the imparting of a soul, and/or conferral of the image of God, at a distinct point in time; and (3) the selection of a specific pair of hominids to become the first humans—though the latter is at times viewed as occurring through the gift of a spiritual relationship rather than any facet of ontological origin. EBP3 tends to militate against the inclusion of any of these as modifying factors to a human pair or group. Instead, EBP3 proposes an evolution of religiosity: through an evolutionary process or processes concurrent with evolution, man enters into conscious relationship with God. Some EBP3 proponents reject a body-soul distinction, and with it the doctrine of an intermediate state between death and the final judgment.

Despite the variety among EBP models, all diminish the inherent distinctiveness of man from the rest of God's creation, particularly through their partial or complete denial of Genesis 2:7 as a literal reality. Adam is not an entirely new and distinct creation, which has at least potential implications for what it means to be an image-bearer.

The lack of a temporally immediate, special creation also serves to erode a biblical ethic of human life: if Adam and/or Eve were at one point hominid and then became human, then they were not fully human for the totality of their existence but became human at the point of endowment with soul or upon becoming image-bearers. In positing this, EBP models present a weakening of scriptural testimony to the sanctity of human life from its first origin. It also necessitates that animal and hominid suffering, violence, and death are part of the "good" and "very good" realities of God's creation prior to Adam and Eve's fall into sin and the ensuing curse on man and creation. According to EBP models, it is an open question, unaddressed by Scripture, at what point hominids became humans; by implication, there is no firm answer at what point a fetus, potentially a child, becomes human. If our ancestors, under divine sovereignty, became human at some point after they began living, why should it be any different for an embryo that has not yet developed to a mature human form? This stands in stark contrast to the literal view's necessary implication: human life begins at the moment of conception for Adam and Eve's descendants, just as it began at the first moment of life for our first parents. The potential impact of the weakness of EBP views is in one case expressed by Francis Collins's arguments for the legitimacy of embryonic stem cell research.[24]

Marriage and Unity of Race

The literal understanding of the Genesis 2 account of Adam and Eve's creation, particularly the account of God's creation of Eve from Adam to be his wife as the first pair of humans, is the God-given origin of and paradigm for marriage as a union of male and female, husband and wife. This creation ordinance of marriage with its description of monogamous, heterosexual marital intimacy and desire is described as very good and sinless—made by God. A complementarian view of marriage, with its distinct roles of husband and wife, finds its foundation in the creation of Eve from, for, and with Adam.[25] In its description of marriage, family unit, one man, and one woman, Genesis 2:24–25 establishes patterns as literal and normative by virtue of the special, immediate creative action of God. They stand as an expansion and implication of what is revealed in Genesis 1:27.

The literal reading of the Genesis 2 creation account in declaring that Adam and Eve were the first pair of humans, without ancestry or fellow humans in creation prior to the fall, is an explicit testimony to unity of race.

---

24. Peter J. Boyer, "The Covenant," *The New Yorker* (September 6, 2010), http://www.newyorker.com/reporting/2010/09/06/100906fa_fact_boyer; Francis Collins, "Statement by NIH Director Francis S. Collins, M.D., Ph.D., on Supreme Court's decision regarding stem cell case," *National Institutes of Health*, January 7, 2013, http://www.nih.gov/about/director/01072013_stemcell_statement.htm.

25. "The Danvers Statement," *Council on Biblical Manhood and Womanhood*, 1987, http://cbmw.org/uncategorized/the-danvers-statement/.

All mankind, whether Australian Aborigines, Asian, Caucasian, African, etc., are descended from Adam and Eve. Thus, all human beings bear God's image. Due to Eve's creation from Adam's rib, there is a complete unity of race in Adam. Rather than multiple races, with some being potentially in a more advanced evolutionary stage than others, there is one human race, under one curse, with one Savior.

EBP models are not unified on this point. EBP1 models, where they posit a creational transition of one "hominid" to a human (Adam) or a "hominid" pair to a human pair (Adam and Eve), potentially allow for unity of race through an argument for the extinction of hominids as an animal species. It does so, however, with a significantly weakened exegetical warrant due to its hermeneutical approach. EBP2 and EBP3 models, where they hold to the mainstream consensus on human evolutionary origins and development, open the potential for the loss of the doctrine of unity of race. At the least, they provide logical opportunity for arguments for evolutionary superiority and inferiority between ethnicities. This is true for the "out of Africa" evolutionary models of human origins, despite their effort to maintain a unity of the human race, and even more so for the multiple regional models of human origins. Due to the fluidity of EBP models, and their ad hoc Adam, EBP proponents can claim to answer this simply by positing a relatively recent origin of humanity.

All of the EBP models, even those that posit Adam and Eve as the sole pair for hominid-to-human transition and the head of all humanity, weaken the created normativity of complementarian roles, heterosexual desire, and monogamous marital intimacy. Animal sexual behaviors are widely varied in the present state of creation. If suffering, violence, and death are normative realities of a prefall creation in the EBP models, why should one assume that present patterns of animal sexuality are less than "good" and "very good"? While the Genesis 1 paradigm of "male" and "female" and reproductive patterns may be assumed as God's general intent through ordinary, providential guidance of the evolutionary process, there is no ground in a nonliteral early Genesis to argue that hominids, or in the case of EBP2–3 models, humans, are innately structured for sexual relations limited to monogamous marriage. The EBP1 model suffers from the same weakness as it posits a physical continuity from hominid to human.

The most that can be argued in the EBP models is that when Adam and Eve become human and the image-bearers of God, they are brought together by God and instructed toward a monogamous marital sexuality. Extramarital, homosexual, bisexual, and polyamorous sexual desires within the EBP models may be construed as innate to original humanity, and not inherently sinful.[26]

Human Language

The literal understanding of the creation of Adam and Eve entails that they were specially and immediately created with the inherent ability to communicate with God and each other through language. When God spoke to them, there was no lack of ability on their part to understand, nor was there anything lacking in the means of communication—language. Speech, divine command, was the means by which God created all things. The process of man's creation is even more intimate, including conversation and communication: "Then God said, 'Let Us make man in Our image, according to Our likeness'" (Gen. 1:26).

God revealed Himself and His will to Adam and Eve through language, which they understood. Language was a vehicle of both perfect communication and communion from the beginning. In Genesis 3, with Satan's entry into the garden, we see the first distortions of language. Satan twists God's clear communication and uses language to deceive, incite sin, and foster rebellion against God. Adam and Eve's consequent choice to pursue sin, and the fall and its effects, now necessitate the work of the Holy Spirit with God's Word to bring both understanding and acceptance of it. This is not because of anything lacking in the Word of God, but because of the effects of sin on humanity. The Spirit illuminates the hearts and minds of fallen men and women who otherwise suppress the truth in unrighteousness. The Holy Spirit enables the spiritually deaf to hear, the spiritually blind to see what is plainly evident in God's Word and creation.

The original context of man's creation, with its inherent connection to the creation and use of human language by God, forms an essential basis for the doctrine of special revelation. God, the Creator of man and language is the One who spoke with perfect clarity and truth for salvation "at various times and in various ways...by the prophets" and has "spoken to us by His Son...through whom also He made the worlds" (Heb. 1:1–2). Hebrews tells us this means that

---

26. Joan Roughgarden, *What Jesus and Darwin Have in Common: Evolution and Christian Faith* (Washington, D.C.: Island Press, 2006), 115–24. Calvin College, a strong center of theistic evolutionary approaches to human origins, reflects a collegial environment with some movement in this direction. Christian Bell, "Calvin College Statement about Homosexuality Draws Fire," *The Banner*, January 18, 2011, http://www.thebanner.org/news/2011/01/calvin -college-statement-about-homosexuality-draws-fire. See also "FAQs about Calvin College, LGBT Students, and Homosexuality," *Calvin College*, http://www.calvin.edu/student-life/ss /faq.html.

"we must give the more earnest heed to the things we have heard, lest we drift away…. How shall we escape if we neglect so great a salvation, which at the first began to be spoken by the Lord, and was confirmed to us by those who heard *Him*" (Heb. 2:1–3).

The Scripture's veracity, inerrancy, and perspicuity are bound up in the fact that it is the Word of the Holy Creator, who "never lies" as He speaks to man. He speaks to us at our level, condescending or "accommodating" us, but never in a manner that obscures the truth and reality that He communicates to us. He has confirmed and confirms His Word to us in many ways (cf. Ps. 19; Eccl. 3:18–20; Rom. 5:12–15; 6:23; Heb. 2:3–4); He has had it written down and providentially preserved through the ages of human history. In harmony with the continuous testimony of all creation to His glory (Acts 14:17; Rom. 1:20), by His Word, God reveals Himself, His works (creation, redemption, etc.), and His will to us.

A literal understanding of Adam and Eve's creation does not negate the development of diverse languages, nor the reality of changes within languages. A further literal tradition reading of Genesis holds the phenomenon of the diversity of languages as being historically rooted in the confusion of languages at Babel (Genesis 11), enacted by God as a means to divide and slow the postflood rebellion of mankind, partly for the preservation of the church. This confusion is shown to begin to be undone through the risen and ascended Son of God sending the Holy Spirit to the church at Pentecost. The early church's reception of the Holy Spirit and the gift of tongues enables the Word of God to go out to and be understood by "every tribe and tongue and people and nation" (Rev. 5:9).

Understanding the creation of man and language as wholly good in the beginning, as in the literal tradition, provides an essential background to the character and nature of God's special revelation for salvation. It does so allowing for historical contextual insights (whether of archaeology, literature, geography, etc.), understanding that God inspired human authors to pen His Word, but it tends to do so with greater reserve and care for the unique authority, inerrancy, sufficiency, and perspicuity of Scripture.

EBP models lay an inherent foundation for an evolutionary view of the origins of language, which in turn can profoundly impact present understandings of language. An evolutionary model of the origins of language can serve to erode the doctrines of the authority, inspiration, inerrancy, sufficiency, and perspicuity of Scripture. According to EBP models, God's creative activity in Genesis 1 and 2 was carried out through lengthy evolutionary processes that included both positive and negative mutations and advances, as well as declines and extinctions. The apparent existence of communicating "homi-nids" (and by some theistic evolutionary estimates, even religious "hominids") prior to the existence of Adam and Eve, raises questions about their spiritual nature, condition, and capability.

EBP models leave it to the whims of theologians and scientists to decide whether language was necessarily created by God immediately with man's creation (whenever or however that occurred) for communion between God and man, communication between humans, and dominion over creation. God's first communication with Adam and Eve, recorded in Genesis 2 and 3, ostensibly occurs long after their ancestors developed linguistic abilities. If the mechanisms of evolutionary biological processes hold true for language, then language in its prefall (Genesis 3) origins is necessarily imperfect—allowing for an innate uncertainty on the part of Adam and Eve in response to Satan's question: "Has God indeed said...?" (Gen. 3:1). It also raises the question as to whether God's creation of language was indeed "very good" from the beginning.

Not only do EBP models open a Pandora's box of potential problems in relation to the origins and early use of language, but they also carry impli-cations for present linguistic theory in relation to the understanding of the doctrine of Scripture and the interpretation of Scripture. Where human ori-gins and language are rooted in EBP, a logical consistency is to then posit an evolutionary model of religion, similar to the stages that Auguste Comte outlined. Rather than moving from human perfection to fallenness with des-perate need for divine revelation that God perfectly meets (1 Pet. 1:23–25), there is a movement from primitive to sophisticated man. The ancient Hebrew is regarded as significantly more primitive in knowledge and capacity than modern humans.

Evolutionary linguistics inform hermeneutical approaches that strongly emphasize contextualization in approaching early texts: contextualization is viewed as key to understanding texts as much as fossils and strata layers are key in evolutionary biology. Contextual studies are of great benefit in reading texts. However, evolutionary linguistics can also formatively influence a phil-osophical foundation for a hermeneutic toward Scripture—and a doctrine of Scripture—that makes little or no qualitative differentiation between the Old and New Testaments and other ancient writings like the *Epic of Gilgamesh*. Too often, the result in approaches that utilize ancient Near Eastern linguistic and cultural studies to interpret Scripture is to place a definitive emphasis on Sume-rian, Ugaritic, and other contexts, instead of seeing the uniqueness and authority of Scripture as definitive for not only surrounding historical contexts, but also for created reality in every time and place. Positioning the weight of scriptural interpretation in this wider historical contextual setting can quite effectively place it not only under the interpretive authority of pagan sources but also under the vicissitudes of shifting historical opinions regarding the meanings of those pagan sources. The more recent hermeneutical approaches of EBP proponents such as Peter Enns, John Walton, and John Collins, reflect this problem.

God, the Creator

In the literal view of the early chapters of Genesis, creation is not only a historical account of the beginnings of created reality, but also a revelation of God's creative activity. It shows the relation of creation to God and tells of God Himself. His sovereignty over creation and His omnipotence in creation are powerfully emphasized in the literal view, as is the Creator/creation distinction. God is infinite and eternal; creation is finite with a distinct beginning in its whole and parts. God is autonomous and self-existent; creation exists under His sovereign rule and is upheld by His power.

Subsequent created existence comes through mediate processes such as reproduction. The God who creates and sustains is no removed deity, nor an immanent one, setting into motion, or sustaining and guiding near eternal processes, in enacting His work of creation. He acts in sudden power and glory. The literal tradition's understanding of Genesis 1 and 2 provides a profound contextual emphasis on God's glory and power displayed through word or speech action and their glorious creative results, along with temporal immediacy and close intimacy in the creation of Adam and Eve. The literal approach sets the creation of Adam and Eve and their existence into the context of this self-revelation of God.

The EBP models, while they may still place Adam and Eve into the context of a creation under a sovereign and omnipotent God, primarily move God's creative activity to the realm of secondary causes or ordinary providence. The result is that God is effectively either further removed, possibly to a distant first cause, or more hidden in a mediate activity of creation. When merged with theistic evolution, a Reformed doctrine of God's sovereignty can tend toward a deistic model of the doctrine of God. Where an Arminian doctrine of sovereignty merged with theistic evolution can do the same, it can also move toward open theism or pantheism—in contrast to a literal-grammatical-historical hermeneutic in relation to Genesis, which stands in opposition to deism, open theism, or pantheism.

Within EBP models, there is no direct immediacy of God's omnipotence displayed through word, or speech, or declarative power as the literal understanding of the Genesis account of creation. The surrounding context of Adam and Eve's transition to humanity differs dramatically from a literal view, at least for the EBP models that hold to a specific Adam and Eve. Some EBP3 proponents argue that such a view of the immediacy of God in His omnipotence and sovereignty and active work of special creation, while harmonizing with Moses (if they believe he is the writer of Genesis) and Paul, is primitive. Others argue that while primitive, the Genesis account of human origins was never understood as literal but rather as archetypal or figurative. Not only does this EBP3 view, with parallels in EBP1–2, make God's power a more distant, obscure power, but it also implies that He is not as close and intimate in the work of creating "Adam and Eve" as a literal reading suggests.

The Goodness of Creation

The literal view of the Genesis 1 account of God's creative work places a high value on the nature of God's original creation as "good" and "very good" (Gen. 1:4, 10, 12, 18, 25, 31). It sees the reality of creation, prior to the temptation, as being free of sin, suffering, violence, and death—paradigmatic of the intended existence of the created order, including humanity in relation to God, one another, and the rest of creation.[27] It sees the fall and curse as a point of drastic change into a world of continued sin, along with disorder, suffering, violence, and death—a creation now groaning for the restoration of all things (Rom. 8:20–25).

Scripture also makes it clear that animal suffering is not neutral (cf. Prov. 12:10; Isa. 11:6–9; Jonah 4:11) but is connected to the fallen state, curse, and judgment—and man bears responsibility in alleviating and minimizing animal suffering.[28] Again, Genesis includes revelation not only of God's creative

---

27. Ambrose of Milan, "On Belief in the Resurrection," in *Nicene and Post-Nicene Fathers, Second Series* (Peabody, Mass.: Hendrickson, 1995), 10:181.

28. After the fall, animal sacrifice, as ordained by God, was a sign of grace and mercy through substitutionary judgment to death. The first indicators of actual death and bloodshed are found in God's clothing of Adam and Eve in Genesis 3:21 (animal death), and then Cain's murder of Abel in Genesis 4:8–10. At the same time, Scripture reveals a shift from a vegetarian diet, prior to the fall, to one which includes eating meat afterwards. Intriguingly in Genesis 6, God's judgment is one of death for humans, animals, and birds, but not sea creatures. In God's sight "all flesh" is corrupt in Genesis 6, with "all flesh" clearly referring in this context to humans, animals, and birds (cf. Gen. 7:15, 16, 21; 8:17). But there is hope, and great contrast, in God's gracious design to keep some alive: Noah, his family, and some of the animals and birds. Again the indication is that human and animal death are not neutral. They are the result of judgment. The narrative of the end of the flood in Genesis 8 ends with animal and bird sacrifice, followed by God's promise.

activity but also of the relation of creation to God, and revelation of God Himself. The God who creates in acts of temporal immediacy, who creates a perfect creation without sin, suffering, violence and death, is Himself very good. He is the One who will bring about a new creation without sin, disorder, suffering, violence, and death. He is the One who is holy and the One who will restore to holiness.

EBP models tend to devote surprisingly little attention to explaining how prefall creation via EBP, under normal providence, was "good" and "very good." The EBP1 model makes the simple assertion that suffering, violence, and death in creatures including hominids, fall within a good creation. Ostensibly, even by the EBP1 model, Adam and Eve witnessed the suffering and deaths of hominid parents, grandparents, uncles, aunts, cousins, siblings, or more distant relations. These would have been hominids significantly similar to themselves, by whom they were nurtured, with whom they lived, laughed, and conversed, possibly argued, fought, and had sexual relations with. There would be no moral reason why Adam could not kill his hominid relations. The EBP1 model, if consistently held, ought to conclude that animal suffering remains morally neutral. This would imply that efforts to minimize it—such as veterinarians using anesthetics in animal surgery—are misguided. Yet, such a position fails to cohere with God's call for humane treatment of animals.

For the EBP2–3 models, suffering, violence, and death among humans are also normative and part of good creation prior to the fall into sin and the curse.[29] The EBP models posit that sin became sin by virtue of God's declarative delineations in the midst of a life already including a range of desires and behaviors—some of which from the "garden" onward became moral transgressions by virtue of being acts of disobedience toward God, but not because they are also violations of His created order. The consequence of such sin in some of the EBP models is simply spiritual death, not physical and spiritual death; physical death was simply a part of the good creation.

Other EBP model variants, like that of John Walton, argue that upon becoming human and being placed in the garden, Adam and Eve entered into a conditional immortality by which they had the opportunity to gain immortality for all their (already existing) contemporary human mortals, but failed to do so. Meanwhile, another EBP proponent, William Dembski, suggests that a solution may be found in a scenario in which the effects of the fall were

---

29. Keith Miller, "And God Saw That It Was Good: Death and Pain in the Created Order," Parts 1–4, *BioLogos*, November 21–24, 2012, http://biologos.org/blog/series/death-and-pain -in-the-created-order.

retroactive to all previous existence, and as such existed outside the garden of Eden prior to the fall—a position fraught with theological and practical difficulties, and devoid of any scriptural warrant.[30]

In the varied EBP views, Romans 5:12 does not correspond directly with Romans 8:20–25, and is not contrasted with Genesis 1 and 2. However, if God has declared suffering, violence, and death as inherently good, this declaration is accurate not only to the created order, but also to God Himself. If God declared formerly "good" created desires and behaviors to be sin, this declaration reflects His own character: He is then changeable and may be seen as capricious. EBP models of creation prior to the fall, in contrast with the literal understanding of the creation of Adam and Eve, question God's nature and attributes. His goodness, holiness, faithfulness, wisdom, and purity are undermined, raising significant issues of theodicy.

In Adam's Fall Sinned We All?

The literal reading of Genesis 1–3 indicates that Adam and Eve were created sinless and very good and continued in an original state of conditional immortality until the fall. According to this tradition, until the fall into sin and the ensuing curse on the serpent, man, and creation, there was no suffering or death. With the fall into sin came the wages of sin—spiritual and physical death, the loss of immortality, and separation from God. Then came God's declaration of the need for covering and His provision that pointed to redemption: the first reference to animal death in Scripture (Gen. 3:21).

The reality of sin, suffering, and death is now inherent to humanity as the natural descendants of Adam and Eve (Rom. 5:12–21), all of whom are now conceived in sin, in spiritual death, destined for physical death. The hard new realities of sin, suffering, and death are explicit in Adam and Eve's sons, Cain and Abel (Genesis 4). Suffering and death also extend more broadly in creation.

EBP models 1–2 of Genesis 1–3 indicate that Adam and Eve's sinlessness and goodness are not inherently connected to their origins but rather to a special declaratory, relational, transformative act of God at the point of their endowment with a soul and placement in the "garden." In EBP1 models, the fall into sin leads to a loss of conditional immortality and spiritual death—a situation in many respects that returns to Adam and Eve's prefall condition as hominids, except that there is now the weight of guilt of having broken and

---

30. William Dembski, *The End of Christianity: Finding a Good God in an Evil World* (Nashville: B&H, 2009), 10, 39, 129–30. See also Tom J. Nettles, review of *The End of Christianity*, by William Dembski, *The Southern Baptist Journal of Theology* 13, no. 4 (2010): 80–100.

fallen from their more recent existence in the "garden." Concurrent with the creation of humanity in EBP1 models, a divine sentence of extinction falls on their "non-but-nearly-human" ancestor hominids.

EBP models holding to a particular Adam and Eve who exist among a broader human society at the point of the fall must also posit that the rest of humanity, who had not engaged in this sin in the garden and who were not descended from Adam and Eve, suddenly also become sinners. This is the case apart from personal involvement and apart from being conceived and born in sin.

Some proponents of EBP2 models argue that covenant theology, with Adam as a federal head and representative for his tribe of contemporaries, as John Collins suggests, solves the difficulties that EBP models pose for the doctrine of the fall and sin. However, in following this approach, EBP2 models that posit a prefall human population extending beyond Adam and Eve effectively posit an Adam and Eve who are raised from a low condition among their contemporaries to an exalted godlike, savior status; they then turn out to be failed saviors in the garden, with an even more miserable existence after the fall than prior to their creative "adoption" by God. After the fall, they faced spiritual death and judgment in addition to physical mortality. EBP2 models with a historical, representative Adam, however, effectively have man falling back to what looks remarkably similar to his original evolutionary state: a life that includes sufferings and misery and ends in physical death. The only difference is that God lifted them up out of an existence separate from Him (to which they return in the fall), to gain an added spiritual dimension now broken by the fall.

In EBP3 models and EBP variants positing a previous wider continuity of humanity, the problems become even more acute with a large number of contemporaries falling under the rubric of the literary representation of "Adam and Eve" and the question of what happened to those who died prior to the fall. To whom did God proscribe the limits of what might be eaten in the perhaps figurative garden? What exactly was the fall? Why was all of existing humanity included? Were they? What happened to those who, according to EBP3, died prior to the *protoevangelium* in Genesis 3?

Hans Madueme, in a review essay focusing on Peter Enns's EBP3 model rejection of a historical Adam, states that Enns "introduce[s] a number of distressing theological problems":

> The first problem relates to the doctrine of the fall. One of its crucial functions within Christian dogmatics is to offer an account of the *origin*

of sin within the human story. As N. P. Williams remarked in his 1924 Brampton Lectures, take away the "fall" and you are left with only two options, either Dualism or Monism. In the first case (e.g. Manicheism), evil becomes a second eternal principle that exists alongside God—Light and Dark; Good and Evil. No one is responsible for sin because it is simply the ontological way of things, or as some might say, God is the author of sin. In the second case (e.g. Taoism), God himself is both good and evil (or transcends them); sin becomes a meaningless concept....

The second problem for Enns is that he needs to tell us why men and women are *sinful* people. In the theological jargon, this is "originated" or inherited sin, a condition we all find ourselves in from birth because we somehow participated in Adam's first sin. Having no recourse to Adam, Enns cannot appeal to that tradition. How will he explain the human predicament of sin? One option is to look to evolutionary theory for help.... The challenge...will be to resist reducing sin to a merely *biological* problem.[31]

The latter option is no real option at all: where Genesis 1 and 2, in relation to human origins, have been mythicized and interpretive weight falls to a philosophical theology engaged with an evolutionary model, there is no longer inherent ground to view any particular early human behavior as "sin." Once the doctrine of human sin has lost its revealed point of origin in time and space, and its character as a specific historical event, subsequent theologizing will prove to be arbitrary and merely at the whims of the theologian engaged in such an endeavor.

The "evil" of many early hominid or human behaviors might be seen as natural and positive survival mechanisms, while other apparently "good" behaviors might be viewed as the opposite. Madueme notes that many EBP3 proponents have moved to jettison an Augustinian formulation of the doctrine of original sin, searching for alternatives. Some, like Enns, have turned to Irenaeus, "describing sins as morally childlike; sins are growing pains, part of the path to maturation."[32] However, even Irenaeus fails to provide what EBP3

---

31. Hans Madueme, "Some Reflections on Enns and the Evolution of Adam: A Review Essay," *Themelios* 37, no. 2 (July 2012): 283–84.

32. Madueme, "Reflections on Enns," 284. Madueme cites the following as examples of this trend: Mark Worthing, "The Emergence of Guilt and 'Sin' in Human Evolution: A Theological Reflection," in *Sin and Salvation*, ed. Duncan Reid and Mark Worthing (Adelaide, Australia: Australian Theological Forum, 2003), 113–29; Ted Peters, "The Genesis and Genetics of Sin," in *Sin and Salvation*, 89–112; Gregory R. Peterson, "Falling Up: Evolution and Original Sin," in *Evolution and Ethics: Human Morality in Biological and Religious Perspective*, ed. Philip Clayton and Jeffrey Schloss (Grand Rapids: Eerdmans, 2004), 273–86; Stephen J. Duffy, "Genes, Original Sin and the Human Proclivity to Evil," *Horizons* 32 (2005): 210–34; Ian McFarland, *In Adam's Fall: A*

proponents need, "because Irenaeus, like all the church fathers, believed that Adam and Eve were two historical people who gave rise to the entire human race. And even though Irenaeus described Adam as an 'infant' in this regard, he viewed him as 'without sin until he disobeyed God.'"[33] From the patristic era, Pelagius may well prove to provide the best potential for theological synthesis of EBP3 on human origins and a concept of sin. However, even Pelagius, in contrast to EBP3 proponents, believed in a specific, specially created, historical Adam.

Christ as Creator and Redeemer

The literal view of creation, with the profound and awesome supernatural immediacy of God's creative activity, establishes a significant foundation for the understanding of Christ's redemptive and re-creative work in coherence with the paradigm of Colossians 1:15–17, which presents the relationship of creation and redemption in Christ, who is "the image of the invisible God, the firstborn over all creation. For by Him all things were created that are in heaven and that are on earth, visible and invisible, whether thrones or dominions or principalities or powers. All things were created through Him and for Him. And He is before all things, and in Him all things consist."

Hebrews 1 reiterates this truth, stating that through the Son, God created the world; it is the Son who upholds "all things by the word of His power" (Heb. 1:2–3). Ephesians 3:9 similarly states, "God…created all things through Jesus Christ." If Christ is the One by whom all things were created, and life, including Adam's and Eve's, did not come into being through the mediation of a providentially guided evolutionary process, but through supernatural, temporally immediate acts, this provides a paradigm of expectation in harmony with both the curse and promise of Genesis 3:15.

God's curse supernaturally brings about a profound change in the created order: sin, as rebellion and disobedience, brings misery. Its end is death. The whole creation now groans with decay, disease, and disorder, while at the same time remaining sovereignly sustained, ordered and governed by God. And yet there is also the promise, the *protoevangelium* of Genesis 3:15. The Triune God, including the person of the creating, preincarnate Christ,

---

Christian Meditation on the Christian Doctrine of Original Sin (Malden, Mass.: Wiley-Blackwell, 2010); and the relevant essays in R. J. Berry and T. A. Noble, eds., *Darwin, Creation and the Fall: Theological Challenges* (Nottingham: Apollos, 2009); and Michael S. Northcott and R. J. Berry, eds., *Theology after Darwin* (Colorado Springs, Colo.: Paternoster, 2009).

33. Madueme, "Reflections on Enns," 284.

begins to progressively unfold the work of redemption in a fallen, curse-constrained creation.

In the literal view of creation, the reading of early Genesis provides every ground to recognize and expect that the work of redemption of fallen men will be marked, illustrated, pursued, and confirmed with supernatural activity in history—activity in the midst of the natural order whose nature and/or timing can only be attributed to God. It is inexplicable by scientific method, though its effects were, and may still be, discernible by scientific methods. And so a global flood, the plagues of Egypt, the collapse of Jericho's walls, the miracles of prophets such as Elijah and Elisha, are all expected indicators of divine sovereignty, presence, and activity. These, and many more, are markers that confirm God's holy and gracious unfolding of redemptive history in Christ—each serving to reaffirm the veracity of God's special revelation by His Word.

For those who hold to a literal view of early Genesis, passages like Isaiah 35:5–6, where the eyes of the blind are opened and the ears of the deaf are unstopped, are a glorious prophecy of God's saving re-creation. These passages are fully congruent with the greater revelation of salvation in and through the incarnate Son: there is literal fulfillment of these prophesies of miraculous, supernatural activity as the New Testament Gospels repeatedly indicate. Why? Because it is Christ, the One by whom all things were created who is both revealing and accomplishing redemption by His sovereign and omnipotent work confirmed by actions that are immanent in, yet transcend, the created, and now fallen and cursed order. The Creator who has revealed His work of creation in Genesis turns water to wine, feeds thousands with a few loaves and some fish, heals, restores, raises from the dead, stops wind and waves, and transforms sinners from spiritual death to life. And so when John's disciples ask whether He is the One, Jesus tells them, "The blind see, the lame walk, the lepers are cleansed, the deaf hear, the dead are raised, the poor have the gospel preached to them" (Luke 7:22).

The great mystery of Christ's condescension and humility in the incarnation is His willing participation in our flesh and frailty, dwelling as the Holy One in the midst of sinners, through His sufferings and death bearing the just penalty for the sin of His people. The wonder is that the One who created ex nihilo by the power of His speech, formed the man from the dust, breathed into him the breath of life, and placed rebel man under the curse places Himself under the curse and penalty as the second Adam.

The supernatural glory and wonder of the resurrection and ascension seal and crown Christ's work as Creator and Redeemer. The One who created all things gains victory over death and the grave, rising from the dead completely contrary to the fallen, cursed state of the natural order (1 Cor. 15:54–57). He is the one Man, the beloved eternal Son, in whom the Father is "well-pleased"— the present natural reality of death in the created order has no grip on Him (Matt. 3:17). He is the "first-fruits," the One who has borne the curse in Himself and who has begun the literal, physical work of re-creation in and through Himself. The pattern of Christ's supernatural, re-creative activity throughout the New Testament is one of immediacy, rather than a providential use of processes of the natural order, since those processes themselves remain bound to decay and death. There remains the longing and expectation for the full completion of redemption and re-creation, when all creation will be set free from its bondage to decay (Romans 8) and when God's people will experience bodily resurrection, and the heavens and the earth will be made new, free from sin and curse.

EBP models of human origins, with their attendant views of cosmological and earth history, remove most, if not all, of the supernatural, temporally immediate aspects of creation. While a number of old earth and biological evolution proponents do not extend a hermeneutic informed by a naturalist view of creation origins and development beyond Genesis 2:3, most who hold or give latitude to models of human origins do. This is evident in the writings of theologians ranging from John Collins to Peter Enns on Genesis 2–5, Meredith Kline on the flood account, and others on the Exodus accounts of the plagues and Red Sea crossing.[34]

Wherever in the text such theologians choose to shift away from a more providential hermeneutic to one that is both providential and supernatural in view of the divine activity of the history of redemption, the earlier approach nonetheless impinges on the person and work of Christ, "by whom all things were created." Many mainline Protestant proponents of EBP models have long accepted that a significantly naturalist hermeneutic applies not only to the Old Testament accounts of divine redemptive activity, but also to those of the New Testament—their quest for the historical Adam standing in complete continuity with their quest for the historical Jesus. In this case, the end result is the complete loss of the gospel of our Lord Jesus Christ.

---

34. Meredith Kline and Ted Hildebrandt, "Kingdom Prologue, Lecture 29," *Biblical Studies Lecture Series*, http://faculty.gordon.edu/hu/bi/ted_hildebrandt/DigitalCourses/00_DigitalBiblical StudiesCourses.html.

Adam, Christ, and the Covenants

Another aspect of the doctrine of Christ and salvation connected with the creation of Adam and Eve is federal or covenant theology. Federal theology deals with the themes of covenant relationship between God and man, and the promises of God across the Old and New Testaments. Particularly in the Reformed tradition of theology, the literal reading of Genesis 1–3 is seen as integral to the covenant of works and covenant of grace. This is especially true in the relation of the early chapters of Genesis to New Testament passages like Romans 5 and 1 Corinthians 15, which speak extensively to the parallels, patterns, and differences between Adam and Christ in relation to sin and salvation. Richard B. Gaffin states,

> Without the "first" man, Adam, there is no place for Christ as either "second" or "last." The integrity and coherence of redemptive history in its entirety depends on this contrast. It is simply not true, as some claim, that whether or not Adam was the first human being is a question that leaves the gospel unaffected, at least if we accept the clear teaching of these passages. Paul is elsewhere similarly clear: Christ's resurrection, the final judgment, and the attendant call for all people everywhere to repent, all stand or fall with the fact that God has made from one man every nation of mankind (Acts 17:26–30).[35]

A stream of theologians within the literal tradition have argued for another connection between a literal reading of the creation origins of humanity and the person and work of Christ as the second Adam. Drawing on John 1:3 and Colossians 1:15, these theologians see the Genesis 2 narrative as including revelation of the preincarnate Christ. Christ is intimately involved in creating the first man and woman—creating in Adam the human nature He will take to Himself in the incarnation. Where "the Lord God" acts or reveals Himself in anthropomorphic ways, including "walking in the garden" (Gen. 3:8), speaking with Adam and Eve (Genesis 3), and in visiting with Abraham (Genesis 18), this is understood as a self-revelation of the preincarnate Christ. Christ is seen as making Himself visibly and audibly present in human form through redemptive history in the Old Testament in preparation for the time when "the Word became flesh and dwelt among us" in the incarnation (John 1:14). These redemptive, covenantal themes of biblical theology stand in unity with both a literal Genesis reading of the origins of the first Adam, and the incarnation of Christ, the Redeemer, as the second Adam.

---

35. Richard B. Gaffin Jr., "All Mankind Descending from Him…?," *New Horizons* 33, no. 3 (March 2012): 3–5.

EBP models vary in their use and recognition of federal theology. Some EBP1 proponents are strong supporters of federal theology, holding to it with their hominid-human distinction. As seen in our discussion of the fall and sin, EBP2 proponents at times seek to use federal theology, particularly its representative aspect, to attempt to answer the problem of human contemporaries of Adam and Eve. However, they do so in a way significantly unlike the traditional formulations and understanding of federal theology—often adopting a theological construct similar to La Peyrère's. Those who propose an Adam who serves as a federal representative for his contemporaries and who transitions from mortality to conditional immortality in the garden place the hope for a salvation for co-Adamites in the mediatorial work of Adam, erasing a significant discontinuity between Adam and Christ.[36]

In addition, EBP3 models that deny the existence of a real Adam or Eve face even more significant theological difficulties in relation to passages like Romans 5 and 1 Corinthians 15, where Paul grounds his understanding of the reality of the covenant of grace and the person and work of Jesus Christ in the historical reality of the first man. Negation of the reality of Adam as the first human, specially created by God in His image, undermines redemptive history and the reality of the person and work of Christ. Here the quest for the historical Adam begins to erode the historical, and present, Jesus.

Adam and Accountability: The Last Things
The literal reading of Genesis 1–3, with the special temporally immediate creation of Adam and Eve in the context of a recent, broader creation, brings a great imminence to the coming reality of judgment and death ensuing from the fall and curse. The realities of physical and spiritual death are not merely a return to prior hominid or human conditions, as proponents of EBP must posit, but are rather a profound supernatural action of God consequent to man's sin, with enduring physical and spiritual ramifications. Reading Genesis according to the literal tradition, the horror of death as God's judgment is stark and profound, a sudden reality. It is not original to the "very good" created order but rather a decisive, divine answer to Adam and Eve's willful sin.

The awesome reality of the day of Christ's return in judgment, salvation, and re-creation stands in harmony with the reality that by the same Word, the world was created: "The heavens and the earth which are now preserved by the same word, are reserved for fire until the day of judgment and perdition of

---

36. To answer the question of what happened to the already dead pre-Adamite humans would require deeper forays into the realm of speculative theology.

ungodly men" (2 Peter 3:7). For those who are Christians, the curse of death, borne by and conquered in Christ, the second Adam, is answered in resurrection glory and eternal life. Scripture indicates that like the initial work of creation, God's work of resurrection and re-creation will occur with temporal immediacy. Christianity has historically anticipated a day of resurrection, rather than a slow process of resurrection over eons of time.

A literal understanding of the beginnings of history and humanity fosters an eschatological sense of immediacy and anticipation for the end of present history, the day when "The Lord Jesus is revealed from heaven with His mighty angels, in flaming fire taking vengeance on those who do not know God, and on those who do not obey the gospel of our Lord Jesus Christ. These shall be punished with everlasting destruction from the presence of the Lord and from the glory of His power, when He comes, in that Day, to be glorified in His saints and to be admired among all those who believe" (2 Thess. 1:7–10).

EBP models tend to either implicitly or explicitly minimize the nature of death as a divine judgment; the physical deaths of humans and animals stand in continuity with their original "very good" existence prior to the fall. Proponents of EBP see physical death as less of a stark reality of God's judgment than do those who hold to the literal tradition. A potential consequence is that the full, gracious, eschatological realities of resurrection glory and eternal life for believers are also eroded. While proponents of EBP models do not necessarily reject eschatological realities including the coming day of resurrection and final judgment, their reading of the early chapters of Genesis can also create the sense that "all things continue as they were from the beginning" (2 Peter 3:4), diminishing anticipation for and awareness of the day of Christ's return.

Concluding the Quest for the Historical Adam

In his *Institutes of Elenctic Theology* (1679–1685), Francis Turretin criticized one of the earliest proponents of pre-Adamism, Isaac La Peyrère:

> Although the Preadamic fiction is so absurd in itself and foreign to all reason (no less than to the Scripture revelation itself) as to deserve rather the contempt and indignation of believers than a laborious refutation, yet in this very latest age (so productive of the most dangerous heresies) there was found not so long ago one who did not blush to obtrude this fiction or fable upon the world.... Thus the question must be touched

upon briefly that not only its folly and falsity, but also its impiety may be the more clearly seen.[37]

Turretin spoke with blunt accuracy regarding the implications of this alternate view of human origins in his day. The issue resurfaced with increasing influence in subsequent centuries and has not gone away. The challenge of diverging views on Genesis, hermeneutics, and human origins—both outside and within the church—remains with us to the present.

The quest for the historical Adam—and how it is pursued—impacts a wide range of doctrinal and practical issues. This is evident not only in the history of Genesis interpretation on human origins, but also from a short comparative survey of the differences between the literal tradition on human origins and evolutionary biological models. Examination of these models clearly demonstrates that there are significant theological implications in moving away from the literal, specially created Adam and Eve of Genesis. Issues range from the doctrines of Scripture and God, to man, ethics, marriage, linguistics, covenant theology, the person and work of Christ, and eschatology. These issues are of profound, gospel importance; these issues are vital to the grace and glory of God.

Proponents of models of human origins by theistic evolution are united in their criticism of a literal understanding of early Genesis and in the pursuit of compatibility with modern scientific models of origins; however, they present little internal coherence beyond those features. In fact, they reveal more of a Pandora's box of speculative and diverging theologies, with "twenty doctors expounding one text twenty ways," each resting on the exegetical credence provided by their alternative hermeneutical models for the interpretation of Genesis.[38] The "Adams" they "find" as they survey the sweep of evolutionary history are ad hoc. As Peter Enns has (ironically) stated, "The irony…is that in expending such effort," to reconcile evolution and Christianity by positing a first human pair (or group) at some point in the evolutionary process, is that in order "to preserve biblical teaching, we are left with a first pair that is utterly foreign to the biblical portrait."[39] The resulting multiple Adams, much like the multiple Jesuses reflected on by Albert Schweitzer, bear little semblance to the historical Adam.

---

37. Francis Turretin, *Institutes of Elentic Theology*, ed. James T. Dennison (Phillipsburg, N.J.: P&R), 1:457.

38. William Tyndale, "The Four Senses of the Scripture," in *Works of William Tyndale* (Edinburgh: Banner of Truth, 2010), 1:305.

39. Enns, *The Evolution of Adam*, xvii.

By contrast, the literal tradition on Genesis and human origins coheres with the Genesis text and the Adam it reveals. In doing so, it maintains the beginning components of a revealed unity of truth: a holistic, historic Christian theology from the Word of God.[40] In the literal tradition, God's glory and grace are steadfastly proclaimed.

---

40. R. L. Dabney in his essay "Geology and the Bible" states, "All truths are harmonious *inter se*. If one proposition contradicts another, no matter from what field of human knowledge it may be brought, manifestly, both cannot be true. If, then, the Bible, properly understood, affirms what geology denies, the difference is irreconcilable; it cannot be evaded by any easy expedient like that described above; it can only be composed by the overthrow of the authority of one or the other of the parties." R. L. Dabney, "Geology and the Bible," in *Discussions by Robert L. Dabney, D.D.* (Harrisonburg, Va.: Sprinkle Publications, 1996), 3:95.

Epilogue:
Literal Genesis and Science?

If special revelation and general revelation form a coherent testimony, why does the literal tradition on Genesis and human origins conflict with the mainstream of contemporary scientific interpretation? The answer is multifaceted. To some degree, since the late Enlightenment and Industrial Revolution, there has been a naïve cultural optimism, an overly high regard for the ability and willingness of the scientific community to pursue impartial objectivity in its mechanisms of review and consensus. A lack of awareness of the role of philosophy and religion in scientific interpretation—in approaching, assessing, organizing, and drawing conclusions from evidence—is also an influence. Significant challenges continue to exist in pursuing research and presentation of alternatives to accepted models in the now predominantly post-Christian academy of science—a reality profoundly felt in matters of origins.

Questions that both comprehend and go beyond issues of appropriateness and error in method and interpretation are considered less often. Contemporary scientific interpretation is extrapolated into the distant past with a spirit of high certainty, often equated with truth, and is typically done without any impetus to consider whether human ability, the tools of science, and the way those tools are used may be more limited than is commonly believed. This is true in respect to the mainstream study of origins and geological, biological, and human history; it can also be true of those who pursue varieties of young-earth creation science.

We need to ask whether general revelation is an insufficient means of accessing the modes and events of creation and human origins. This insufficiency might exist not merely by lack of discovery but by consequence of the nature of the finitude and creatureliness of man and/or the fall and curse. To put the question another way, are there aspects of the history of the present natural order that require not merely general revelation, but also special revelation in order for us to accurately understand them? I believe the simple answer is yes. Special revelation is required because general revelation is insufficient for fallen minds.

Can the literal tradition on Genesis and human origins be harmonized with scientific interpretation of the testimony of general revelation to natural history and origins? Vern Poythress suggests that "three major alternatives offer themselves":

> (1) Unusual, supernatural action of God at the time of the flood or the fall, or else a change in God's governance at the end of the sixth day of creation, has thrown off mainstream calculations based on continuity of scientific laws; or

> (2) there is continuity of law, but some major causal influences (such as, for example, a hypothetical preflood "ice canopy") have been left out by the mainstream; or

> (3) the real laws (for the speed of light or radioactive decay, for example), are subtly or radically different from what the mainstream has taken them to be.[1]

The first alternative, particularly in relation to God's action of causing the Noahic flood, is often understood by young-earth creationists as a universal and catastrophic event with significant influence on both geology and fossilization. Typically, scientists pursuing flood models for the interpretation of existing natural evidence view this as a "natural" event occurring through divine, possibly supernatural initiative—allowing for the pursuit of the construction of detailed explanatory theory. Proposed varieties of flood models view the flood as a significant, though not exclusive, period of fossilization. Many proponents of such models are skeptical of mainstream geological and fossil dating methods; some proffer alternatives including the hypothesis that the physical processes involved in the flood, including massive tectonic shifts and changes in the earth's crust, may have created conditions for rapid "aging."

A key factor not mentioned in Poythress's first alternative is original creation maturity. Although only a few theorists, such as Philip Henry Gosse, consider fossils to have been native to God's original work of creation, much of the literal Genesis tradition through the millennia has held that God's original work of creation produced an immediately mature creation. Adam himself stands as one

---

1. Vern S. Poythress, *Christian Interpretations of Genesis 1* (Phillipsburg, N.J.: P&R, 2013), 31–32. In his prior volume, *Redeeming Science* (Wheaton, Ill.: Crossway, 2006), 113–47, Poythress evaluates and dismisses a mature creation argument as needless, primarily due to his rejection of a literal reading of Genesis 1 in favor of C. John Collins's analogical rendering of the days.

example, created not as a zygote but as a mature man; although perhaps only hours old when he woke and saw the newly created Eve, Adam was an adult.

Modern proponents of the literal tradition have argued that although fossils cannot be included within the rubric of this factor because of a lack of death prior to the fall, nonetheless, geological or molecular "age" aspects of biological maturity and appearance of "age" among living things during the prefall period stand in harmony with the revelation of the Genesis text and the testimony of the rest of the Scriptures. Believing a supernaturally created maturity is no different than believing Jesus' miracle of instantly changing water into fine, "vintage" wine.

The implications of the fall gain far less attention than the flood among scientists seeking to defend a young-earth creation model. Attention is usually focused on the entrance of disease, violence, and death into the created order. Genesis 3 and following provide evidence of changes in the natural order under the weight of the curse. Yet there is ground to posit that God's curse, with ensuing death, involved a supernatural weight of change upon the entire fabric of creation. The apostle Paul speaks of the whole creation groaning and laboring with birth pangs because of "the bondage of corruption" (Rom. 8:21–22). Such a supernatural shift in the cosmos, potentially with a sudden, great increase of decay, could well be an additional factor misinterpreted on uniformitarian principles as a linear past extending into distant time. In reality, some of what we may consider "age" and "decay" may rather be a profound declaration of the weight of the curse of God resting upon a now significantly altered creation, in contrast to its original condition.

Taken together, an originally mature, pristine, and "very good" creation, with God's curse coming upon it at the time of the fall, followed some millennia later by a catastrophic, universal flood, with both uniformitarian change, and occasional other catastrophic changes occurring prior to and after that flood, provide substantive, general answers to many of the aspects of contemporary evolutionary and geological theories of creation history and origins that challenge the literal Genesis tradition. Ignoring or minimizing real and potential factors indicated by special revelation can easily lead to a significant misreading of general revelation on creation history and origins.

Much like Geerhardus Vos, and in contrast to his good friend B. B. Warfield, I believe that the quest not only for the historical Adam, but also for creation history and origins, is too often pursued without due reflection on these considerations. Efforts to understand natural and human history, including origins, too often reinterpret special revelation in a way that distances or even removes it from the equation. Like many in the long history of the literal tradition, I believe that exegetical and theological considerations point to special revelation's abiding validity and truth.

The consequence of this position is that proponents of alternative hermeneutics, while having some poignant insights into the text of Genesis 1 and 2 that cohere with the literal tradition, in other aspects, they interpret the Word poorly.[2] To the degree they do, they err in their exposition—and in their understanding of creation history and origins.[3] Like Simon Patrick, B. B. Warfield, and Meredith Kline, many remain capable exegetes and expositors of much of the riches of God's Word and the gospel of Jesus Christ. As fellow believers, they are to be loved, and the positive substance of their work appreciated. Those committed to the literal tradition must realize that the views of proponents of alternative hermeneutical approaches on Genesis 1–2 only rise to the level of heresy "when on principle they raise the so-called results of science to grant precedence to them over the Word of God," encroaching on human origins and history.[4]

In any pursuit to harmonize our knowledge of God's special and general revelation, we must walk humbly—this is true for all of us. We are called to be watchful in love for one another, and where there is error to respond in a spirit of Christlike faithfulness. At the same time, we all need to be aware that too often the tensions of disagreement and concern drive us to avoid contested passages of Scripture, leading to an even greater obscuring of the greatness of God's Word and works and the glory that is His. As we seek to grow together in understanding God's handiwork in creation and His gracious Word to us, may it lead us to wonder and worship.

> Oh, the depth of the riches both of the wisdom and knowledge of God!
> How unsearchable are His judgments and His ways past finding out!
> "For who has known the mind of the LORD?
> Or who has become His counselor?"
> "Or who has first given to Him
> And it shall be repaid to him?"
> For of Him and through Him and to Him are all things, to whom be glory forever. Amen. (Rom. 11:33–36)

---

2. Geerhardus Vos, "Dogmatiek van G. Vos. Ph.D. D.D., Deel I. Theologie" (unpublished manuscript), Heckman Library Archives, Calvin College, Grand Rapids, Michigan, 1910, 170.

3. Vos, "Dogmatiek," 170.

4. Vos, "Dogmatiek," 170.

Bibliography

Aalders, Gerhard Charles. *De Goddelijke Openbaring in de Eerste Drie Hoofdstuk-ken van Genesis.* Kampen: Kok, 1932.

———. *Genesis.* Grand Rapids: Zondervan, 1981.

Abecassis, Deborah. "Reconstructing Rashi's Commentary on Genesis from Citations in the Torah Commentaries of the Tosafot." PhD diss., McGill University, 1999.

Ainsworth, Henry. *Annotations Upon the First Book of Genesis.* Amsterdam, 1616.

Alexander, Denis. "How Does a BioLogos Model Need to Address the Theological Issues Associated with an Adam Who Was Not the Sole Genetic Progenitor of Humankind?" Biologos. December 2010. http://biologos.org/resources /essay/how-does-a-biologos-model-need-to-address-the-theological-issues.

Allan, Verity. "Bede's Commentary on the Six Days of Creation and the Six Ages of the World in *In Genesim* I. 1093–1224: Sources and Analogues." BA thesis, Cambridge University, 2000.

———. "Theological Works of the Venerable Bede and Their Literary and Manu-script Presentation, with Special Reference to the Gospel Homilies." MLitt thesis, Oxford University, 2006.

Allison, Gregg R. *Historical Theology: An Introduction to Christian Doctrine.* Grand Rapids: Zondervan, 2011.

Almond, Philip C. *Adam and Eve in Seventeenth Century Thought.* Cambridge: Cambridge University Press, 1999.

Alter, Stephen. "Review of *Adam's Ancestors: Race, Religion and the Politics of Human Origins* by David N. Livingstone." *Fides et Historia* 41, no. 2 (Summer–Fall 2009): 118–20.

Ambrose of Milan. "Hexaemeron, Paradise, Cain and Abel." In vol. 42 of *Fathers of the Church*, translated by John J. Savage. Washington, D.C.: Catholic University of America Press, 1986.

———. "On Belief in the Resurrection." In vol. 10 of *Nicene and Post-Nicene Fathers: Second Series*, 174–98. Peabody, Mass.: Hendrickson, 1995.

Ames, William. *Lectiones in CL Psalm os Davidis*. Amstelodami, 1635.

———. *The Marrow of Theology*. Grand Rapids: Baker, 1997.

———. *Sententia de Origine Sabbati & die Dominico…*. Franeker, 1653.

———. *The Substance of Christian Religion*. London, 1659.

Anselm. *St. Anselm: Basic Writings*. Translated by S. N. Deane. La Salle, Ill.: Open Court, 1962.

The Apostolic Fathers. 3rd ed. Edited and translated by Michael Holmes. Grand Rapids: Baker, 2007.

Aquinas, Thomas. Vol. 4 of *Summa Theologica*. London: Burns, Oates & Washbourne, 1922.

Associate Reformed Presbyterian Church. "Minutes of the General Synod of the Associate Reformed Presbyterian Church." Greenville, S.C.: Associate Reformed Presbyterian Church, 2012.

Augustine. *On Genesis*. Hyde Park, N.Y.: New City Press, 2006.

———. *The City of God*. New York: Modern Library, 2000.

———. *The Retractations*. Translated by M. Inez Bogan. Washington, D.C.: Catholic University of America Press, 1999.

Baier, Johann Wilhelm. *Compendum Theologiae Positivae*. Lipsiae: Ex Officina Jo. Frid. Gleditshii, 1750.

Barker, William S. "The Westminster Assembly on the Days of Creation: A Reply to David W. Hall." *The Westminster Theological Journal* 62, no. 1 (Spring 2000): 1–16.

Barlow, Nora. *The Autobiography of Charles Darwin 1809–1882*. London: Collins, 1958.

Barton, Stephen C., and David Wilkinson, eds. *Reading Genesis after Darwin*. Oxford: Oxford University Press, 2009.

Basil of Caesarea. *The Hexaemeron*. In vol. 8 of *Nicene and Post-Nicene Fathers*. Peabody, Mass.: Hendrickson, 1989.

Bavinck, Herman. *God and Creation*. Vol. 2 of *Reformed Dogmatics*. Grand Rapids: Baker, 2004.

———. *In the Beginning: Foundations of Creation Theology*. Grand Rapids: Baker, 1999.

———. *Our Reasonable Faith: A Survey of Christian Doctrine*. Grand Rapids: Baker, 1977.

Baxter, Richard. *The Practical Works of the Rev. Richard Baxter*. London, 1830.

Beale, Gregory K. *The Erosion of Inerrancy in Evangelicalism: Responding to New Challenges to Biblical Authority*. Wheaton, Ill.: Crossway, 2008.

———. *The Temple and the Church's Mission: A Biblical Theology of the Dwelling Place of God*. Downers Grove, Ill.: InterVarsity, 2004.

Beall, Todd. "Reading Genesis 1–2: A Literal Approach." In *Reading Genesis 1–2: An Evangelical Conversation*, 45–59, edited by J. Daryl Charles. Peabody, Mass.: Hendrickson, 2013.

Beattie, Francis. *The Presbyterian Standards*. Greenville, S.C.: Southern Presbyterian Press, 1997.

Becker, Matthew. "The Scandal of the LCMS Mind: Creationism, Science and Creation in Biblical-Theological Perspective." *The Daystar Journal*. Summer 2005. http://thedaystarjournal.com/the-scandal-of-the-lcms-mind/.

Bédard, Paulin. *In Six Days God Created*. [Maitland, Fla.]: Xulon Press, 2013.

Bede. *Bede on the Nature of Things and on Times*. Translated by Calvin Kendall and Faith Wallis. Liverpool, U.K.: Liverpool University Press, 2010.

———. *On Genesis*. Translated by Calvin B. Kendall. Liverpool, U.K.: Liverpool University Press, 2008.

———. *The Reckoning of Time*. Translated by Faith Wallis. Liverpool, U.K.: Liverpool University Press, 1999.

Beeke, Joel, and Mark Jones. *A Puritan Theology: Doctrine for Life*. Grand Rapids: Reformation Heritage Books, 2012.

Belcher, Richard. "Did Adam and Eve Really Exist? A Review." Reformation 21. February 2012. http://www.reformation21.org/articles/did-adam-and-eve-really-exist-a-review.php.

———. "Genesis to Joshua." Reformed Sermons by Third Millennium Ministries. http://reformedsermons.org/series.asp/srs/Genesis%20to%20Joshua.

Bell, Christian. "Calvin College Statement about Homosexuality Draws Fire." *The Banner*. January 18, 2011. http://www.thebanner.org/news/2011/01/calvin-college-statement-about-homosexuality-draws-fire.

Ben Meir, Samuel. *Rabbi Samuel Ben Meir's Commentary on Genesis*. Translated by Martin I. Lockshin. Lewiston, N.Y.: Edwin Mellen Press, 1989.

Ben Nachman, Moshe. *Ramban (Nachmanides) Commentary on the Torah*. Translated by Charles B. Chavel. New York: Shiloh, 1971.

Bergman, Jerry. *Hitler and the Nazi Darwinian Worldview*. Kitchener, Ontario: Joshua Press, 2012.

Berkhof, Louis. *Systematic Theology*. Grand Rapids: Eerdmans, 1996.

Berkouwer, G. C. *De Heilige Schrift*. Kampen: Kok, 1967.

———. *The Holy Scripture*. Grand Rapids: Eerdmans, 1975.

———. *Man: The Image of God*. Grand Rapids: Eerdmans, 1962.

Berry, R. J., and T. A. Noble, eds. *Darwin, Creation and the Fall: Theological Challenges*. Nottingham: Apollos, 2009.

Beuker, Hendrikus. "Isagogische Schets der Systematische Theologie in het algemeen ter Inleiding tot de Gereformeerde Dogmatiek in 't bijzonder." Lectures presented at Calvin Theological Seminary, October 1897.

BioLogos Editorial Team. "A Survey of Clergy and their Views on Origins." BioLogos Forum. May 2013. http://biologos.org/blog/a-survey-of-clergy -and-their-views-on-origins.

Boston, Thomas. *The Fourfold State of Man*. Edinburgh: Banner of Truth, 2002.

———. "Of the Work of Creation." In *An Illustration of the Doctrines of the Christian Religion*, in vol. 1 of *The Complete Works of the Late Rev. Thomas Boston*. Edited by Samuel M'Millan. London, 1853.

Boyce, James P. *Abstract of Systematic Theology...First Published in 1887*. Cape Coral, Fla.: Founders Press, 2006.

Boyer, Peter J. "The Covenant." *The New Yorker*. September 6, 2010. http://www .newyorker.com/reporting/2010/09/06/100906fa_fact_boyer.

Brakel, Wilhelmus á. *The Christian's Reasonable Service*. Translated by Bartel Elshout. Edited by Joel R. Beeke. Grand Rapids: Reformation Heritage Books, 1999.

Bratt, James D., ed. *Abraham Kuyper: A Centennial Reader*. Grand Rapids: Eerdmans, 1998.

Brenz, Johannes. *Commentary on Genesis*. In *Reformation Commentary on Scripture*, ed. John L. Thompson. Downers Grove, Ill.: InterVarsity, 2012.

Briggs, Charles Augustus. *Biblical History: A Lecture Delivered at the Opening Term of The Union Theological Seminary....* New York, 1889.

Brown, John. *A Dictionary of the Holy Bible*. Edinburgh, 1816.

———. *The Systematic Theology of John Brown of Haddington*. Grand Rapids: Reformation Heritage Books, 2002.

Bullinger, Heinrich. *The Decades of Heinrich Bullinger*. Grand Rapids: Reformation Heritage Books, 2004.

———. *A Hundred Sermons on the Apocalypse of Jesus Christ*. London, 1561.

Bultmann, Christoph. "Creation at the Beginning of History: Johann Gottfried Herder's Interpretation of Genesis 1." *Journal for the Study of the Old Testament* 68 (1995): 23–32.

Burnet, Thomas. *Archaelogia Philosophica, or the Ancient Doctrine Concerning the Originals of Things...translated into English...by Mr. Foxton...Part I. Being a Critique of the Mosaic Creation*. London: Printed for E. Curll in the Strand, 1729.

———. *Of the State of the Dead and of the Resurrection*. London, 1727.

———. *The Sacred Theory of the Earth: Containing an Account of the Original of the Earth, and of all the General Changes which It Hath Already Undergone....* London, 1726.

Burnett, James, Lord Monboddo. *Antient Metaphysics: Or the Science of Universals*. Edinburgh, 1779.

———. *Of the Origins and Progress of Language*. Edinburgh, 1774.

Byzer, Ernst. *Frühorthodoxie und Rationalismus.* Zurich: EVZ Verlag, 1963.

Calhoun, David. *Princeton Seminary.* Edinburgh: Banner of Truth, 1996.

Calov, Abraham. *Commentarius in Genesin.* Wittebergae, 1671.

Calvin College. "LGBT Students and Homosexuality FAQ." http://www.calvin.edu
/offices-services/student-life/programs/sexuality-series/lgbt-homosexuality
-faq.html.

Calvin, John. *Commentaries on the Last Four Books of Moses.* Edited and translated by Charles William Bingham. Grand Rapids: Baker, 1983.

———. *Commentary on the Book of Genesis.* Edited and translated by John King. Grand Rapids: Baker, 2003.

———. *Institutes of the Christian Religion.* Edited by John T. McNeill. Translated by Ford Lewis Battles. Philadelphia: Westminster Press, 1960.

———. *Sermons on Genesis, Chapters 1–11.* Translated by Rob Roy McGregor. Edinburgh: Banner of Truth, 2009.

Capito, Wolfgang. *Hexemeron Dei opus Expicatum.* Argentorati per Vuendelinum, 1539.

Cassuto, Umberto. *A Commentary on the Book of Genesis.* Jerusalem: Magnes Press, 1989.

Chalmers, Thomas. "Natural Theology." In *Selected Works of Thomas Chalmers.* Edinburgh, 1857.

Chrysostom, John. "Homilies on Genesis." In vol. 74 of *Fathers of the Church,* translated by Robert C. Hill. Washington, D.C.: Catholic University of America Press, 1986.

Clark, R. Scott. *Recovering the Reformed Confession: Our Theology, Piety, and Practice.* Phillipsburg, N.J.: P&R, 2008.

Clement. "I Clement." In *The Apostolic Fathers,* 44–131, translated by Michael Holmes. 3rd ed. Grand Rapids: Baker, 2007.

Clement of Alexandria. "The Instructor." In vol. 2 of *Ante-Nicene Fathers,* 207–98. Peabody, Mass.: Hendrickson, 1989.

Clements, Don K. "At the PCA General Assembly: Commissioners Vote on Controversial Overtures." The Aquila Report. June 21, 2012. http://
theaquilareport.com/from-the-pca-general-assembly-commissioners
-vote-on-controversial-overtures/.

Cockburn, William. *A New System of Geology.* London, 1849.

Collins, C. John. "Adam and Eve as Historical People, and Why It Matters." *Perspectives on Science and the Christian Faith* 62, no. 3 (September 2010): 147–65.

———. "Adam and Eve in the Old Testament." *Southern Baptist Journal of Theology* 15, no. 1 (2011): 4–25.

——. *Did Adam and Eve Really Exist? Who They Were and Why You Should Care.* Wheaton, Ill.: Crossway, 2011.

——. "Reading Genesis 1–2 with the Grain: Analogical Days." In *Reading Genesis 1–2: An Evangelical Conversation*, edited by J. Daryl Charles. Peabody, Mass.: Hendrickson, 2013.

——. "Replies to Reviews of *Did Adam and Eve Really Exist?*" *Journal of Creation Theology and Science Series B: Life Sciences* 2 (2012): 43–47.

Collins, Francis. "Statement by NIH Director Francis S. Collins, M.D., Ph.D., on Supreme Court's Decision Regarding Stem Cell Case." National Institutes of Health. January 7, 2013. http://www.nih.gov/about/director/01072013 _stemcell_statement.htm.

Comte, Auguste. *A General View of Positivism; Or a Summary Exposition of the System of Thought and Life, adapted to the Great Western Republic Formed of the Five Advanced Nations, The French, Italian, Spanish, British, and German.* London, 1865.

Craigen, Trevor. "Review of *God's Pattern for Creation: A Covenantal Reading of Genesis 1* by Robert W. Godfrey." *Master's Seminary Journal* 15, no. 1 (2004): 117–18.

——. "Review of *Perspectives on An Evolving Creation*, edited by Keith Miller." *Master's Seminary Journal* 18, no. 1 (Spring 2007): 130–32.

Cugoano, Ottobah. *Thoughts and Sentiments on the Evil and Wicked Traffic of Slavery: The Commerce of the Human Species, Humbly Submitted to the Inhabitants of Great-Britain.* London, 1787.

Currid, John. *Against the Gods: The Polemical Theology of the Old Testament.* Wheaton, Ill.: Crossway, 2013.

——. "Genesis 1–11: The Creation, the Fall, the Promise," parts 1–6. Chapel messages given at Reformed Theological Seminary, Jackson, Mississippi, n.d. http://www.rts.edu/Site/RTSNearYou/Jackson/Chapel/currid _creation.aspx.

——. *Genesis 1:1–25:18.* Vol. 1 of *A Study Commentary on Genesis.* Darlington, U.K.: Evangelical Press, 2003.

Dabney, R. L. *Discussions by Robert L. Dabney, D. D.* Harrisonburg, Va.: Sprinkle, 1996.

——. *Lectures in Systematic Theology.* Richmond, Va., 1871.

——. *Systematic Theology.* Edinburgh: Banner of Truth, 1996.

Dagg, John L. *Manual of Theology.* Charleston, S.C.: Southern Baptist Publication Society, 1857.

Daneau, Lambert. *The Wonderfull Woorkmanship of the World Wherin Is Conteined an Excellent Discourse of Christian Natural Philosophie.* Translated by Thomas Twine. London, 1578.

Dargan, Edwin C. *The Doctrines of Our Faith*. Nashville: Sunday School Board, Southern Baptist Convention, 1905.

Darwin, Charles. *The Descent of Man, and Selection in Relation to Sex*. London, 1871.

———. *On the Origin of Species by Means of Natural Selection, or the Preservation of Favoured Races in the Struggle for Life*. London, 1859.

———. *On the Origin of Species...Third Edition*. London, 1861.

Darwin, Erasmus. *The Botanic Garden*. London, 1825.

———. *The Temple of Nature, or, The Origin of Society*. Baltimore, 1804.

———. *Zoonomia; or, the Laws of Organic Life*. 2nd ed. London, 1796.

Davidson, Gregg. *When Faith and Science Collide*. Oxford, Miss.: Malius, 2009.

Davidson, Gregg, and Ken Wolgemuth. "The PCA Creation Study Committee a Dozen Years Later: What Does Science Say Now?" Seminar presented at Presbyterian Church General Assembly, Louisville, Kentucky, June 20, 2012.

Davidson, William. "Lecture on Natural Christology Delivered before the Students of the Associate Reformed Theological Seminary, Allegany City, Pa., March 19, 1855." *The Pulpit and Intelligencer of the Associate Reformed Presbyterian Church* 5 (1854): 401–60.

De Bruin, C. C. *De Synode van Dordrecht in 1618 en 1619*. Houten: Den Hartog, 1994.

De Foigny, Gabriel. *A New Discovery of Terra Incognita Australis, or, the Southern World*. London, 1693.

Delitzsch, F. *A New Commentary on Genesis*. Translated by Sophia Taylor. Edinburgh: T&T Clark, 1888.

Dembski, William. *The End of Christianity: Finding a Good God in an Evil World*. Nashville: B&H, 2009.

DeYoung, Kevin. "Adam and Eve Follow-Up: A Dialogue with Jack Collins." TGC. July 28, 2011. http://thegospelcoalition.org/blogs/kevindeyoung/2011/07/28/adam-and-eve-follow-up-a-dialogue-with-jack-collins/.

Dick, John. *Lectures on Theology*. Philadelphia, 1841.

Dillenberger, John. *Protestant Thought and Natural Science*. New York: Doubleday, 1960.

Diodore of Tarsus. *Commentary on Psalms 1–51*. Translated by Robert C. Hill. Atlanta: Society of Biblical Literature, 2005.

Donne, John. *Two Sermons Preached Before King Charles, Upon the xxvi verse of the first Chapter of Genesis*. Cambridge, 1734.

Downame, John, ed. *Annotations Upon All the Books of the Old and New Testament*. London, 1645.

Driscoll, Mark. "Answers to Common Questions about Creation." The Resurgence. July 3, 2007. http://theresurgence.com/2006/07/03/answers-to-common -questions-about-creation.

Driscoll, Mark, and Gary Breshears. *Doctrine: What Christians Should Believe.* Wheaton, Ill.: Crossway, 2010.

Duffy, Stephen J. "Genes, Original Sin and the Human Proclivity to Evil." *Horizons* 32 (2005): 210–34.

Edwards, Jonathan. *The Freedom of the Will.* Vol. 1 of *The Works of Jonathan Edwards.* Edited by Paul Ramsey. New Haven, Conn.: Yale University Press, 1957.

———. *A History of the Work of Redemption.* Vol. 9 of *The Works of Jonathan Edwards.* Edited by John F. Wilson. New Haven, Conn.: Yale University Press, 1989.

———. *Sermons and Discourses 1743–1758.* Vol. 25 of *The Works of Jonathan Edwards.* Edited by Wilson H. Kimnach. New Haven, Conn.: Yale University Press, 2006.

———. *The Works of Jonathan Edwards.* Edited by Ava Chamberlain. New Haven, Conn.: Yale University Press, 2000.

Elders, Leo. "Les citations de saint Augustin dans la Somme." *Doctor Communis* 40 (1987): 115–67.

Elliot, Ralph H. *The Genesis Controversy and Continuity in Southern Baptist Chaos: A Eulogy for a Great Tradition.* Macon, Ga.: Mercer University Press, 1992.

———. *The Message of Genesis.* Nashville: Broadman, 1961.

Enns, Peter. *The Evolution of Adam: What the Bible Does and Doesn't Say about Human Origins.* Grand Rapids: Baker, 2012.

———. *Inspiration and Incarnation: Evangelicals and the Problem of the Old Testament.* Grand Rapids: Baker, 2005.

———. "Reading Genesis: Let's Be Adults about This, Shall We." Patheos. September 10, 2012. http://www.patheos.com/blogs/peterenns/2012/09/reading -genesis-lets-be-adult-about-this-shall-we/.

"Epistle of Barnabas." In *The Apostolic Fathers*, 380–441, translated by Michael Holmes. 3rd ed. Grand Rapids: Baker, 2007.

Erikson, Millard J. "The Origin of Humanity." In *Christian Theology*, 496–516. 3rd ed. Grand Rapids: Baker, 2013.

Eriugena, Johannes Scotus. *Periphyseon: On the Division of Nature.* Translated by Myra Uhlfelder. Indianapolis, Ind.: Bobbs-Merrill, 1976.

Estelle, Bryan. "Preachers in Lab Coats and Scientists in Geneva Gowns." *Ordained Servant Online.* November 2010. http://www.opc.org/os.html ?article_id=220&cur_iss.

Evans, William B. "Imputation and Impartation: The Problem of Union with Christ in Nineteenth Century American Reformed Theology." PhD diss., Vanderbilt University, 1996.

Farrer, A. J. D. "William Whiston." *Transactions of the Baptist Historical Society* 4 (1914): 3.

Feenstra, J. G. *Onze Geloofsbelijdenis.* 4th ed. Kampen: Kok, 1966.

Fesko, J. V. "The Days of Creation and Confession Subscription in the OPC." *Westminster Theological Journal* 63, no. 2 (2001): 235–49.

Findley, Samuel, ed. "The Deluge." *The Religious Examiner* 2 (1828): 3–9, 66–71, 130–32.

Fisher, James, Ebenezer Erskine, and Ralph Erskine. *The Westminster Assembly's Shorter Catechism Explained.* Philadelphia: Presbyterian Board of Publication, 1765.

Flinn, Derek. "James Hutton and Robert Jameson." *Scottish Journal of Geology* 16 (October 1980): 251–58.

Flipse, Abraham. "The Origins of Creationism in the Netherlands: The Evolution Debate among Twentieth Century Dutch Neo-Calvinists." *Church History* 81, no. 1 (March 2012): 104–47.

Friesen, J. Glenn. "The Investigation of Dooyeweerd and Vollenhoven by the Curators of the Free University." http://www.members.shaw.ca/herman dooyeweerd/Curators.pdf.

Fulgentius of Ruspe. "To Peter on the Faith." In *Fulgentius: Selected Works,* 57–108. Translated by Robert Eno. Washington, D.C.: Catholic University of America Press, 1997.

Fuller, Russell T. "Interpreting Genesis 1–11." *Southern Baptist Journal of Theology* 5, no. 3 (Fall 2001): 18–27.

Futato, Mark. "Because It Had Rained: A Study of Genesis 2:5–7 with Implications for Genesis 2:4–25 and Genesis 1:1–2:3." *Westminster Theological Journal* 60, no. 1 (Spring 1998): 1–21.

Gaffin, Richard B., Jr. "'All Mankind Descending from Him...'?" *New Horizons* 33, no. 3 (March 2012): 3–5.

Gale, Theophilus. *The Court of the Gentiles: Or A Discourse Touching the Original of Human Literature, Both Philology and Philosophie, from the Scriptures....* Oxon, 1660.

Galilei, Galileo. *Nov-antiqua sanctissimorum patrum....* Strassburg, 1636.

Galton, Francis. *Inquiries into Human Faculty and Its Development.* London: J. M. Dent, 1907.

Garrett, Don, ed. *The Cambridge Companion to Spinoza.* Cambridge: Cambridge University Press, 1996.

Garrett, James Leo, Glenn Hinson, and James E. Tull. *Are Southern Baptists "Evangelicals"?* Macon, Ga.: Mercer University Press, 1983.

———. *Baptist Theology: A Four Century Study.* Macon, Ga.: Mercer University Press, 2009.

———. *Systematic Theology: Biblical, Historical & Evangelical.* Grand Rapids: Eerdmans, 1990.

Geisler, Norman. *Systematic Theology.* Minneapolis: Bethany House, 2003.

Gerhard, Johann. *Loci Theologici Cum Pro Adstruenda Veritate....* Jena: Steinmann, 1611.

Gibbons, Nicholas. *Questions and Disputations Concerning the Holy Scriptures Wherein Are Contained, Briefe, Faithfull, and Sound Expositions of the Most Difficult and Hardest Places....* London, 1601.

Gill, John. *A Body of Practical Divinity.* Atlanta: Turner Lassetter, 1965.

———. *An Exposition of the Old Testament.* London, 1810.

Giltner, John H. "Genesis and Geology: The Stuart-Sillman-Hitchcock Debate." *The Journal of Religious Thought* 23, no. 1 (1996–67): 3–13.

———. *Moses Stuart: The Father of Biblical Science in America.* Atlanta: Scholars Press, 1988.

Godfrey, W. Robert. *God's Pattern for Creation: A Covenantal Reading of Genesis 1.* Phillipsburg, N.J.: P&R, 2003.

Goldsworthy, Graeme. *Gospel-Centered Hermeneutics.* Downers Grove, Ill.: IVP Academic, 2006.

Goodwin, Thomas. *The Works of Thomas Goodwin, D. D.* Edinburgh, 1663.

Gosse, Philip Henry. *An Introduction to Zoology.* London, 1844.

———. *Omphalos: An Attempt to Untie the Geological Knot.* London, 1857.

Graebner, Theodore. *Evolution: An Investigation and Criticism.* Milwaukee: Northwestern, 1922.

———. *God and the Cosmos—A Critical Analysis of Atheism, Materialism, and Evolution.* Grand Rapids: Eerdmans, 1932.

Grafton, Anthony. *New Worlds, Ancient Texts: The Power of Tradition and the Shock of Discovery.* Cambridge, Mass.: Belknap Press, 1992.

Gravemeijer, H. E. *Leesboek over de Gereformeerde Geloofsleer.* Gronigen, 1892.

Gray, Terry. "Being an Evolutionary Creationist in a Confessionally Reformed Church." *An Evangelical Dialogue on Evolution.* http://evanevodialogue.blogspot.com/2010/03/being-evolutionary-creationist-in.html.

———. "Excerpts from the Minutes of the 63rd General Assembly of the Orthodox Presbyterian Church." *Documents Related to the Evolution Trial in the OPC at The American Scientific Affiliation.* http://www.asa3.org/gray/evolution_trial/general_assembly_actions.html#anchor8409563.

———. "A Letter to the Committee of Five in Response to the First Draft of the Charges, March 14, 1994." *Documents Related to the Evolution Trial in the OPC at The American Scientific Affiliation.* http://www.asa3.org /gray/evolution_trial/response_to_PMWcharges.html.

———. "Letter to Rev. Thomas E. Tyson, editor of *New Horizons*" (February 15, 1993): www.asa3.org/gray/evolution_trial/NHevolution.html.

Gregory of Nyssa. "On the Making of Man." In vol. 5 of *Nicene and Post-Nicene Fathers*, 2nd series, 387–427. Peabody, Mass.: Hendrickson, 1989.

Gregory, Mary Efrosini. *Evolutionism in Eighteenth Century French Thought.* New York: Peter Lang, 2008.

Grosseteste, Robert. *On the Six Days of Creation: A Translation of the Hexaemeron by C. F. J. Martin.* Oxford: Oxford University Press, 1996.

Groves, J. Alan. "Review of *Genesis: With an Introduction to Narrative Literature* by George W. Coats." *Westminster Theological Journal* 46, no. 2 (1984): 400–402.

Grudem, Wayne. *Bible Doctrine: Essential Teachings of the Christian Faith.* Grand Rapids: Zondervan, 1999.

———. *Systematic Theology.* Grand Rapids: Zondervan, 1994.

Gunkel, Hermann. *Creation and Chaos in the Primeval Era and Eschaton.* Grand Rapids: Eerdmans, 2006.

Gustafson, Robert Kovitz. "A Study in the Life of James Woodrow Emphasizing His Theological and Scientific Views as They Relate to the Evolutionary Controversy." PhD diss., Union Theological Seminary, Richmond, Va., 1964.

Gutzke, Manford George. *Plain Talk on Genesis.* Grand Rapids: Zondervan, 1975.

Haak, Theodore, trans. *The Dutch Annotations Upon the Whole Bible.* London, 1657.

Haarsma, Deborah B., and Loren D. Haarsma. *Origins: Christian Perspectives on Creation, Evolution, and Intelligent Design.* Grand Rapids: Faith Alive Christian Resources, 2011.

Haeckel, Ernest. *History of Creation: Of the Development of the Earth and Its Inhabitants by the Action of Natural Causes. A Popular Exposition of the Doctrine of Evolution in General.* Translated by E. R. Lancaster. New York, 1876.

Hagopian, David G., ed. *Three Views on the Days of Creation: The G3N3S1S Debate.* Mission Viejo, Calif.: Cruxpress, 2001.

Ha-Levi, Yehudah. *The Kuzari: In Defense of the Despised Faith.* Edited by David Kahn. Nanuet, N.Y.: Feldheim, 2009.

Hamilton, Victor P. *The New International Commentary on the Old Testament— The Book of Genesis: Chapters 1–17.* Grand Rapids: Eerdmans, 1991.

Harlow, Daniel. "After Adam: Reading Genesis in an Age of Evolutionary Science." *Perspectives on Science and Christian Faith* 62, no. 3 (September 2010): 179–95.

Harris, R. Laird. *Man—God's Eternal Creation: Old Testament Teaching on Man and His Culture.* Chicago, Ill.: Moody, 1971.

Harris, R. Laird, Gleason L. Archer, and Bruce K. Waltke, eds. *Theological Wordbook of the Old Testament.* 2 vols. Chicago: Moody, 1980.

Hart, Darryl. "Machen and the End of Princeton." Lecture presented at the Greenville Presbyterian Theological Seminary Spring Theology Conference, Greenville, S.C., March 2012.

Hausmann, William. *Science and the Bible in Lutheran Theology: From Luther to the Missouri Synod.* Washington, D.C.: University Press of America, 1978.

Haykin, Michael. *Rediscovering the Church Fathers.* Wheaton, Ill.: Crossway, 2011.

Heck, Joel D. *In the Beginning, God: Creation from God's Perspective.* St. Louis: Concordia, 2011.

Heidegger, Johann. *Medulla Medullae Theologae Christianae.* Tiguri, 1697.

Hemkes, Gerrit. "De vijf Boeken van Mozes, Rectorale Rede uitgesproken den 5 den Sept. 1895, door Prof. G.K. Hemkes." Unpublished manuscript, Heckman Library Archives, Calvin College, Grand Rapids, 1895.

Henry, Carl F. H. *God, Revelation, and Authority.* 6 vols. Waco, Tex.: Word, 1983.

Henry, Matthew. *Commentary on the Whole Bible.* Peabody, Mass.: Hendrickson, 1994.

———. *A Scripture Catechism.* Vol. 2 of *The Complete Works of Matthew Henry,* 174–263. Grand Rapids: Baker, 1997.

Hepp, Valentine. *Calvinism and the Philosophy of Nature.* Grand Rapids: Eerdmans, 1930.

Herder, Johann Gottfried. *Werke.* Frankfurt: Deutscher Klassiker Verlag, 1985.

Heyns, William. "Bijbelsche Geschiedenis." Unpublished manuscript, Heckman Library Archives, Calvin College, Grand Rapids, Michigan, n.d.

———. "Historia Sacra. Oud Testament." Unpublished manuscript, Heckman Library Archives, Calvin College, Grand Rapids, Michigan, n.d.

———. *Manual of Reformed Doctrine.* Grand Rapids: Eerdmans, 1926.

Hippolytus of Rome. "Fragments from Commentaries." In vol. 5 of *Ante-Nicene Fathers,* 163–203. Grand Rapids: Eerdmans, 1995.

Hirsch, Emil. "Philo." In *The Jewish Encyclopedia.* New York: Funk and Wagnalls, 1925.

Hodge, Archibald Alexander. *A Commentary on the Confession of Faith.* Philadelphia, 1869.

———. Introduction to *Theism and Evolution,* by Joseph S. Van Dyke, xv–xxii. New York, 1886.

Hodge, Charles. "Review of *The Epoch of Creation*." *The Biblical Repertory and Princeton Review* 23, no. 24 (1851): 696–98.

———. *Systematic Theology.* Grand Rapids: Eerdmans, 1997.

———. *What Is Darwinism?* New York, 1874.

Holland, John. *The Smoke of the Bottomless Pit. Or a More True and Fuller Discovery of the Doctrine of Those Men which Call Themselves Ranters: Or, the Mad Crew.* London, 1651.

Hollaz, David. *Examen Theologicum Acroamaticum Universam Theologam Thetico-polemicam complectens.* Lipsiae, 1763.

Home, Henry, Lord Kames. *Sketches of the History of Man.* 2nd ed. Edinburgh, 1778.

Horne, Thomas Hartwell. *An Introduction to the Critical Study and Knowledge of the Holy Scriptures.* 5th ed. London: Cadell, 1825.

Horton, Michael. *Lord and Servant: A Covenant Christology.* Louisville: Westminster, 2005.

Hottinger, Johann Heinrich. *De Ktisis Hexaemeros. Id est, Historiae Creationis Examen Theologico-Phylologicum.* Hiedelbergae, 1659.

———. *Medulla Medullae Theologiae Christianae.* Tiguri, 1697.

Hughes, R. Kent. *Genesis: Beginning and Blessing.* Wheaton, Ill.: Crossway, 2004.

Hume, David. "Of National Characters." In *The Philosophical Works of David Hume.* Edinburgh, 1825.

Hutton, James. *Abstract of a dissertation…Concerning the system of the Earth, Its Duration, Its Stability.* Edinburgh, 1785.

———. *An Investigation of the Principles of Knowledge, and of the Progress of Reason, from Sense to Science and Philosophy.* Edinburgh, 1794.

Huxley, Thomas. "Science and Hebrew Tradition." In *Collected Essays by T. H. Huxley.* New York: D. Appleton, 1903.

Irenaeus. "Against Heresies." In vol. 1 of *Ante-Nicene Fathers,* 309–567. Grand Rapids: Eerdmans, 1989.

Irons, Lee. "The Bruce Waltke Affair and the Westminster Confession." *The Upper Register.* March 2010. http://upper-register.typepad.com/blog/2010/04/the-bruce-waltke-affair.html.

———. "The Framework Interpretation: An Exegetical Summary." *The Upper Register.* http://www.upper-register.com/papers/framework_interpretation.html.

Jackson, Arthur. *A Help for the Understanding of Scripture…The First Part…Containing Certain Short Notes of Exposition upon the Five Books of Moses.* Cambridge, 1643.

Jaki, Stanley. *Genesis 1 through the Ages.* London: Thomas Moore Press, 1992.

John of Damascus. "Exposition of the Orthodox Faith." In vol. 9 of *Nicene and Post-Nicene Fathers, Second Series*, 1–101. Peabody, Mass.: Hendrickson, 1995.

Jordan, James B. *Creation in Six Days: A Defense of the Traditional Reading of Genesis One.* Moscow, Idaho: Canon, 1999.

Josephus, Titus Flavius. *Antiquities of the Jews.* Translated by William Whiston. Project Gutenberg, 2009. www.gutenberg.org/files/2848/2848-h/2848-h .htm#link2HCH0001.

Kant, Immanuel. *Critique of Judgement.* Translated by J. H. Bernard. London: Macmillan, 1914.

Keil, C. F., and F. Delitzsch. *Biblical Commentary on the Old Testament: The Pentateuch.* Translated by James Martin. Grand Rapids: Eerdmans, 2006.

Keischnick, Gerald B. "President-Elect Acceptance Speech." In *2001 LCMS Convention Proceedings*, 114. St. Louis: Concordia, 2011.

Keller, Timothy. "Creation, Evolution, and Christian Laypeople, Part 6." BioLogos Forum. March 30, 2012. http://biologos.org/blog/creation-evolution-and -christian-laypeople-part-6.

Kelly, Douglas F. *Creation and Change: Genesis 1.1–2.4 in the Light of Changing Scientific Paradigms.* Fearn, U.K.: Christian Focus, 1997.

Kidner, Derek. *Genesis: An Introduction and Commentary.* Downers Grove, Ill.: InterVarsity, 1967.

Kirwan, Richard. *Geological Essays.* London, 1799.

Kline, Meredith. "Because It Had Not Rained." *Westminster Theological Journal* 20, no. 2 (May 1958): 146–57.

———. "Genesis." In *The New Bible Commentary*, edited by Donald Guthrie, 54–91. 3rd rev. ed. Downers Grove, Ill.: InterVarsity, 1970.

———. "Space and Time in the Genesis Cosmogony." *Perspectives on Science and the Christian Faith* 48, no. 1 (March 1996): 2–15.

Kline, Meredith, and Ted Hildebrandt. "Kingdom Prologue, Lecture 29." Biblical Studies Lecture Series, Gordon College, Barnesville, Georgia, 2012.

Krabbendam, Henry. "B. B. Warfield vs. G. C. Berkouwer on Scripture." In *Inerrancy*, edited by Norman Geisler, 413–48. Grand Rapids: Zondervan, 1980.

Krey, Philip D. W., and Lesley Smith, eds. *Nicholas of Lyra: The Senses of Scripture.* Leiden: Brill, 2000.

Kruger, Michael J. "An Understanding of Genesis 2:5." *CEN Technical Journal* 11, no. 1 (1997): 106–10.

Kuiper, R. B. "Outlines of Topics Discussed by Rev. R. B. Kuiper at the Meetings of the Advanced Bible Class of the La Grave Avenue Christian Reformed Church, Grand Rapids, Michigan. Season 1928–1929." Unpublished manuscript, Heckman Library Archives, Calvin College, Grand Rapids, Michigan, 1928–1929.

———. "The Reformed System of Theology." Unpublished manuscript, Heckman Library Archives, Calvin College, Grand Rapids, Michigan, n.d.

Kuitert, H. M. *Do You Understand What You Read?* Translated by Lewis B. Smedes. Grand Rapids: Eerdmans, 1970.

———. *Jesus: The Legacy of Christianity.* Translated by John Bowden. London: SCM, 1999.

Kulikovsky, Andrew. *Creation, Fall, Restoration: A Biblical Theology of Creation.* Fearn, U.K.: Christian Focus, 2009.

Kuyper, Abraham. *Evolutie. Rede bij de overdracht van het rectoraat aan de Vrije Universiteit op 20 October 1899 gehouden.* Amsterdam, 1899.

———. "Locus De Creatione." *Dictaat Dogmatiek* 3 (1891): 50–64.

———. *Van de Voleinding.* Kampen: Kok, 1929.

Lactantius. "The Divine Institutes." In vol. 7 of *Ante-Nicene Fathers,* 9–223. Grand Rapids: Eerdmans, 1989.

———. "On the Workmanship of God." In vol. 7 of *Ante-Nicene Fathers,* 281–300. Grand Rapids: Eerdmans, 1989.

Lamarck, Jean-Baptiste. *Hydrogeologie.* Paris, 1802.

Lammerts, Walter E., ed. *Scientific Studies in Special Creation.* Nutley, N.J.: Presbyterian and Reformed, 1971.

Landes, Richard. "The Fear of an Apocalyptic Year 1000: Augustinian Historiography, Medieval, and Modern." *Speculum* 75, no. 1 (January 2000): 97–145.

La Peyrère, Isaac. *Men before Adam, or a Discourse upon the Twelfth, Thirteenth, and Fourteenth Verses of the Fifth Chapter of the Apostle Paul to the Romans....* London, 1656.

———. *A Theological Systeme upon the Presupposition, That Men Were Before Adam.* London, 1655.

Lapidge, Michael. *The Blackwell Encyclopedia of Anglo Saxon England.* Oxford, U.K.: Blackwell, 2001.

Lavallee, Louis. "Augustine on the Creation Days." *Journal of the Evangelical Theological Society* 32, no. 4 (December 1989): 457–64.

Leclerc, George-Louis, Comte de Buffon. *Natural History, General and Particular....* 2nd ed. Translated by William Smellie. London, 1785.

Le Clerc, Jean. *Genesis Sive Mosis Prophetae Liber Primus.* Amstelodami, 1710.

———. *Twelve Dissertations out of Monsieur Le Clerk's Genesis.* Translated by Thomas Brown. London, 1696.

LeCroy, Timothy R. "Thoughts on the 40th PCA GA, Part Two: *In Thesi* Statement on the Creation of Adam." *Vita pastoralis.* June 25, 2012. http://

pastortimlecroy.wordpress.com/2012/06/25/thoughts-on-the-40th-pca -ga-part-two-in-thesi-statement-on-the-creation-of-adam/.

Lee, Hoon J. "Accommodation—Orthodox, Socinian, and Contemporary." *Westminster Theological Journal* 75 (Fall 2013): 335–48.

Leigh, Edward. *A System or Body of Divinity wherein the Fundamentals and Main Grounds of Religion Are Open.* London, 1654.

Leo the Great. "On the Feast of the Nativity." In vol. 12 of *Nicene and Post-Nicene Fathers, Second Series,* 128–44. Peabody, Mass.: Hendrickson, 1985.

Letham, Robert. "'In the Space of Six Days': The Days of Creation from Origen to the Westminster Assembly." *Westminster Theological Journal* 61, no. 2 (1999): 149–74.

Leupold, H. C. *Exposition of Genesis.* Grand Rapids: Baker, 1950.

Lever, Jan. *Creation and Evolution.* Translated by Peter G. Berkhout. Grand Rapids: Grand Rapids International Publishers, 1958.

———. "De Oorsprong van de Mens." *Geloof en Wetenschaap* 53 (1955): 133–67.

———. *Waar blijven we?* Kampen: Kampen-Wageningen, 1969.

Lewis, Gordon R., and Bruce Demarest. *Integrative Theology.* Grand Rapids: Zondervan, 1990.

Liberty University. "Who We Are: Doctrinal Statement." http://www.liberty.edu /aboutliberty/.

Lightfoot, John. *A Few New Observations upon the Book of Genesis.* London, 1642.

———. *The Whole Works of the Rev. John Lightfoot.* Edited by John Rogers Pitman. 11 vols. London, 1822–1825.

Lindsell, Harold. *The Battle for the Bible.* Grand Rapids: Zondervan, 1976.

Livingstone, David. *Adam's Ancestors: Race, Religion and the Politics of Human Origins.* Baltimore, Md.: Johns Hopkins University Press, 2008.

Lombard, Peter. "On the Creation and Formation of Things Corporal and Spiritual and Many Others Pertaining to This." In *The Four Books of Sentences.* Translated by Alexis Bugnolo. http://www.franciscan-archive.org /lombardus/opera/ls2–17.html. (By the time of publication the source had been removed from the Internet.)

Longman, Tremper III, and Ray Dillard. *How to Read Genesis.* Downers Grove, Ill.: InterVarsity, 2005.

———. *An Introduction to the Old Testament.* Grand Rapids: Zondervan, 1994.

———. "Responses to Chapter Two." In *Reading Genesis 1–2: An Evangelical Conversation,* edited by J. Daryl Charles, 60–72. Peabody, Mass.: Hendrickson, 2013.

Lord, Eleazer. *The Epoch of Creation. The Scripture Doctrine Contrasted with the Geological Theory.* New York, 1851.

Lubenow, Marvin L. *Bones of Contention: A Creationist Assessment of Human Fossils.* Grand Rapids: Baker, 2007.

Luther, Martin. *Lectures on Genesis.* Vol 1 of *Luther's Works.* Translated by Jaroslav Pelikan. St. Louis: Concordia, 1958.

Lutheran Church–Missouri Synod. "A Brief Statement of the Doctrinal Position of the Evangelical Lutheran Synod of Missouri, Ohio, and Other States." In *Doctrinal Declarations, A Collection of Official Statements on the Doctrinal Position of Various Lutheran Synods in America,* 1–60. St. Louis: Concordia, 1932.

———. *Convention Proceedings of the Forty-Seventh Regular Convention of the Lutheran Church–Missouri Synod, New York, N.Y., July 7–14, 1967.* St. Louis: Concordia, 1967.

Lyell, Charles. *Principles of Geology....* London, 1830.

Lyell, Katherine. *Life, Letters and Journals of Sir Charles Lyell, Bart.* London, 1881.

MacArthur, John. *The Battle for the Beginning: Creation, Evolution and the Bible.* Nashville: Nelson, 2001.

———. "Creation: Believe it or Not." *Master's Seminary Journal* 13, no. 1 (Spring 2002): 5–32.

———, ed. *The MacArthur Bible Commentary.* Nashville: Nelson, 2005.

Machen, J. Gresham. *Christianity and Liberalism.* Grand Rapids: Eerdmans, 1992.

Mahoney, Edward P., ed. *Philosophy and Humanism: Renaissance Essays in Honor of Paul Oskar Kristeller.* Lyden: Brill, 1976.

Maimonides, Moses. *The Guide for the Perplexed.* Translated by M. Friedlander. 2nd ed. London: George Routledge, 1919.

Manton, Thomas. *The Complete Works of Thomas Manton, D. D.* London, 1873.

Martyr, Justin. "Dialogue with Trypho." In vol. 1 of *Ante-Nicene Fathers,* 194–270. Grand Rapids: Eerdmans, 1989.

Mather, Cotton. *Biblia Americana, vol.1, Genesis.* Edited by Richard Smolinski. Grand Rapids: Baker, 2010.

Madueme, Hans. "Some Reflections on Enns and the Evolution of Adam: A Review Essay." *Themelios* 37, no. 2 (July 2012): 283–84.

Mayhue, Richard. "Editorial: Scripture on Creation." *Master's Seminary Journal* 23, no. 1 (Spring 2012): 1–6.

McEvoy, James. *The Philosophy of Robert Grosseteste.* Oxford: Clarendon, 1986.

McFarland, Ian. *In Adam's Fall: A Christian Meditation on the Christian Doctrine of Original Sin.* Malden, Mass.: Wiley-Blackwell, 2010.

Meijering, E. P. *Melanchthon and Patristic Thought: The Doctrines of Christ and Grace, the Trinity and the Creation.* Leiden: Brill, 1983.

Melanchthon, Philip. *Commentarius in Genesin* in *Corpus Reformatorum.* Edited by Carrolus Gotlieb Bretschneider. Halis Saxonum, 1846.

Mersenne, Marin. *Quaestiones Celeberrimae In Genesim, Cum Accurata Textus Explicatione.* Lutetiae Parisiorum, 1623.

Metaxas, Eric, and Timothy Keller. "Fireside Chat at New Canaan Society 2012 Washington Weekend." http://vimeo.com/42020632.

Methodius. "The Banquet of the Ten Virgins." In vol. 6 of *Ante-Nicene Fathers*, 309–55. Grand Rapids: Eerdmans, 1987.

Mid-America Reformed Seminary. "What the Faculty of Mid-America Reformed Seminary Teaches Regarding the Days of Creation." http://www.mid america.edu/about/docstandards.htm.

Miller, Hugh. *The Testimony of the Rocks.* Boston, 1857.

Miller, Keith. "And God Saw That It Was Good: Death and Pain in the Created Order." Biologos Forum. November 21–24, 2012. http://biologos.org /blog/series/death-and-pain-in-the-created-order.

Mohler, R. Albert, Jr. "Adam and Eve: Clarifying Again What Is At Stake." Albert-Mohler.com. August 31, 2011. www.albertmohler.com/2011/08/31/adam -and-eve-clarifying-again-what-is-at-stake/.

———, ed. "Debating Adam." *The Southern Baptist Journal of Theology* 15, no. 1 (Spring 2011): 1–107.

———. "False Start? The Controversy Over Adam and Eve Heats Up." Albert Mohler.com. August 22, 2011. www.albertmohler.com/2011/08/22/false -start-the-controversy-over-adam-and-eve-heats-up/.

Molenaar, D. *Handleiding voor Mijne Leerlingen.* Amsterdam, 1852.

Mook, James R. "The Church Fathers in Genesis, the Flood, and the Age of the Earth." In *Coming to Grips with Genesis: Biblical Authority and the Age of the Earth*, edited by Terry Mortenson and Thane H. Ury, 23–52. Green Forest, Ariz.: Master Books, 2008.

———. "The Church Fathers: Young Earth Creationists." Address given at the Origins 2012 Conference, Patrick Henry College, Purcellville, Virginia, July 28, 2012.

Moore, James. *The Darwinian Controversies: A Study of the Protestant Struggle to Come to Terms with Darwin in Great Britain and America 1870–1900.* Cambridge: Cambridge University Press, 1979.

Morris, Henry M. *Biblical Creationism: What Each Book of the Bible Teaches about Creation and the Flood.* Grand Rapids: Baker, 1993.

———. *The Genesis Record: A Scientific and Devotional Commentary on the Book of Beginnings.* Grand Rapids: Baker, 1976.

Muller, Richard. "Scripture as Word of God and *Principium Cognoscendi Theologiae.*" In *Post-Reformation Reformed Dogmatics*, 151–223. Grand Rapids: Baker, 2003.

Mullins, E. Y. *The Christian Religion in Its Doctrinal Expression*. Valley Forge, Pa.: Judson, 1917.

Murdoch, Brian. *The Medieval Popular Bible: Expansions of Genesis in the Middle Ages*. Suffolk, U.K.: Boydell & Brewer, 2003.

Murray, John. "Calvin's Doctrine of Creation." *Westminster Theological Journal* 17, no. 1 (November 1954): 21–43.

———. *The Epistle to the Romans*. Grand Rapids: Eerdmans, 1968.

———. "Immediate and Mediate Creation." *Westminster Theological Journal* 17, no. 1 (November 1954): 22–43.

———. "The Origin of Man." In vol. 2 of *Collected Writings of John Murray*, 3–13. Edinburgh: Banner of Truth, 1977.

Musculus, Wolfgang. *In Genesim Mosis Comment Arij plenissimi: In quibus veterum et recentiorum sententiae diligenter expenduntur....* Basel, 1554.

Nettles, Tom J. "Review of *The End of Christianity*, by William Dembski." *Southern Baptist Journal of Theology* 13, no. 4 (2010): 80–100.

Nicholas of Lyra. *Postilla super totam Bibliam*. Rome, 1471–1472.

Noll, Mark, and David Livingston, eds. *What Is Darwinism? and Other Writings on Science & Religion*. Grand Rapids: Baker, 1994.

Noordtzij, Arie. *Gods Woord en Der Eeuwen Getuigenis: Het Oude Testament in Het Licht der Oostersche Opgravingen*. Kampen: Kok, 1924.

Northcott, Michael S., and R. J. Berry, eds. *Theology after Darwin*. Colorado Springs, Colo.: Paternoster, 2009.

Novak, David. "Maimonides and Aquinas on Natural Law." In *St. Thomas Aquinas and the Natural Law Tradition*, edited by John Goyette, Mark Larkovic, and Richard Myers, 43–65. Washington, D.C.: Catholic University of America Press, 2004.

Numbers, Ronald L. *The Creationists: The Evolution of Scientific Creationism*. New York: Knopf, 1992.

O'Conner, Ralph. "Young Earth Creationists in Early Nineteenth Century Britain? Towards a Reassessment of 'Scriptural Geology.'" *History of Science* 45 (2007): 357–403.

Oecolampadius, Iohannes. *An Exposition of Genesis*. Translated by Mickey L. Mattox. Milwaukee: Marquette University Press, 2013.

Offenberg, A. K. "The Earliest Printed Editions of Rashi's Commentary on the Pentateuch." In *Rashi 1040–1105, Hommage à Ephraim E. Urbach*, edited by Gabrielle Sed-Rajna, 493–505. Paris: Éditions du Cerfs, 1993.

Olinger, Danny E., ed. "Adam: Man or Myth?" *New Horizons* 33, no. 3 (March 2012).

Oosterhoff, B. J. *Hoe lezen wij Genesis 2 en 3? Een hermeneutische studie*. Kampen: Kok, 1972.

Origen. *Contra Celsum*. Cambridge: Cambridge University Press, 1980.

———. *Homilies on Genesis and Exodus*. Washington, D.C.: Catholic University of America Press, 1981.

Orr, James. "The Early Narratives of Genesis." In vol. 1 of *The Fundamentals: A Testimony to the Truth*, edited by R. A. Torrey and A. C. Dixon, 228–40. Grand Rapids: Baker, 1988.

Orthodox Presbyterian Church. *Report of the Committee to Study the Views of Creation to the 71st General Assembly of the Orthodox Presbyterian Church*. Willow Grove, Penn.: Orthodox Presbyterian Church, 2004.

Ostling, Richard N. "The Search for the Historical Adam." *Christianity Today* 55, no. 6 (June 2011): 27.

Owen, John. *The Works of John Owen*. Edinburgh: Banner of Truth, 2000.

Papazian, Mary Arshagouni, ed. *John Donne and the Protestant Reformation: New Perspectives*. Detroit: Wayne State University Press, 2003.

Park, Jae-Eun. "Theophilus Gale's Reformed Platonism: Focusing on His Discourse of 'Creation' and 'Providence' in The Court of the Gentiles." *Mid-America Journal of Theology* 24 (2013): 121–42.

Pascal, Blaise. *Pensées*. Edited by A. J. Krailsheimer. London: Penguin, 1995.

Patrick, Simon. *A Commentary on the Historical Books of the Old Testament*. London, 1851.

Patton, Corrine. "Lyra's Commentary on Genesis 1–3." In *Nicholas of Lyra: The Senses of Scripture*, 19–43. Leiden: Brill, 2000.

Perkins, William. *An Exposition of the Symbole or Creed of the Apostles*. Cambridge, 1608.

———. *A Golden Chain or the Description of Theology.…* Cambridge, 1597.

Perman, Matt. "Science, the Bible, and the Promised Land: An Analysis of John Sailhamer's *Genesis Unbound*." Desiring God. January 1, 1998. http://www.desiringgod.org/articles/science-the-bible-and-the-promised-land.

Peterson, Gregory R. "Falling Up: Evolution and Original Sin." In *Evolution and Ethics: Human Morality in Biological and Religious Perspective*, edited by Philip Clayton and Jeffrey Schloss, 273–86. Grand Rapids: Eerdmans, 2004.

Phillips, Richard, Nick Batzig, and Kenneth Kang-Hui. "The Historical Adam." Reformed Forum. January 27, 2012. www.reformedforum.org/podcasts/ctc212/.

Philo, Alexandrinus. *On the Account of the World's Creation Given by Moses*. Vol. 1 of *Philo: In Ten Volumes*. Translated by F. H. Colson and G. H. Whitaker. Cambridge, Mass.: Harvard University Press, 2001.

Pictet, Bernard. *Christian Theology*. Translated by Frederick Reyroux. Philadelphia, 1890.

Pieper, Francis. *Christian Dogmatics*. St. Louis: Concordia, 1950.

Pipa, Joseph A., Jr., and David W. Hall, eds. *Did God Create in Six Days?* Greenville, S.C.: Southern Presbyterian Press, 1999.

Playfair, John. *Illustrations of the Huttonian Theory of the Earth*. Edinburgh, 1802.

Poole, Matthew. *Annotations upon the Holy Bible*. London, 1683.

———. *Synopsis Criticorum…Sacrae Scripturae*. Francofurti a Moemum, 1678.

Pope, Alexander. "Essay on Man: Epistle II." In *Representative Poetry Online*. Toronto: University of Toronto Libraries, 2013. http://rpo.library.utoronto.ca/poems/essay-man-epistle-ii.

Popkin, Richard H. *Isaac La Peyrère (1596–1676): His Life, Work, and Influence*. Leiden: Brill, 1987.

———. "The Pre-Adamite Theory in the Renaissance." In *Philosophy and Humanism: Renaissance Essays in Honor of Paul Oskar Kristeller*, edited by Edward P. Mahoney, 50–69. Leiden: Brill, 1976.

———. "Spinoza and Bible Scholarship." In *The Cambridge Companion to Spinoza*, edited by Don Garrett, 303–407. Cambridge: Cambridge University Press, 1996.

Poythress, Vern S. "Adam versus Claims from Genetics." *Westminster Theological Journal* 75, no. 1 (Spring 2013): 65–82.

———. *Christian Interpretations of Genesis 1*. Phillipsburg, N.J.: P&R, 2013.

Presbyterian Church of America. *Report of the Creation Study Committee to the 28th General Assembly of the Presbyterian Church in America*. Lawrenceville, Ga.: Presbyterian Church of America, 2000.

Price, George McCready. *Genesis Vindicated*. Washington, D.C.: Review and Herald, 1941.

———. *Outlines of Modern Christianity and Modern Science*. Oakland, Calif.: Pacific Press, 1902.

Ramm, Bernard. *The Christian View of Science and Scripture*. Grand Rapids: Eerdmans, 1954.

Rana, Fazale, with Hugh Ross. *Who Was Adam?: A Creation Model Approach to the Origin of Man*. Colorado Springs, Colo.: NavPress, 2005.

Reid, Duncan, and Mark Worthing, eds. *Sin and Salvation*. Adelaide, Australia: Australian Theological Forum, 2003.

Repcheck, Jack. *The Man Who Found Time: James Hutton and the Discovery of Earth's Antiquity*. Cambridge, Mass.: Perseus, 2003.

Reymond, Robert. *A New Systematic Theology of the Christian Faith*. 2nd ed. Nashville: Nelson, 2001.

Richards, Robert J. "Ernst Haeckel and the Struggles over Evolution and Religion." In *Annals of the History and Philosophy of Biology* 10 (2005): 89–116.

Ridderbos, Jan. *Het Verloren Paradijs: Een woord met het oog op de aangaande Genesis 2 and 3 gerezen vragen.* Kampen: Kok, 1925.

Ridderbos, Nicholas Herman. *Is There a Conflict between Genesis 1 and Natural Science?* Grand Rapids: Eerdmans, 1957.

Ridgley, Thomas. *Body of Divinity.* Edited by John M. Wilson. New York, 1855.

Rimmer, Harry. *The Harmony of Science and Scripture.* Grand Rapids: Eerdmans, 1954.

———. *Modern Science and the Genesis Record.* Grand Rapids: Eerdmans, 1954.

Roberts, Alexander, and James Donaldson, eds. *Ante-Nicene Fathers.* Peabody, Mass.: Hendrickson, 1989.

Roehrs, Walter. "The Creation Account of Genesis." *Concordia Theological Monthly* 36, no. 5 (May 1965): 320.

Roger, Jacques. *Buffon: A Life in Natural History.* Translated by Sarah Lucille. Ithaca, N.Y.: Cornell University Press, 1997.

Rogland, Max. "*Ad Litteram*: Some Dutch Reformed Theologians on the Creation Days." *Westminster Theological Journal* 63, no. 2 (Fall 2001): 211–35.

Rosenberg, A. J., ed. *The Complete Tanach with Rashi's Commentary.* Brooklyn, N.Y.: Judaica Press, 2012.

Roughgarden, Joan. *What Jesus and Darwin Have in Common: Evolution and Christian Faith.* Washington, D.C.: Island, 2006.

Sailhamer, John. "Creation, Genesis 1–11, and the Canon." *Bulletin for Biblical Research* 10, no. 1 (2000): 89–106.

———. "Exegetical Notes: Genesis 1:1–2:4a." *Trinity Journal* 5 (1984): 73–82.

———. "Genesis." In *The Expositor's Bible Commentary*, 21–332. Grand Rapids: Zondervan, 1990.

———. *Genesis Unbound: A Provocative New Look at the Creation Account.* Sisters, Ore.: Multnomah, 1996.

———. *The Meaning of the Pentateuch: Revelation, Composition and Interpretation.* Downers Grove, Ill.: IVP Academic, 2009.

Sanlon, Peter. "Augustine's Literal Adam." The Gospel Coalition. June 14, 2011. http://www.thegospelcoalition.org/article/augustines-literal-adam.

Scaliger, Joseph Justus. *Opus de Emendatione temporum.* Geneva, 1629.

Schaeffer, Francis A. *Genesis in Space and Time.* Downers Grove, Ill.: InterVarsity, 1972.

Schaff, Philip. *The Creeds of Christendom.* Grand Rapids: Baker, 1996.

———, ed. *Nicene and Post-Nicene Fathers.* Peabody, Mass.: Hendrickson, 1989.

Schaff, Philip, and Henry Wace, eds. *Nicene and Post-Nicene Fathers. Second Series.* Peabody, Mass.: Hendrickson, 1989.

Schleiermacher, Friedrich. *The Christian Faith in Outline*. Edinburgh: William F. Henderson, 1922.

Schweitzer, Albert. *The Quest of the Historical Jesus: A Critical Study of Its Progress from Reimarus to Wrede*. Translated by W. Montgomery. London: Adam and Charles Black, 1910.

Seidl, Horst. "Is Aristotle's Cosmology and Metaphysics Compatible with the Christian Concept of Creation?" In *Divine Creation in Ancient, Medieval, and Early Modern Thought*, edited by Willemien Otten, Walter Hannam, and Michael Treschow, 35–100. Leiden: Brill, 2007.

Simmons, David L. "Poetry, Religion and History: Johann Gottfried Herder on Genesis 1–11." PhD diss., University of Chicago, 2010.

Sinnema, Donald. "Aristotle and Early Reformed Orthodoxy: Moments of Accommodation and Antithesis." In *Christianity and the Classics: The Acceptance of a Heritage*, edited by Wendy Helleman, 119–48. New York: University Press of America, 1990.

Smith, David P. *B. B. Warfield's Scientifically Constructive Theological Scholarship*. Evangelical Theological Society Monograph Series, no. 10. Eugene, Ore.: Wipf and Stock, 2011.

Smith, George. *The Chaldean Account of Genesis*. New York, 1876.

Smith, Morton H. *Harmony of the Westminster Confession and Catechisms*. Taylors, S.C.: Presbyterian Press, 1990.

———. *Systematic Theology*. Vol. 1. Greenville, S.C.: Greenville Seminary Press, 1994.

Sproul, R. C., ed. *New Geneva Study Bible*. Nashville: Nelson, 1995.

———, ed. *Reformation Study Bible*. Phillipsburg, N.J.: Ligonier Ministries, 2005.

———. *The Triune God*. Vol. 1 of *Truths We Confess: A Layman's Guide to the Westminster Confession of Faith*. Phillipsburg, N.J.: P&R, 2006.

Spurgeon, Charles. "The Power of the Holy Ghost: A Sermon Delivered on Sabbath Morning, June 17, 1855…at New Park Street Chapel, Southwark." The Spurgeon Archive. http://www.spurgeon.org/sermons/0030.htm.

Stillingfleet, Edward. *Origines sacrae, or, A Rational Account of the Grounds of Christian Faith…*. London, 1675.

Streane, A. W., trans. *A Translation of the Treatise Chagigah from the Babylonian Talmud*. Cambridge, 1891.

Street, T. Watson. "The Evolution Controversy in the Southern Presbyterian Church with Attention to the Theological and Ecclesiastical Issues Raised." *The Journal of Presbyterian History* 37, no. 4 (1959): 237.

Swierenga, Robert P. "Burn the Wooden Shoes: Modernity and Division in the Christian Reformed Church in North America." Paper presented at University of Stellenbosch Conference, South Africa, International Society for the Study of Reformed Communities, June 2000. http://www.swierenga .com/Africa_pap.html.

Sytsma, David. "Calvin, Daneau, and *Physica Mosaica.*" Paper presented at Calvin Theological Seminary Colloquium, November 12, 2013.

———. "Richard Baxter's Philosophical Polemics: A Puritan's Response to Mechanical Philosophy." PhD diss., Princeton Theological Seminary, 2013.

Tattersall, Ian. *The Fossil Trail: How We Know What We Think We Know about Evolution.* Oxford: Oxford University Press, 1995.

Taylor, Justin. "On Theistic Evolution and Professor Waltke's Resignation." TGC. April 9, 2010. http://thegospelcoalition.org/blogs/justintaylor/2010/04/09 /on-theistic-evolution-and-professor-waltkes-resignation/.

Ten Hoor, Foppe. *Compendium der Gereformeerde Dogmatiek.* Holland, Mich.: A. Ten Hoor, 1919.

———. "Dogmatiek." Unpublished manuscript, Heckman Library Archives, Calvin College, Grand Rapids, Michigan, n.d.

———. "Lectures on Systematic Theology." Unpublished manuscript, Heckman Library Archives, Calvin College, Grand Rapids, Michigan, 1895.

Tertullian. "Against Hermogenes." In vol. 3 of *Ante-Nicene Fathers*, 477–502. Grand Rapids: Eerdmans, 1989.

———. "On the Resurrection of the Flesh." In vol. 3 of *Ante-Nicene Fathers*, 545– 96. Grand Rapids: Eerdmans, 1989.

Theodore of Mopsuestia. *Theodore of Mopsuestia.* Translated by Frederick G. McLeod. London: Routledge, 2009.

Theodoret of Cyrus. *Commentary on the Psalms, 73–150.* Translated by Robert C. Hill. Washington, D.C.: Catholic University of America Press, 2001.

Theophilus of Antioch. "Theophilus to Autolycus." In vol. 2 of *Ante-Nicene Fathers*, 85–122. Grand Rapids: Eerdmans, 1989.

Theunissen, Bert. *Eugene DuBois and the Ape-Man from Java.* Dordrecht, Netherlands: Kluwer Academic Publishers, 1989.

Thornwell, J. H. *The Collected Writings of James Henley Thornwell.* Edinburgh: Banner of Truth, 1974.

Tobin, Thomas H. *The Creation of Man: Philo and the History of Interpretation.* The Catholic Biblical Quarterly, Monograph Series 14. Washington, D.C.: Catholic Biblical Association of America, 1983.

"Traditions of the Elders." In *The Apostolic Fathers*, edited by Michael Holmes, 769–73. 3rd ed. Grand Rapids: Baker, 2007.

Turretin, Francis. *Institutes of Elenctic Theology.* Edited by James T. Dennison. Phillipsburg, N.J.: P&R, 1992.

Tyndale, William. *Doctrinal Treatises and Introductions to Different Portions of Holy Scripture.* Vol. 1 of *Works of William Tyndale.* Edinburgh: Banner of Truth, 2010.

Ussher, James. *The Annals of the World Deduced from the Origin of Time....* London, 1658.

———. *A Body of Divinity or The Summe and Substance of Christian Religion.* London, 1653.

———. *Immanuel, or Mystery of the Incarnation of the Son of God.* London, 1638.

———. *The Principles of Christian Religion.* London, 1644.

Van den Honert, Taco Hajo. *Dissertations Historicae....* Lugduni Batavorum, 1739.

Van der Mijle, Abraham. *De Origine Animalium et Migratione Populorum.* Geneva, 1667.

Van der Schuit, J. J. "Het Bijbelsch Wereldbeeld." *De Wekker* 9 (June 30, 1933): 4–6.

VanDixhoorn, Chad, ed. *Minutes, Sessions 604–1163 (1646–1652).* In vol. 4 of *Minutes and Papers of the Westminster Assembly.* Oxford: Oxford University Press, 2012.

Van Genderen, J., and W. H. Velema. *Concise Reformed Dogmatics.* Translated by G. Bilkes and E. M. van der Maas. Phillipsburg, N.J.: P&R, 2008.

Van Huyssteen, J. Wentzel. "Human Origins and Religious Awareness." Nobel Conference, Gustavus Adolphus College, 2008. http://www.youtube.com/watch?v=7QQXfiPtR0M.

Van Kooten, George H., ed. *The Creation of Heaven and Earth: Re-interpretations of Genesis 1 in the Context of Judaism, Ancient Philosophy, Christianity, and Modern Physics.* Leiden: Brill, 2005.

Van Oosterzee, J. J. *Christian Dogmatics: A Text-Book for Academical Instruction and Private Study.* New York, 1874.

Van Til, Cornelius. *The Defense of the Faith.* 4th ed. Phillipsburg, N.J.: P&R, 2008.

Van Till, Howard. *The Fourth Day.* Grand Rapids: Eerdmans, 1987.

Van Till, Howard, Robert E. Snow, John H. Stek, and Davis A. Young. *Portraits of Creation: Biblical and Scientific Perspectives on the World's Formation.* Grand Rapids: Eerdmans, 1990.

Venema, Herman. *Institutes of Theology.* Translated by Alex W. Brown. Edinburgh, 1850.

Vermigli, Pietro M. *In primum librum Mosis qui volgo Genesis.* Zurich, 1579.

———. *Loci Communes.* Londini: Ex Typographia Ioannis Kyngystoni, 1576.

Versteeg, J. P. *Adam in the New Testament.* Translated by Richard B. Gaffin Jr. Phillipsburg, N.J.: P&R, 2012.

Visser, Rob P. W. "Dutch Calvinists and Darwin." In *Nature and Science in the Abrahamic Religions: 1700–Present*, edited by Jitse M. van der Meer and Scott Mandelbrote, 293–316. Leiden: Brill, 2008.

Voltaire. "Philosophical Dictionary." In *The Works of Voltaire. A Contemporary Version*, vols. 3–7. Translated by William F. Fleming. New York: E. R. DuMont, 1901.

Von Harnack, Adolf. *What Is Christianity? Lectures Delivered at the University of Berlin during the Winter Term, 1899–1900*. 2nd ed. New York: G. P. Putnam's Sons, 1908.

Vos, Geerhardus. "Dogmatiek van G. Vos. Ph.D. D.D., Deel I. Theologie." Unpublished manuscript, Heckman Library Archives, Calvin College, Grand Rapids, Michigan, 1910.

———. *Reformed Dogmatics: Theology Proper*. Translated by Richard B. Gaffin Jr. Bellingham, Wash.: Lexham Press, 2014.

———. "Systematische Theologie van G. Vos, Ph.D., D.D, Compendium." Unpublished manuscript, Heckman Library Archives, Calvin College, Grand Rapids, Michigan, 1900.

———. "Theologie Naturalis." Lecture notes taken by L. J. Veltkamp. September 27, 1898, Grand Rapids, Michigan." Unpublished manuscript, Heckman Library Archives, Calvin College, Grand Rapids, Michigan, 1898.

Vos, J. G. *Genesis*. Pittsburgh, Pa.: Crown & Covenant, 2006.

Vossius, Isaac. *Dissertatio de Vera Aetate Mundi*. Hague, 1659.

Walaeus, Antonius, Antonius Thysius, Johannes Polyander, and André Rivet. *Synopsis purioris theologiae*. 3rd ed. Leiden, 1642.

Walhout, Edwin. "Tomorrow's Theology." *The Banner*. May 3, 2013. http://www .thebanner.org/features/2013/05/tomorrow-s-theology.

Waltke, Bruce. "Barriers to Accepting Creation by an Evolutionary Process." The Biologos Forum. November 17, 2009. http://biologos.org/blog/barriers -to-accepting-creation-by-an-evolutionary-process.

———. "Why Must the Church Come to Accept Evolution?" The Biologos Forum. March 24, 2010. http://biologos.org/blog/why-must-the-church-come-to -accept-evolution.

Waltke, Bruce, and Cathi J. Fredricks. *Genesis: A Commentary*. Grand Rapids: Zondervan, 2001.

Walton, John. "Creation in Genesis 1:1–2:3 and the Ancient Near East: Order Out of Disorder after *Chaoskampf.*" *Calvin Theological Journal* 43 (2008): 48–63.

———. *Genesis 1 as Ancient Cosmology*. Winona Lake, Ind.: Eisenbrauns, 2011.

———. "Human Origins and the Bible." *Zygon* 47, no. 4 (December 2012): 875–89.

———. *The Lost World of Genesis One: Ancient Cosmology and the Origins Debate.* Downers Grove, Ill.: InterVarsity, 2009.

———. "Reflections on Reading Genesis 1–3: John Walton's World Tour, Part 2." The Biologos Forum. September 18, 2013. http://biologos.org/blog /john-waltons-world-tour-part-2.

———. "Reflections on Reading Genesis 1–3: John Walton's World Tour, Part 3." The Biologos Forum. September 18, 2013. http://biologos.org/blog /john-waltons-world-tour-part-3.

Ward, Benedicta. "Bede the Theologian." In *The Medieval Theologians*, edited by G. R. Evans, 57–64. Oxford, U.K.: Blackwell, 2001.

Warfield, B. B. *B. B. Warfield, Evolution, Science and Scripture: Selected Writings.* Edited by Mark Noll and David Livingstone. Grand Rapids: Baker, 2000.

———. "On the Antiquity and Unity of the Human Race." In *Studies in Theology*, edited by John E. Meeter, 235–58. Edinburgh: Banner of Truth, 1988.

Webb, R. A. "The Evolution Controversy." In *The Life Work of John L. Girardeau, Late Professor of the Presbyterian Theological Seminary, Columbia, S.C.*, edited by George A. Blackburn, 231–84. Columbia, S.C.: State Company, 1916.

Weber, Robert, and Roger Gryson, eds. *Biblia Sacra Iuxta Vulgatam Versionem.* Stuttgart, Germany: Deutsche Bibelgesellschaft, 1994.

Weeks, Noel. "Background in Biblical Interpretation: Part 1." Reformation 21. October 2012. http://www.reformation21.org/articles/background-in -biblical-interpretation-part-1.php.

———. "Background in Biblical Interpretation: Part 2." Reformation 21. October 2012. http://www.reformation21.org/articles/background-in-biblical -interpretation-part-2.php.

Weeks, Stuart, Simon Gathercole, and Loren Stuckenbruck, eds. *The Book of Tobit: Texts from the Principal Ancient and Medieval Traditions: With Synopsis, Concordances, and Annotated Texts in Aramaic, Hebrew, Greek, Latin, and Syriac.* New York: de Gruyter, 2004.

Wegner, Walter. "Creation and Salvation, A Study of Genesis 1 and 2." *Concordia Theological Monthly* 37, no. 8 (September 1966): 528–29.

Whiston, William. *A New Theory of the Earth….* London, 1737.

Whitcomb, John, and Henry M. Morris. *The Genesis Flood.* Philadelphia: Presbyterian and Reformed, 1961.

White, John. *A Commentary on the Three First Chapters of the First Book of Moses Called Genesis.* London, 1656.

Williams, Michael D. "First Calling: The *Imago Dei* and the Order of Creation—Part I." *Presbyterion* 39, no. 1 (Spring 2013): 30–44.

———. "Man and Beast." *Presbyterion* 34, no. 1 (Spring 2008): 15.

Wills, Gregory A. *Southern Baptist Theological Seminary, 1859–2009.* Oxford: Oxford University Press, 2009.

Wilson, John M. *The Heavens, the Earth, and the Sea, or, The Hand of God in the Works of Nature.* London, 1860.

———. *Nature, Man and God: A Contribution to the Scientific Teaching of Today.* London, 1885.

Winchell, Alexander. *Adamites and Preadamites: Or, A Popular Discussion Concerning the Remote Representatives of the Human Species and Their Relation to the Biblical Adam.* Syracuse, N.Y., 1878.

Wisse, G. *Gereformeerde Geloofsleer.* 3rd ed. Kampen: J. H. Bos, 1911.

Witsius, Herman. *Sacred Dissertations on the Apostles' Creed.* Grand Rapids: Reformation Heritage Books, 2010.

Wood, A. Skevington. "Nicholas of Lyra." *Evangelical Quarterly* 4 (1961): 196–206.

Wood, Todd C., and Megan J. Murray. *Understanding the Pattern of Life: Origins and Organization of the Species.* Edited by Kurt P. Wise. Nashville: Broadman & Holman, 2003.

Wood, Todd C., Kurt P. Wise, Roger Sanders, and N. Doran. "A Refined Baramin Concept." In *Occasional Papers of the Biology Study Group* 3 (2003): 1–14.

Woodrow, James. "Address on Evolution." In *My Life and Times 1810–1899*, edited by John B. Adger, 431–56. Richmond, Va., 1899.

Woodward, John. *An Essay Toward a Natural History of the Earth…With an Account of the Universal Deluge and the Effect It Had Upon the Earth.* London, 1695.

Young, Davis A. "The Antiquity and the Unity of the Human Race Revisited." *Christian Scholar's Review* 24, no. 4 (May 1995): 380–96.

———. *John Calvin and the Natural World.* Lanham, Md.: University Press of America, 2007.

Young, Davis A., and Ralph F. Stearley. *The Bible, Rocks and Time: Geological Evidence for the Age of the Earth.* Downers Grove, Ill.: IVP Academic, 2008.

Young, E. J. "The Days of Genesis—I." *Westminster Theological Journal* 25 no. 1 (November 1962): 1–34.

———. "The Days of Genesis—II." *Westminster Theological Journal* 25, no. 2 (May 1963): 143–71.

———. "The Interpretation of Genesis 1:2." *Westminster Theological Journal* 23 (November 1960–May 1961): 151–78.

———. *In the Beginning.* Carlisle, Pa.: Banner of Truth, 1976.

———. *Studies in Genesis One.* Grand Rapids: Baker, 1973.

Youngblood, Ronald F., ed. *The Genesis Debate: Persistent Questions about Creation and the Flood.* Grand Rapids: Baker, 1990.

Zanchi, Girolamo. *De operibus Dei intra spatium sex dierum*. Neostadii in Palatinorum, 1601.

———. *H. Zanchius His Confession of Christian Religion*. Cambridge, 1599.

Zaspel, Fred. *The Theology of B. B. Warfield*. Wheaton, Ill.: Crossway, 2010.

Zimmerman, Paul, ed. *Darwin, Evolution, and Creation*. St. Louis: Concordia, 1959.

Zwingli, Huldrych. *Annotations on Genesis*. In vol. 1 of *Reformation Commentary on Scripture*, edited by John L. Thompson, 1–113. Downers Grove, Ill.: InterVarsity, 2012.

———. *Commentary on True and False Religion*. Edited by Samuel Jackson and Clarence Heller. Durham, N.C.: Labyrinth, 1981.

———. *Farragi annotationum in Genesim*. Tiguri, 1527.

Index